PUBLICATIONS

OF THE

NAVY RECORDS SOCIETY

VOL. 150

THE CUNNINGHAM PAPERS. VOLUME II

The NAVY RECORDS SOCIETY was established in 1893 for the purpose of printing unpublished manuscripts and rare works of naval interest. The Society is open to all who are interested in naval history, and any person wishing to become a member should apply to the Hon. Secretary, Pangbourne College, Pangbourne, Berks., R98 8LA. The annual subscription is £30, which entitles the member to receive one free copy of each work issued by the Society in that year, and to buy earlier issues at much reduced prices.

SUBSCRIPTIONS and orders for back volumes should be sent to the Membership Secretary, 1 Avon Close, Petersfield, Hants GU31 4LG.

THE COUNCIL OF THE NAVY RECORDS SOCIETY wish it to be clearly understood that they are not answerable for any opinions and observations which may appear in the Society's publications. For these the editors of the several works are entirely responsible.

Admiral of the Fleet Sir Andrew Cunningham, listening to Admiral Harold R. Stark, US Navy, Commander of the US Naval Forces in Europe, 1945.

THE CUNNINGHAM PAPERS

Selections from the private and official
Correspondence of Admiral of the Fleet Viscount
Cunningham of Hyndhope, O. M., K. T., G. C. B.,
D. S. O. and two bars

VOLUME II

THE TRIUMPH OF ALLIED SEA POWER
1942–1946

Edited by

MICHAEL SIMPSON, M. A., M. Litt., F. R. Hist. S.,
Reader (ret.) in History, University of Wales Swansea

PUBLISHED BY ASHGATE
FOR THE NAVY RECORDS SOCIETY
2006

This book has been published with the help of funds provided by the Social Sciences and Humanities Research Council of Canada.

Published by
Ashgate Publishing Limited
Gower House
Croft Road
Aldershot
Hants GU11 3HR
England

Ashgate Publishing Company
Suite 420
101 Cherry Street
Burlington, VT 05401-4405
USA

Ashgate website: http://www.ashgate.com

British Library Cataloguing in Publication Data

Cunningham of Hyndhope, Andrew Browne Cunningham, Viscount, 1883–1963
The Cunningham papers : selections from the private and official correspondence of Admiral of the Fleet Viscount Cunningham of Hyndhope
Vol. II: The triumph of Allied sea power, 1942–1946. – Navy Records Society publications)
1.Cunningham of Hyndhope, Andrew Browne Cunningham, Viscount, 1883–1963 – Correspondence 2.Great Britain. Royal Navy – History – World War, 1939–1945 3.Admirals – Great Britain – Correspondence 4.World War, 1939–1945 – Mediterranean Sea – Naval operations, British
I.Title II.Simpson, Michael (Michael A.) III.Navy Records Society (Great Britain)
940.5'45'941'092

Library of Congress Cataloging-in-Publication Data

Cunningham, Andrew Browne Cunningham, 1st Viscount, 1883–1963
The Cunningham papers : selections from the private and official correspondence of Admiral of the Fleet Viscount Cunningham of Hyndhope / edited by Michael Simpson.
(Publications of the Navy Records Society : vol. 150)
Contents: v. II. The Triumph of Allied Sea Power 1942–1946
1. Cunningham, Andrew Browne Cunningham, 1st Viscount, 1883–1963—Correspondence. 2. World War, 1939–1945—Campaigns–Participation, British. 3. Great Britain—History, Naval—20th century. 4. Admirals—Great Britain—Correspondence—Mediterranean Sea. I. Simpson, Michael (Michael A.) II. Navy Records Society (Great Britain) III. Title. IV. Series.
DA70.A1 vol. 150   [DA89.1.C8]   98–6909
940.54'594'092—dc21   CIP

ISBN-10: 0 7546 5598 9

Printed on acid-free paper

Typeset in Times by Manton Typesetters, Louth, Lincolnshire, UK.
Printed and bound in Great Britain by MPG Books Ltd, Bodmin, Cornwall.

In Memoriam

Professor David Syrett
(1939–2004)
Distinguished Professor of History,
Queens College, City University of New York,
Member of Council and editor of several of these volumes

CONTENTS

BUCKINGHAM PALACE.

I was very interested to learn that the publication of *The Cunningham Papers Volume II, 1942–1946* happened to be the 150th volume to be published by the Navy Records Society. It so happens that I served for a short time in 1941 as a Midshipman in *HMS Valiant* in the Mediterranean Fleet under his command. I was lucky enough to be in charge of her searchlight control on the night of the action at Cape Matapan on 28/29 March, arguably his greatest triumph against the Italian Navy.

Later on, I served as First Lieutenant in *HMS Wallace*, once Cunningham's Flotilla Leader in 1922–1924, in home waters and in the Mediterranean. By coincidence, we were involved with the invasion of Sicily in June 1943, for which Cunningham was partly responsible for the planning.

Unless they happen to be serving in the Flagship, junior officers would only know of their Commander-in-Chief by reputation. I can recall that 'ABC' as he was generally known, was perceived as an aggressive and energetic leader, with the obvious ambition of destroying the Italian Navy as soon as possible. This certainly communicated itself to everyone in the Fleet.

Lord Cunningham enjoyed a very distinguished career in the Royal Navy. He was among the very senior leaders during World War II and one of the major architects of the final victory. This volume of his papers shows just what an important contribution he made to the national war effort.

MAPS AND ILLUSTRATIONS

Frontispiece: Admiral of the Fleet Sir Andrew Cunningham, listening to Admiral Harold R. Stark, US Navy, Commander of US Naval Forces in Europe, 1945. Courtesy of the Imperial War Museum.

MAPS

PREFACE

Admiral Sir Andrew Cunningham had gained a formidable reputation during his command of the Mediterranean Fleet between June 1939 and March 1942; he had become known as a 'fighting sailor' as a consequence of his fleet's triumphs at Taranto and Matapan and its courageous and grim fight against the Italian fleet and air force and the *Luftwaffe* and U-boats in the latter part of his command. As a result, Cunningham remarked early in 1942, 'there is now no fleet to go to sea in'. The deeds of Cunningham and the Mediterranean Fleet during this stirring time are dealt with in volume I of these papers.[1]

Following America's entry into the war, there was a necessity for the Royal Navy to strengthen co-operation with the United States Navy. To achieve this, the First Sea Lord, Admiral of the Fleet Sir Dudley Pound, turned to Cunningham, believing his great prestige and experience of combat conditions as a commander in a ferocious war zone would carry great weight with the Americans.[2] Cunningham's brief term as head of the British Admiralty Delegation in Washington was to endear him to the Americans, so much so that they proposed him as Allied Naval Commander of the Expeditionary Force which was to invade North Africa in November 1942.[3] The 'Torch' expedition was the start of almost two years of landings in the Mediterranean, embracing 'Husky' (the invasion of Sicily) in July 1943 and the 'Baytown' and 'Avalanche' landings in Italy in September 1943. His role as ANCXF was abruptly terminated in October 1943, when he was summoned to replace the dying Pound as First Sea Lord.

Cunningham was First Sea Lord from October 1943 to his retirement from active service in June 1946. In that time he presided over the invasion of Normandy ('Neptune/Overlord'), operations in the Medi-

---

[1]M. A. Simpson (ed.), *The Cunningham Papers*, volume I, *The Mediterranean Fleet, 1939–1942* (Aldershot, 1999). The quotation is from document 322, p. 583.

[2]AoF Sir A. Dudley P. R. Pound (1877–1943): ent RN 1891; CO of a torpedo boat 1897; Cdr 1909; Capt 1914; *Colossus* Jutland 1916; DOD (H) 1917; *Repulse* 1920–2; DPD 1922; CoS, Med F 1925; RA 1926; ACNS 1927; BCS 1929; VA 1930; 2SL 1932; Adm 1935; C-in-C Med 1936–9; FSL 1939–43. R. Brodhurst, *Churchill's Anchor: Admiral of the Fleet Sir Dudley Pound* (Barnsley, 2000).

[3]BAD, from 1941, part of JSM.

terranean, the sinking of the *Scharnhorst* and *Tirpitz*, the defeat of a late surge of U-boat activity, the British Pacific Fleet, and the problems of manpower, the futures of the Royal Marines and the Fleet Air Arm, and the conversion of the Royal Navy from its swollen wartime strength to a much-reduced peacetime cadre.

Having suffered a heart attack in the spring of 1946, the result of accumulated stress, being generally worn out and despondent, and disliking the task of downsizing the fleet, he retired that June, handing over to his chosen replacement, Admiral Sir John H. D. Cunningham (no relation).[4] He retreated to his much-loved home at Bishop's Waltham, within easy reach of Portsmouth. He and his wife enjoyed gardening, fishing and hosting family and friends. He remained concerned over the future of the country's defence and that of the Royal Navy and, since he had been raised to the Viscountcy in January 1946, he was able to speak in major defence debates in the House of Lords. Following a visit to the Admiralty and lunch at the Athanaeum, in June 1963, he died suddenly and was buried at sea. Thus passed one of Britain's great sailors, a worthy successor to Nelson, whom he admired and many of whose qualities he displayed.

Separating Cunningham's activities from those of the Allied commands, the strategic direction of the war, or the work of the Admiralty has proved just as difficult as it was with the first volume. Many of the documents which bear his signature were drafted for him. There are, however, many letters to his family and brother officers that exhibit his feelings, as well as his illuminating diary entries from April 1944 onwards. This volume has been based on Lord Cunningham's papers, deposited mainly in the British Library (Manuscripts Division), the National Maritime Museum, the Churchill Archives Centre and the Imperial War Museum. Other papers written by him have been found in the collections of Admirals Blake, Cowan, Kelly, Manley Power, Somerville, Whitworth and Willis and other officers. Extensive use has been made also of the Admiralty, Cabinet and Prime Minister's records in The National Archives (formerly the Public Record Office). Contributions of material and memories have been made by those who served with him and by members of his family.

---

[4]AoF Sir John H. D. Cunningham (1885–1962): ent RN 1900; Lt 1905; navig spist; Med & Grand F 1914–18; Cdr 1917; Navig Sch 1922–3; Master of F 1923; Capt 1924; staff cmds; N War Coll; DP; *Adventure, Resolution*; RA & ACNS 1936; ACNS (Air) & then 5SL 1937–9; RA & 1CS, Med F 1939; VA & 1CS, Home F 1939–40; N Cdr 'Menace', Dakar 1940; 4SL 1941–3; C-in-C Levant & later Med, & Adm 1943; 1SL 1946–8; AoF 1948; Chmn, Iraq Pet Co 1948–58. M. H. Murfett, 'Adm J. Cunningham', in Murfett (ed.), *The First Sea Lords: From Fisher to Mountbatten* (Westport, CT & London, 1995), pp. 217–28.

Once again, editing of the documents has been done with as light a touch as possible. Punctuation marks have been inserted on occasion to clarify passages or to mark omissions. At times, numbered paragraphs in official communications have been omitted, resulting in breaks in their sequence. Missing words are indicated thus: [-]. If there is some doubt about a word, it is expressed thus: [? word]. Place names are contemporaneous. Places and dates of origin, where known, are placed at the head of documents. All Admiralty communications originated from London. Details of ships and aircraft have been obtained from a variety of sources, such as *Lloyd's List, Conway's All the World's Fighting Ships 1922–1946* and *Jane's Fighting Ships*; dates given are for the first flight of an aircraft and for completion in the case of ships.

ACKNOWLEDGEMENTS

I am indebted to colleagues in the Navy Records Society for encouraging me to edit the second volume of the Cunningham papers. I owe particular thanks to the Society's Publications Committee and to the General Editor, Dr Roger Morriss. I am grateful, too, to Lt Cdr Jock Gardner of the Naval Historical Branch for supplying information. Captain Hugh Lee, formerly Cunningham's Flag Lieutenant, has once again been of invaluable assistance, as has Commander John Somerville, who served in the Mediterranean Fleet and who also kept in touch with Cunningham after the war.

The bulk of Cunningham's papers are held by the Manuscripts Division of the British Library, while others are in the National Maritime Museum and the Churchill Archives Centre, Churchill College, Cambridge, and I have enjoyed exemplary and cheerful service from the staffs of those repositories. Admiralty, Cabinet and Prime Minister's papers have been consulted at The National Archives, from which I have also received admirable service; Crown Copyright material there has been reproduced by kind permission of the Controller of Her Majesty's Stationery Office. Mr Roderick Suddaby, Keeper of the Archives at the Imperial War Museum, has been, as ever, a source of sage advice and has drawn my attention to material in his care. The Librarian of Christ Church College, Oxford, has kindly made available to me the papers of Marshal of the RAF Viscount Portal. Dr Vincent Orange of the University of Canterbury, New Zealand, has generously provided me with much material on Marshal of the RAF Lord Tedder. The Embassies and Defence Attachés of Greece, Norway and Russia and the Service historique de la Marine, Vincennes, and Library and Archives Canada have amiably answered several queries. I have used extensively the archives of the Franklin D. Roosevelt Presidential Library, Hyde Park, New York, the Naval War College, Newport, Rhode Island, the Navy Library and the Operational Archives at the Naval Historical Center, Washington Navy Yard, the Manuscripts Division of the Library of Congress, and the U. S. Navy archives at the National Archives, College Park, Maryland; at all of these places, I have received a warm welcome and most efficient service.

My former Head of Department, Professor Noel Thompson, and former colleagues in the History Department at the University of Wales Swansea, have been very supportive of my research and have made valuable points. My research students Mr Martin Jones, Mr Stan May and Dr James Levy have provided me with important insights. Mr Tim Fearnside, Cartographer in the Department of Geography, has drawn the maps with his usual cheerfulness and expertise.

The British Academy has borne the brunt of the financial support of my research and I am also indebted to the Scouloudi Foundation, the Franklin and Eleanor Roosevelt Institute, and departmental funds for their assistance.

Admiral Cunningham's family have been of particular assistance and I should like to thank Sir Hugh and Lady Fiona Byatt, Mr Robin Byatt, Mr David Byatt, Mrs Hilda Mckendrick, Admiral Sir Jock Slater and the late Professor Colin Matthew. My former college, Fitzwilliam, kindly accommodated me when I was working in Cambridge. My daughter Alison, her husband Neil and grandson Harry welcomed me while I was undertaking research in London, and latterly Neil's brother, Aleister Smith, has genially hosted me. As ever, my greatest debt is to my wife, Sue, the compiler of the index, who has provided a safe and comfortable harbour and also much love.

GLOSSARY OF ABBREVIATIONS

AA	Anti-Aircraft
ABDA	American-British-Dutch-Australian [strategic area, 1942]
AB	Able Bodied [seaman]
ABC	Andrew Browne Cunningham
a/c	aircraft
A/Cdr	Acting Commander
ACM	Air Chief Marshal
ACNS	Assistant Chief of Naval Staff (Air, Foreign, Home, U-boat Warfare and Trade)
ADC	Aide de Camp
Adm	Admiral
AF	Atlantic Fleet
AM	Admiralty Message
AM	Air Marshal
AM	Air Ministry
AM	Auxiliary Minesweeper [US Navy]
AMC	Armed Merchant Cruiser
ANCXF	Allied Naval Commander Expeditionary Force
AOC	Air Officer Commanding
AoF	Admiral of the Fleet
A/S	Anti-Submarine
ASV	Air-to-Surface Vessel [radar]
ASW	Anti-Submarine Warfare
AVM	Air Vice Marshal
BAD	British Admiralty Delegation
BAOR	British Army of the Rhine
BPF	British Pacific Fleet
Capt	Captain
Capt (D)	Captain (Destroyers)
Capt (S)	Captain (Submarines)
CAS	Chief of the Air Staff
CCO	Chief of Combined Operations
CCS	Combined Chiefs of Staff [UK-US]

CCOS	Combined Chiefs of Staff [a misnomer]
CIGS	Chief of the Imperial General Staff
Cdr	Commander
Cdre	Commodore
Cdre (D)	Commodore (Destroyers)
CEx	Chancellor of the Exchequer
C-in-C	Commander-in-Chief
CINCPAC	Commander-in-Chief Pacific [US Navy]
Cmd	Command
CNO	Chief of Naval Operations [US]
CNR	Chief Naval Representative [at Ministry of Aircraft Production]
CNS	Chief of Naval Staff
CNSO	Chief Naval Staff Officer
Cntrlr	Controller and Third Sea Lord
CO	Commanding Officer
CO	Combined Operations
COHQ	Combined Operations Head Quarters
COMINCH	Commander-in-Chief [of US Fleet]
COPP	Combined Operations Pilotage Party
COS	Chiefs of Staff [UK]
CoS	Chief of Staff
CS	Cruiser Squadron
CSMR	Controller of Shipbuilding Maintenance and Repair
CSO	Chief Staff Officer
DAUD	Director of the Anti-U-boat Warfare Division
DCO	Deputy Chief of [Combined] Operations
DC	District of Columbia
DCSR	Deputy Controller of Shipbuilding Repair
D-day	day of landings [and also D-1, before, or D+1, after]
DDOD (M)	Deputy Director of Operations Division (Mining)
DEMS	Defensively Equipped Merchant Ship
DF	Destroyer Flotilla
DFSL	Deputy First Sea Lord
D/B	Dive Bomber
DM	Destroyer Minelayer *or* Destroyer Minesweeper [US Navy]
DMO	Director of Military Operations
DOD (H)	Director of Operations Division (Home)
DoP	Director of Plans
DoP (Q)	Director of Plans (Quartermaster)
DPS	Director of Personnel Services

DSC	Distinguished Service Cross
DSO	Distinguished Service Order
DTSD	Director of Training and Staff Duties
DUKW	D= model year; U= amphibian; K= all wheel drive; W= dual rear axle
EF	Eastern Fleet
EIF	East Indies Fleet
FAA	Fleet Air Arm
F/B	Fighter Bomber
FDR	[President] Franklin Delano Roosevelt
FDR	Fighter Direction Radar
FL	Flotilla Leader
FM	Field Marshal
FO	Foreign Office
FO	Flag Officer
FO (Air)	Flag Officer (Air)
FOAT	Flag Officer Air Training
FOC	Flag Officer Commanding
FOIC	Flag Officer in Command
FOIS	Flag Officer Inshore Squadron
FONAS	Flag Officer Naval Air Stations
FOO	Fire Observation Officer
FL	First Lord of the Admiralty
FSL	First Sea Lord
GEE	An air navigation device
Gen	General
GHQ	General Head Quarters
GOC	General Officer Commanding
GR	General Reconnaissance
gt	gross tonnage [merchant vessels]
HA	High Angle
HAA	Heavy Anti-Aircraft [gun]
HACS	High Angle Control System
HA/LA	High Angle/Low Angle [dual purpose gun]
HDML	Harbour Defence Motor Launch
HE	High Explosive
H/E	Hydrophone Echo
HF	Home Fleet
HF/DF	High Frequency Direction Finding
H-hour	Hour of landing [also H-1, before, and H+1, after]
HM	His Majesty
HMG	His Majesty's Government

HMS	His Majesty's Ship
HNMS	Her Netherlands Majesty's Ship
HQ	Head Quarters
JCS	Joint Chiefs of Staff [US]
JIC	Joint Intelligence Committee
JPC	Joint Planning Committee
JSM	Joint Staff Mission [UK, in Washington, DC]
k	knots
LA	Low Angle [gun]
LAA	Light Anti-Aircraft [gun]
lbs	pounds [aircraft bomb load]
LCG	Landing Craft Gun
LCI	Landing Craft Infantry
LCT	Landing Craft Tank
LS	Leading Seaman
LSI	Landing Ship Infantry
LST	Landing Ship Tank
Lt	Lieutenant
Lt Cdr	Lieutenant Commander
Lt Col	Lieutenant Colonel
Lt Gen	Lieutenant General
m	miles [aircraft range]
Maj Gen	Major-General
MAP	Ministry of Aircraft Production
MAS	Italian motor torpedo boat
MDG	Medical Director General
mg	machine guns [aircraft]
MGB	Motor Gun Boat
MF	Mediterranean Fleet
ML	Motor Launch
M/L	Minelayer
MN	Merchant Navy
mph	miles per hour [aircraft]
M/S	Minesweeper
MTB	Motor Torpedo Boat
MWT	Ministry of War Transport
NA	Naval Attaché
NAA	Naval Air Arm
NC	Naval Commander
NAWI	North America and West Indies Station
NCXF	Naval Commander Expeditionary Force

NCTF	Naval Commander (Central *or* Eastern *or* Western) Task Force
NSHQ	Naval Staff Head Quarters
OC	Officer Commanding
ORP	Polish ship
OS	Ordinary Seaman
PBY	Patrol Bomber [US; floatplane]
PC	Patrol Craft [US]
PM	Prime Minister
PoW	Prisoner of War
PRU	Photographic Reconnaissance Unit
(R)	(Repeat)
RA	Rear Admiral
RAA	Rear Admiral Air
RAAC	Rear Admiral Aircraft Carriers
RA (D)	Rear Admiral (Destroyers)
RAAF	Royal Australian Air Force
RAF	Royal Air Force
RAFT	Rear Admiral Fleet Train
RAN	Royal Australian Navy
RCN	Royal Canadian Navy
RDF	Radio Direction Finding [radar]
RFA	Royal Fleet Auxiliary
RMS	Royal Mail Ship
RN	Royal Navy
RNB	Royal Naval Barracks
RN (Emgcy)	Royal Navy (Emergency)
RNR	Royal Naval Reserve
RNVR	Royal Naval Volunteer Reserve
RNZN	Royal New Zealand Navy
SAC	Supreme Allied Commander
SACSEA	Supreme Allied Commander South East Asia
SCAEF	Supreme Commander Allied Expeditionary Force
SEAC	South East Asia Command
SF	Submarine Flotilla
SHAEF	Supreme Headquarters Allied Expeditionary Force
S/M	Submarine
SNO	Senior Naval Officer
SNSO	Senior Naval Staff Officer
SO	Staff Officer; Senior Officer
SOCRM	Senior Officer Commanding Royal Marines
SO (O)	Staff Officer (Operations)

SOS	Save Our Souls
Sqdn	Squadron
SS	Steamship
SWPA	South West Pacific Area
t	tonnage [displacement]
tt	torpedo tubes
T/B	Torpedo Bomber
TBR	Torpedo Bomber Reconnaissance
TBS	Talk Between Ships
TF	Task Force
TG	Task Group
TLC	Tank Landing Craft
TOO	Time of Origin
UK	United Kingdom
UN	United Nations
UNO	United Nations Organisation
USA	United States of America
USAAF	United States Army Air Force
USSR	Union of Soviet Socialist Republics
VA	Vice Admiral
VAC	Vice Admiral Commanding
VAEF	Vice Admiral Eastern Fleet
VA (Q)	Vice Admiral (Quartermaster)
VC	Victoria Cross
VCNS	Vice Chief of Naval Staff
V/S	Visual Signalling
W Apps	Western Approaches
WRNS	Women's Royal Naval Service
W/T	Wireless Telegraphy
WW1	A CCS strategic paper of 1942
1st Lt	First Lieutenant
1SL, 2SL, etc.	1st, 2nd, etc., Sea Lords

CHRONOLOGY OF THE LIFE AND CAREER OF ADMIRAL OF THE FLEET VISCOUNT CUNNINGHAM OF HYNDHOPE

(From Admiral Cunningham's service record in ADM 196/8, The National Archives, his autobiography and other sources).

For the period from his birth on 7 January 1883 to his leaving the Mediterranean Station on 3 April 1942, the details are given in volume I.

9 April 1942	The Cunninghams arrived in London from Alexandria.
11 June 1942	Created a baronet.
23 June 1942	The Cunninghams flew to the United States.
August 1942	Appointed Allied Naval Commander, Expeditionary Force.
11 October 1942	Cunningham left Washington for London.
8 November 1942	Landings in North Africa ('Torch').
21 January 1943	Appointed Admiral of the Fleet.
5 February 1943	Appointed C-in-C, Mediterranean, for a second time.
12 May 1943	End of fighting in North Africa.
10 July 1943	Landings in Sicily ('Husky').
8 September 1943	Surrender of Italy.
9 September 1943	Landings in Italy ('Baytown' and 'Avalanche').
10 September 1943	Italian Fleet surrendered at Malta.
5 October 1943	Appointed First Sea Lord.
16 October 1943	Left Mediterranean and assumed duties as First Sea Lord.
14 November–11 December	Attended summit conferences at Cairo and Tehran.
26 December 1943	Destruction of *Scharnhorst* by Home Fleet under Fraser.
5 June 1944	Landings in Normandy ('Neptune' and 'Overlord').
5–25 September 1944	Attended summit conference at Quebec.

12 November 1944	*Tirpitz* capsized following RAF bombing.
1 January 1945	Appointed a Knight of the Thistle.
3 February 1945	Attended summit conference at Yalta.
23 March 1945	British Pacific Fleet in action.
8 May 1945	Fighting in Europe ended.
15–25 July 1945	Attended summit conference at Potsdam.
8 August 1945	Created a baron.
14 August 1945	Japan surrendered.
1 January 1946	Created Viscount Cunningham of Hyndhope.
31 March 1946	Hospitalised at Haslar, Portsmouth.
6 June 1946	Left Admiralty and ceased active service. Retired to his home, The Old Palace House, Bishop's Waltham, Hampshire.
13 June 1946	Appointed to the Order of Merit.
12 June 1963	Died suddenly in London.
18 June 1963	Buried at sea, south of the Nab Tower, The Solent.

A BRIEF BIBLIOGRAPHY

C. Barnett, *Engage the Enemy More Closely: The Royal Navy in the Second World War* (London, 1991).

Admiral of the Fleet Viscount Cunningham of Hyndhope, *A Sailor's Odyssey* (London, 1951).

Vice Admiral Sir Peter Gretton, *Former Naval Person: Winston Churchill and the Royal Navy* (London, 1968).

R. L. Ollard, *Fisher and Cunningham: A Study of the Personalities of the Churchill Era* (London, 1991).

S. W. C. Pack, *Cunningham the Commander* (London, 1974).

S. W. Roskill, *The War at Sea*, 3 volumes (London, 1954–61).

——, *Churchill and the Admirals* (London, 1977).

M. A. Simpson, 'Admiral Viscount Cunningham of Hyndhope (1943–1946)', in M. H. Murfett (ed.), *The First Sea Lords: From Fisher to Mountbatten* (London, 1995), pp. 201–16.

—— (ed.), *The Cunningham Papers*, volume I, *The Mediterranean Fleet, 1939–1942* (Aldershot, 1999).

——, *A Life of Admiral of the Fleet Viscount Cunningham of Hyndhope* (London, 2004).

O. Warner, *Cunningham of Hyndhope: Admiral of the Fleet* (London, 1967).

J. Winton, 'Admiral of the Fleet Viscount Cunningham', in S. Howarth (ed.), *Men of War: Great Naval Leaders of World War II* (London, 1992), pp. 207–26.

J. Winton, *Cunningham: The Greatest Admiral since Nelson* (London, 1998).

PART I

THE BRITISH ADMIRALTY DELEGATION,
WASHINGTON, D.C.
MARCH TO SEPTEMBER 1942

The First Sea Lord, Admiral of the Fleet Sir Dudley Pound, had several motives for moving Cunningham from Alexandria to Washington. The fact that the United States was now a co-belligerent was to be welcomed but the American forces would now clamour for resources with more urgency and their shopping lists would be virtually endless; it was vital that the British should retain a major share of American industrial production. Secondly, America had been ushered into war most violently by the attack on Pearl Harbor (7 December 1941) and her other Pacific possessions; it was natural that the American people and their Navy would want to avenge themselves upon Japan, and leave Germany and Italy till later – an option which Britain could not countenance, for though she too had suffered greatly at Japan's hands, she knew that Germany alone possessed the strength to defeat her, while the collapse of Italy might well open a way to re-enter the European continent from the south. Finally, Admiral Ernest J. King, an enigmatic figure who seemed to the Royal Navy to embody anti-British features and appeared unlikely to be 'a good co-operator', became Chief of Naval Operations on 26 March.[1] King's priorities seemed to be the rapid expansion of the U. S. Navy, the annihilation of the Japanese fleet, and the concentration of American naval effort in the Pacific. To counter this prospect, a forceful, resolute British Admiral who commanded respect in Washington for his fighting qualities and successes was required, someone who could engage the single-minded, dedicated and determined King on equal terms. No one in the Royal Navy fulfilled the criteria so completely as Cunningham.

Cunningham was most reluctant to go. He did not wish to leave his men and women in the Mediterranean in their hour of adversity. He

---

[1]Adm (later F Adm) Ernest J. King, US Navy (1878–1956): US N Acad 1897–1901; Lt 1906; instr., staff and eng. appts; staff of Adm Mayo, C-in-C, Atl F 1915–19; S/M Div 11 1922–6; Capt & CO *Wright* 1926; qualified as pilot 1927; Bur Aeronautics and other aviation cmds; *Lexington* 1930–2; N War Coll 1932; RA & Chief Bur Aeronautics 1933–6; further aviation cmds; Cdr Patrol Force Atl Dec 1940; Adm & C-in-C Atl F Feb 1941; COMINCH Dec 1941; CNO March 1942–Dec 1945; T. B. Buell, *Master of Sea Power* (Boston, 1980).

was essentially a sea-going rather than a desk-bound admiral. He felt he lacked the qualities and interest required for astute maritime diplomacy, though he believed that he could match King's reputed toughness and bluntness [1]. Churchill was also most reluctant to let him go.[1] He had become convinced that Admiral Sir John Tovey was too recalcitrant and too defensively-minded to continue as Commander-in-Chief of the Home Fleet and, though he had had sharp differences with Cunningham, too, he was attracted, as always, by the aura of aggressiveness about him.[2] He tried to persuade Cunningham, the First Lord, A. V. Alexander, and Pound, that the Royal Navy's best interests would be served by making Cunningham Commander-in-Chief of the Home Fleet and sending Admiral Sir Percy Noble, at that time C-in-C, Western Approaches, to Washington (Noble succeeded Cunningham as head of BAD), replacing him with Tovey.[3] There was never any doubt about Cunningham's steadfast refusal to relieve Tovey; Pound and Alexander also stood firm and Churchill agreed, rather grudgingly, to a short stay for Cunningham in Washington. Questions of status and allowances, on which Cunningham proved obdurate, delayed his move to Washington until 23 June [2–5,7–8].

Once there, and having rekindled relations of mutual admiration with Field Marshal Sir John Dill, head of the Joint Staff Mission, and met the other senior American and British figures, Cunningham settled down to a life that was away from the gunfire and thus uncongenial, rather full of parties and public speaking (neither of which appealed to him), not over-burdensome in terms of work, and somewhat uncomfort-

---

[1](Sir) Winston L. S. Churchill (1874–1965): brief career as Subaltern, India & Sudan 1890s; war correspondent Cuba & Boer War 1898–1900; MP Con, Lib & Con again, most of 1900–65; Pres BoT, Home Sec & 1st Lord 1906–15; Col, W Front 1915–16; M Muns 1917–19; S War and Air 1919–21; C Ex 1924–9; pol wilderness 1931–9; 1st Lord Sept 1939–May 1940; PM & M Defence 1940–5; Ldr of Oppn 1945–51; PM 1951–5.

[2]AoF Lord (Sir John) Tovey (1885–1971): ent RN 1900; destroyer cmds, incl. Jutland, 1914–18; RN Staff Coll 1919–20; OD 1920–2; Capt (D) 1923–5; IDC 1927; N Asst to 2SL 1928–30; *Rodney* 1932–4; Cdre, RNB, Chatham 1935; RA 1936; VA 1939; 2nd-in-C, Med F 1940; Actg Adm & C-in-C, Home F 1940–3; Adm 1942; C-in-C Nore 1943; AoF 1943.

[3]Albert V. (later Earl, of Hillsborough) Alexander (1885–1965): local govt officer; Capt Artists' Rifles, WWI; lay preacher, leader in co-op & union movts; Lab MP Hillsborough, Sheffield 1922–31 & 1935–50; Parl Sec BoT 1924; 1st Lord 1929–31 & May 1940–Dec 1946; M Defence 1946; Chllr Duchy of Lancaster & Visct 1950; Lab Ldr, H Lords 1955; Earl 1963.

Adm Sir Percy Noble (1880–1955): ent RN 1894; *Ribble* i/c 1907–8; signal spist; Cdr 1913; Grand F 1914–18; Capt 1918; *Calliope, Calcutta* 1919; *Barham* 1922; *Ganges* (training), *St Vincent* 1925–7; DOD 1928–9; RA 1929; D N Eqpt 1931; 2CS, Home F 1932; VA & 4SL 1935; C-in-C China 1937–40; Adm 1939; C-in-C W Apps 1941; BAD Oct 1942–June 1944; ret 1945.

able in the sticky summer heat of Washington [9–13, 18–19].[1] He
headed the British Admiralty Delegation, though, as for the most part
that consisted of a myriad of detailed local contracts for a vast variety
of equipment, it ran itself. His chief function was to reinforce and
pursue detailed strategic discussions initiated by the First Sea Lord,
though occasionally he was required to straighten out negotiations on
matters of *matériel* [6, 15]. He found the Americans, newly at war,
somewhat confused strategically and organisationally; the Army and
Navy continued to fight each other for control of resources and operations. They had conflicting strategic priorities – the Navy intent on
revenging themselves on the Japanese, while the Army visualised an
immediate march on Berlin. Cunningham found the whole experience
exasperating and frustrating. The Joint Staff Mission, representing the
Chiefs of Staff, sat with the newly-formed (and hardly harmonious)
Joint Chiefs of Staff, but since decisions were taken by the Combined
Chiefs of Staff (the Chiefs of Staff meeting with the Joint Chiefs of
Staff), it could only counsel and inform – 'we are only liaison officers
with no power to order a man or a dinghy to move', as Cunningham put
it [16].[2]

Cunningham's fiercest encounters were with the equally unbending
Ernest King, a real case of the immovable object meeting the irresist-
ible force. He had some straight-talking encounters with King but one
'very stormy interview' cleared the air [17]. King had been represented
generally in the United Kingdom as 'anti-British' and certainly
Cunningham came close to believing that. King had a low opinion of
the Admiralty and the Royal Navy arising from his unfavourable contact with them in 1917–18, when he was a member of the staff of
Admiral Mayo, C-in-C of the Atlantic Fleet.[3] He made his opinions
clear to Cunningham and normally he had to be coaxed or forced into
co-operation with the Royal Navy (and the U. S. Army). Nevertheless,

[1]FM Sir John Dill (1881–1944): Brig Gen 1918; I Corps BEF 1939–40; VCIGS Apr
1940; CIGS May 1940–Dec 1941; Head JSM, Washington, DC Dec 1941–Nov 1944;
member CCS.
[2]The US did not have a chiefs of staff (JCS) cttee till entering war 1941; formed to
counter British COS; together COS, JSM and JCS formed CCS. JSM formed Dec 1941
to represent UK services in USA. D. Rigby, 'The Combined Chiefs of Staff and American Strategic Co-ordination in World War II' (unpub. Ph.D. thesis, Brandeis U., 1997);
A. Danchev, 'Being Friends: The Combined Chiefs of Staff and the Making of Allied
Strategy in World War II', in L. Freedman (ed.), *War, Strategy and International Politics: Essays in Honour of Sir Michael Howard* (Oxford, 1992).
[3]Adm H. T. Mayo (1856–1937): grad from US N Acad 1876; hydrography spist; Capt
1908; CO *California* 1909–10; Cdt, Mare I N Yd, S Francisco 1911–13; RA & Aide for
Personnel to S Navy 1913; CO Bat Div 4 1913–14; VA & 2nd-in-C Atl F & C-in-C 1916–
19; ret 1920. On visit to UK 1917, Cdr King accompanied Mayo.

there were several occasions, both before and after Cunningham's time in Washington, when King volunteered U. S. naval co-operation, even to the extent of placing American forces under the White Ensign [15]. King was not anti-British as such, however; he is best described as ultra-nationalistic and wedded to the U. S. Navy. Having just succeeded to the top post and having to settle in amidst an organisational reshuffle, as well as a world war which was going badly for the Allies, he was much preoccupied with re-arranging commands, finding ships for both Atlantic and Pacific, planning a massive expansion and adjusting to a new inter-service structure. The increasingly importunate British were an additional burden.

Fortunately for Cunningham, relief from the oppressive heat and unwholesome atmosphere of Washington came swiftly, with the commitment of the United States to the Mediterranean policy advocated by the British, beginning with the 'Torch' landing in North Africa, scheduled for 30 October 1942. Cunningham was put forward by the Americans as Allied Naval Commander of the Expeditionary Force (ANCXF). His fighting reputation, dignity, conscientiousness, unselfishness and exemplary leadership of his staff had earned the warm respect of Americans (including King). They appreciated, too, his dedication to the most effective means of winning the war in combination with the United States and other members of the United Nations. He had, furthermore, an unparalleled knowledge of the Mediterranean. As ANCXF-designate, he returned to Britain on 11 October 1942 and at the beginning of November to the Mediterranean.

1.   *To Admiral Sir Howard Kelly*[1]

Alexandria,
29 March 1942

. . . it is proposed that I should go to Washington and deal with the American CNS who is being difficult.

I don't know why the Admiralty have chosen me for this job. I am no use at it but I daresay I can give the Yank some straight speaking. . . .

2.   *A. V. Alexander to Churchill*

3 June 1942

. . . Moreover it seems clear that unless he [Cunningham] is entitled to maintain a certain state and entertain fairly freely, which would be quite impossible on the pay at present attaching to the post, he will be unable to take full advantage, in his dealings with the Americans, of the prestige attaching to his name as a result of the achievements of the Mediterranean Fleet under his Command.

3.   *Churchill to A. V. Alexander*

4 June 1942

1. As you know, I do not think the arrangement of Commands is the best that could be made. I thought that Cunningham should command the Home Fleet, Admiral Noble should go to Washington, and that Admiral Tovey should go to Liverpool and manage Western Approaches. I am sure that this is what the true interests of the Service and the war require, and I hope it may soon be brought about.

2. However, I think there are certain advantages in Admiral Cunningham paying a short visit to the US, as they will pay great attention to what he says on account of his having actually commanded ships against the enemy, so frequently and on so a large scale. I hope that in say a couple of months he will be put in his rightful place as the Head of the Home Fleet. All that you say about him shows how wrong it is to send him off out of the war. You know well that all important Anglo-

---

[1] Adm Sir W. A. Howard Kelly (1873–1952): Capt *Gloucester* in pursuit of *Goeben* 1914; liaison France 1916–17; Cdre 8CS & UK force, Adriatic 1917–19; Head, UK N Mission, Greece 1919–21; 2CS 1925–7; Ady rep L of N 1927–9; 1BS, Med F 1929–30; C-in-C China 1931–3; ret 1936; UK N rep, Turkey 1940–4.

American decisions are taken between the First Sea Lord and Admiral King.

3. I could not agree to the course you propose of making Admiral Cunningham Deputy to Field Marshal Dill. Dill's position is exceptional. Admiral Cunningham has been appointed by you merely to fill Admiral Little's place.[1] If he were treated exceptionally, the Air Force would demand a similar rise for Air Marshal Evill.[2] In fact they have a better case as far as the importance of their business actually transacted in the US is concerned.

4.   *Pound to A. V. Alexander*

8 June 1942

6. Important Anglo-American decisions are arranged in the first place between Admiral King and myself, but there is great work in front of Admiral Cunningham to obtain complete co-operation between the two Services. This does not exist at the present time.

Admiral Little has done a great deal to forward this co-operation, but it requires someone with Admiral Cunningham's prestige to bring it to a really satisfactory conclusion.

5.   *A. V. Alexander to Churchill*

9 June 1942

... I am more than ever convinced that my desire to have Admiral Cunningham at Washington, to improve and expedite our co-operation with the US Navy is sound.

There can be no doubt as to the part which plans must play, now and during the rest of the War, and the importance of having the fullest understanding and working arrangement with Admiral King and his staff. That the USA recognise the position is indicated by the appointment of Admiral Stark.[3] They have given him a position he is able to maintain, and I cannot think we should do less. . . .

---

[1]Adm Sir Charles J. C. Little: ent RN 1897; Capt 1917; RA 1929; VA 1933; Adm 1937; 2SL 1938–41; Head, BAD, Washington, DC 1941–2; C-in-C Portsmouth 1942.

[2]Air Mshl Sir Douglas Evill (1892–1971): b. Australia; RNAS, W Front 1914–18; RAF 1919; 20 Sqdn, Iraq 1932; Wing Cdr, RAF Staff Coll 1929, & Group Capt & Asst Cdt 1932; AVM, Bomber Cmd 1938; Snr Air SO, France 1940; SASO, Fighter Cmd 1940; AM and head RAF delegn, Washington 1942–3; ACM & VCAS 1943; ret 1947.

[3]Adm H. R. ('Betty') Stark, US Navy (1880–1972): destroyer & staff service, Med & UK 1917–18; N War Coll; Navy Dept; battleship cmd; Chief, Bur of Ordnance; cruiser

6.   *A. V. Alexander to Sir Kingsley Wood*[1]

10 April 1943

... The appointment of Admiral Cunningham paid us handsomely as events have proved.

7.   *To Aunt Doodles*[2]

London,
11 June 1942

... I am having rather a riot with the powers that be. They will not give me proper status in Washington and are trying to pay me less than our Naval Attaché over there.

So I have refused to go and have written a letter requesting permission to withdraw my acceptance of the appointment. Although I have shown it to the First Lord I have not actually sent it in, giving him time to see what he can do. Of course as usual it is Winston Churchill who is the nigger in the woodpile and he has undoubtedly some ulterior motive.

I lunched with him and Mrs Churchill at 10 Downing Street on Tuesday. I liked her very much.[3] I tried to bring him to the point but he slid out of it every time though I made it quite clear to him that the question of my going to the USA was not yet settled.

He has asked me to dine and sleep at Chequers on Sunday and I am going.[4] I know he has some proposition to put to me which at lunch he didn't think I was in the mood to accept. He's in for the surprise of his life when he makes it as I know what it is – nothing to do with going to the USA.

cmd; CNO 1 Aug 1939–26 March 1942; C-in-C, US Naval Forces in Eur Waters 1942–5; ret.1946. B. M. Simpson III, *Admiral Harold R. Stark: Architect of Victory, 1939–1945* (Colombia, SC, 1989).

[1]Sir Kingsley Wood: Con MP; Post Mr Gen 1931–5; M Health 1935–8; S Air 1938–40; C Ex 1940–3.

[2]Doodles & Connie May: Cunningham's maiden aunts, who looked after him as a schoolboy in Edinburgh but by this time were ensconced in Barmouth, N Wales.

[3]Lady Clementine Spencer-Churchill (1885–1977): neé Ogilvy Hozier; m WSC 1908; much charity work; independent spirit; raised to peerage 1965.

[4]Chequers: country house for PMs, Buckinghamshire.

8. *To Aunt Doodles*

London,
16 June 1942

... Well I won my battle but for myself only not for any further
incumbent of the Washington job.

A very small party down there [Chequers] this time. Major and Mrs
Lloyd George – he a very nice man.[1] A Mr Watt and a Scot parliamen-
tary Private Secretary to Winston and evidently a friend of Alan's.[2] Air
Marshal Harris the bomber king whom I cordially disliked and General
Ismay the Imperial Defence Secretary.[3]

... then to the great man's study. He cleared everyone else out and
we had a heart to heart talk for about one and a half hours. We found
many points both of agreement and disagreement and I found him quite
ready to listen. We went to bed at 2.30 a.m.

9. *From Pound*

1 June 1942

There are three things I should like you to take up with Admiral King
when you get an opportunity.

A. *Invasion of Australia*

We have said that in the event of Australia being invaded we would
send the Eastern Fleet to join up with the [US] Pacific Fleet.

By the Eastern Fleet we mean Force A of that Fleet, e.g., *Warspite,
Valiant, Nelson, Rodney* and three carriers.[4]

---

[1]Major Gwilym Lloyd George (1894–1967): s of DLG, PM; W Front 1914–18;
Lib MP 1922–4; Con MP, Pembrokeshire 1929–50; PPS, BoT; M Food & Power
1942–5; Con MP, Newcastle 1951; M Food 1951–4; Home S 1954–7; Viscount
Tenby 1957.

[2]Probably Dr (Sir Robert) Watson Watt, the father of radar, and Jock Colville, a
private sec to the PM.

[3]ACM Sir Arthur Harris (1892–1984): b. Rhodesia; RFC in WW1; Sqdn Ldr RAF
1918; cmd 5 Group, Bomber Cmd 1939; DCAS 1940; head RAF delegn Washington
1942; ACM & C-in-C Bomber Cmd Feb 1942–5; M of RAF 1946 & ret.

Gen Sir Hastings Ismay (1887–1965): Indian Army 1905; E Africa 1914–20; Staff
Coll Quetta; HQ Staff India; RAF Staff Coll 1924–5; Asst Sec CID 1925–30; Mil Sec
India 1933; SO; Dep Sec CID 1936; Sec CID 1938; Maj Gen 1939; link between COS &
PM; Head of Mil Secretariat; Lt Gen 1942; Gen 1944; ret & baron 1946; served
Mountbatten, India 1947–8; Sec St Commonwealth Relns 1951; 1st Sec-Gen NATO
1952–7. Lord Ismay, *The Memoirs of General the Lord Ismay* (London, 1960).

[4]*Warspite*: 1915, 30600t, 24k, 8×15in, 8×6in, 8×4in, fully mod 1930s; *Valiant*: 1916,
32700t, 24k, 8×15in, 20×4.5in, fully mod 1930s.

Nelson, Rodney: 1927, 33950t, 23k, 9×16in, 12×6in, 6×4.7in, 2×24.5in tt.

We do not know however, whether it is the American intention to send their Fleet to Australian waters in these circumstances. If it is then we should have a rough plan as regards areas of concentration, bases to be used, etc.

I attach a rough appreciation of this problem [not reproduced] and I do not think we can get any further until we know what the US intentions are.

B.   *Offensive versus Japan*
  1.   Working through the Islands:

I believe the American plan is to work to the westward, and north-westward, commencing from Northern Australia, going step by step as shore-based air protection is provided, e.g., the same method as the Japanese adopted in the southward movement. This would be a very slow business as combined operation after combined operation would be required.

  2.   I attach a copy of JP (42) 537 [not reproduced], in which the Joint Planners propose taking Truk.[1] The COS have not yet considered this paper, but as it gives a good survey of the whole problem I thought you would like to have it.

C.   If at any time we have to reinforce the [US] Pacific Fleet we should know exactly what is required to enable the ships of the two nations to work together. I am asking Tovey about his experiences with TF 99 and will then ask you to get something arranged with the Americans.[2]

10.   *To Aunt Doodles*

Washington,
29 June 1942

. . . I got a bit mixed up with the PM. He obviously bears me no malice. He himself took me into the President on Friday afternoon. I was much struck by Roosevelt. Such a charming man and of course he hardly moves out of his chair. He was off to the country for a weekend but he has asked me to come and see him and have a talk when he comes back.[3] . . .

Illustrious, Formidable, Indomitable: 1940–1, 23000t, 31k, 54–60 aircraft, 16×4.5in. *Nelson* appears to have been 'back up' for, and *Rodney* did not serve in, Eastern F.
[1]Joint Planning Staff (JPS): The heads of Planning Depts of all 3 Services.
[2]TF99: US Navy force serving with Home F 1942, cmd by R Adm R. C. Giffen, US Navy.
[3]President Franklin D. Roosevelt (1882–1945): Dem poln; NY St Sen 1911–13; Asst S of N 1913–20; V-Pres cand 1920; severe polio 1921; Govr N Y 1929–32; Pres 1933–45.

11.   *To Aunt Doodles*

6 July 1942

... It's an interesting but annoying job this. You don't have anything at all under your command and all you do is sit at a desk and on committees.

12.   *To Aunt Doodles*

13 July 1942

... One seems a long way off the war here. ...

Whether we have the best organisation for winning the war is another question. I don't myself think we are close enough together yet, but it will doubtless come.

13.   *To Aunt Doodles*

25 July 1942

... [Following his address to the Overseas Press Club] I have fairly stirred things up about the shipping losses from submarines, which I took as my principal theme. Unfortunately there were two or three US naval officers there and they did not like hearing that there were shortcomings. ...

14.   *To Pound*

31 July 1942

B.   There is no doubt Little built up quite a unique position for himself, and was most highly thought of; I am not sure that his underlings command the same respect.

Patterson and Dick have very quickly established themselves, particularly the former. I think the Americans like his downright attitude. They are both on excellent terms with the American staff.[1]

---

[1]Adm Sir Wilfrid M. Patterson (1893–1956): ent RN 1906; RA & Dep Hd BAD 1941–2; Adm 1949; ret 1950.

R Adm Royer M. Dick: Cdr 1933; SO (P) Med F 1939; Capt 1940; BAD 1942; Cdre 1st Cl & CoS to C-in-C Med 1943; *Belfast* 1944–5; RA 1949; ret 1953; later at NATO HQ.

King I have not found very easy. He announces his decisions without giving reasons which I find a little trying. I will doubtless in time wean him from this bad habit.

D.   Our RAF people here are very upset about the lack of co-ordination of the aircraft against the submarine and asked for my assistance in getting the Americans to establish something analogous to our Coastal Command.

The trouble is that the majority of anti-submarine aircraft are Army bombers and the Army is quite intolerant of naval control of their aircraft. The Navy is afraid to bring it to a head on account of the greater political pull exercised by the Army.

Willson himself asked me if I could help him on the CCS level.[1] The fact is they are in a mess. The Army have, I believe, demanded that they should conduct the aerial anti-submarine war and I believe at one time demanded that our Hudson squadron be put under them. If this latter is seriously put forward we shall easily defeat it.[2]

The line I have suggested to them on the main issue is that it really doesn't matter who is the head of the aerial anti-submarine effort provided it is all under one organisation and that that organisation is under the operational control of the Navy Department.

15.   *To Pound*

12 August 1942

As I signalled to you I had a very stormy interview with King about submarines for the Mediterranean. He was abominably rude and I had to be quite firm with him and I told him that the remarks he made got us no further in winning the war. I do not think the breeze did any harm and he made a lame sort of apology when I left but if he says the same things about us to his underlings as he said to me, as I have no doubt he does, it makes things very difficult. . . .

I hear Russell Willson is to be relieved from CoS to King. Edwards, at present Deputy CoS, has been promoted to Vice Admiral and is relieving him. This is I think all to the good as the former is rather what they call over here 'a stuffed shirt' – a nonentity – and the latter is a livewire, very ready to work with us in every way. . . .[3]

---

[1] R Adm Russell Willson, US Navy: Supt N Acad 1942; Deputy C-in-C Aug 1942; Jt Strat Svy Ctee, JCS Nov 1942.

[2] Lockheed Hudson: 1938, coastal patrol bomber, 2×120ohp, 253mph, 2500mls, 5 crew, 5–7mg, 1400lbs bombs.

[3] V Adm R. S. Edwards, US Navy: R Adm & DCoS & CoS 1942.

16. *From Pound*

24 August 1942

4. I am sorry you had to have a 'bust-up' with King but my own opinion is that it will have done no harm. It was really quite amazing that he should say that we never discussed the submarine question because we did so for some considerable time. . . .

I do not quite understand your remark about King having a fixed determination not to place any US ships under British command because we have had their ships working under C-in-C, Home Fleet for a very long time. . . .

17. *To Howard Kelly*

17 August 1942

. . . I have been here just two months and frankly I don't like it. The façade is that we represent the COS and that we sit in council with the US COS and discuss high policy and take decisions.

Actually we are only liaison officers with no power to order a man or a dinghy to move. We see the US COS once a week and register approval of minor matters. Sometimes we have to try to persuade them to do things they don't want to do but naturally these matters are mostly done by signal.

Otherwise I am the head of a vast organisation for processing the manufacture of weapons of war and the building of ships and I spend a large part of my time arguing about who has the most right to them, the US or ourselves.

The Navy Department officials are very nice and polite to us but they are quite determined not to be run by us, in fact rather than benefiting by our experience they prefer to have a disaster of their own to learn by.

In some ways they are very good. Their FAA is excellent, as good as our own and of course with far superior weapons. Some of their technical stuff such as AA control is ahead of ours.

But they are poor in A/S work and the sinkings on this coast have made the situation rather critical as far as shipping is concerned. In this line they are paying some attention to us. But as most of the aircraft engaged in A/S work belong to the army and as the jealousy between the two services is extreme, rather worse than our own relations with the RAF, it is difficult to get them to make progress, but they are coming along.[1]

The cross currents here are rather astonishing. The army wants to fight the Huns, the navy wants to fight the Japanese, and I am not really sure that we and the USA have the same ideas on how to conduct the war. . . .

18.   *To Aunt Doodles*

23 August 1942

. . . On Tuesday we had an important dinner party – to my opposite number in the USA Navy. I asked all the heads of our mission to meet him. A party of ten.

We thought it was going to be a very sticky party but the American admiral after three or four glasses of wine became quite lively and we had quite a cheery evening.

I had another interview with the President during the week. He is a most delightful man but rather inclined to sweep difficulties away with a wave of the hand. A very good trait in wartime however. You'll never do anything if you let the difficulties overawe you. . . .

19.   *To Aunt Doodles*

30 August 1942

. . . We had a dinner party on Wednesday. Some interesting people. A man Butler and his wife. He is head of British publicity over here. It's frightful that we have to go in for that sort of thing but the American press are so obsessed with the doings of their own armed forces that one would think Great Britain was taking no part in the war at all. . . .[2]

---

[1]In the first half of 1942, U-boats sank at will along the virtually defenceless US eastern seaboard, known as 'the Second Happy Time'. R. J. Love, Jr., *History of US Navy*, vol II (1942–91) (Harrisburg, PA, 1992) and M. Gannon, *Operation Drumbeat* (New York, 1990) give opposing points of view.

[2]Probably N. M. Butler (1893–1973): Scottish Horse 1916–18; FO 1920; Pte Sec 1920s; 1st Sec 1929; Pte Sec to PM 1930–5; Chargé d'Affaires, Tehran 1935; Berne; Cnslr & Minr, Br Emb, Washington Dec 1939–Aug 1942; Head N Am Dept; Asst US St 1944–7; Amb Brazil 1947–51; Amb Netherlands 1952–4.

20.   *To Aunt Doodles*

6 September 1942

. . . I also went to dine at the New Zealand legation. . . . I sat next the Canadian minister and Admiral Leahy the President's Chief of Staff a very courteous old Admiral and delightful to talk to.[1] After dinner I was about an hour with Mr Stimson the War Secretary and a most interesting talk. A most delightful man. . . .[2]

[1]Canadian Minister: Leighton McCarthy (1869–1952): lawyer; Lib MP, N Simcoe 1898–1908; Minister to USA 1941–3 & Ambassador 1943–5.

F Adm William D. Leahy, US Navy (1875–1959): R Adm 1927; CNO 1937–9; Govr Puerto Rico; Amb to Vichy France 1941–2; President's CoS & Chmn JCS July 1942; F Adm 1944; ret 1949. W. D. Leahy, *I Was There* (New York, 1950).

[2]Henry L. Stimson (1867–1950): Repubn; Sec War 1911–13; Sec State 1929–33; Sec War 1940–5. H. L. Stimson with McG. Bundy, *On Active Service in Peace and War* (London, 1947).

PART II

RETURN TO THE MEDITERRANEAN

SECTION A

'TORCH':

THE LANDINGS IN NORTH AFRICA
JULY 1942–MAY 1943

Operation 'Torch', a series of Anglo-American landings in North Africa in November 1942 designed to clear the southern shore of the Mediterranean of Axis forces, was a great success, but its origins were marked by deep division between American and British military leaders. The source of their dispute lay in their nations' differing strategic traditions. The Americans plunged straight for the enemy's heart but the British preferred an indirect approach, wearing down their opponent in a series of marginal campaigns, which used the superiority of British sea power. In 1942 the Americans, already distracted by a desire to seek vengeance in the Pacific for the surprise Japanese attack on Pearl Harbor, also sought an early end to the European war. Through operation 'Bolero' they proposed to build up forces in Britain with which to invade northern Europe, either in 'Sledgehammer', a diversionary invasion of western France in 1942 designed to relieve pressure on a collapsing Soviet Union, or in 'Roundup', a full-scale landing across the Channel in 1943, which intended a rapid march on Berlin. The British thought that the German army and air force were too strong for any invasion the western alliance could mount in 1942 or 1943; ministers, military leaders and public opinion feared a repeat of the Western Front's bloody stalemate of 1914–18. They pressed for an attritional campaign which would weaken German military and aerial power, leading to a return to the continent in 1944, when German strength in the air and on the ground would be more manageable. They had invested heavily, in prestige as well as military resources, in the Mediterranean, where their position in the first half of 1942 was parlous; a successful campaign in that region would restore British morale, prestige, control – and her economic and diplomatic position in the post-war Middle East and Balkans. Almost every British minister and service chief supported the idea of an early Mediterranean expedition, Cunningham included [21, 25]. It was President Franklin Roosevelt, interested in securing control of Morocco to aid the Battle of the Atlantic and realising that the British were unalterably opposed to a landing in France in 1942, who tipped the strategic balance in favour of 'Torch' in July 1942.

The Mediterranean Sea, 1942–44

American service chiefs accepted their Commander-in-Chief's decision but rather reluctantly, causing Cunningham to complain that they
were dragging their feet, dangerously so, on preparation in the summer
of 1942. He himself had no complaints, for, on American initiative, he
had been appointed Naval Commander of the Allied Expeditionary
Force (ANCXF), setting out clearly his terms [23, 26]. Cunningham
was keen to get out of the hothouse atmosphere of Washington and
back to the 'real war', and to do so in the Mediterranean, with which he
had been identified for a quarter of a century, was doubly satisfying. He
had an unavailing struggle to persuade the Americans to recognise the
crucial importance of Tunis, finding they were more obsessed with the
less important Moroccan ports and a safety-first approach to the problem of communications through the Strait of Gibraltar. He and his
colleagues were unable to shift the JCS; the 'Torch' landings, at Casablanca, Oran and Algiers, therefore represented a compromise between
the American and British points of view [25].

Vice Admiral Sir Bertram Ramsay, who as Vice Admiral, Dover, had
masterminded the evacuation from Dunkirk in 1940, was the chief planner for 'Torch'.[1] Ramsay, a mercurial, meticulous man, worked happily
with Cunningham, to whom he had to cede the limelight. Cunningham,
notoriously irked by staff detail and jargon, was fortunate in having
Ramsay at his side, for the plans, which led to almost total success, were
almost entirely the latter's brainchild. Cunningham recognised Ramsay's
invaluable contribution with warm words of praise tinged with guilt,
having come to his post rather late in the preparations [27–9]. Cunningham
for his part magnanimously waived seniority to serve under the untried
and relatively junior American Commanding General, Dwight D. Eisenhower, to whom he gave subtle tutelage in the arts of war and unwavering
support in the negotiation of the North African political maze [30].[2]

The landings passed off remarkably well, but it was as much a matter
of good fortune as of careful planning. French North Africa was gov-

[1]Adm Sir Bertram Ramsay (1883–1945): ent RN 1898; Lt 1904; signal spist; N War
Coll 1913; Grand F 1914–15; *M25* 1915–17; *Broke* 1917–18; Capt 1923; *Weymouth*,
Danae; N War Coll 1927–9; *Kent*, China 1929–31; IDC 1931–3; *Royal Sovereign* 1933–
5; RA 1935; CoS to Adm Sir R. Backhouse, Home F but felt redundant & left Dec 1935;
ret 1938; VA Dover 1939–42; chief planner, Med landings 1942–3 & Normandy Dec
1943; ANCXF 1944–5; d air accident 2 Jan 1945. W. S. Chalmers, *Full Cycle: The
Biography of Admiral Sir Bertram Ramsay* (London, 1959).
[2]Gen of Army Dwight D. Eisenhower, US Army (1890–1969): able staff officer; Col
March 1941; Brig Gen Sep 1941; chief War Plans, then Ops, Dec 1941; Cmdg Gen, US
Forces in Eur June 1942; Cmdg Gen, N Af, Sicily, Italy 1942–3; Gen Feb 1943; Sup
Cdr, AEF 1944–5; Gen of Army Dec 1944; CoS Dec 1945–8; Pres, Columbia U 1948–
50; Sup Cdr, NATO 1950–2; Pres (Repub) 1953–61. S. E. Ambrose, *Eisenhower the
Soldier, 1890–1952* (London, 1984).

erned and garrisoned largely by men loyal to the Vichy regime.[1] The Americans had convinced themselves that, while the British had no more than a negative equity with Vichy, they enjoyed a close relationship, likely to be rewarded by an enthusiastic welcome for the mainly American expedition; British opinion, including that of Cunningham, was rather more sceptical [38]. The British were proved right; French resistance was generally instant, fierce and, in operations 'Reservist' and 'Terminal' (attempts to seize undamaged the harbours of Oran and Algiers), successful. In addition, many landing craft, in largely unschooled hands, were casualties of surf or mishandling. There were shortcomings in anti-aircraft defence, communications and refuelling and had the opposition been German, the invaders might well have received a very bloody nose. However, the French were divided, their weapons often out of date, their training neglected and, crucially, Darlan was there to order a ceasefire after a day of hostilities.[2] The first great Anglo-American combined operation had begun, somewhat fortuitously, on the credit side [31–6, 105].

Darlan, unloved by almost everyone in Britain and America because of his collaboration with the Germans and apparent political ambition, was in Algiers ostensibly to visit his sick son, though perhaps he had observed the turning of the tide in the war and wished to switch sides [40, 48, 50, 57, 67]. It soon transpired that only Darlan could command the support of most Frenchmen [40, 55]. The ceasefire was a matter of mutual interest between the western allies and Darlan. He was granted a political fiefdom in North Africa while the allies, secure in the centre of the resident French population, could bend their energies to the task of racing the Germans to Tunis. For this exercise in *realpolitik*, the green Eisenhower was widely pilloried in the British and American governments and the media of both countries, though military opinion was almost universally in favour of the deal [44–5, 47–8, 52]. Churchill and Roosevelt were forced to state, hurriedly, that the Darlan ceasefire and resulting political arrangement was but temporary and for the purposes only of saving life and expediting 'Torch's' military aims [47–8].

Cunningham shared the widespread allied distaste for Darlan but came to respect and work with him in some amity, even socialising with him [43–6, 50, 55, 58–9]. Importantly, Cunningham gave unstinting support to Eisenhower, though this and subsequent French political and

---

[1]Republic established at Vichy in neutral unoccupied S France June 1940.
[2]Adm Jean-François Darlan, French N (1881–1942): creator of modern French N; Adm & C-in-C 1939; Vichy Mins of Defence, For Affs, etc., & C-in-C Armed Forces June 1940–Nov 1942; collaborated with Germans, then with Allies; assassinated by Royalist fanatic 24 Dec 1942.

military turmoils were to cost them a great deal of time and effort [40–1, 48, 54, 60]. There is a note of exasperation with French navel-gazing, but the bizarre behaviour of French political and military leaders reflected their confused loyalties, aims and rivalries, which had been given scope for fruition by the consequences of defeat in 1940. Moreover, divisions within and between the British and Americans served only to muddy further the French waters [41, 44–5, 52, 62–4, 66]. Cunningham was initially concerned to bring French units over to the Allied side, a hope sadly terminated by the Toulon fleet's ignominious scuttling and the prevarication of Godfroy at Alexandria [38–9, 41, 50, 67].[1] His second aim was to secure ports, preferably undamaged, but where they were wrecked, to restore them quickly, and to obtain the co-operation of senior French officers. With Darlan's help, this aim was largely achieved [46, 50, 83].

Like most British military leaders, Cunningham was extremely uncomplimentary about other French leaders, notably Giraud, who lacked political sense, and de Gaulle, who had rather too much of it [48, 55, 62–4].[2] The Frenchman who caused Cunningham and his successor as C-in-C, Mediterranean, Admiral Harwood, most heartache was Vice Admiral Godfroy, commanding the demilitarised French squadron at Alexandria.[3] Several political and naval envoys tried to persuade Godfroy to join the western allies – which he did but only after months of patient negotiation and much personal agonising [42, 49, 51, 53, 56, 59, 61, 65]. It is ironic that the unsavoury Darlan should prove the most useful French ally in the whole 'Torch' operation.

In hindsight, Cunningham appears to have been over cautious in hanging on to a major fleet to deal with possible Italian or Vichy capital ship sorties. Both fleets adopted a supine posture and, given the experience of the previous two years, little more was to be expected. One must remember, however, the nature of Cunningham's responsibility.

[1]VAdm R. E. Godfroy, French N (1885–1981): ent N 1901; Lt de V 1913; cruisers & gunboats 1914–18; naval aviation 1920s; Capt de V 1931; cmded cruisers 1931–5; Contre Amiral 1936; DCNS 1936–7; 4 C Div 1937; VA 19 June 1940; joined Free French N May 1943; removed from cmd 1943 but this annulled 1955.

[2]Gen Henri Giraud, French A (1879–1949): CO 7 & 9 Armies 1939–40; captured but escaped April 1942; cmdr French forces N Af Nov 1942; H Cmnr N Af Dec 1942; ousted Nov 1943.

Pres Charles de Gaulle, French A (1890–1970): ent army 1909; wounded and captive 1914–16; 4 Arm Div March 1940; Brig-Gen & U Sec Natl Def June 1940; launched Free French 18 June 1940; Pres 1944–6 & 1958–69;

[3]Adm Sir Henry Harwood (1888–1950): ent RN 1903; t spist; Grand F 1914–16; IDC; Capt 1928; *Exeter, Ajax* & Cdre, S Am Div 1936–9; VA & ACNS (F) Dec 1940; C-in-C Med March 1942; C-in-C Levant Feb 1943; invalided home March 1943; FOIC Orkney & Shetland April 1944; Adm & ret Aug 1945.

'Torch' was a major Allied expedition, the first of several. Large numbers of merchantmen and even greater numbers of landing craft were involved, together with 150,000 troops. The landings were on potentially hostile shores. The Americans were rather nervous about the success of their first 'big show'. The enemy and Vichy had an enormous target before them. The stakes were high – 'Torch's' success would open up the 'soft underbelly of the Axis'. As Cunningham realised, if the Axis or Vichy were going to counter-attack, 'Torch' represented a golden opportunity. One major raid by the opposition could have been disastrous. Cunningham could not afford to take the risk, nor, as he pointed out, could air power fill the gap if his major vessels were withdrawn [68, 73–4, 88].

For the most part, operations after the landings consisted of logistic support by the Inshore Squadron, constant anti-aircraft action in port and at sea, intensive anti-submarine patrols by air and sea, attempts to disrupt enemy communications by air strikes, submarines, coastal forces and Force Q, and sweeping and salvage in captured ports. The interruption of enemy convoys represented a difficult and prolonged task, not the easy matter suggested by Churchill [71–2, 77, 79, 91]. The anti-submarine effort was ultimately effective, though there were major losses. Much of the burden of anti-aircraft work was shouldered by the warships and merchant vessels, aided by radar, fighter cover and direction, much improved close range armament and a ring of confidence [98, 105]. Determined action by naval and air forces eventually shut down the enemy's seaborne route to Tunis and Bizerta. As it turned out, the most important ships were 'the militia of the sea' – trawlers, landing craft, minesweepers, motor launches, AA ships, escort vessels and submarines; maritime warfare in the Mediterranean had shifted inexorably to the little ships [70]. The Allies occupied and opened up successive ports and the soldiers were capably assisted in their long slog towards the glittering prize – Tunis [75–6, 81, 84, 94, 96–7, 105].

Cunningham turned in a masterful performance – experienced, assured, thoroughly at home in Mediterranean conditions, a strong prop to the tyro Eisenhower [69, 82, 86, 92, 101]. He seems to have been somewhat dictatorial but he throve on the whole experience [87]. Though he no longer commanded a battle fleet and was shore-bound much of the time, with most of his journeys made in an uncomfortable Beaufighter, he directed the vast armada and ships of several nations, notably those of the USA, with aplomb, certainty and shrewdness.[1] In

[1]Bristol Beaufighter: 1940–5, 2-eng, 2-seat torpedo/fighter/night ftr/bomber, 4 cannon, 7mg, 320mph, 1470m.

February 1943 he became only the second man to become C-in-C, Mediterranean, for a second time – a wise move designed to accord with the progress of the campaign and the decisions of the other services [82, 85–6].

The end came swiftly in May 1943, Cunningham ensuring with utter ruthlessness the inability of the Axis to do a Dunkirk; for him and for many Mediterranean veterans, it represented macabre revenge for the evacuations of Greece and Crete in 1941. A swarm of destroyers and coastal craft, at the last shielded by fighters, blocked seaward escape routes for the enemy [96–7, 99, 106]. The one major regret he had was the failure of the American JCS to agree to a landing deep inside the Mediterranean, making possible the early seizure of Tunis, rightly identified by Cunningham and other British service chiefs as the key to North Africa [105]. By the time the Axis surrender marked the campaign's conclusion, Cunningham and his fellow commanders were already planning the next amphibious landing.

1. The Preparations

21. *To Pound*

21 July 1942

... I am more than ever convinced that conditions this year lie in Mediterranean. There seems almost every advantage in an operation to obtain hold in North Africa now. It would go a long way towards solving our shipping problem once the short route through the Mediterranean was gained. It would jeopardise the whole of Rommel's forces and relieve anxiety about Malta.[1] It would shake Italy to the core and rouse the occupied countries. To intervene effectively Hitler would have to act through Spain and/or unoccupied France thus involving him in most unwelcome fighting and transport commitments.[2] The troops for purpose would have to be withdrawn from France thus weakening those defences. The effect on Russian situation might well be conclusive.

Finally it would put us in a position to attack later through southern France as well as north west or to go for Italy. If we wait until 1943 it may mean facing a Germany in Europe free of Russian commitments and immeasurably stronger.

2. If we consider North African project we should plan to land at least as far east as Algiers, though I am strongly in favour of including surprise to Bizerta (which could so [easily?] be done under cover of a Malta convoy). I discussed these ideas with King who though implacably opposed to Casablanca project gave me impression that an operation along North African coast and at Bizerta in particular would be much more likely to have his support.

3. I am naturally unable to weigh up shipping commitments implied but feel they could surely be met if reward is control of Mediterranean and quick route to Middle East.

---

[1]FM Erwin Rommel, German A (1890–1944): W Front 1914–16; armr cdr France 1940; cmded Afrika Korps 1941–3; Italy 1943; i/c defences in NW France Jan–July 1944; forced suicide after being implicated in bomb plot against Hitler.
[2]Adolf Hitler (1885–1945): Corporal WWI; right-wing Putsch 1923; Nat Socst (Nazi) Chllr Germany 1933–45.

22. *To Pound*

31 July 1942

A. I was much puzzled by the discrepancy between your personal telegram to me and CCS94.[1]

I thought CCS94 a most poisonous document. . . .

I gather the President has decided that 'Torch' must be carried out by 30 October which is a great advance and in line with your message and ensures that not only the planning but the preparations must be started forthwith.

Smith is apparently going as CoS to the Supreme Commander.[2] . . . He told me that the reason that he had come to see me was to have a naval opinion as to the effect of the capture of North Africa on the naval and shipping situation. King had apparently stated that it would have little or no effect, hence Smith's desire for an independent opinion. I explained to him that the gain from complete success was just incalculable from every point of view. I fear King is going to be a difficulty, particularly if he insists on implementing the paragraph in CCS94 with regard to the reduction of US naval forces in the European theatre. Smith is also an enthusiast for 'Torch' and he told me that Eisenhower was too. Marshall also appears to be full out.[3]

Incidentally, Smith sounded me out as to whether I would take on the job of Naval Commander in the Operation. I don't suppose there was anything behind his query but he stressed that it was important to get a naval officer who was wholeheartedly in favour of the operation.

I replied that if it was thought that I could be of use I should be proud to serve under an American Supreme Commander.

I don't know what you think of all this. You probably have someone already in your mind, but if it was considered that I could be of use I should be more than willing. At the same time I don't want to push myself forward. . . .

[1]CCS 94: the strategic document by which the JCS agreed to 'Torch'.

[2]Gen W. Bedell ('Beetle') Smith, US Army (1895–1961): AEF 1917–18; Lt Col April 1941; Maj Gen Dec 1942; Lt Gen Jan 1943; CoS to Eisenhower 1942–5; Gen 1951.

[3]Gen of Army George C. Marshall, US Army (1880–1959): AEF 1917–18; Brig Gen 1936; chief War Plans 1938; DCOS & COS 1939; Gen of Army Dec 1944; ret Nov 1945; China mission 1946; S State 1947–9; S Def 1950–1.

23. *To Pound*

12 August 1942

... The trouble is that the US COS returned from London with a feeling of frustration particularly on the Army side. ... the Navy saw the chance of getting on with the war in the Pacific and leapt at it.[1] There is no doubt that the US COS and British COS interpret that direful document, CCS94, quite differently.

There was a stormy meeting of the Joint Planners over the British COS' amendments to the Strategical Hypothesis. Our representatives had to put up with some pretty hard remarks including accusations of ingratitude for all that had been done for the UK by the US.

At the last CCS meeting King was quite impossible and just objected to everything, his cry being that it was contrary to everything that had been agreed in London. Even the British COS's suggested directive to Eisenhower he objected to as not in accordance with CCS94.

None of this would matter a row of pins but it reacts on 'Torch', for which there are few signs of enthusiasm, and they do not seem to be getting down to it though they pay lip service to the usefulness of the operation. I may be overstressing this but I feel that at the moment there is not that wholehearted enthusiasm so necessary to produce success. I am quite sure that King is dead against it and that he has given it as his opinion that it is of no value to the UN war effort and this opinion of his is reflected all through the Navy Department.[2]

Leahy is I think a steadying influence; he takes the chair at the CCS meetings and does not seem to agree very well with King but he is all in favour of 'Torch' provided everything is done to ensure success.

The command question was discussed by Leahy, Marshall, King, Dill and myself. As I did not know your views on the Naval command I was very guarded and only put forward views as my own, committing no one. The whole affair is coloured on the US side by King's fixed determination not to place any US ships under British command He considers the operations of landing outside and inside the Mediterranean should be completely separate, the US C-in-C, Atlantic to command the former though he was prepared to yield some small measure of control of the Naval forces to the Supreme Commander.[3] Their method

---

[1]Cunningham habitually referred to the JCS as 'US COS'.
[2]UN: all the wartime allies, 1942–5.
[3]Adm Royall E. Ingersoll, US Navy: grad N Acad 1905; OpNav WWI; ONI; CO *Nokomis* 1924; Battleship Force; Capt & Dir, War Plans 1935–8; mission to UK 1938; RA 1938; Asst CNO 1940; CoS to King, Atl F 1941; VA & cmdr Atl F 1 Jan 1942; Adm 1 July 1942.

differs somewhat from ours in that until the soldiers are ashore the Naval Commander is invariably in sole charge. I have put on paper how I see it after hearing King's and Leahy's views and enclose it. I fear this letter is rather a diatribe against King but in my view he is a determined non-collaborator and means to work entirely for his own naval ends except in so far as he is forced to work with us. . . .

[Enclosure]

Command

The Command in forthcoming operations will evidently be one of the main points at issue. At present the matter is in the melting-pot and although the military commanders are nominated the question of the other services and of the appointment of a Deputy Supreme Commander remains open.

In so far as the Navy is concerned there are three possible arrangements–

(a) A Naval C-in-C subordinate to the Commanding General of the whole expedition and directing naval operations alongside the latter in consultation.

(b) A Naval Officer of comparatively junior rank (say Rear Admiral) on the staff of the Commanding General.

(c) A Naval officer of high standing on the staff of the Commanding General as his naval advisor or Naval Chief of Staff.

(a) Is the normal chain of command (except that the Supreme authority of the Commanding General is accepted). It has great advantages from the fact that it will give confidence to the naval forces in that they will know that they are receiving orders through their 'legal' Commander instead of directly from a General Officer of another nation. I doubt, however, if this arrangement will be acceptable to the US Navy although it seems to have been that in force between General Wavell and Admiral Hart in the ABDA area Supreme Command. . . .[1]

---

[1] ABDA: American-British-Dutch-Australian cmd in SW Pac Jan–Feb 1942.

FM Earl Wavell (1883–1950): ent A 1900; Black Watch; Boer War; India; Staff Coll; A/Maj, W Front 1914–16; Lia O, Russia 1916–17; Brevet Col Palestine 1917–18; WO 1921–6; Col & GSO I, 3 Div 1926; Brig, 5 Inf Bde 1930–4; Maj Gen 2 Inf Div 1935–7; GOC Palestine 1937–8; GOC S Cmd 1938–9; GOC-in-C ME 1939–41; C-in-C India 1941–3; Viceroy 1943–7; Visct 1943; Earl 1947.

Adm Thomas C. Hart, US Navy (1877–1951): grad N Acad 1897; Sp-Am-Cuban War 1898; Capt & s/m divs 1916–18; A & N War Colls; CO *Mississippi* 1925; cdr Atl F s/m 1927; RA 1929; Supt N Acad 1931; Scoutg Fc csrs 1935; Gen Bd 1936; cdr Asiatic F 1939–42; ABDA N cdr Jan 1942.

(b) This arrangement is not very acceptable from our point of view. A
     Naval Commander at sea on receiving orders issued on the advice
     of a comparatively junior officer may feel that his own greater
     experience and actual knowledge of a given situation make it
     necessary for him to query particular decisions. From the US
     point of view the scheme may have the merit that the Command-
     ing General will probably be able more quickly to make his
     decisions if he is not hampered by having to defer to the opinions
     of a highly placed naval officer. I consider any suggestion to
     adopt this arrangement should be strongly resisted.

(c) This scheme has not the advantages of (a) but from the US view-
     point it has the profound attraction that it avoids putting US naval
     forces under British command. It ensures experienced naval ad-
     vice with weight behind it. There may be disadvantages unless
     Naval Commanders at sea and the Naval Advisor are carefully
     chosen. It is a compromise and as such it has the weaknesses of
     compromises.

24. *From Pound*

24 August 1942

2. None of us liked CCS94 very much but we felt having got the
American COS to our way of thinking as regards 'Torch' it was a pity
to be too critical of the actual wording under which they have given
their assent.

There was no suggestion that this document, which was headed
'Operations in 1942–43', in any way superseded WW1 and it came as a
great shock to us that the American COS thought that it did.[1] Perhaps
we were too confiding, but I must say I would have imagined that they
would have made it clear to us at the time had they intended anything
of the kind.

I have now come to the conclusion that not only is a Supreme Naval
Commander necessary [but that we should] put in the most suitable
Naval Commander, and you already know who that is.

I never for one moment intended that Ramsay should have control of
Force H.

---

[1] WW1: COS strategic policy agreed to by JCS at 'Arcadia' conf Dec 1941, essentially
'Germany first'.

25. *CCS 38th Meeting Supplementary Minutes*

28 August 1942

Admiral Cunningham said it was difficult to put forward further arguments to those already advanced by the British COS and the Prime Minister. As he saw it, the original operation 'Torch' was intended to relieve German pressure on Russia.

Admiral King said that he did not agree that this was the original intention though it would now appear to be accepted as one of the objects.

Admiral Cunningham said the essence of the operation was, in the British view, the early capture of Tunisia. The capture of Tunisia would threaten the Mediterranean position of the enemy. Further advantages of clearing the whole northern coast of Africa were that it would provide a point of departure for a subsequent entry into Europe, ease the shipping situation by opening the Mediterranean, relieve the dangers to Malta, and ensure a satisfactory outcome of the battle for Egypt

Operation 'Torch' in any form entailed risks. The French might come in against us, and the Spanish might cast in their lot with the Germans, but the new directive proposed by the US COS would produce all these disadvantages without the corresponding advantages. Only two landings, one on each side of Morocco, were most likely to cause the Spaniards to go in against us and allow the Germans to enter Spain. Moreover, the proposed landings were so far to the west and communications to the eastward so bad it would be months before our forces could reach Tunisia. The Germans would thus be given time to continue their attack in Russia and then withdraw forces to aid the French in Algeria and Tunisia if indeed the French alone could not hold our forces. To hold Morocco might well prove impossible in view of the speed with which the Germans, using French ports, could build up forces in Algeria and Tunisia.

If determined efforts were not made to carry out the operation as originally contemplated, we would lose our one opportunity of wresting the initiative from Hitler.

Admiral Leahy said he agreed with the points made by Admiral Cunningham, but there was one additional point he wished to stress – the difficulties of supporting the Allied Army via the Strait of Gibraltar. Since it appeared that the occupation of Spanish Morocco was a necessary corollary to the invasion of French Morocco in order to ensure continuous use of the Strait, the result might be 150,000 Frenchmen and 130,000 Spaniards would be matched against 150,000 Allied troops. Even that risk could be accepted if it were certain that our forces inside the Mediterranean could be supplied by sea through Gibraltar. However, if this proved impracticable, they would starve.

In reply to a question by Admiral Cunningham, Admiral King said that he anticipated that within one month, the German Air Force could be established in Spain, and together with their submarines operating in the narrow waters of the Strait of Gibraltar, this would render our positions in North Africa untenable because of lack of continuous supply. The supply problem would be comparable with to that now experienced in regard to Malta.

Admiral Cunningham said he felt that the supply ships could be got through the Strait of Gibraltar provided the southern shore was in our hands. It would be difficult but certainly not impossible, to pass convoys through, as was being done continuously through the Straits of Dover, where difficulties were comparable.

General Marshall, in reverting to Admiral Cunningham's opening statement, said it was not accurate to describe 'Torch' as originally designed to relieve pressure on Russia. The US COS had always urged a cross-Channel operation to achieve this object. 'Torch', as he saw it, had been primarily designed to relieve the Middle East convoy routes and to deny to the enemy naval bases from which they could attack our South Atlantic convoy routes.

The seizure of Tunisia, as now contemplated, was certainly aimed at relieving the Middle East situation. Relief to the Russians was a secondary consideration. In the original discussions in London, the logistic situation had been given only cursory examination, and it had been thought that the British could produce all the naval and mercantile tonnage required for operations inside the Mediterranean, with the possible assistance of four or five US combat loaders for the landings of the 1st US Division. In the plan now put forward, it was proposed to use every available US transport and naval vessel for Mediterranean operations. The additional escorts, shipping and combat loaded transports required both for an attack on Casablanca and securing the north coast could not be found from US Navy resources.

He appreciated fully the views of the British COS. He did not fear the hazards of the landings nor the danger to Gibraltar air staging field, but he did fear greatly the attrition to naval and shipping resources which he felt would be inevitable in the build up period subsequent to the initial landings. These dangers had been brought forcibly to his attention by the losses sustained by the convoy of tanks and guns recently despatched to the Middle East. Four weeks' production of resources for armoured divisions had been sent and one torpedo had cost us one-third of this quantity.

Another consideration was that success in this operation was essential, since the reputation of the US Armed Services was at stake. Lack of shipping was making it impossible to meet urgent operational needs in the Solomons, New Caledonia and Australia. The British COS had strongly emphasized the hazards of 'Sledgehammer' but were making no mention of similar hazards incident to 'Torch'.

Admiral King agreed with the points made by General Marshall.

Admiral Cunningham pointed out that a North African venture was far easier than a landing on the coast of France. In North Africa, the country would be divided, some French forces might come in on our side, and the French Air Forces had only antiquated aircraft.

General Marshall replied that he was not worried as to the success of the landings, subsequent fighting or even the possible loss of Gibraltar airfield. His chief concern was the dangerous effects of subsequent naval and shipping losses, with its attendant effect on operations in other parts of the world.

Admiral Cunningham pointed out the difficulty of subsequent operations based on Casablanca and Oran only. He was not alarmed at the prospect of the closing of the Strait of Gibraltar. Spanish Morocco could be taken if the Germans entered Spain. He agreed that Casablanca should, if possible, be taken approximately simultaneously with the operations inside the Mediterranean, and it might be possible to use the naval forces from inside the Mediterranean for an attack on Casablanca some days later.

General Marshall pointed out that this delay would give the French in Casablanca adequate time to make preparations. He had investigated the possibility of landing small forces either at Rabat, Agadir or Fedhala, in order to obtain a foothold for a subsequent attack on Casablanca. This had not so far proved possible, though he was continuing the studies.

Air Marshal Evill said that a reasonable fighter force working from Spanish Morocco could ensure the safety of shipping through the Strait from air attack and that bomber forces based at Rabat or Oran could neutralise German air forces operating from Spanish bases. Further to the eastward the problem of safeguarding our shipping was even less difficult, the German air bases were further away. In spite of all their efforts the Germans had been unable to prevent continuous use of the Straits of Dover and the ports of Southampton and London.

General Macready suggested that the weak French Air Force would be beaten within four or five days and that after this period Casablanca might be reduced by bombardment and air attack.[1]

General Marshall reiterated the importance of success in the first large US expedition. A failure in 'Sledgehammer', for which the public had been adequately prepared, could have been accepted, but failure in 'Torch' would only bring ridicule and loss of confidence. The British felt it was essential to press on to the eastward. The US felt it was essential to have secure lines of communication.

Admiral Leahy also emphasised the effect on the whole world if the US failed. Patriots in all the other countries were waiting for the American effort. The political consequences of US failure would be appalling both for the patriots and for the peoples of China and Russia. He felt sure that the landings were possible, but secure lines of communication were essential and to obtain these, Casablanca must be captured.

General Macready pointed out that the port of Casablanca could only maintain about seven divisions. If the Germans were able to use all the ports of Tunisia and Algeria, they might maintain a much larger number of divisions, thus making certain the final eviction of the Allied forces.

General Marshall said that the US plan included an attack to the eastward and he favoured a landing at Algiers if this proved possible. But we must not, by only occupying the North African coast, suffer crushing rates of naval attrition through lack of secure communication.

Admiral Cunningham said that as he understood the US point of view, the whole operation stood or fell on the simultaneous occupation of Casablanca and North African ports.

Admiral King agreed and said that the case, in the American view, hinged on the necessity of secure lines of communications.

Admiral Cunningham said that if the operation was worth doing at all, it must be done with all the available resources of both nations. If we went into it wholeheartedly, he felt sure that the necessary resources could be provided, either by one or the other nation, or by both together.

Admiral King said that the US Navy had very heavy commitments in the Pacific, and the idea that the US should relax its efforts there was untenable. He could not agree to diminish the US forces in the Pacific unless ordered to do so.

[1]Lt Gen Sir Gordon Macready (1891–1956): of mil fam; W Front 1914–18; Versailles, Berlin, Poland 1919; Brevet Maj 1919; Asst S, CID 1926–32; IDC 1933; GSO I, WO 1934–6; DDSD 1936–8; Asst CIGS 1940–2; Chief, Br Army Staff, Washington 1942; ret 1946; Reg Cmnr, Lwr Saxony 1946–7; Econ Advsr, Control Cmn, Germany 1947–51.

Admiral Cunningham repeated that only a wholehearted effort could result in providing the necessary resources.

In conclusion, Admiral Leahy said that the discussion had been most beneficial. The proposed operation is worth doing, and great risks will have to be accepted. But a risk that cannot be accepted is the dependence on one insecure line of communications, and therefore, efforts must be made to find means of providing an alternative.

26. *To Pound*

12 September 1942

Had an encouraging interview with King today Friday on his return from a visit to C-in-C, Pacific Fleet.[1]

2. He considers that Casablanca operation and Oran and Algiers operations must be treated as one and therefore US Navy forces must come under Naval Commander.

3. His general idea appears to be and this is I think shared by other members of US COS that each operation should be entrusted to a task force under a Naval Commander responsible to Allied C-in-C the command to pass to Army General concerned when he sets up on shore to include such Naval Forces as may be left for local duty.

4. He hopes any US forces used inside the Mediterranean may be used at Oran and he accepts that all naval forces are in the pool and can be interchanged.

5. With minor alterations he agrees with suggested directive.

Although argument set out in (2) above is not entirely in accordance with our ideas I think it can be accepted as I shall be at Allied C-in-C's elbow to keep him straight on Naval Affairs.

I hope to avoid rigid definitions of scopes of Commands as I feel it will be a simple matter to reach working agreement with Eisenhower.

6. The Command position is however still obscure to the extent that intention to appoint me is on the Presidential level and is only known to [King?] unofficially. He is anxious to have matter confirmed on COS level and intends raising it in US COS today Friday. This will be sound I consider because system of command can be cleared up at same time and whole matter regularised.

7. Vice Admiral Russell Willson has been put in charge of co-ordination of whole US Navy side of 'Torch' over here so far as Navy

---

[1] FAdm Chester W. Nimitz (1885–1966): s/m; RA 1938; chief Bur Navig 1939; Adm & C-in-C Pac F Dec 1941; F Adm Dec 1944; CNO Nov 1945.

Department is concerned. This is satisfactory as he is easy to work with. . . .

27. *Vice Admiral Ramsay to his wife*[1]

London,
22 September 1942

. . . Cunningham has come over with me for a week. . . I have to try and put him in the picture and arrange everything for him. It is quite clear that all the work of this great affair will continue to devolve on me right up to the end, with him only dealing with a few of the more interesting and easier parts; and finally I will drop out and he will take on the carefully prepared and I hope smoothly running machine! He is not a man of detailed knowledge and so hasn't and [never] will have much knowledge of what is going on behind the scenes. His CoS is very junior and I doubt whether they are quite capable of running it, except that the machinery will be running and it is so much easier to run a show than construct it.[2]

28. *From Ramsay*

Norfolk House,
Grosvenor Square,
London,
2 November 1942

. . . There is no one I would rather have done my work for and I have done it with real pleasure. And I am confident that success awaits you and that it will be a short cut to the appointment of First Sea Lord.

All has gone well since your departure: I've watched the passage of the various convoys with interest and some anxiety but so far all our decisions have been successful and therefore I hope correct.

As the day approaches the interest and anxiety will no doubt increase. Everyone in the Admiralty is most helpful. . . .

I have sensed that underground intrigue is going on by CCO to regain the position he held previous to my entry on the scene, of representing the naval side of future overseas operations.[3] He has got C.

---

[1]Lady Ramsay: b 1904, née (Helen) Margaret Menzies; m 1929.
[2]Cdre Royer Dick.
[3]AoF Earl Mountbatten of Burma (1900–79): ent RN 1913; s of Pr Louis of Battenberg, FSL 1914; *Lion* 1916; Capt 1937; Capt (D) 5DF & *Kelly* 1939–41; *Illustrious* June

Lambe and I think K[ennedy] P[urvis] on his side by, I suspect, 'opera suijui', but I've told Charles Lambe straight what I think about it and D[udley] P[ound] who knows K. P. is going to tackle him. Meanwhile I will see to it that VCNS and CNS are well briefed.[1]

29. *To Ramsay*

Gibraltar,
3 November 1942

... To say that things here are chaotic would be an exaggeration but they are certainly a bit confused.

The signalmen appear to have made everything so intricate that no one, including themselves, knows what to do.

A bad mistake is that some of the Task Force commanders' orders have been distributed with no restrictions as to opening them, the fault of the secretaries of Burrough and Troubridge, I fear.[2] So even some of the MLs are aware of the detailed orders.

The chat going on in the bars is most alarming and I have threatened to put the American colonel in *Furious* in a cell for giving the show

1941; A/Cdre, CO Oct 1941; VA & Chief of CO April 1942; A/Adm & Sup Cdr SE Asia Oct 1943; Viceroy, Gov-Gen & earl 1947–8; RA 1CS 1948; VA 1949; 4SL 1950; C-in-C Med 1952; Adm & SACMED 1953; FSL 1954; AoF 1956; Chief of Def Staff 1959–65; assassinated in Ireland 1979. I. McGeoch, *The Princely Sailor: Mountbatten of Burma* (London, 1996).

[1]AoF Sir Charles Lambe (1900–60): ent RN 1914; t spist & pilot; *Vernon* i/c 1935; Capt 1937; *Dunedin* 1939–40; ADP, DDP & DP 1940–April 1944; *Illustrious* 1944–5; RA & ACNS (Air) & FO (Flying Training) 1947–9; RA 3 Carrier Sqdn 1949–51; VA 1950; FO (Air) Home 1951–3; C-in-C Far E 1953–5; 2SL 1955; C-in-C Med 1957–9; FSL May 1959; AoF 1960; resigned, ill health.

Adm Sir Charles Kennedy-Purvis: Capt 1921; RA 1933; Pres RNC Greenwich 1938; Asst to DCNS (ABC) 1938; C-in-C NAWI April 1940; DFSL 1942; d May 1946.

VCNS was Adm Sir Henry Moore (1886–1978): ent RN 1902; Lt 1908; Grand F 1914–18; Capt 1926; IDC 1927; DDP & DP 1930–3; *Neptune* 1933–5; Cdre 1st Cl & CoS to C-in-C Home F 1936–8; CoS to C-in-C Portsmouth 1938–9; RA 1938; ACNS (T) 1940–1; VA & VCNS 1941–2; 2-in-C Home F 1943–4; Adm & C-in-C Home F 1944–5; Head of BAD Dec 1945–Sept 1948; C-in-C Nore 1948–50.

[2]Adm Sir Harold M. Burrough (1888–1977): ent RN 1903; gun spist; Jutland 1916; Capt 1928; *London*; Tac Sch; 5DF; *Excellent* i/c; RA & ACNS (T) 1939; 10CS April 1940; Russian & Malta convoys 1941–2; VA Oct 1942; NCETF Nov 1942; FOC Gib & Med Apps 1943–4; ANCXF 1945; FO Germany 1945–6; C-in-C Nore 1946; ret 1949.

Adm Sir Tom Troubridge (1890–1949): of a long line of distinguished RN officers; ent RN 1908; Lt Jutland 1916; staff spist; army staff coll; Capt 1934; NA Berlin 1936–9; *Furious* 1940; *Nelson* Force H 1941; *Indomitable* E F & Malta convoy 1942; Cdre CTF Nov 1942; RA Sicily landgs 1943; Anzio Jan 1944; CVE force 'Anvil-Dragoon' Aug 1944; 5SL May 1945; Adm (Air) Sept 1946; 2-in-C Med F & FO (Air) Jan 1947–8.

away by chat in her wardroom.[1] Why on earth did RAA ask for them – this craze for liaison officers is in my opinion getting out of hand.[2]

... The harbour is absolutely stiff with shipping, cruisers, carriers and small fry. How on earth the enemy are expected to take no notice beats me.

You will have seen the request of that lunatic to postpone the business for 14 days. I got the wind up, not about Eisenhower, but about what might happen in the stratosphere!

Things are damned slack in this place. ... I want to lay my hands on some of the young officers to be seen in half dozens drunk in the streets at night. It is reported to me that they are worse than the sailors.

All this sounds a bit disgruntled but I'm not a bit. I'm thoroughly enjoying myself but the fact of not being able to act normally yet as one's own self is a bit galling.

Good luck old boy. I still feel a sense of shame that I am where I am after you have done all the chores. You know I hope how very grateful I am to you.

30. *From General Eisenhower*

Supreme HQ,
Allied Expeditionary Force,
Office of the Supreme Commander,
10 May 1945

... Incidentally, just the other day someone asked me what period I would probably remember longest in this war. The subject was interesting enough to demand an hour's conversation and out of it I came to the conclusion that the hours that you and I spent together in the dripping tunnels of Gibraltar will probably remain as long in my memory as will any other. It was there I first understood the indescribable and inescapable strain that comes over one when his part is done – when the issue rests with fate and the fighting men he has committed to action. Moreover, it was during those hours that I first became well acquainted with you and really learned that I had a partner in that campaign to whom I could always look with admiration, confidence and affection.

---

[1] *Furious*: 1917, 22450t, 31k, 33 a/c, 12×4in. The US col is not identified.
[2] Adm Sir Lumley Lyster (1888–1957): ent RN 1903; Instr *Excellent* 1912; Dardanelles, N Sea & Baltic 1914–18; Capt 1928; *Danae, Despatch* 1931–2; 5DF 1933–5; *Excellent* i/c 1935–6; DTSD; *Glorious* 1937–8; RA 1939; Norway 1940; RAA Med F Sept 1940–Feb 1941; 5SL 1941–2; RAA Home F 1942; VA Oct 1942; N Af landgs Nov 1942; ret 1943; FO Corvette Training & Adm i/c Largs 1943–4.

2. The Landings

31. *To Lady Cunningham*[1]

10 November 1942

We have had such wonderful luck and Bertie Ramsay's organisation has proved itself. I am so sorry for him – to have taken it so far and then to have to give it up to someone else. I don't know how it would have gone without my three old Eastern Meds though. Dick, Power and Brownrigg have the whole thing on their shoulders and to a slightly less degree Barnard and Laurie [Durlacher].[2] They are surprising everyone by their efficiency and capacity. I must say I like working with these Americans[,] we all get on famously. Roy Dick is surprising even me and all the high up Americans think he is a great man.

32. *From Ramsay*

11 November 1942

. . . I must first send you my warmest congratulations on the phenomenal success achieved in reaching the objectives, with comparatively no losses, at the date and time specified. No one, who has not detailed knowledge of the implications concerned, can have any conception of the amount of staff work this involved or the care necessary to see that everything had been thought of.

I reckon that the Navy has done a great thing and deserves well of the UN in general and the army in particular.

I watched the progress of the convoys daily with fascination and thrill and it's gratifying to know now that our decisions in regard to their movements *vis-à-vis* known or estimated submarine positions

---

[1]Lady Cunningham (1889–1978): née Nona Byatt, b Midhurst, Sussex, dtr of a headmaster, an energetic worker for naval welfare.

[2]VAdm Sir Manley Power (1904–81): ent RN 1917; Lt 1926; Cdr June 1939; SO (O) Med F Aug 1939; *Opportune* 1942; 'Torch' plans 1942; A/Capt *Hannibal* 1943; Capt Dec 1943; Capt (D) 26DF & *Saumarez*, sank *Haguro* 1945; RA 1953; VA 1956; DCNS & 5SL 1957–9; C-in-C Portsmouth 1959–61.

VAdm Sir Geoffrey Barnard (1902–74): Cdr June 1935; FGO Med F Dec 1938; *President* 1942; DCoS Med F 1943; *Aurora* Dec 1943; *Victory* 1944–5; CSO to FO (Air) 1946–7; Dir Tac Sch 1948; Indian N 1950–1; RA 1951; ACNS 1952–3; DCNS 1953–4; JSM 1954–6; Pres RNC Greenwich 1956–8; ret 1959.

Capt T. M. Brownrigg: Cdr Dec 1936; Mr of F, Med F June 1939; *President* 1942; Capt Dec 1942; *Merganser* (Peterhead) 1944–5.

Cdr Laurie Durlacher: Cdr June 1939; *Victory* Nov 1940, for Sig Sch; F Sig O, Med F Jan 1943; *Volage* March 1944.

proved correct. It looked impossible, from the submarine chart, that convoys could escape detection. The *Spey* affair was a gallant effort and I liked your signal to her. It was a blow later to learn that all but two of her landing craft had to be abandoned. The towing of the *Thomas Stone* by *Wishart* was a good effort too.[1] The Algiers assault seems to have been highly successful and we were thankful to know that the Port was open and undamaged and the ships berthing inside and being speedily unloaded. There's a bit of luck finding Darlan there. It looks as though he was there of a purpose, but perhaps it wasn't. At the moment we are anxiously awaiting news of the French Fleet and in particular whether the *Strasbourg* got out of dock and away in time.[2] You always said that the French C-in-C was a bad man, so perhaps he will not obey Darlan's orders.[3] I hope he will, however! What fools they are! Blocking Oran and Bizerta and no doubt Casablanca; allowing the Huns to land planes in Tunis and setting up air and naval HQ. Even the Germans could hardly have counted on this much. Now, it seems we shall have to fight our way, it being dangerous to project our paratroops down on to an airfield occupied in advance by the Hun. . . .

. . . You will doubtless have a chance of testing out Darlan's announcement that you were the only British Admiral that he would shake hands with. But you might remind him what I did for the French at Dunkirk (129,000 of them) and the letter and telegram he sent me.

I'm sorry that we've lost those two combat loaders, as well as *Viceroy of India* and *Nieuw Zealand, Cathay, Roberts*, etc.[4] But we've been awfully lucky on the whole, the critical period having passed before the enemy really got going. I'm sure they were awaiting us further east, expecting an attack on Sardinia, or Sicily or Italy! . . .

It is clear that the expected submarine concentration is taking place in the Western Mediterranean and you must be anxious for Force H. I'm not surprised that you've stopped the independent sailing of personnel ships. They are most valuable ships and serious losses would

---

[1]*Spey*: escort, 1942, 1370t, 19k, 2×4in.

Wishart: destroyer, 1920, 1550t, 32k, 5×4.7in, 5×21in tt.

USS *Thomas Stone*: 1941, 10120t, 18.4k, 4×3in. She was torpedoed on 7 Nov; her landing craft were shepherded by *Spey*; she was towed into Algiers by *Wishart* and the tug *St Day*. It was an outstanding example of bravery and persistence on the part of all concerned. The troops were safely landed.

[2]*Strasbourg*: Fr b/csr, 1938, 26500t, 29.5k, 8×13in, 16×5.1in; scuttled Toulon, 27 Nov 1942.

[3]Adm de la Borde, French N: FO Toulon 1939–42.

[4]*Viceroy of India*: P & O, 1929, 19627gt, 19k.

Nieuw Zealand: KPM, Batavia, 1928, 11069gt, 15k.

Cathay: P & O, 1925, 15295gt, 16.5k.

Roberts: monitor, 1941, 7970t, 12k, 2×15in. Damaged but not sunk.

affect the build up very gravely. As it is we are short for KMF4.[1] We don't know at the moment what the harbour situation at Oran is and whether the ships sunk there by those bally idiots the French are going to prevent the port being used or to what extent it can be used. Altogether you must be having an anxious time, though I know you thrive on it. . . .

. . . I feel that more could and should be done to impress the naval side on the public, as so much is being made of the fact that it is an all American show. . . .

33.   *To Ramsay*

12 November 1942

Nobody has contributed more to the success of this show than you have and I hope everyone knows it.

Things go well on the whole and we have got further in the last five days than I expected. But we are not moving fast enough. Tunis is anybody's who cares to walk in but the Huns are beating us in the race. I cannot understand why our soldiers do not embus and get on but they are methodically piling up POL and amm[unition] and haven't really got going yet.[2]

We have started having heavy losses from the U-boats and air attacks but not out of the way for what has been achieved.

There is I think a concentration of 20–30 of the former between here and Algiers and they are picking off our shipping rather too rapidly. They are not however getting away with it unscathed. I think we have already sunk about six and there are also many headaches. . . .

Eisenhower is good but terribly mercurial. He was in the depths of despair because Oran did not fall at once. But his ideas are good. He does not seem to me to take enough part in directing the operations, but perhaps I am an interfering person.

Troubridge did very well and thoroughly justified your choice of him. Burrough is good but obstinate and hasn't yet realised that he is dealing with someone even more pigheaded than himself. I am off to Algiers to sort him [out] in a day or two.

All the best, old boy, we all realise the steady hand on the home helm.

[1]KMF4: fast convoy from UK to N Africa.
[2]POL: Petrol, Oil and Lubricants.

34. *Ramsay to his wife*

14 November 1942

... ABC thoroughly appreciates it [Ramsay's work] and no one could have been nicer about it or done more to try and get me a good appointment in compensation.

He is doing excellently out there and is undoubtedly the best man for the job.

35. *To Aunt Doodles*

19 November 1942

... Very busy and delighted to get down to some active work again. ...
... there is no doubt that for the first time in this war we have got ahead of Hitler.

36. *To Ramsay*

21 November 1942

All goes well here and we are meditating an early move to Algiers. I paid no attention to the air signal. I could see Dreyer writing it and I made rather a snappy reply.[1]

Not a few of the Admiralty signals are pretty futile. I got one today which indicates that someone has got it in what he doubtless calls his head that you can turn operation 'Torch' off like a tap. Wanting to know whether we can cut down 'Torch' commitments, when I can part with Force H destroyers and when I can part with the Gibraltar escort force.

I sent a signal to the CNS giving an appreciation of the naval forces required but I doubt it went into his drawer and no one saw it otherwise the above signals could not have been made.

Have you read Mountbatten's puff on the news page of *The Times* of 18 [November]? I see he lays claim or an American pressman does for him, to having made the plans for 'Torch'. Really he ought not to be

---

[1]Adm Sir Frederick C. Dreyer (1878–1956): ent RN 1891; gun spist; Lt 1898; *Dreadnought* 1903–7; Capt 1913; F Capt *Iron Duke* 1915–16; DNO 1916–19; Dir Gun Div 1920–2; *Repulse* 1922–3; RA 1923; ACNS 1924; BCS 1927; VA 1929; DCNS 1930; Adm 1932; C-in-C China 1933–6; ret 1939; convoy cdre 1939–40; Inspr merchant ship gunnery 1941; 5SL 1942; DCN Air Eqpt 1943.

allowed to advertise like this. If you see the CNS you might point it out.
. . .

Malta has failed us over 'Breastplate'. I wish old Dobbie had been there[;] he would have landed carrying his Bible, opposition or no opposition.[1] It is good they have a convoy. I hear my shares with the COS are at a very low ebb. I made a signal to Dick at Gibraltar from Algiers giving him Anderson's ideas on 'Breastplate' and repeated it to VA (Malta) who showed it to Gort who took it as a direction and blew up.[2] The COS made a signal to Eisenhower saying my signal was unauthorised and I sent one to Dudley Pound asking for an explanation of the COS language. I got my apology from Pound but I doubt if he ever showed the COS how they had been misled. Damned funny really but I was annoyed at the time.

I have had Force H using Mers-el-Kébir the last four days[;] it is a good anchorage and even at the moment fairly safe and it will be better shortly.

I took a trip to Oran and Algiers last week in *Aurora*.[3]

Bennett has done well at Oran and strangely enough is playing well.[4] Morse has the port of Algiers in the palm of his hand and all the French are working cheerfully with him.[5] . . .

James Somerville comes through here tomorrow and I am looking forward to a talk with him – he can do a bit of candid friend with the Admiralty too.[6]

[1]'Breastplate': a planned occupation of Sousse, launched from Malta; cancelled owing to lack of assault craft.

Lt Gen Sir Frank Dobbie, RE: 2Lt 1899; Boer War 1901–2; Capt 1908; W Front 1914–18; SO, WO 1919–20, & Aldershot 1920–4; Col 1926; Brig, Egypt 1928–32; Maj Gen 1932; Cdt Sch Mil Eng 1933–5; GOC Malaya 1935; Govr & C-in-C Malta 1940–2.

[2]VA, Malta: VAdm Stewart Bonham-Carter: Capt 1927; RA & N Sec to FL Jan 1939; RA Halifax, NS Jan 1940; apptd RA 3BS, EF, under V Adm Phillips Oct 1941, but did not serve; 18CS Jan 1942; Arctic convoys; VA June 1942; VA Malta Dec 1942–Sept 1943; ret Dec 1943; Convoy cdre 2cl, *Eaglet* (Liverpool) May 1944.

FM Lord Gort, VC (1886–1946): Gren Gds 1905; Capt & ADC to Gen Haig 1914; Lt Col 1917; VC 1918; Staf Coll 1919–21; Col 1935; India 1932; Cdt, Staff Coll 1936; Gen & CIGS 1937; C-in-C BEF 1939–40; Inspr Gen 1940–1; Govr & C-in-C Gib 1941, & Malta 1942–4; FM 1943; H Cmnr & C-in-C Palestine & Trans-Jordan 1944–5.

[3]*Aurora*: lt csr, 1937, 5270t, 32.5k, 6×6in, 8×4in, 5×21in tt.

[4]RAdm A. C. Bennett, US Navy: RA & CO Adva Grp, Amph Fce, Atl F 1942; i./c Oran Nov 1942.

[5]R Adm J. A. V. Morse: Capt June 1934; *Neptune* & F Capt & CoS to C-in-C Africa July 1937; CSO, *Pyramus*; NOIC Kirkwall June 1940; MNBDO (1) May 1941; NOIC Syria & Lebanon Ports July 1941; *Hannibal* Nov 1942; RA July 1943; FO W Italy Sept 1944; FO N Area Med Oct 1944.

[6]AoF Sir James Somerville (1882–1949); ent RN 1897; Lt March 1904; sig spist; W/T O, E Med 1915; F W/T O, Grand F Jan 1917; Capt Dec 1921; *Benbow* Aug 1922; DSD Feb 1925; Tac Sch March 1927; *Barham*, *Warspite* May 1927; IDC staff June

All the best old boy[;] it is a great comfort to us to know that you are watching over our interests at home.

37. *From Pound*

27 November 1942

Many congratulations on your part of 'Torch' which was a great success. I am sure you had as anxious a time as we did here, and I had visions of large convoys waltzing up and down both outside and inside the Mediterranean with the weather too bad to land and the U-boats buzzing around. We really did have remarkable luck. . . .

3. The French

38. *To all British warships*

7 November 1942

US Commanding General will broadcast message to French land, sea and air forces at intervals throughout day of assault to the following effect:
1.   We come as friends not as enemies and will take no offensive action unless French do so first.
2.   French who are willing to co-operate with us should signify this by displaying day Tricolor with US Flag or failing that two Tricolors; Night as well – search beam held vertically.
3.   Following instructions must be obeyed by French or we shall infer hostile intent:
   (a)   Warships and Merchant ships are not to move.
   (b)   No attempt to scuttle.
   (c)   Defences not to be manned.
   (d)   Aircraft must be kept on ground in normal positions.
   (e)   All instructions by commanders of Allied units to be proclaimed.

1929; Tac Sch Sept 1931; *Norfolk* Dec 1931; Cdre RN Barracks, Portsmouth Oct 1932; RA Oct 1933; DPS May 1934; Tac Sch Feb 1936; RA (D) Med F April 1936; VA Sept 1937; C-in-C E Indies Oct 1938; invalided home, suspected TB April 1939; ret July 1939; pioneered N radar 1939–40; asstd Ramsay in Dunkirk evacuation May–June 1940; Force H June 1940; C-in-C EF Feb 1942; Active List Aug 1944; Head BAD Oct 1944–Dec 1945; AoF May 1945; ret April 1946. D. Macintyre, *Fighting Admiral* (London, 1961); M. A. Simpson, (ed.), *The Somerville Papers* (Aldershot, 1996).

B.   *Treatment of Vichy merchant ships*

... all Vichy merchant ships encountered during 'Torch' will be taken under Allied control and with exception of coastal vessels will be cleared to westwards as quickly as possible.

2.   Any Vichy ships which fall into our hands during 'Torch' will not (R) not be treated as prize and will continue to sail under the French Flag.

3.   If Vichy declares war all Vichy shipping wherever encountered is, if possible, to be intercepted and sent to a UN port.

39.   *To Vice Admiral Burrough*

11 November 1942

We have a big chance here and should exploit it to the full. Urge necessity of all French getting together with us and building up a formidable force to whip the Axis.

Tell Darlan to get the [fleet] to Gibraltar (R) Gibraltar.

40.   *To Pound*

11 November 1942

Following comments by my CoS who was present on Clark-Darlan negotiations are forwarded for your personal information begins: First round has been gained but situation will obviously not be satisfactory till wholehearted co-operation obtained.[1]

Large number of French already out to help but Darlan clique will need watching. This is in hand.

2.   Darlan still hostile to us and in lesser degree to Americans but consider he sees position gone in France and wishes to control from North Africa. I think he is genuine in that he will not let French Fleet fall into German hands but will move them only in last emergency.

3.   It is intended to continue work on this as also question of Alexandria squadron.

4.   Clark was magnificent. . . .

---

[1]Gen Mark Clark, US Army (1896–1984): AEF 1917–18; II Corps, UK June 1942; Lt Gen & D Cmdg Gen, 'Torch'; 5 Army, Italy 1943; Cdr 15 Army Grp Dec 1944; Gen March 1945.

41.   *To Ramsay*

12 November 1942

... Clark has gone to Algiers to try and sort out the rival claims of Giraud, Darlan, Juin, Noguès, etc. and I have sent Dick with him.[1] It is indeed a tangled skein. I begin to wonder are there any patriotic Frenchmen, de la Borde whom I would have sworn by appears to have let his fleet just remain in Toulon without making any effort to escape the Huns.

Esteva is in a difficult position and I have hopes of him yet – if we can only get on.[2] ...

42.   *From Admiral Harwood*

14 November 1942

Following is extract from my 2026B/14 to Admiralty about interview I had today with Godfroy.

He will not come over to us yet but I have not completely given up hope. He made the following points:

1.   [Godfroy] wanted to know what has happened regarding Pétain, Darlan, Esteva, etc. I told him all I knew.[3]
2.   He is extremely anti-Gaullist for the harm they have done to France by their propaganda.
3.   It would be easier to come over if a French Government were formed in Algeria.
4.   He sincerely hopes Giraud will act independently of de Gaulle, as if the latter gets into North Africa it will wreck French opinion.
5.   His officers and ships' companies are so bitter because our action has caused Hitler to occupy Vichy and for the loss their navy has incurred.

[1]Mshl A. Juin, French A (1888–1967): Cdr 15 Mot Div 1940; CO Morocco 1941; Lt Gen, Land Forces, N Af Nov 1941; jnd Allies Nov 1942; CO Fr forces, Tunisia 1943; Gen Feb 1943; C-in-C Land Forces, C Eur, NATO; Mshl 1952.

Gen A. Noguès, French A (1876–1971): C-in-C Fr forces N Af Sept 1939; Res Gen Morocco; jnd Allies Nov 1942; resigned June 1943; sentenced after war for collaboration.

[2]Adm Jean-Pierre Esteva, French N (1880–1951): Adm Sud 1939–40; Res Gen, Tunisia 1942; capt by Germans; imprisoned after war for failure to prevent German seizure Tunisia but released 1950.

[3]Mshl Henri Philippe Pétain, French A (1856–1951): hero of Verdun 1916; Mshl 1918; Vice PM May 1940; PM 16 June 1940; headed govt at Vichy July 1940–Aug 1944; condemned to death post war but commuted to life imprisonment.

6. He would be greatly influenced by a message from Esteva in whom he has great faith; possibly by Darlan but I am not so sure. He hopes for a message from de la Borde but I warned him cipher probably compromised by Germans. I fear de la Borde's influence if he is still in Toulon will be adverse.

Your 2236/13 [not reproduced] just received. Anything Darlan will do to ginger up Godfroy will be useful but Esteva will have more weight. I fear he will pay more attention to de la Borde than anybody else.

43. *To Lady Cunningham*

15 November 1942

I met Darlan – embarrassingly cordial. Shook me warmly by the hand and said 'Thank you for Admiral Godfroy'. I wouldn't trust him an inch but I think he meant that.

44. *From Vice Admiral Whitworth*[1]

Admiralty,
16 November 1942

P.S: I was particularly interested in your account of Darlan. He is the subject of heated arguments in all the clubs, and leading articles in the papers. Everybody is trying to sum him up. I am inclined to the view that he is not quite such a snake as we all thought he was. An article in today's *Daily Sketch* recalls that he praised you as being the only gentleman among British Admirals on account of your handling of Godfroy and his ships, which accounts for the cordial handshake. Looks as though you alone can handle him, and get the best out of him. . . .

45. *To Pound*

18 November 1942

I am concerned that the state of affairs in North Africa is apparently not fully realised at home. This may be due to the fact that insufficient

[1]Adm Sir W. ('Jock') Whitworth: Capt 1925; Capt of F, Med F, *Resolution* 1935; RA 1936; BCS, Home F 1939; VA 1940; 2nd Battle of Narvik 1940; 2SL 1941–4; Adm Dec 1943; C-in-C Rosyth Feb 1944.

information on certain aspects may have been given. It appears for instance that there is some doubt that Allied internees are to be released.

The following points may be of use therefore:

2. (a) Our service and merchant seamen internees totalling about 900 were promptly released and surprisingly expeditiously sent to Algiers from their camps some 300 miles away in the interior. The large majority of these men have already passed Gibraltar on their way home. All internees from Sacomis in Hebajce numbering 600 also released and have left Casablanca.

(b) Darlan was definitely responsible for stopping hostilities at a moment of vital importance to us and when our troops in Algiers were far too weak to have moved east had there been even lack of co-operation.

(c) Giraud's appointment was quickly announced despite initial strong French opposition to him.

(d) French troops were ordered to resist Axis and help us. Both have been done.

(e) The French are actively co-operating with us and giving practical assistance at ports, use of railroads and W/T communications.

(f) *Stork* is in process of being fitted with a false bow for passage by French Naval Constructors at Algiers.[1]

(g) Darlan signalled to the French Fleet to come over and though this has so far been ineffective the game is not yet over.

(h) Darlan has summoned leading personalities from Dakar to bring them into active collaboration with us.

(i) US-French relations in Oran and Morocco are excellent.

3. All the above are positive evidence that Darlan is genuinely working with us for the moment whatever his underlying motives may be . . . none, least of all myself, like dealing with this skunk but above all we must have stability in North Africa and have it speedily till the Axis is flung out of that continent. I gravely fear repercussions of President's message; with our forces strung out as at present in the race for Tunisia we simply can't afford a renewal of hostile feeling. The prize is too great and too close to our reach to risk it.

4. I fully understand how difficult a position it is for the two Governments and how distasteful the set up must be, but for the moment it presents the one hope of quick success. It is all in Darlan's interest now to work with us and while he has power to be of extreme use to us, his potentiality for harm is small while in power and under our thumb.

---

[1]*Stork*: 1936, 1190t, 18.75k, 6×4in, later famous as Capt F. J. Walker's ship, 2EG.

5.   So long as Darlan plays the game along the lines shown in paragraph 2 we should not disturb the existing delicate balance. As soon as
we are really strong then will be the moment to act rapidly and without
compunction. We can meanwhile restrain the insertion of more Vichy
men into the Government.
6.   I feel that the COS and HMG should be aware of the above and I
am not quite sure if it has been fully put to them.

46.   *To Pound and Harwood*

18 November 1942

Yesterday attended ceremony of hoisting British and US colours at HQ
in Algiers and had long conversation with Darlan. He is very hopeful of
bringing in the Dakar party. Three representatives from there were due
to arrive in Algiers today Wednesday to confer with him. Darlan told
me that Admiral Auphan who has apparently taken command of Toulon
Fleet had sent him a private message from Marshal Pétain to the effect
that the Marshal thoroughly approved of all that he was doing but could
not say so publicly.[1] Darlan also said that he Darlan was looked upon
generally as the natural successor to the Marshal. I look on these
statements with considerable doubt. Darlan said he wished to send a
message to Godfroy and I assured him that I would have it delivered
through the C-in-C, Mediterranean. I also met Michelier who has been
appointed in command of all the French Navy in North Africa. His HQ
are and will be at Casablanca. He was most cordial.[2] At Oran I had a
most frosty interview with Admiral Ripult who was full of complaints.
I hope he was more friendly inclined when I left him.[3]

47.   *To Lady Cunningham*

20 November 1942

I came back and found the general rather in despair over our politicians
not much liking his dealings with Darlan. They are curious people,

---

[1] Adm Gabriel Auphan, French N: b 1894; ent N 1911; Lt de V May 1919; Capt de V
Oct 1936; *Jeanne D'Arc* Aug 1937; Admy staff June 1939; RA & M Merchant Marine
June 1940; S St Marine April 1942; ret Sept 1944; imprisoned after war; amnesty 1957.
[2] Adm F. Michelier, French N (1887–1966): ent N 1904; Lt de V Nov 1916; Capt de V
July 1931; csrs *Foch*, *Colbert*, staff posts 1931–7; RA Feb 1937; head Fr N aviation Aug
1938; VA May 1940; cdr French N Morocco Oct 1942; ret Dec 1943.
[3] Adm Ripult, French N: unidentified.

always wanting to have it both ways. Of course our obligations to de Gaulle make it difficult for them to justify dealings with the snake – Darlan. I hope they won't allow the former or any of his emissaries down here – they would properly upset the apple cart.

48.   *To Ramsay*

21 November 1942

. . . We have been heavily shot at from home over allowing Darlan to be the head of the government out here. . . . They [politicians and diplomats] were perfectly willing to use him to produce the armistice, otherwise why did they not tell us not to negotiate with him – they knew about it four days before agreement was reached.

The fact is that as usual our intelligence was much at fault. They gambled on Giraud's influence and thought Darlan was hated and had no influence. The exact contrary was the case. Giraud cut no ice at all and consented at once to work under Darlan who is the only man who can deliver at least some of the goods. . . .

I would like to ask the FO what they would have done in Eisenhower's position.

. . . Smuts came through two days ago and Eisenhower and I had an interview with him. He rather set Eisenhower's mind at rest over the political set up here.[1] Of course it was the PM being badgered in the House. I don't myself believe the great British Public care a damn who we work through provided the war is brought nearer to an end. . . .

49.   *From Pound*

27 November 1942

. . . There was never any doubt amongst the COS as to Eisenhower not having taken the right line with Darlan. Some of the politicians were a bit difficult because they felt tied up to that nuisance de Gaulle who is behaving like a spoilt child.

I agree with you that it was a pity to attempt to rush Godfroy at the moment we did, but the politicians are feeling very bold at the moment and the Cabinet decided that action was to be taken at once, in spite of

---

[1]FM J. C. Smuts (1870–1950): Boer cdo 1899–1902; Lt Gen, clearing Germans from SW Af 1914–17; UK War Cab 1917; PMUn S Af 1919–24, 1939–48; F M 1941; UK War Cab 1943; a founder of UNO.

my protest that what we wanted was floating ships and not ones resting on the bottom of Alexandria harbour with holes in them. However, I hope it works out all right but just like you I am not at all sanguine that Godfroy will not scuttle them. When I told the Cabinet that Godfroy had the whip hand of us as he could scuttle his ships at any time they wanted to tell him that if he did he would be shot. However, I managed to keep them off anything so idiotic.

50. *To Lady Cunningham*

Algiers,
28 November 1942

The fate of the Toulon fleet has caused considerable depression here. My *quondam* friend Darlan is very upset. Of course Hitler meant to cheat them from the word go. My old friend Admiral de la Borde has been badly sold. However it will I hope unite all the French and I can't see Godfroy standing out any longer.

Darlan, unpopular as he seems to be in the UK and US, has certainly delivered some of the goods in the shape of Dakar.

It is a pity he failed over the fleet.

51. *To Lady Cunningham*

1 December 1942

I am daily hoping to hear that Godfroy and the Alexandria fleet have come over. They have no excuse now for remaining inert except perhaps that all Frenchmen at the present time appear to have lost all their spirit. It will come again doubtless but the will to fight for their country is at the moment completely absent. (Rather sweeping but true enough generally speaking).

52. *From Dill*

JSM, CCS Offices,
Washington, DC,
1 December 1942

. . . What a tangle this Darlan problem is! No one doubts your wisdom of using him full out, and Marshall has just told me that Win[ston] sent Ike a helpful answer to the 'squeezed lemon' letter. . . The political talk is that it is quite impossible to fit de Gaulle into the Darlan picture and whatever one may think of de Gaulle he did stand firm when all else in France crumbled and broke. However one can only live from day to day in this matter and Darlan is at the moment absolutely indispensable. . . .

53.   *From Harwood*

3 December 1942

. . . Godfroy is very tiresome, he won't take the slightest risk and wants 100% certainty so that not only his conscience but also those of his officers can feel perfectly clear. . . . After a very long session and much rather brutal frankness I gingered him up one night to have a meeting of his Captains after which he came off the fence in a five volume novel full of ifs, buts, etc. The next morning he was extremely fussed and asked that his letter should be washed out as a new situation had arisen. It appears that they had listened to Pétain's broadcast. The broadcast was quite innocuous . . . but my efforts to point this out did not meet with much success. Undoubtedly at least half of his officers want to do nothing. A good part of the other half want to renew the fight. A large part of the men want to fight. . . . Godfroy is 100% Pétain and looks upon any dissidents of any sort as traitors. . . . I can best sum him up by saying that he is the worst time waster I have ever met in my life. . .

54.   *To Ramsay*

4 December 1942

. . . Our principal troubles are political. You would have thought that when Dakar fell into our hands our FO would not look a gift horse in the mouth but they are being sticky about releasing the prisoners de Gaulle has.

We just must get all these Frenchmen working together. Darlan is I think very desirous of coming to an agreement with them but they don't care much about de Gaulle.

55.   *To Pound*

5 December 1942

. . . I feel that the FO should keep de Gaulle in order and not allow him to impede the advantageous agreements we are getting out of Darlan.

C. We had a big do at the local War Memorial on Wednesday. Darlan, Eisenhower and I placed wreaths in memory of the men killed in the late operations.

It may amuse you to know that the representative of *perfide Albion* got quite an ovation from the large crowd present. Darlan was heartily cheered – perhaps he had rigged the crowd. . . .

56. *From Harwood*

9 December 1942

. . . In the end I feel sure that Godfroy will come around to Darlan but I can't say when. If he remains inactive much longer then I think his hand will be forced by desertions.

57. *From Whitworth*

15 December 1942

. . . I have passed on your views about Darlan to D[udley] P[ound]. The majority of the British public don't want him at any price, and fail to see why the French should be allowed to select their own leader!

58. *To Lady Cunningham*

26 December 1942

What times we are living through out here. I only lunched with the Darlans on Wednesday and he was murdered next day. A bad business. I rather liked the little man. In his dealings with us here he has been quite honest.

I attended his funeral this morning. First an hour in the Cathedral. Then his coffin was taken outside the chapel where he was lying in state and about half the French Army and Navy marched past and also some of our sailors and marines and detachments of the American Army. Then into the chapel where we all had to sprinkle holy water on the coffin!! Eisenhower and I went together and he was astounded. He had never taken part in a Roman Catholic service before and was horrified and thought he was back in the Middle Ages.

I told him he was very lucky it wasn't Malta otherwise he would have had a douche of holy water himself!

59. *From Pound*

28 December 1942

D.I wonder how Darlan's assassination strikes you who are on the spot? . . . I am also wondering what effect his assassination will have on Godfroy. I may be maligning the latter but it seems to me that he is using every imaginable excuse for not coming to help us fight.

60. *Chiefs of Staff*

28 December 1942

COS 357: Darlan

[Sir Dudley Pound referred to a telegram from Admiral Cunningham] regarding the lack in British pronouncements of any appreciation of Darlan's actions in support of the Allied cause in North Africa, and suggesting that a statement by a leading British statesman on the lines of that made by Mr Cordell Hull would have a favourable effect, particularly on the French Navy.[1]

61. *From Godfroy*

24 May 1943

I thank you very much for the kind and friendly words of your message about my decision to join the remainder of the French Navy in North Africa.

As you may suppose, it is after a harsh struggle with myself that I made up my mind, but I feel confident to have chosen the right step without disloyalty. . . .

62. *To Aunt Doodles*

6 June 1943

. . . You will have seen that Giraud and de Gaulle have reached agreement – just about time too. . . . the PM . . . lectured them on making use

---

[1]Cordell Hull (1871–1955): Reprv (Dem), Tenn 1907–21, 1923–31; Sen 1931–3; S St 1933–44.

of it and working together for the good of France. I must say I have little use for de Gaulle. Eisenhower described him as looking like a shark that had been hauled up out of water and left to die. Not a bad description either.

63. *To Aunt Doodles*

13 June 1943

. . . Our de Gaulle and Giraud party are still scrapping. They are marvellous these Frenchmen[,] they cannot see that for the good of France they must get together, but de Gaulle is very difficult. . . .

64. *To Aunt Doodles*

29 June 1943

. . . The French don't seem to be getting together as well as they ought. They don't trust each other and I am not surprised. De Gaulle is quite unaccountable and the others seem to think he is out for power for himself. Giraud is honest but rather stupid. . . . I have a lot to do with the French Admiral so I have to keep my eye on both in case they mess up what I have arranged. . . .

65. *To Aunt Doodles*

5 September 1943

. . . I had my old friend Godfroy . . . to lunch . . . He looked a new man but rather annoyed that he had been placed on the retired list. This Committee of Liberation has got rid of all the good French admirals and I rather tremble for the future of the French navy. . . .

66. *Diary*

14 March 1945

. . . The trial of the French Admiral Esteva started yesterday in Paris. He seems to be putting up a good defence. He mentioned his relations with me having been very cordial. He maintains that he was saying one thing and acting another and I think this was probably true. He did several things for us notably in connection with the *Manchester* ship's company.[1] Further his telephoned message to Darlan a few days after we landed at Algiers 'that he was entirely with us but had a tutor at his elbow'. I have always maintained his honesty and his hatred for the Germans. It is to be hoped that he gets away with it but the jury is packed.[2] . . .

67.   *To Admiral John Godfrey*[3]

26 April [1954?]

. . . Darlan was a queer fish. I am not sure that history will not clear him of many of the accusations made against him. Certainly he was absolutely square with us in Algiers. And he would have had the whole fleet out of Toulon if that charming but idiotically obstinate man Admiral de la Borde had not hated Darlan so much. . . .

4.   The Campaign

68.   *To Pound*

20 November 1942

Forces required to deal with Italian Fleet, etc.

2.   As long as the Italian Fleet is in being and in a position to interfere a considerable force of capital ships and therefore cruisers is required. This applies even more strongly if we attempt any operations against Sicily, Sardinia or France. Even if we do not do so the Italian fleet will be a constant nuisance and menace to through convoys in the Mediterranean and it must be our object to render it ineffective as soon as possible otherwise we shall lose much of the value from the 'Torch' operation.
3.   Apart from the above there remains the requirement of a force for work in the Atlantic and until the fate and future activities of the French Toulon Fleet and the force at Dakar are definitely known. For this purpose a small capital ship force appears desirable.
4.   In regard to the Malta convoy it is proposed to await the result of 'Stoneage' and of the operation in Tunisia.[4] Should neither of these

---

[1]*Manchester*: csr, 1938, 9400t, 32k, 12×6in, 8×4in, 6×21in tt; t MAS boats, off Tunisia, 13 Aug 1942.
[2]Esteva was imprisoned but released in 1950.
[3]Adm J. H. Godfrey: DNI 1939–43; FO cmdg RIN 1943–6; blamed for mutiny 1945.
[4]'Stoneage': convoy from Alexandria to Malta, Nov 1942.

come up to expectations it will be necessary to fight the western convoy through.

5.   If, however, we can get a proper scale of trained shore-based aircraft we shall be in a much better position to get rid of the carriers which apart from other calls on them are much better out in open waters. It would also be possible to withdraw some capital ships. It may not perhaps be realised but we have at present no (R) no anti-ship striking force at all if one excepts six Swordfish at Algiers.[1]

6.   When 'Torch' was planned we pressed hard on this subject but all that we could obtain was a nebulous promise of one Beaufort torpedo bomber squadron from the Middle East. . .[2] We are feeling this lack of an air striking force very seriously at this moment with the Axis running supplies at this critical moment into Tunisia by day by sea virtually unhindered.

7.   I feel it is of primary importance not to reproduce the situation we had in the Eastern Mediterranean in 1941, when owing to carrier losses, we had neither a sea-borne nor a shore-based air striking force with the results of which we are aware. I must earnestly press therefore for every effort to be made to have adequate air operationally under Naval control before my only striking force in the shape of capital ships and carriers is removed.

8.   To summarise, the following is my view of the Naval Forces both major and minor which are needed. It is based on the assumption that we have effectively occupied Tunisia, that Spain remains neutral and the French Fleet passive.

A.   Carriers can be dispensed with as soon as an effective and trained naval co-operation group is established on similar terms to 201 Naval Co-operation Group.[3] Adequate reconnaissance, striking and fighter forces essential to include torpedo aircraft.

B.   Carriers would again be required for assault of Sardinia, to be withdrawn on establishment of RAF there.

C.   When I am satisfied practically that the Naval Co-operation Group is up to the job I consider capital ships could be withdrawn except for one to work westward from Gibraltar with attendant cruisers and destroyers. A carrier very desirable with this force.

---

[1]Fairey Swordfish: TBR, 1934, 690hp, 138mph, 546m, 3 crew, 1500lbs/1610lb t, 2mg.
   [2]Bristol Beaufort: TBR,1938, 2×1130hp, 265mph, 1035m, 4 crew, 2000lbs/1610lb t, 4mg.
   [3]201 Naval Co-operation Group was established in Alexandria in the autumn of 1941, at Cunningham's instigation and despite strong RAF objections.

D.   Four good cruisers and a Flotilla of 'Tribals' or 'M's' should be retained, based on Algiers or perhaps Bizerta as surface striking force.[1]
E.   'Hunts' to be maintained at present level being particularly suitable for convoys past Malta.[2]
F.   Minesweeper and A/S Trawler forces to be maintained at present level pending experience.
G.   Flotilla of MTBs and MGBs most desirable for operation from Bizerta.
H.   Most important additional MLs or HDMLs be sent as soon as possible.
J.   AA ships required for work in convoy.
K.   Gibraltar escort force remain at present level pending experience but can probably be eventually reduced.

69.   *Ramsay to his wife*

21 November 1942

. . . ABC is doing extremely well and handling the difficulties in masterly fashion.

70.   *To Ramsay*

Algiers,
4 December 1942

. . . We are trying to get settled in here. At the moment I am in *Bulolo*, I found I was too far removed from the fighting and becoming nothing but a convoy king back at Gibraltar.[3]

I hope to get the shore communications going the end of the week and then I shall come ashore. I have a small but rather lovely villa up the hill over the town looking out over the bay about three-quarters of a mile from the hotel where we have our Allied HQ. Eisenhower and I are proper buddies and I think he likes to have me by him. I like him very much and he is very good at deferring to my opinion not only on naval matters.

---

[1] 'Tribals': destroyers, 1938–9, 1870t, 36.5k, 8×4.7in, 4×21in tt.
    'M' class: destroyers, 1941, 1920t, 36.5k, 6×4.7in, 8×21in tt.
[2] 'Hunts': destroyers, 1940–3, 27k, 1000–1050t, 4–6×4in.
[3] For the first time, there were HQ command ships, packed with communications: *Bulolo*: Burns, Philp, 1938, 6500t, 15k, (as AMC) 7×6in, 2×3in.
    Also present *Largs*: 1938, 4504t, 17k, (formerly OBV).

... As for the military operations we are hung up. Our logistics have gone all wrong. Railhead is choked, the wharves are littered up all for want of transport to take away the stuff.

The aerodromes become unfit in rain and we have not yet brought all our air to bear. I keep on telling them that with only two second class ports [in enemy hands] it should be an easy matter to put them both out of action but we just haven't put the necessary weight of bombs on to them. . . .

What I want is MTBs and MGBs. Harwood is lending me a few but I can't see why they can't ship a few out in *Argus* or a fast tanker.[1]

You ask if I can spare Burrough. I am not sure. I have him in charge of the advanced operations but I am not at all certain he is not redundant. He and Anderson don't hit it off, chiefly Anderson's fault, he is a non-co-operator and has a narrow soldier's mind but as you know Burrough is also difficult at times.[2] However he has and is doing very well. I hope to get him forward to Bône shortly and send *Bulolo* home.

Yes, I consented to Gerald Dickens going to Bizerta – when we get it. He is very good with the French and a very capable officer. But it's no good thinking of him coming out yet.[3] I hope you manage to clip the wings of the CCO operation.

It is undoubtedly wrong and frightfully wasteful besides spreading the doctrine in the three services that combined operations are a black art. Of course the COS are frightened to tackle the PM about it.

I shall be quite happy about Tom Troubridge as the next NCTF, he did very well at Oran and all the Americans like him.

... I haven't had a single letter or paper from the UK since I left. I am fair mad about it.

71.   *To Pound*

5 December 1942

Things are not going too well out here militarily but on the whole it is not surprising. . . .

---

[1]*Argus*: 1918, 14450t, 20k, 20 a/c, 6×4in.
[2]Gen Sir Kenneth Anderson (1891–1959): b India; Seaforth Highlanders 1911; W Front, Palestine 1914–18; much service in India; Col 1934; Maj Gen 1 Div, II & VIII Corps, E Cmd 1940–2; 1 Army, N Af 1942–3; 2 Army 1943; E Cmd Jan 1944; GOC-in-C E Af 1945–6; Gen 1949.
[3]Adm Sir Gerald Dickens (1879–1962): ent RN 1894; Lt 1902; Dardanelles 1915; ID; Capt 1919; DDP 1920–2; *Carlisle* 1922–4; IDC 1926–9; *Repulse* 1929–31; RA 1932; DNI 1932–5; Res F 1935–7; VA 1936; ret 1938; NA The Hague 1940; SNLO, Allied Navies 1940; FO Tunisia 1943; FO Netherlands 1945.

Today, nearly a month after Algiers was taken, *Alynbank* in the Bay
still represents the long range [air raid] warning.[1] . . .

. . . the enemy are building up too and we do not seem to be able to
interrupt his sea communications to Bizerta and Tunis.

Our submarines, for some reason, have been unsuccessful, probably due to the bad hunting they are undergoing, though they have
fired plenty of torpedoes. The air from Malta, with the exception of
one good Albacore strike, do not appear to be having much luck in
sea strikes.[2]

It should be an easy problem to stop the enemy's supplies, particularly as he only has two seaports worth the name. But, like all generals,
Anderson believes in bombing the aerodromes primarily and it is only
lately that I have succeeded in making him go for the ports with any
weight.

Force Q did well and I was glad that Harcourt had Agnew at his
elbow as, good man as he is, he is a bit ignorant about night work and
dealing with night torpedo bombers in these narrow waters. He will
quickly learn.[3]

Quentin's loss was most unfortunate and I have not got to the bottom
of it yet. The aircraft was never detected or fired at which in these days
is quite inadmissible.[4]

Of course the result of Force Q's success is that the enemy ships are
coming over by day only.

Harwood is lending me some MTBs which should perhaps deal with
the smaller craft which are being used at night but, as you know, I could
do with many more.

B.   I am finding Eisenhower and the Americans increasingly easy to
deal with. The former particularly so. He is much worried by the
political side, and was today very grateful when I told him what you
said in your letter that the COS had never any doubt that he had taken
the right line with Darlan. It is rather the hesitations and hair splitting
of our FO that worries him.

---

[1]*Alynbank*: A. Weir, 1925, 5151t, 12k, 8×4in; blockship 9 June 1944.

[2]Fairey Albacore: TBR, 1940–4, 1065hp, 161mph, 930m, 3 crew, 2000lbs/1610lb t,
2mg.

[3]RAdm C. H. J. Harcourt: Capt June 1933; DOD (H) Aug 1938; Ord D Sept 1939;
Duke of York April 1941; RA July 1942; Force Q Oct 1942; *Cleopatra* May 1943; N Sec
to FL Feb 1944; RA, 11 Carrier Sqdn, *Venerable* March 1945.

VAdm Sir William G. Agnew (1898–1960): gun spist; Capt 1937; AMC *Corfu* 1939;
Aurora 1940; SO, Force K 1941; Cdre 12CS 1943; *Excellent* i/c 1943; *Vanguard* 1946;
RA & DPS 1947–9; VA & ret 1950.

[4]*Quentin*: destroyer, 1942, 1705t, 36k, 4×4.7in, 8×21in tt; sunk by a/c off Galita 2
Dec 1942.

He is good enough to consult me always and I attempt to keep the British point of view well to the fore as in these latest Dakar negotiations. The difficulty that I at times find myself in is that I don't know how the COS view the particular question so can only speak for myself.

D.   Force H is rather on my conscience. They do not appear to be doing very much but I do not see how they can be abolished while the Italian squadron is in a position to come on to our coast.

It is at the moment the only thing we have to hit them with, but they rather buy up the destroyers.

At the same time it is the fate of all capital ships to sit in harbour and wait on events.

Actually they are organising Mers-el-Kébir as a fleet base and not wasting their time.

We are being expensive in small craft, I fear. *Ithuriel* is in a bad way, with her back broken but I hope to save her.[1]

Manxman was sheer bad luck, just when she had done so well. Her minefield has already claimed a victim. She will be towed to Gibraltar and probably patched up for towing home.[2]

72.   *Churchill to Pound*

6 December 1942

. . . this is the week of all others when the Malta surface force (Force K) must strike upon the communications of the Axis forces in Tunis[ia]. A week or 10 days later will be too late. Infinite harm will be done and the whole battle compromised.

2.   This is also the time for Admiral Cunningham to use his cruisers and destroyers even at heavy risk against enemy convoys. These vessels could never play so useful a part as in stopping the reinforcements of the enemy during the battle. The first duty of the Navy for the next 10 days is to stop the reinforcements to Tunis[ia]. This duty should be discharged even at a heavy cost.

---

[1]*Ithuriel*: destroyer, 1942, 1360t, 35.5k, 4×4.7in, 4×21in tt; ex-Turkish; irreparably damaged, Bône 28 Nov 1942.
[2]*Manxman*: fast minelayer, 1941, 2650t, 39.75k, 6×4.7in, 100–156 mines.

73. *From Pound*

6 December 1942

A.   We are sending *Victorious* to join the [US] Pacific Fleet and hence Home Fleet will be left without a carrier.

B.   The French Fleet is out of the picture and as the Italian Fleet showed no inclination to take action even when our Air was weak in North Africa, it seems unlikely that they will come sufficiently far west to interfere with our convoys to Algiers.

C.   It has occurred to me whether it is now necessary to maintain two carriers with Force H as apart from giving Home Fleet a carrier it is necessary to avoid risk to our carriers as far as possible.

D.   Please consider the possibility of releasing *Formidable*.

E.   Until Mers-el-Kébir is reasonably safe against attack by human torpedoes it would seem that its use by Force H should be avoided as far as possible.

74. *To Pound*

8 December 1942

I am anxious to dispense with the carriers which I appreciate are not at the moment pulling their weight. On the other hand they provide at present my only mobile torpedo force and fighter cover in the absence of long-range fighters and also a measure of trained naval reconnaissance.

2.   *Furious* alone is not adequate to provide the necessary fighter strength in face of serious attack (air) and it is therefore questionable whether she is worth retaining by herself. In fact if *Formidable* goes the justification of retaining any heavy forces in the Western Mediterranean other than for Atlantic duty is questionable.

3.   It then becomes a matter of gambling on the inactivity of the Italian Fleet. Knowing that we have no heavy forces [or] carriers in the Western Mediterranean might galvanise it to life and such easy targets as the bombardment of Bône present little risk in the absence of shore-based torpedo-bomber forces. With the knowledge that no heavy forces are available to interfere the Italians could cause us serious difficulties on the coastal flank were they so minded.

4.   To balance I am prepared to part with *Formidable* now, but I should like to keep her Albacores shore-based here in default of a better striking force and would again urge most strongly the need of a properly trained naval co-operation group in this area.

5.   The weighing up therefore of the disadvantages of taking *Formidable* away against the requirements for her elsewhere must be done at the Admiralty as I am not in a position to judge the latter.
6.   I am anxious not to reduce destroyer strength at present. *Formidable's* homeward escort would therefore be somewhat of a problem.
8.   As for the safety of Mers-el-Kébir I think it is no less secure than Gibraltar. My policy has been that the Fleet should not stay long enough in either to allow a planned attack to be mounted.

75.   *To Lady Cunningham*

13 December 1942

Things go on steadily here but I fear that the first rush having been unsuccessful it may take us a little time. We have a lot to learn and one or two airmen and soldiers with Middle East experience would be most valuable.

76.   *To Lady Cunningham*

25 December 1942

Here we are having the most frightfully wet weather[,] rain every day and it hampers our business badly. We're having a pretty lively time at sea and the ominous telephone against my bed rings fairly often. Do you remember it during the Crete time? I can hear it still.

77.   *From Pound*

28 December 1942

. . . How thankful we all are that you are where you are, not only because we feel we are in safe hands with you in command but also because it is evident that you have obtained Eisenhower's confidence, which means so much.
B.   . . . I rather hoped it would be easier to cut his [the enemy's] lines of communication to Tunisia than it is. However, as there are only two ports he can use, we . . . should be able to knock them about to such an extent that they are practically useless. We must do so in fact and I will bring this up before the COS tomorrow to see what more can be done in this direction.

C.   . . . these protracted operations [owing to rain] will result in the loss of a lot of small craft which we can ill afford.

E.   As far as ability is concerned, I consider that Willis rather than Syfret should have relieved Moore, but I am convinced that he would not have been a success with either the PM or the Cabinet.[1] However, now that he is to have Force H, I am sure he would consider that he has got the best of the bargain.

H.   You need not worry about Force H not doing anything. It is only the politicians who imagine that ships are not earning their keep unless they are madly rushing about the ocean. . . .

78. *To Aunt Doodles*

10 January 1943

I took a trip in a destroyer up to the east just to see the sailors in one port that had been having a poor time. It was grand getting into a little ship again although it was quite rough and I had some difficulty in keeping myself in my bunk. . . .[2]

79. *Pound to Churchill*

12 January 1943

The stoppage of this traffic [convoys from Italian ports to North Africa] is a matter in which both Naval and Air Forces are concerned.

When the enemy endeavour to run their convoys across at night it gives the Naval forces a great opportunity, as was proved by the destruction of the convoy by Force Q last week.

As a result of this disaster the enemy are now running their convoys so that they arrive at Bizerta or Tunis in the later part of the afternoon,

---

[1]AoF Sir Algernon Willis (1889–1976): ent RN 1903; Lt 1909; t spist; Grand F 1916–18; Capt 1929; N War Coll 1930–2; *Kent*, China 1933–4; *Nelson*, HF 1934–5; *Vernon* i/c 1935–8; *Barham*, Med F 1938; Cdre & CoS, Med F 1939–41; RA 1940; A/VA & C-in-C S Atl Sept 1941–Feb 1942; VA, 3BS & 2-in-C, EF March 1942; FOIC, Force H 1943; C-in-C, Levant 1943; 2SL 1944–6; Adm 1944; C-in-C Med 1946–8; C-in-C Portsmouth 1948–50; AoF 1949.

Adm Sir E. Neville Syfret (1889–1971): ent RN 1904; Lt 1909; gun spist; Harwich 1914–18; Capt 1929; N Sec to FL Nov 1939; RA, 18CS 1940; cmd Force H Feb 1942; Malta convoys 1941–2; Madagascar 1942; N Af Nov 1942; VA & VCNS 1943; Adm 1946; C-in-C Home F 1945–8; ret 1948.

[2]*Lookout*: destroyer, 1941, 1920t, 36.5k, 6×4.7in, 1×4in, 4×21in tt.

Bône had over 70 air raids in the winter of 1942–3.

which means that at daylight on that day they are some 200 miles from Bône, which is the most advanced base our ships can work from.

Force Q could, therefore, leave Bône after dark and if, by air reconnaissance or special intelligence, information is known of the time of arrival of the convoy and its route, there should be a reasonable chance of the convoy being intercepted in the early morning, either just before or just after daylight. This means, however, that Force Q will have to carry out more than half of its retirement to Bône in daylight without fighter cover.

Considering that there are 120 torpedo aircraft in Sicily, in addition to some 200 to 300 long-range bombers and some dive-bombers, it is hardly to be expected that Force Q will arrive at Bône without serious loss or damage to its ships.

There is no doubt that Admiral Cunningham is fully alive to the necessity of stopping this traffic, and he has been given an additional cruiser to enable Force Q to work in two watches.

What it really comes to as regards the stoppage of this traffic by surface forces is that it should be possible to stop one convoy, but this means accepting such losses as would practically wipe out half of Force Q, and a second convoy might be stopped by sacrificing the other half.

We have no more suitable ships with which to build up another Force Q.

I should say, therefore, that Admiral Cunningham, sitting alongside General Eisenhower as he is, would wish to be quite certain, before he decides to sacrifice part of his force, that he is doing so for some more adequate object.

The action which Admiral Cunningham has taken as regards the ships which are due to arrive at Bizerta at 3.0 tomorrow afternoon is that he has ordered that part of Force Q which is now at Bône to have steam up by 5.0 this evening, but not to leave harbour without orders. Whether he has since ordered this force to sea we do not know.

The stoppage of this traffic by air is not an easy matter, as owing to the short distance between Sicily and Bizerta the convoy can be fully protected by enemy short-range fighters during the whole of its passage. On the other hand, owing to the distance of the Sicily/Bizerta line from Malta and Bône, we are unable to give short-range fighter protection to any of our Air Forces attacking the convoy. . . .

80. *To Lady Cunningham*

21 January 1943

Now I am indeed the 'veteran admiral' as announced in the Washington Press. . . .

81. *To Pound*

31 January 1943

6. You left Algiers just in time to escape three air raids, not of any great weight, but we were lucky to escape with only one merchant ship hit and minor damage to others. The enemy seems to be organising their attacks on our convoys and ports. It is wonderful what they do with so few aircraft and I fear that our convoys may be in for a rough ride east of Algiers. You will have seen that in the last convoy to Bône, we had *Pozarica* and *Avon Vale* torpedoed and badly damaged, and a corvette sunk.[1] The only bright feature being that the convoy was unscathed at Bône.

82. *To Lady Cunningham*

1 February 1943

In a few days' time I shall assume the old title again. It's funny coming in through the back door so to speak and it was none of my making. . . .

83. *From Rear Admiral F. H. Pegram*[2]

Office of the FOC West Africa,
Freetown, [Sierra Leone],
1 February 1943

. . . I think I can sum up the results of my visit to Dakar as follows:
We have made a sound agreement which will leave the operational direction in British hands whilst paying sufficient attention to French

---

[1]*Pozarica*: McAndrews, AA ship, 1938, 1893t, 6×4in; severely damaged and sank off Bougie 13 Feb 1943.
  Avon Vale: 'Hunt', 1940.
  Marigold: corvette, 1941, 925t, 16k, 1×4in; sunk off Algiers 9 Dec 1942.
  [2]VAdm F. H. Pegram: Capt 1932; Cdre 2Cl, S Am Div, *Glasgow*, July 1939; RA Jan 1941; *Eland* March 1942; 4SL & Chief of Supplies & Transport, May 1943; VA Aug 1943; d 8 March 1944.

amour propre, and which will allow them as they become better equipped and more efficient to play an increasingly effective part in operations in this area.

At present they are not able to do much and I am afraid for some months they will be more of a liability than an asset, nevertheless the will to play their part is clear. At present they appear to agree to everything, including the use of their ships on blockade runner patrol, but this is not quite the same as getting them to do the job. All sorts of difficulties were immediately produced when I wished to send the *Gloire* and the *Georges Leygues* to sea.[1] However, the latter has gone, though only for a short time. I have sent my technical experts to Dakar to inquire into the present state of the French asdics and minesweeping equipment, and from initial reports it appears that it is not very efficient. I hope soon to be able to give the Admiralty the information they require in order to get the small craft suitably equipped. We are already training some of the French here in our A/S methods.[2]

I am very much afraid that the U-boats seeking, as always, a new soft target, will hit on the West African routes, and should they do so in any force we shall be in for a bad time. As you know my escort forces are very small, mostly worn out, and owing to the fact that they never stop running at all, very lacking in training. I have of course constantly shouted for reinforcements but they, quite naturally, have not been forthcoming, in fact the reverse has occurred. Other theatres of war and in particular yours have had to be supplied first. . . .

84. *From Commodore H. G. Norman*[3]

Royal Navy,
GHQ, Middle East Forces,
Cairo,
1 February 1943

. . . Malta was at once the saddest and bravest sight I've seen. No account or photograph can give the true picture though Ricci's little book gives something of the atmosphere.[4]

---

[1]*Georges Leygues, Gloire, Montcalm*: Fr csrs, 1937, 7600t, 31k, 9×6in, 4×21.7in tt.
[2]Asdic: anti-submarine detection device, later called 'sonar'.
[3]RAdm H. G. Norman: Capt 1938; IDC 1939; Cdre & Addnl CoS, Med F 1940; *Queen Elizabeth*, EF 1943–4; RA.
[4]Capt A. da C. Ricci: *Victoria & Albert* June 1932; Pay Capt Dec 1935; NID Sept 1939; ret June 1941; a well-known naval writer.

... The dockyard was like a vast waste returning to life. ... They've done tremendous work and much remains to be done.

As regards the air side, the island is really like a vast carrier, with fighter protection taking its correct perspective as a *sine que non* for the operation of overseas air strikes. Park agreed with this view and said he wouldn't have missed such a command for worlds.

Tripoli is an anxiety but after a very unpleasant complaint by the Army Commander against the Navy – which reached the PM's ears incidentally – it is I think being shown that we haven't failed them in speed or supplies. The figures for the first six days since sweepers got in here have averaged 650 tons per day, with 750, 1100 and 1450 for the last 3 days.[1] The blockade is thorough though.

85.   *Chiefs of Staff Committee*

2 February 1943

COS (43) 35: Naval Command in the Mediterranean

In view of the progress of the 8th Army, the appointment of an AOC Mediterranean who will be alongside the Allied C-in-C at Algiers, and the fact that General Alexander will shortly be conducting operations over the whole of the Tunisia area, I am of the opinion that the time has come to make the change in Naval Command in the Mediterranean which was approved in principle by the CCS at Casablanca.[2]

2.   At the present time it is not desired to extend what will be the new Mediterranean Command further to the east than is necessary . . .

3.   It is for consideration whether General Eisenhower should be informed in advance of this proposed change in the Naval Command and whether it will be necessary to inform the Cabinet. . . .

---

[1]FM Visct (Sir Bernard) Montgomery of Alamein (1887–1976): R Warks R 1908; W Front 1914, severely wounded; staff 1915–18; India, Egypt, Palestine 1919–39; 3 Div April 1939; Lt Gen, V, XII Corps July 1940; SE Cmd Dec 1941; 8 Army Aug 1942; 2nd Battle of Alamein & Gen Oct 1942; Sicily, Italy 1943–4; 21 Army Grp, 'Overlord' 1944–5; CIGS 1946.

[2]Eighth Army: the British & Commonwealth Army in Egypt.

M of RAF Lord (Sir Arthur) Tedder (1890–1967): Army & RFC; Sqdn Ldr 1919; AVM & AOC, Far E 1937; Dir Gen Research & Development 1938; DAOC ME Dec 1940; AM & AOC May 1941; ACM & VCAS 1942; Cdr, Med AF Feb 1943; DSup Cdr, 'Overlord' Dec 1943; M of RAF Sept 1945; CAS Jan 1946. V. Orange, *Tedder: Quietly in Command* (London, 2004).

FM Visct (Sir Harold) Alexander of Tunis (1891–1961): Maj Gen 1937; 1 Div 1939; Lt Gen, S Cmd Dec 1940; Gen & Burma retreat March–April 1942; C-in-C ME Aug 1942; Cdr Tunisian campaign 1943; C-in-C 15 Army Grp, Sicily & Italy 1943–4; Sup Cdr Med Nov 1944–5; S Def 1951; Gov-Gen Canada 1951–2.

[Attachment]

1 February 1943: Draft Signal: Naval Command in the Mediterranean

The Mediterranean will be divided into two Commands:
  (a) The area to the west of a line A to B to be the Mediterranean Command.
  (b) The area to the east of the above line to be the Levant Command which will include the Red Sea.
2. For the present the line A to B will be the line running from the Tunisian/Tripolitanian border to a position in Latitude 35°N, Longitude 16°E thence to Cape Spartivento (Italy).
3. The FOC of the area to the west of the line A to B to be the C-in-C, Mediterranean, the FOC to the east of the area of the line A to B to be the C-in-C, Levant.
4. The C-in-C, Mediterranean, as defined above, will co-ordinate all movements and matters which affect the Mediterranean as a whole and will be responsible for the distribution of forces between the Mediterranean and Levant commands.
5. The C-in-C, Levant, will assume the responsibility, at present carried out by C-in-C, Mediterranean, subject to the limitations of his Command as given in para. 3 above.
6. Until such time as Malta and the Middle East military forces at present in the Middle East command can be supplied from the west, the C-in-C, Levant, will be responsible for organising the supplies which are carried by sea.[1]

86. *To Lady Cunningham*

14 February 1943

. . . Harwood is not pleased and I don't blame him. But I was quite impersonal about it and told Dudley Pound I would stand down with pleasure for anyone. But apparently they want me while Eisenhower is here but I won't stay for ever. . . .

[1]VAdm Sir Henry H. Harwood

87.   *Ramsay to his wife*

Gibraltar,
15 February 1943

... Cunningham is thriving on it and is in great form. He is very autocratic, sees only his side of any matter and dictates his orders and decisions accordingly. It has many advantages to see only one side of a question. But it doesn't make for all-round contentment. Nevertheless it saves him much wear and tear. ...

88.   *To the Admiralty*

17 February 1943

May I call Admiralty attention to paragraph 3 of Ministry of Information telegram EMPAX No.94 to Cairo which suggests exploiting the inactivity of the Italian Fleet. I now have convoys of between 15 and 20 merchant ships very lightly escorted and covered by only two Cruisers and two or three Fleets [destroyers] running every 10 days to Tripoli, Libya and Malta. Under these conditions one deprecates any action that might goad the Italian Fleet into activity.

89.   *From Pound*

27 February 1943

We have had a good talk with Ramsay and he seems to be fairly happy about things. I think you have got four very good Naval Task Force Commanders in Troubridge, McGrigor, Mack and Oliver.[1] As you know,

---

[1]AoF Sir Rhoderick McGrigor (1893–1959): destroyers, Dardanelles, Jutland 1914–18; t spist; Capt 1933; Cdre 1Cl & CoS, China & *Kent* i/c 1938–40; *Renown* Feb-Sept 1941; RA & ACNS (Weapons) 1941; Sicily landgs & SNO S Italy 1943; 1CS, Home F 1944–5; VCNS 1945–8; Adm & C-in-C, Home F 1948–50; C-in-C Plymouth 1950–1; FSL 1951–5; AoF 1953. E. J. Grove, 'Admiral Sir Rhoderick McGrigor', in M. Murfett (ed.), *The First Sea Lords: Fisher to Mountbatten* (London & Westport, CT, 1995), pp. 249–64.

RAdm P. J. Mack: Capt 1934; Capt (D), 7DF, *Jervis*, Home F March 1939; Med F 1940–2; *Duke of York* May 1942; *King George V* Sept 1942; RA Jan 1943; d in air crash April 1943.

Adm Sir Geoffrey N. Oliver (1898–1980): ent RN 1915; gun spist; destroyer cmds 1934–6; Capt 1939; SD 1939–40; *Hermione* 1940–2; cdr, landg craft, 'Torch', Nov 1942; NOIC Bône 1943; Sicily & Italy landgs 1943; 'Neptune' June 1944; carriers off Greece 1944; EI F 1945; RA 1945; Adm (Air) 1946; ACNS 1946; Pres, RNC Greenwich 1948; VA 1949; C-in-C E Indies 1950–2; Adm 1952; C-in-C Nore 1953–5.

it is a terrific strain on the Second Sea Lord to provide all the personnel for these businesses, but he is playing up magnificently.[1] I do not know what we shall do about escort craft on account of there being so many.
. . .

I was glad to see that in the Western Mediterranean Air Organisation there was a Coastal Force and I only hope that Tedder is playing up and giving you what is necessary.

90. *To Aunt Doodles*

3 March 1943

[visited Malta] . . . . The dockyard which I thought was just grand and was working flat out. . . . The children were all looking very well[,] in fact none of the populace showed signs of what they had been through.
. . .

91. *To Pound*

15 March 1943

A.   The figures of submarine sinkings for February were certainly satisfactory but we can do better than that yet. I am not clear how the merchant ship sinkings are going but we seem to be losing a lot.
B.   I had a very interesting visit to Malta.

I was most impressed by what was going on in the Dockyard and how they were overcoming the difficulties. I think Mackenzie has done, and is doing, a real good job which should be recognised.[2]

Bonham-Carter is settling in well and certainly appears to have his head screwed on the right way.[3] Leatham is looking much better and is enjoying a well-earned rest as Deputy Governor at San Anton. He will be glad to come away.[4]

Admiralty House, although the Auberge de France is flat, hasn't a crack in it and wants but a little glass!! It houses about 40 officers.

---

[1]Adm Whitworth.
[2]RAdm K. H. L. Mackenzie (1888–1970): ent RN 1904; navig spist; Capt 1930; RA 1941; Adm Supt, Malta DY Jan 1941–Nov 1943.
[3]VAdm S. S. Bonham-Carter.
[4]Adm Sir Ralph Leatham (1886–1954): ent RN 1900; Capt 1924; CO *Yarmouth, Durban, Ramillies, Valiant*; RA 1BS 1938–9; VA 1939; C-in-C EI 1939–41; VA, Malta 1942–3; Adm 1943; C-in-C Plymouth 1943–5; ret 1946; Govr & C-in-C Bermuda 1946–9.

C.   I had a very good meeting with Harwood and we quickly reached agreement on all points.

Incidentally he is very upset at being relieved, and puts it down to two things:

1.   He withstood the PM on the question of the French Fleet at Alexandria. Quite rightly in my opinion – so did I when the PM was here and subsequent events have shown how right we were.
2.   Montgomery claimed that there was dilatoriness in opening up Tripoli. This I know is quite untrue. In my opinion Tripoli was most expeditiously cleared and opened up and any statement to the contrary is quite untrue.

Later: I now gather that the latter reason is correct and I feel that Harwood has been very hardly dealt with. Nor will this tend to improve relations between the Navy and the Army which are usually excellent. Montgomery, I gather, is not given to appreciate what the Navy does for him and wants pulling up.

D.   The difficulty in Washington over the A/S measures west of Gibraltar was evidently a case of the RAF getting hoisted with their own petard.

The AOC Gibraltar has constantly tried to get the Casablanca PBYs under his orders and obviously complained to some air official who brought it up at the Convoy Conference by saying the A/S measures west of Gibraltar were inefficient.[1] In actual fact, although the co-ordination with the PBYs leaves something to be desired, the A/S measures west of Gibraltar have been most efficient and efficacious.

Tedder and I will get down to the better co-ordination problem when the US Admiral Hewitt arrives.[2]

There are several warring factions to be placated. The American Army Air [Force] over the B24s, the US Navy air and the RAF with ourselves as a very interested party to see that an efficient arrangement [will] be come to.[3]

Eisenhower took a bit of convincing that he must stand out of it but with Bedell Smith's help all is peace as far as he is concerned.

---

[1]Consolidated PBY (Catalina): f/boat, 1936, 2×1200hp, 179mph, 3100m, 8 crew, 5mg, d/c.

[2]Admiral H. Kent Hewitt, US Navy: grad N Acad 1907; CO *Cummings*, N Atl convoys, 1917–18; gun spist; NW Coll 1928; Capt & N Acad 1933; *Indianapolis* 1936; RA & Spl Svc Sqdn & csrs, Atl F 1939; cded W NTF, 'Torch' 1942; VA Nov 1942; Cdr US N Forces, NW African Waters & Cdr 8 F 1943; Cdr Allied N Forces, 'Avalanche' & 'Anvil' 1943–4; Adm & Cdr, US Naval Forces Eur 1945; ret 1949.

[3]Consolidated B24 (Liberator): bomber, a/s, 1939, 4×1200hp, 300mph, 2100m, 12 crew, 10mg, 5–12800lbs bombs.

The air situation is slowly getting better but Lloyd, who is to command the Coastal Group, has not yet arrived and it badly wants pulling together.[1] I had a collision with Tedder over a sea striking force permanently attached to the Coastal Group and he gave way.

The Air have reached the decision that no reconnaissance over the Sicilian narrows in daylight is possible with which I don't agree and the reconnaissance in the Tyrrhenian Sea is still quite inadequate.

Fortunately we get on well with the Americans who are always ready to place squadrons at our disposal. They seem to realise the importance of sinking ships *at sea* much better than do our RAF.

The Coastal Group *will* function satisfactorily but it's hard slogging getting them going. Neglect to make an all-weather aerodrome between Bône and Algiers is also exposing our shipping to most unnecessary risks. Yesterday, Sunday, the cruisers and the LSIs carrying troops to Bône spent the day dodging torpedoes fired by T/B aircraft boldly within 10 miles of our coast. Eisenhower has got on to this himself and his Chief Engineer has orders to give this aerodrome first priority.[2]

F.   Losing *Lightning* was sheer bad luck. *Aurora* had got the E-boats on the RDF and was firing 6-inch barrage but somehow *Lightning* got in the way of a torpedo which stopped her and then another which broke her in half.[3] . . .

92.   *Ramsay to his wife*

15 March 1943

. . . We played ping-pong for one and a half hours after dinner last night. ABC is extraordinarily good at it. . .

93.   *To Lady Cunningham*

25 March 1943

Things go on slowly here. Though the Eighth Army did not over-run the Mareth line at the first onslaught they and others further north have

---

[1]ACM Sir Hugh Lloyd (1894–1981): RE 1914; RFC 1917; Sqdn Ldr , 2 Flyg Sch 1930; India 1931–4; Instr, Army Staff Coll 1936–8; Snr Air SO, 2 Group, Bbr Cmd; A/ AVM & AOC Med, June 1941–July 1942; AOC NW Af Coastal AF March 1943–Feb 1944; IDC 1945–7; AOC Far E 1947–9; Bbr Cmd; ACM 1951; ret 1953.

[2]Chief Engineer: not identified.

[3]*Lightning*: destroyer, 1941, 1930t, 36.5k, 6×4.7in, 1×4in, 4×21in tt; sunk by MAS boat, off N Af 12 March 1943.

done quite well and we shall get going again soon. In the latest battle
the Americans have done well and are finding their feet. So I am full of
optimism.

94.   *To Lady Cunningham*

20 April 1943

I spent most of my day feeding with Ike yesterday. Alex[ander] and
Monty were in to lunch with him. My first meeting with the latter and I
wasn't impressed though I think he did his best. Too much 'I' about it
altogether. . . .

95.   *From Pound*

23 April 1943

C.   As regards Harwood's relief, the French Fleet at Alexandria had
nothing to do with it. He was relieved on my recommendation as I
came to the conclusion that someone – J. H. D. Cunningham – could
do the job much better.[1] The actual work of the salvage party at
Tripoli was very good and they were commended, but the staff arrangements left too much to chance which was quite unacceptable
when one takes into consideration what the clearing of Tripoli meant
to the Army. As a matter of fact, Montgomery has been most appreciative of what the Navy has done and took the trouble to visit every
ship at Tripoli. I am very sorry for Harwood but with a blood pressure
of 255, which no one knew about until after Tripoli, it is not surprising that he was not up to the mark. I am surprised at your expressing
such a definite opinion about his relief when you only know one side
of the case.
E.   King now pretends that he never agreed to provide capital ships for
the Mediterranean, though the paper in which this was put down as a
possible US requirement was considered by the CCS and he made no
comment. However, he says he is going into the matter and will try to

[1]AoF Sir John H. D. Cunningham (1885–1962): ent RN 1900; Lt 1905; navig spist;
Med F & Grand F 1914–18; Cdr, Navig Sch 1922–3; Mr of F 1923; Capt 1925; staff
cmds; N War Coll; DP; *Adventure, Resolution*; RA & ACNS 1936; ACNS (Air) & 5SL
1937–9; RA, 1CS, Med F 1939; VA & 1CS, Home F 1939–40; N cmdr, 'Menace',
Dakar, 1940; 4SL 1941–3; C-in-C Levant & then Med & Adm 1943; FSL 1946–8; AoF
1948; Chm, Iraq Pet Co, 1948–58. M. H. Murfett, 'Admiral Sir John Cunningham', in
Murfett (ed.), *The First Sea Lords*, pp. 217–28.

help, but I expect it will be by sending ships to the Home Fleet, which should be the best arrangement.

G. I did not butt in about the Gibraltar-Casablanca air business because it looked as if you were getting an agreed arrangement locally, and without knowing definitely how I could help, I might have done more harm than good.

I. It must be a great relief to you to be operating in an area where we have air supremacy. Marshall has got some wild scheme for doing part of 'Husky' between the end of May and the middle of June, but it is so obviously impracticable that I do not think you will even have it referred to you for your remarks.[1]

96. To Pound

28 April 1943

B. Things otherwise are not going too badly. With the air we seem to have pretty well stopped shipping going to Tunisia, but there is a continual stream of Siebel ferries and lighters that we have not hit hard yet, though the MTBs have had some little success.[2]

I am moving up a division of 'Hunts' on each flank, who I hope, when the enemy air is a little more tamed, will be able to look after themselves in daylight and at any rate increase the threat to the line of supply. The mines are, however, a nuisance.

G. The loss of *Splendid* and *Sahib* is a bad blow; two of the best CO's; the latter you saw on *Maidstone*.[3] I hope the worsening of the Asdic conditions which should take place in a week or two now, will make things easier for our submarines, though of course it cuts both ways.

D. I am most grateful for the four 'T' destroyers coming to the Levant.[4] I have refrained, knowing full well the difficulties, from asking

---

[1]'Husky': the invasion of Sicily in July 1943 – see next section.
[2]Siebel ferry: a German motorised barge.
[3]*Maidstone*: s/m depot ship, 1938, 8900t, 17k, 8×4.4in.
Splendid, Sahib: 'S' cl s/m, 1942, 715/1000t, 14.5/10k, 6–7×21in tt, 1×3in; *Splendid* lost off Corsica 21 April & *Sahib* off Sicily 24 April 1943; both damaged & scuttled, almost all crew becoming PoWs. See S. May, 'The British Submarine Campaign in the Mediterranean, 1940–1943', unpub. M.Phil. thesis, U. Wales Swansea, 2000.
CO *Splendid*: Lt I. McGeoch: Lt May 1937; *Clyde* Aug 1937; *Triumph* Aug 1940; *St Angelo* (Malta) Sept 1941; *P228 (Sahib)* May 1942; sunk & PoW 24 April 1943; escaped Sept 1943; Lt Cdr May 1944; *Swiftsure* Jan 1945; later VAdm Sir Ian McGeoch & FO (S).
CO *Sahib*: Lt J. S. Bromage.
[4]'T' cl destroyers: 1943, 1710t, 36k, 4×4.7in, 8×21in tt.

for more fleets, but it is a fact that most of the ones out here are on their last legs. I do not think the 'Tribals' can be kept going much longer.

97. *To Pound*

8 May 1943

C. . . . Oliver was, I think, in Bizerta this forenoon and while the fighting at sea and the heavy minesweeping programme is going on it is as well to have him in charge with all the experience he has accumulated. He is a grand man and imbues everyone with his own energy.

We have the Strait packed with destroyers and MTBs every night and tomorrow the air has promised to cover so they will be there by day as well. They get bombed but so far happily without damage.

There appears a tendency for the remnants of the enemy to try to hold the Cape Bon peninsula but I can't see how he can supply himself there for long. He is already using German submarines and maybe we shall bag one or two.

D. . . . I feel myself that we should attempt to maintain a reasonable standard of smartness in dress on the part of both officers and men. To allow personnel to be sloppily dressed is, in my opinion, the first step to indiscipline.

E. . . . I think we should look forward to the time when the whole Mediterranean is again a single command. Not, however, for the benefit of the present incumbent.

There is not room for two Cs-in-C. I feel there should be one only with Gibraltar, Malta and the Levant as subordinate but semi-independent commands.

This is a purely objective view and has not arrived as the result of any disagreement. Leatham has been splendid.

98. *To Captain Edelsten*[1]

15 June 1943

. . . I wished you were out here the other day when our destroyers were going unscathed (except by our own air force) off Tunisia. They are regaining the confidence in themselves which I think they lost at Crete.

---

[1]Adm Sir John Edelsten (1891–1966): Lt 1913; Capt 1933; DPD 1938; SNO, Somaliland 1940; Cdre & CoS Med F 1941; RA & ACNS (UT) 1942; RA (D) BPF 1945; VA, 1BS 1945; 4CS 1946; VCNS 1947; Adm & C-in-C Med 1950; C-in-C Portsmouth 1950–2; ret 1954.

Two or three of the little 'Hunts' are quite prepared to take tea with a reasonable number of Ju88s and even with dive-bombers.[1] The older ones, Eaton, Tyrwhitt and others are taking more time over it but it's coming and I have hardened my heart and denied them high priority fighter support on several occasions.[2] We must just get back our confidence in ourselves and our weapons. . . .

One young 'Hunt' captain told me he thought it was too dangerous to stop and pick up one boatload so he ran over them. I shook him warmly by the hand and left him without enquiring further. I trust there were more like him.

5. The End in Africa

99. *To Aunt Doodles*

16 May 1943

Well the job is finished. No one in their wildest hopes thought we should catch the lot but we have and I doubt if more than 2 or 3 hundred got away and that mostly by air.

The sight of the destroyers off the Tunisian coast cannot have given much encouragement to them to go boating.[3] . . .

100. *To Aunt Doodles*

6 June 1943

. . . I have had Winston staying in my house for about eight days, much too long in these busy times and a perfect nuisance interfering with the work. I just cleared out and lived on board a ship in the harbour. . . .

I must say he's very amusing and his memory is quite amazing[,] he never forgets anything you say to him but it's a bit wearing after dinner never getting to bed till after one.

---

[1]Junkers Ju88: bomber, 1939–45, 2×1410hp, 273mph, 1550m, 4 crew, 2 cannon, 4mg, 3960lbs.

The dive-bomber was the Junkers Ju87: 1939–45, 1400hp, 255mph, 620m, 4mg, 3960lbs.

[2]Capt J. W. M. Eaton: Cdr Dec 1937; *Venetia* July 1939; *Mohawk* Oct 1939; Capt Dec 1941; *Eskimo* Nov 1942; *Sheffield* Jan 1945.

Cdr StJ. R. J. Tyrwhitt: L Cdr 1936; *Defender* April 1939; Cdr June 1940; *Tartar* June 1942; D N Asst, 2SL's Off, April 1944.

[3]600 escaped by sea; some 700 were captured. On land, 238,000 became captive.

I made him visit the submarines and he made a very delightful speech to them. But he was very affected talking to the very young captains and came away with tears streaming down his face and talking of the 'boys walking in the valley of the shadow of death'. . . . It is a little sad to see all these gay lads and know what danger they are in constantly and that their losses have been frightful[,] much heavier than any other branch of any of the services.

101. *From Dill*

11 June 1943

When lunching alone with Marshall today, he dilated on how much your successful support to Eisenhower had meant to him and, more important, to the smooth running of affairs in North Africa.

I do not tell you this for your personal gratification! but that you may know how completely the Americans (including King!) trust your judgement and will accept your considered opinion. You will still, I feel, have a vastly important part to play in keeping the balance in all that lies ahead.

102. *To Aunt Doodles*

13 June 1943

. . . We got hold of Pantelleria with less trouble than I expected . . . we got Lampedusa with little trouble . . . It is very satisfactory to have cleared those two hornets' nests and so made the passage for our convoys safer.[1]

103. *To Aunt Doodles*

24 June 1943

. . . He [the King] persuaded me to let him go to Malta. . . I thought a visit to Malta would have a great effect all over the British Empire.[2]

---

[1]Pantelleria and Lampedusa were Italian islands off the coast of Tunisia.
[2]King George VI (1895–1952): RN; at Jutland 1916; Duke of York; King 1936, on abdication of Edward VIII, his brother.
Malta, the principal peacetime base of the Med F, was under heavy air attack from the start of the war in June 1940 and experienced extremely heavy 'aerial sieges' in Jan–April 1941 and Dec 1941–Sept 1942. In April 1942 King George VI awarded the island the GC.

... We entered the Grand Harbour shortly after eight and it was a fine sight to see the old walls and battlements black with cheering people. ... And as he stepped ashore all the bells in the island started ringing and the churches are very many. ... his reception was wildly enthusiastic everywhere. ...

104. *From Rear Admiral J. L. Hall, Jr, US Navy*[1]

Casablanca,
3 December 1943

The salvage experts have been somewhat disappointing, for the problem seems to impress them as bigger than I had believed. They are now talking in terms of months.

I was glad to get *Winnooski* to Gibraltar. She is quite a favourite with Admirals Ingersoll and Sharpe, experienced and well-equipped for fueling ships at sea and for keeping up with the fleet.[2]

Hambledon is still awaiting the raising of the dry dock, which is proving to be more of an undertaking than we thought.[3] We are finding many holes from bomb and shell fragments in the deck. It is my hope that we may be able to fit the destroyer for the voyage to home waters under her own power.

Electra's engine room is dry after 12 days' submersion, but we hope to repair her temporarily here.[4]

I am pleasantly surprised that submarines have given us so little trouble recently. Whether the patrol planes and the minefields have kept them at a distance or they are busy elsewhere remains to be seen. ...

Perhaps my only just cause for irritation is this: to have in this port one French Vice Admiral and four Rear Admirals who have no real

[1]Adm J. L. Hall, Jr, US Navy: b 1891; grad N Acad 1913; battleships 1917–18; N Acad 1920–2; Capt *Arkansas* 1940–1; RA & Cdr, Adva Base Unit, Atl F, & then Sea Frontier Forces, WTF, Casablanca Nov 1942; XI Amph Force, UK Nov 1943; cmd, 'Omaha' beach, 'Neptune' June 1944; amph forces, Pac F Oct 1944; S Atk Force, Okinawa 1945; post-1945, amph forces Pac F, 14 N Dist, Cdt Armed Forces Staff Coll, Cdr W Sea Frontier; ret 1953. S. H. Godson, *Viking of the Assault: Admiral J. L. Hall, jr, and Amphibious Assault* (Washington, DC, 1982).
[2]USS *Winnooski*: HQ ship, 1941, 5985t, 16.7k, 1×5in.
VAdm Alexander Sharp, Jr, US Navy: grad N Acad 1906; destroyers, Queenstown, 1918–20; Capt & BuNav 1931–3; *Concord* 1933–5; Dir of Officer Peronnel 1937–8; *Idaho* 1938–9; CNO office 1939–41; RA & BS Div 5 & BS Atl F 1941–2; A/VA & cmd Service Force, Atl F Aug 1942–4; RA & Cdr, Minecraft, Pac F 1944–5; admin posts 1945–6; VA & ret 1946. Adm R. E. Ingersoll, see note 3, page 28 for biography.
[3]*Hambledon*: 'Hunt' cl, 1940 later cmd by L Cdr G. McKendrick, husband of Cunningham's niece Hilda.
[4]USS *Electra*: cargo ship, 1941, 4500gt, 12.5k, 1×5in, 1×3in.

ships to operate, and to have to see their efforts to maintain a place in the sun, when their presence is really nothing more than a cause for extra red tape. . . .

Admiral Ingersoll is calling for the return of the fast minesweepers which are my only real ocean escort vessels (five DM's and three AM's). This will leave me only the eight 173-foot PCs, and the small minesweepers and inshore patrol craft.[1] I do not doubt you have noted the order he gives all convoy escorts, that while in these waters they are available for local escort only, and for no other operations. I do not interpret that to mean I could not send them out to sink a submarine if the opportunity arises or can be created. I have used two for escort duty to Gibraltar.

I am still hopeful that it will not be long before General Cannon can let me have from four to six B17s or B24s to give them an extra day's cover to convoys arriving and departing. Port Lyautey can support these planes when they become available.[2] They have much greater range than PBY-5A's. . . .

105. *Cunningham's Report of Proceedings on Operation 'Torch'*

30 March 1943

I have the honour to tender the attached report on Operation 'Torch' covering the period 22 October to 17 November 1942, from the sailing of the assault convoy from the UK until the occupation of Bône. This report deals mainly with the British naval assaults. . .

2.   The early stages of the operation prior to D-Day were remarkable for lack of incident. This was indeed fortunate since, in the course of this vast and complex movement delays caused by casualties or stress of weather would have rendered the timely delivery of the assaults improbable.

3.   The movement of the assault convoys and Force H through the Strait of Gibraltar on the 5/6 November and the continuous entry and departure of all classes of ships for refuelling placed a heavy strain on the resources and organisation of Gibraltar. The manner in which this strain was withstood reflects credit on the Vice Admiral, Gibraltar, and Commodore Superintendent and their staffs.[3]

[1]DM= Destroyer Minelayer; AM= Auxiliary Minesweeper; PC= Patrol Craft.
[2]Gen Cannon, USAAF: unidentified.
    Boeing B17 (Fortress): bomber, 1935, 4×1200hp, 300mph, 1850m, 10 crew, 13mg, 17600lbs.
[3]VAdm, Gibraltar: VAdm Sir Frederick Edward-Collins: Capt 1925; RA 1935; 2CS

4.   It is also a tribute to the skill and seamanship of individual COs that this continuous flow of movements and berthing in a congested harbour and anchoring in the dark was accompanied with but a single minor collision.

5.   The only major incident inside the Mediterranean before the assault was the torpedoing of the USS *Thomas Stone* at 0535 on 7 November. A notably courageous decision was taken by Capt O. R. Bennehoff, US Navy, to send on his escort and boats to the assault, leaving his ship defenceless; tenacity and seamanship was displayed by *Wishart* (Cdr H. G. Scott) in towing USS *Thomas Stone* to Algiers.[1]

6.   Reconnaissance by submarine and Folbot parties prior to the assaults were in the main successfully carried out. Inshore reconnaissance by Folbot had already been viewed with misgiving as endangering security.[2] That these fears were well grounded was proved at 'A' Beach when two officers were captured. Fortunately they kept their heads and the pre-arranged cover plan was adequate. The work of Lt-Cdr Willmott, both in active reconnaissance and in his painstaking training and preparation before the operation is worthy of special note.[3] Credit is also due to the Captain (S), 8SF and the COs of *P45*, *P48*, *P221*, *P54* and *Ursula* for their efficient co-operation.[4]

7.   The arrival of the assault forces at their initial positions off the beaches proceeded without a hitch. Contacts were made with beacon submarines as planned. In fact the operation up to this point proceeded with a flawless accuracy which reflected high credit on Task Force Commanders, COs of HM Ships and Masters of Merchant Vessels alike.

8.   Assault at Oran beaches passed off without a hitch, but at Algiers 'B' and 'C' Beaches things went awry and delay and confusion resulted, which might have endangered success had the opposition been

April 1938; VA 1939; VAC N Atl, Gibraltar Jan 1941; Adm & ret 1943; *Forte*, Falmouth 1944.

Cdre Supt: RAdm A. J. Robertson (ret June 1941).

[1]Capt O. R. Bennehof, US Navy: when his ship *Thomas Stone* was torpedoed on 7 Nov 1942, bravely launched his landing craft while wallowing helpless at sea.

Cdr H. G. Scott: Cdr Dec 1938; *Wishart* 1942; *Victory* for RN Barracks 1943; Capt June 1945.

[2]Folbot: a folding canoe, launched from s/m, for beach reconnaissance, etc.

[3]Cdr H. N. C. Willmott: Lt Dec 1932; *Wellington* Dec 1937; Lt Cdr Dec 1940; *Nile* June 1941; Comb Ops, *Monck* Greenock July 1942; Cdr June 1944; PD (Q) Sept 1944.

[4]Capt (S), 8SF: Capt G. B. H. Fawkes (1903–67): ent RN 1920; s/m spist; Capt 8 SF 1941–2; CoS to Adm (S) 1944; *Sheffield* 1946 NAWI; DOD 1949; Cdre & CoS Home F 1951; *Vanguard* 1952; RA 1952; FO (S) 1954–5; ret 1956.

P45 (Unrivalled), *P48* (sunk 25 Dec 1942 off Tunis), *P54 (Unshaken)*, *Ursula*: all 'U' cl s/m, 1938–42, 630/732t, 11.25/10k, 4–6×21in tt, 1×3in.

P221 was an 'S' cl s/m, later named: 1941/2, 842/990t, 14.75/9k 1×3in, 7×21in tt.

determined or alert. These points are well brought out in the reports of the Naval Commander, Eastern Task Force (Vice Admiral Sir Harold Burrough) and that of Lt-Cdr H. N. C. Willmott. I would only wish to state my entire concurrence with the remarks of the former and re-emphasise that these difficulties are not 'lessons learnt', but recognised and foreseen disadvantages which had reluctantly to be accepted owing to the speed with which the operation was staged and the consequent short time available for training, coupled with the difficulty of co-ordination of units scattered initially from Scapa to Sierra Leone.

9.   The actual landings when the troops reached their beaches appear to have gone according to plan and the work of the beach parties was excellent, but unnecessarily large numbers of landing craft were crippled as the disembarkations proceeded. These losses were mostly avoidable and due to lack of training and bad seamanship. In this connection it is recommended that the use of new entries, not properly disciplined, in this type of operation be avoided.

Various suggestions have arisen, chiefly from US Army reports, that landing craft should be manned and operated by the Army on the score of improved co-ordination and training. In fact it is felt that it matters little what uniform the crews wear provided that they are disciplined, trained and practical *seamen* and provided they are organised and operated by officers competent in their jobs and in close touch with the requirements of the troops they are required to land and maintain. As, however, the ships taking part in an assault are tied to a great degree to their landing craft during the period of unloading it remains essential that the control of the latter should rest in the hands of those responsible for the safety of the ships.

10.   The direct assaults planned against the harbours of Algiers and Oran (Operations 'Terminal' and 'Reservist') were in no sense planned as imitations of Zeebrugge but were intended to be launched just before the surrender or capture of the ports with the purposes of preventing sabotage of ships and port installations.[1] The choice of the correct moment for entry was a difficult one, depending on the existing situation and the large degree of resistance encountered.

In the event neither operation was successful in its object but both were remarkable for the determination and gallantry with which all concerned tackled their task, and both were successful in forcing an entry through the booms.

---

[1]Zeebrugge, an outlet for U-boats and light forces, was the scene of a partially successful blocking operation in the spring of 1918.

Operation 'Terminal'

11.   *Broke* (Lt-Cdr A. F. C. Layard) succeeded in getting alongside in Algiers and disembarked her troops but they were pinned by machine gun fire and did no good. It is considered that the CO's decision to retire from a position rapidly becoming untenable was a correct one. It is much to be regretted that an underestimate of the damage sustained should have led to the subsequent foundering of this ship when she might by then have been safely berthed in Algiers harbour.[1]

Operation 'Reservist'

12.   The choice of the ships for this operation had rested on their American appearance, and their chance of a friendly reception lay largely in this appearance and in the use of the American Ensign. In the face of serious opposition it could not be expected that they would succeed in their task. In the event, the moment chosen could hardly have been less fortunate, since the French alarm to arms was in its first full flush of Gallic fever and they had not yet been intimidated by bombing or bombardment, while darkness prevented an American complexion to the operation being apparent.

The expedition was a failure, redeemed by the gallantry displayed by officers and men of both nations as they strove to achieve their object in the face of hopeless odds. It is much to be regretted that Capt F. T. Peters, VC, DSO, DSC, the leader, having survived this ordeal, lost his life in an aircraft accident on his way to the UK.[2]

Support Fire

13.   The experience of units detailed to provide supporting fire for soldiers ashore served only to re-emphasise the well-known fact that ship gunfire cannot be expected to knock out forts by obtaining direct hits on gun positions. Ships' gunfire is capable of very considerable moral effect when using heavy calibre guns, and of smothering effect from the rapid volume of medium calibre fire of any gun at close range, but that is the most that should be expected. Cases reported of delays in responding to calls for fire are attributable to two main causes, namely inability of military authority to appreciate that a ship cannot remain

---

[1]Cdr A. F. C. Layard: *Excellent* Aug 1937; Lt Cdr Feb 1938; *Broke* April 1942; A/Cdr *Salisbury* Aug 1943; 2i/c Swansea, July 1944; Cdr Nov 1944. The other destroyer was *Malcolm*: 1919, 1530t, 31k, 2×4in, 1×3in, 3×21in tt. See his article, 'Algiers, 8 November 1942', *Naval Review* (1978), pp. 156–71.

[2]Capt F. T. Peters, VC: Cdr Sept 1929; Capt ret; *Lord Stanhope* Oct 1939; *Victory* June 1941; *Walney* 1942; d in air crash Nov 1942.

Walney, Hartland: ex-US CG cutters (Lend Lease 1941), 1546t, 16k, 1×5in, 2×3in.

indefinitely in her bombarding position in submarine infested waters, and failure to make proper use of the support wave for rapid communication.

Air Support

Fighters

14. Taken as a whole the provision of fighter support over the shipping and beaches left little to be desired. It suffered from all the known limitations of carriers operating aircraft, but was fully effective within these limitations. In general, it is considered that the operation of carrier-borne fighters reflected great credit on the foresight and planning of the RAAC, on the spirit and training of the FAA and the efficiency of the carriers alike.

Bombers

15. The provision of close support bombing by carrier-borne aircraft suffers from similar limitations to those referred to in paragraphs 13 and 14 above. In spite of these drawbacks it proved remarkably effective whenever opportunity was given.

In particular the dive-bombing of La Senia aerodrome was most striking not only for its accuracy and effect, but also for the extremely gallant and determined manner in which it was carried out.

Communications

17. The complication of the communications inherent in any Combined Operation was enhanced in 'Torch' by the fact that a W/T organisation had to be evolved for a new station concurrently with carrying out a major operation therein.

18. Further difficulties were the number of services involved and the manner in which they were inextricably mingled in both the Eastern and Central Task Forces. The mounting of the Western Task Force in the USA added considerably to the troubles of the planning stage.

19. Naval communications were generally satisfactory and stood up well to the heavy load of traffic which was considerably increased by the failure of certain W/T lines of the other services.

20. The two HQ ships – *Bulolo* (Capt R. L. Hamer) and *Largs* (Cdr E. A. Divers, RNR) – were of inestimable value.[1]

---

[1]Capt R. L. Hamer: ret Jan 1929; *Bulolo* Nov 1942; NOIC, Thurso, March 1944.
A/Capt E. A. Divers, RNR: Lt Cdr 1936; *Discovery II* Nov 1939; A/Cdr *Registan* Nov 1940; Cdr Dec 1941; *Largs* Nov 1942; A/Capt *Glengyle* Jan 1944; A/Capt, Hbr Craft, *Lanka* 1944–5.

Naval Operations

21.   The complaisant attitude of the Italian Fleet, and the inactivity of the French main Fleet, unfortunately gave Force H no scope for action. This powerful force had in fact to be kept cruising idly in an area where it was subject to sporadic air attack and faced with an increasing concentration of U-boats. We were perhaps fortunate that torpedo casualties were limited to two destroyers, *Martin* and HNMS *Isaac Sweers*.[1]

22.   The value of Force R was amply demonstrated. These two oilers, RFA *Dingledale* and RFA *Brown Ranger*, did yeoman service. It was not my intention that large cruisers should fuel from this force, nor should I have permitted it except in emergency. It is considered very fortunate that *Bermuda* (Capt T. H. Back) escaped damage in her prolonged fuelling at dead slow speed on a steady course inadequately screened.[2]

23.   In this connection it has been observed from numerous reports that many COs without Mediterranean experience lacked appreciation of the problem with which they were faced in these narrow submarine and aircraft infested waters. It is clear that advice on this subject should have been promulgated beforehand. This has now been done within the 'Torch' area, and will be available for future operations.

24.   Such surface operations as did take place were somewhat distasteful and one-sided encounters with the French destroyers trying to break out of Oran. *Brilliant* (Lt-Cdr A. G. Poe) fought a satisfactory duel with the French destroyer *La Surprise*.[3] *Aurora* (Capt W. G. Agnew) polished off her opponents on each occasion with practised ease. The performance of *Jamaica* in expending 501 rounds to damage one destroyer was less praiseworthy.[4]

Unloading

25.   The weather only held in our favour long enough to enable the smooth working of the assault and early maintenance. The breaking of

---

[1]*Martin*: 'M' cl destroyer; sunk by *U-431*, off Algiers, 10 Nov 1942.

HNMS *Isaac Sweers*: destroyer, 1940, 1604t, 37.5k, 6×4in, 8×21in tt; completed UK; sunk by *U-431* 13 Nov 1942.

[2]RFA *Brown Ranger*: 1941, 3417gt, 14k.

RFA *Dingledale*: 1941, 17000gt, 11.5k.

Bermuda: csr, 1942, 8525t, 33k, 12×6in, 8×4in, 6×21in tt.

Capt T. H. Back: Capt June 1938; *Capetown* July 1939; *Sultan* Nov 1941, for addnl services; *Bermuda* July 1942; *President* 1945.

[3]*Brilliant*: destroyer, 1931, 1360t, 35k, 4×4.7in, 8×21in tt.

Cdr A. G. Poe: Cdr Dec 1942; *Dipper* (Henstridge, Somerset) April 1943; Cdr (F) *Owl* Feb 1944.

La Surprise: m/l sloop, 1938, 630t, 20k, 2×3.9in; sunk 8 Nov 1942.

[4]*Jamaica*: cruiser, 1942, as *Bermuda*.

the weather on D+1 was not sufficient to stop disembarkation, but speedily reduced the flow of supply and served to show up the need for greater robustness in the landing craft and for training in rough water and surf conditions for the crews.

26.   The early seizure of Arzeu and the surrender of Algiers were invaluable in assisting unloading of the convoys. Even so, we were left with the great anxiety of vast masses of shipping anchored in open roadsteads for many days. Had the enemy shown more enterprise with his U-boats or had more torpedo aircraft been at his call, our losses might have been uncomfortably high. This had of course been recognised as an unavoidable and acceptable risk.

Shipping Casualties

27.   I was concerned to get shipping away as soon as possible from these crowded anchorages. Orders had been issued on this subject in accordance with which the fast troopships were sailed independently for Gibraltar as soon as empty. We were most unfortunate, I consider, in that two of these ships blundered on to U-boats and were destroyed. It was an even chance whether they would be safer at sea proceeding at high speed for Gibraltar alone, or anchored in the mass, escorts not being available.

28.   This ill-fortune with the big troopships persisted with the destruction of *Ettrick* and *Warwick Castle* in convoy MKF1 after they had passed clear of the Mediterranean.[1]

29.   Other personnel ship losses, notably *Narkunda*, *Cathay* and HMS *Karanja* (A/Cdr D. S. Hore-Lacy, RN (Emergency)) were part of the price which may be expected to be paid for taking such large and valuable vessels into the forward area in order to ensure the early occupation of a port, in this case Bougie.[2] These losses and the damage suffered by various ships at Algiers serve to point again to the essential importance of establishing properly directed fighter protection at the earliest moment. This was the lesson well learned in the Western Desert Campaigns, which now had to be demonstrated again by bitter experience in a new theatre.

AA Gunfire

30.   A striking feature of the operation at Algiers and to eastward of that port was the number of enemy aircraft shot down by ships' gunfire,

---

[1]*Ettrick*: P & O, 1938, 11279gt.
Warwick Castle: Union Castle, 1931, 20107gt, 20k.
[2]*Narkunda*: P & O, 1920, 16632gt, 17.5k.
    Karanja: LSI (L), 1930, 9890gt, 17k, 1×6in, 1×3in, 1500 troops.
    Cdr D. S. Hore-Lacy, RN (Emgcy): RN ret; Lt Cdr RAN Sept 1926; *Lady Sharazad* Jan 1941; *LST30* Dec 1942; Cdr 3LST Flo, *LST322*.

warships and merchant vessels alike. This was perhaps the first great undertaking by our seaborne forces in which ships entered the area of operations adequately armed. We suffered loss, but the toll paid by the enemy was high.

31.   The presence of the AA ships at occupied ports was invaluable.

Administrative Arrangements

32.   The administrative arrangements for this operation worked well, due chiefly to the detailed planning carried out by Admiralty departments and the administrative staff at Norfolk House.

The efficiency with which the administrative section of the Plans Department at the Admiralty met all my requirements and interpreted them to the Supply Departments, where they were well implemented, fully justified the establishment of this section and together with the assistance rendered by the Second Sea Lord's Office and the department of the DPS, contributed greatly to the success of the operation.

In future operations the planning should ensure an adequate supply of clothing for naval and merchant seamen from D-Day.

The Naval and Victualling Store Departments at Gibraltar were inadequately manned to achieve their full functions.

Advance to the East

33.   No sooner was Algiers occupied than the FOIS in co-operation with the GOC, First Army, pressed on urgently with the task of extending the operation eastward.[1] The acquiescence of the French enabled the occupation of Bône to be quickly undertaken, but the tide of advance reached but little beyond that port.

34.   It is a matter of lasting regret to me that the bolder conception for initial assault in that area or even further eastward was not implemented. Had we been prepared to throw even a small force into the eastward ports, the Axis would have been forestalled in their first token occupation and success would have been complete. They were surprised and off their balance. We failed to give the final push which would have tipped the scales.

35.   To sum up. There were few new lessons learnt, but many old ones received fresh emphasis. Those which require most firmly to be borne in mind are:

(a)   The need for boldness and the value of holding even a small highly mobile reserve to exploit success daringly.

[1]FOIS: Cdre G. N. Oliver.

(b)   The importance of not over-estimating the enemy's resources, exemplified in this case by the infra-red bogey, which led us to lie too far offshore at the initial landings.

(c)   The importance of training in a service which is no longer manned by a majority of prime seamen, and the need for combined training with the soldiers with whom they are to work.

(d)   The importance of carrying out such beach reconnaissance as is required well in advance, to gain security.

(e)   The vital necessity for immediate installation of a proper air defence system at occupied ports.

(f)   The need of co-ordination in the various elements of Naval port parties who would be assembled and organised under one command before embarkation.

(g)   The necessity for promulgating experienced advice about conditions in a theatre of operations to units joining from other stations.

36.   That the operation achieved the success was due, in so far as general operations are concerned:

(a)   To the high measure of secrecy achieved, which enabled us to gain some surprise.

(b)   To the sound planning and forethought shown in the Naval sphere by Admiral Sir Bertram Ramsay, who made a contribution not easily measured, to the smooth running of the seaborne operations.

(c)   To the excellent co-operation which existed through all ranks of the services of both nations, the foundations of which were laid during the period of combined planning at Norfolk House.

(d)   To the compact and efficient arrangement of the Combined HQ at Gibraltar.

(e)   To the high standard of seamanship and technical efficiency which is mercifully still maintained in the units of the Fleet. In this connection the value of the Western Approaches training is outstanding.

(f)   To the courage, determination and adaptability of the Merchant Navy.

37.   In conclusion I feel it should be placed on record that in this most difficult of all types of operation with a number of services involved and despite the difficulties inherent in welding together the systems of command and organisation of two nations, there reigned a spirit of comradeship and understanding which provided that vital force which brought success to our undertaking. The embodiment of that spirit was exemplified in our C-in-C, General Dwight Eisenhower, we counted it a privilege to follow in his train.

Appendix 1: Narrative

8 November 1942: D-Day.

1. *NXCF*
The Flag of Sir Andrew Cunningham, as NXCF was hoisted in *Nelson* at 0800.[1]

2. *Meteorological Report*
At 0100 pressure was high over the essential area. Winds in these areas were and continued nil all day.

3. *Eastern Task Force*
(i) *Landing Operations:* . . . NCETF . . . reported that landings had been successful at 'A', 'B' and 'C' beaches, and that little resistance was encountered, except on 'B' beach, Red Sectors 2, 3 and 4, where it was later reported that landings had been badly shot up. By 0300/8 Fort Sidi Ferruch had been captured without opposition.[2] At 0340 Cap Matifou battery opened fire on the western transports. *Zetland* opened fire, extinguishing a searchlight.[3] *Zetland* closed the shore and exchanged shots with the Fort until 0400. About 0530 *Broke* charged the boom and entered Algiers harbour. *Malcolm* was hit and retired to the north east with three boilers out of action (Operation 'Terminal').

. . . During the forenoon French resistance generally stiffened.

About 0930 *Broke* withdrew as she was being shelled, and got clear of the harbour under cover of smoke from *Zetland* but was badly damaged. At 1112 *Zetland* asked NCETF for bombing support at 1300 for troops trying to enter West Matifou – and this was arranged – but resistance continued. Fort Dupere was also holding out, but surrendered at 1600 after being bombed.

At 1655 NCETF found the situation improved and *Sheffield* and *Berwick* were informed that they were no longer required for bombardment. *Berwick* was subsequently told that bombarding at 12 knots in submarine waters was to be deprecated and that speed should have been 18 knots.[4]

During the afternoon the wind freshened from the north east, and in 'C' Sector the landing of stores was delayed, there being heavy casualties among landing craft, although in other Sectors landing proceeded

---

[1]*Nelson, Rodney*: battleships, 1927, 33950 & 33900t, 23k, 9×16in, 6–8×4.7in, 2×24.5in tt.
[2]VAdm Burrough.
[3]*Zetland*: 'Hunt' cl, 1942.
[4]*Sheffield*: csr, 1937, 9100t, 32k, 12×6in, 8×4in, 6×21in tt.
Berwick: csr, 1928, 10900t, 31.5k, 8×8in, 8×4in, 8×21in tt.

at fair speed, and it was anticipated that disembarkation would be completed to permit of sailing at least three LSI (C) to the westward on 9 November.

Appendix 3: Surface Actions and Bombardments

Surface Action

Time & Date	Ship	Enemy	Result
0537/8	*Aurora*	*La Tramontaine* (destroyer)	sunk
0630/8	*Brilliant*	*La Surprise* (escort)	sunk
0650/8	*Aurora, Calpe, Boadicea*	*La Tornade, Le Typhon* (destroyers)	*La Tornade* beached; on fire *Le Typhon* damaged, Oran
0959/9	*Aurora, Jamaica*	*Épervier Le Typhon*	*Épervier* on fire, beached, *Le Typhon,* scuttled.[1]

Remarks on Surface Action

2.   These actions took place against opponents who fought courageously against heavy odds but were in a poor state of training. In most cases the French tried to take refuge under the shelter of shore batteries, which attempted to embarrass our forces. The presence of high land behind the target generally precluded the successful use of RDF for ranging and spotting, and no experience was gained in this direction.

3.   The manner in which *Aurora* used her gun armament successfully to stop destroyers breaking out of Oran was commendable and reflected credit on a well organised fighting unit.

4.   The fact that *Aurora* frequently straddled without hitting, however, stresses the need for taking all possible measures to reduce spreads both by training of personnel and by improvements in equipment. It is again emphasised that minute attention to detail in matters such as

[1]*Calpe*: 'Hunt' cl, 1941.
Boadicea: destroyer, 1931, 1360t, 35k, 4×4.7in, 8×21in tt; sunk by a/c 13 June 1944.
Tramontane, Typhon, Tornade: destroyers, 1924–7, 1319t, 33k, 4×5.1in, 6×21.7in tt.
Épervier: destroyer, 1931, 2441t, 36k, 5×5.5in, 7×21.7in tt.

ramming [ammunition], director tests and pointer following may make a vital difference in hitting the enemy.

5. *Jamaica's* heavy expenditure of ammunition was quite disproportionate to the results achieved and can be largely attributed to the excessive use of helm wheel, which made it practically impossible to hold range or line and never gave the guns a chance.

6. *Brilliant's* suggestion of resorting to quarters firing at very short range when the enemy is beaten is concurred in.

Bombardments

7.

Date & Time	Ship	Target	Result	Remark
8–10/various	*Rodney*	Ft du Santon	Capitulated, 3rd day	Indirect fire, EMM gear, FOO observation
8/1237, 1500	*Berwick*	Fts Matifou, D'Estrees	Capitulated	Indirect fire, FOO observation
8/0340, 0450, 0950	*Zetland*	Ft Matifou	Temporary cease fire, or search-lights doused	Direct fire & observation
8–9/various	*Aurora, Farnworth, Brilliant*[1]	Enemy troops		

Remarks on Bombardments

8. Once again this operation proved that naval bombardments, however accurate, do not get direct hits on guns in protected emplacements. The moral effect of rapid and heavy naval bombardment remains as great as ever.

9. Bombardment used to support dive-bombers proved decisive in reducing one fort (*Berwick* against Fort D'Estrees). This is evidently a most effective combination.

10. The mere appearance of a man-o'-war in more than one case was sufficient to cause troops to surrender in the field, and in other cases a

[1]*Farnworth*: 'Hunt' cl, 1941.

few rounds satisfied military honour. *Farnworth* did good work in assisting an uncomfortably situated US battalion.

11.   As a technical feat *Rodney's* intermittent bombardment for three days of Fort du Santon with 16-inch must rank as a performance of a high order. The fort, which was awkwardly situated on the top of a hill 1,000 feet high, capitulated shortly after the 16-inch fire was augmented with rapid and accurate fire with 6-inch guns.

12.   *Rodney's* bombardment of Fort du Santon and *Berwick's* accurate bombardment of Fort Manitou and Fort D'Estrees suggest that better results can be achieved by firing 6-inch full gun broadsides with a high rate of fire into a small area than by deliberate fire with heavier shell, observing that the reduction is usually brought about by terrorism, rather than by direct hits on small objects. The employment of strengthened fuzes now allows this and is a great advance.

13.   It is not suggested that bombardments of this nature by guns smaller than 6-inch will achieve the same results. Bombardments by 'Hunt' class destroyers during assaults have a high nuisance value (vide *Zetland's* at Matifou), and more cannot be expected.

Co-operation with the Army

14.   Ships universally speak well of the benefit of Liaison Officers on board, and these officers together with most of their FOO party colleagues ashore carried out their duties with distinction.

15.   Both at Oran and Algiers reports of how the battle was progressing ashore depended almost entirely on FOO reports. It was significant that information about the progress of American assaults in the Casablanca area where no FOOs were operating was almost negligible.

19.   Some complaints about the speed of ships in answering calls for fire have been made by military authorities who do not seem to realise that ships cannot be expected to be in a position to bombard every target in their area at short notice especially as they must keep moving owing to the submarine and bomber menace. Whenever possible a prearranged time for a bombardment to take place should be made some hours ahead. . . .

Appendix 4: Air Operations

A/S Escort and Patrols

1.   A/S escorts and patrols were flown in accordance with plans from 1 November by aircraft from Gibraltar. Except on 4 November, when all sorties were cancelled due to bad weather, the RAF exerted an intense A/S effort.

2.   On 1 November, one squadron of Hudson aircraft moved to Oran and on 19 November to Algiers, this rapid move ensuring good A/S cover to shipping, and resulted in many attacks on U-boats, including three certain kills.[1]

3.   No ships were lost in convoy while under A/S protection.

4.   Co-operation with the RAF was uniformly excellent. The completion of the naval-air operations room in the Tunnel at Gibraltar in time for the assault stage was a great help.

This co-operation was continued at Algiers by the establishment of the GR Wing in a combined operations room.

5.   The endurance of Catalina aircraft permitted escort of convoys by day at a distance of 400 miles from Gibraltar. Full advantage could not always be taken of this endurance as rough water conditions at Gibraltar Bay limits take-offs and landings to daylight only.

Short Range A/S Patrols

6.   Until the installation of A/S underwater defences was complete, harbour A/S patrols were an urgent requirement.

7.   No 813 (TBR) Squadron, equipped with Swordfish, was available at Gibraltar. One flight of the Squadron was moved to Oran on 10 November armed with depth-charges. This flight was relieved by the second flight on 11 November and moved to Algiers.

8.   Additional harbour patrols at Algiers were provided by 6 Walruses disembarked from Force H to form No 700 Squadron, Algiers.[2]

9.   Local A/S patrols at Gibraltar were taken over by No 835 (TBR) Squadron disembarked from *Biter* and *Dasher*.[3]

Torpedo Striking Forces

15.   The only shore-based torpedo striking force in Algeria up to 26 January 1943 has been No 813 Squadron.

16.   This Squadron was also required to provide local A/S escorts at Algiers so that the strike force available in the forward area has normally been three Swordfish, whose endurance renders them incapable of operating beyond the close approaches to Bizerta and then only by night and with a wind speed of less than 30 knots.

17.   No 813 Squadron has operated in a most determined manner and

---

[1]Lockheed Hudson: GR, 1938, 2×1200hp, 253mph, 2800m, 5 crew, 5–7mg, 1400lbs.
    Four U-boats sunk appear to have been sunk by Hudsons: *U-605* (14 Nov), *U-595* (14 Nov), *U-259* (15 Nov), *U-331* (17 Nov).
[2]Supermarine Walrus: seaplane, 1933, 775hp, 135mph, 600m, 4 crew, 2mg.
[3]*Biter, Dasher*: escort carriers, 1942, 12150t, 16.5k, 20 a/c, 1×4in; *Dasher* blew up, Clyde, 27 March 1943; *Biter* became Fr N *Dixmude* 1945.

has had at least two successes against shipping in the Lake of Bizerta, but has been unable to attack the supply lines to Bizerta and Tunis since the movements of enemy ships have been very neatly timed to avoid night air attacks within Swordfish range.

Air Reconnaissance

19.   PRU reconnaissance of enemy and French ports was carried out according to plan, although several sorties to Toulon were abortive due to low cloud.

21.   It is considered that in future operations it is imperative that PRU of enemy ports should be carried out from a base in the near vicinity of the Naval Commander, sufficient aircraft being provided to meet his requirements.

22.   SAP were flown as planned to the northward of the Balearics and of Dakar, to prevent unobserved movement of enemy forces between PRU sorties. These patrols were very expensive in Catalina sorties to provide adequate cover. ... The Toulon Fleet was, in the event, unenterprising, but definite risks were taken due to lack of full air reconnaissance in this direction at certain critical times.

Fighter Protection of Shipping

24.   ... the development of fighter protection of shipping was extremely slow.

25.   The following were the causes of the delay:

(a)   Bad communications.

(b)   Inexperienced Squadrons. .... Visual turn-overs by relieving sections were the exception rather than the rule. Patrols almost invariably arrived after and withdrew before the dusk and dawn danger periods.

(c)   Unserviceable Airfields. Insufficient provision appeared to have been made for the production of all-weather airfields. As a result, during a prolonged spell of wet weather, the coastal airfields at Bougie, Djidjelli and Philippeville were unserviceable and shipping in this area received no protection.

(d)   Lack of Night Fighters. The scale of Beaufighters provided was inadequate to protect convoys along a 300-mile coastline.

26.   It is suggested that in future operations extra officers should be provided for Naval Liaison at Fighter Sector HQ during the assault and consolidating stages.

Ship-Borne Aircraft

28.   The operation of ship-borne aircraft was carried out according to plan. Fighter protection of ports and airfields was extended to D+1

because, although RAF fighters had arrived, servicing facilities were lacking.

29.   The Seafire proved a satisfactory fighter, except for the weakness of the undercarriage.[1] It is much to be regretted that the lifts in *Victorious* and *Formidable* are too small to accommodate these aircraft, thus forcing the use of the relatively slow Martlet.[2]

31.   The protection of TBR by modern fighters presents a difficult problem. . . .

32.   Dive-bombing attacks by TBR aircraft were accurate, and effective morally, although the material damage was slight when the target was shore fortifications. Against other airfields dive-bomber attacks were accurate and destructive.

33.   Tactical reconnaissance was carried out by Fulmar aircraft. The use of these obsolescent aircraft is not considered acceptable against serious opposition.[3] It is suggested that single-seat fighter squadrons should be trained in Tactical Reconnaissance duties.

Appendix 5: Gunfire

General

. . . It was refreshing for once to have ships taking part with somewhat appropriate close range armament.

2.   Evidence shows that enemy aircraft were using ASV at night, and the threat of night and dusk torpedo-bomber attacks against shipping has considerably increased. The correct combination of night fighters, smoke and gunfire in the defence of shipping at sea is the most urgent current problem in the Mediterranean.

AA Gunfire by Day

3.   There were few opportunities during 'Torch' of using HACS or FKC systems in the roles for which they were designed, that is, against moderately high flying aircraft at a steady height and on a steady course in daylight.[4] It appears that this form of attack will become more and more the exception rather that the rule, and training to combat high level bomber attacks . . . should have lower priority in the future.

5.   As a rule the 1500-yard barrage by destroyers has been confirmed as the most suitable in self-defence and was often successfully em-

---

[1]Supermarine Seafire: FAA fighter, 1936 (Spitfire), 1941 (Seafire), 1470hp, 352mph, 465m, 2 cannon, 4mg.
[2]Grumman Wildcat (Martlet): FAA fighter, 1937, 1200hp, 328mph, 1150m, 4mg.
[3]Fairey Fulmar: FAA 2-seat fighter, 1940, 1080hp, 280mph, 800m, 8mg.
[4]FKC: evidently an AA control mechanism.

ployed by auxiliary AA ships and 'Hunt' class destroyers off the beaches, and later at Bône and Bougie.

6.   Many enemy aircraft showed an unwarranted contempt for our small craft and merchant ships and paid for it at the hands of the Oerlikon and single pom-pom crews, who handled their guns by day resolutely and skilfully.[1]

7.   It was disappointing that *Delhi* had so few opportunities for opening fire by day with her American equipment.[2]

AA Gunfire at Night

8.   The outstanding feature of the operations in the assault stage has been the ample confirmation that the accuracy of bombers and torpedo-bombers at night falls off very rapidly if fire is opened with plenty of tracer and flash in the general direction of the attacking aircraft. Prisoners confirm the difficulty of approaching convoys in the face of a sustained barrage. The standard 1500-yard barrage is still considered the best, although others have been tried.

9.   Successful attacks by torpedo-dropping aircraft have usually taken place when the aircraft were undetected by RDF and fire was not opened until too late. The Type 281 set has been disappointing in picking up low-flying aircraft, particularly near land.

Air Defence of Harbours

11.   The defence of harbours fell heavily on the Navy in the early stages and the arrangements laid down in TADO 20 worked well.[3] It was most unfortunate that the services of two auxiliary AA ships, *Tynwald* and *Pozarica*, were lost so early.[4]

Merchant Ship Gunfire

13.   The equipment carried by Merchant Ships and the greatly improved standard of training of DEMS crews made these vessels formidable objects for air attacks by day. During the heavy attacks on merchant shipping unloading at Algiers and Bougie immediately after the assaults, DEMS crews distinguished themselves by their accurate shooting and devotion to duty when their ships had been hit.

14.   The problem of controlling merchant ship fire by night causes some concern. Fire at present is generally opened with all weapons on

---

[1]Oerlikon: Swiss 20mm AA gun.
[2]*Delhi*: AA cruiser, 1918 (converted New York 1940), 4850t, 29k, 5×5in.
[3]TADO 20: probably 'Tactical Air Defence Order'.
[4]*Tynwald*: I of Man Line, 1937, 2376gt, 21k, 6×4in; sunk by It s/m off Bougie 12 Dec 1942.

the noise of unseen aircraft at all heights with consequent unlikelihood of hitting. Admittedly the moral effect may be great for the gun crews and possibly moderate on the enemy. At the same time the wastage of ammunition is great, and the danger to adjacent ships and personnel appreciable. . . .

Appendix 6: Report on A/S Operations

General

The U-boat strength available to the enemy was amply sufficient to have caused a very serious threat to the assault convoys had the true nature of our intentions been appreciated.

2.   Fortunately this was not the case, and although the assault convoys appeared to pass through concentrations of some 20–25 U-boats west of Gibraltar no attacks on them developed. The strength and continuity of A/S air patrols contributed largely to this fact. Convoy SL125 which was passing through the area just before the assault convoys sustained heavy losses but was instrumental in driving off a U-boat pack from the path of the 'Torch' convoys.[1]

3.   Subsequent to the assault it is possible that about eight U-boats entered the Mediterranean, and U-boat activity along the North African coast became considerable, reaching a climax on 12 November when five U-boats were attacked by surface vessels in that area.

Convoy Escorts

4.   A large proportion of escort vessels was drawn from the Western Approaches command and, although it was not always possible to avoid some splitting of the Escort Groups, their previous experience and their 'team spirit' were of the greatest value.

A/S Fitted Minesweepers

8.   The majority of these ships had little experience of U-boat warfare and this was very apparent in the initial stages. There has since been a considerable improvement.

9.   *A/S Minesweeping Trawlers.* The dual equipment of these trawlers proved of great value.

10.   *Endless Chain Patrols . . .* were established to cover assault convoys whilst unloading on the beaches, and proved effective in averting any U-boat attacks during these operations.

---

[1]SL125 was a convoy from UK to Sierra Leone which cut across 'Torch' routes and attracted heavy U-boat attention.

11.   *Operating Conditions*. Asdic operating conditions throughout the area were good, and at times exceptional. Non-submarine contacts even on inshore patrols were few.

12.   *Attacks on U-boats*. Thanks to the excellent work and considerable strength of A/S air patrols operated from Gibraltar, U-boats were prevented from approaching convoys on the surface and almost every attack was made submerged.

13.   There were a number of very spirited attacks on U-boats: *Lord Nuffield* on 10 November and *Starwort* on 12 November being worthy of mention.[1]

14.   The latter included a Hedgehog attack.

15.   The loss of *Hecla* on the other hand was most regrettable, as no warning of the attack was given by the A/S escort.[2]

16.   *U-boat Tactics*. U-boats inside the Mediterranean were slow to take advantage of the situation as it developed or to adapt their tactics in the face of heavy air reconnaissance over the area. There was, in fact, a decided 'casualness' in U-boat tactics during the first few days.

18.   The use of *Pillenwerfer* was suspected in one instance but was not definitely established.[3]

19.   *Conclusion*. The operation emphasised once again the prime importance of good teamwork amongst convoy escorts which enables them each to act to the best advantage with a minimum of signals in moments of emergency.

20.   Successes against U-boats were achieved by escorts with well-drilled 'A/S teams'. Lack of team work in others let slip some golden opportunities.

21.   The results were as follows:

Attacks:	29.
Sunk:	5.
Probably Sunk:	5.
Severely Damaged:	4.[4]

---

[1]*Lord Nuffield*: trawler; no U-boat sinking attributed to her.

Starwort: corvette, 1941: *U-660* was sunk by the corvettes *Lotus* and *Starwort* on 12 Nov 1942, N of Oran.

[2]*Hecla*: destroyer depot ship, 1941, 11000t, 17k, 8×4.5in; sunk by *U-515* off Morocco 12 Nov 1942.

[3]*Pillenwerfer*: s/m tube through which to eject decoy canisters.

[4]U-boats sunk: *U-660* (*Lotus* & *Starwort*), *U-605*, *U-595*, *U-259*, *U-331* (all by Hudsons).

106. *Cunningham's Report on Operation 'Retribution'*

13 November 1943

3.   The possibility that the enemy might attempt a large scale evacuation of Tunisia had been foreseen some months previously, and orders had been issued, under the code name 'Retribution', for the concentration of naval forces to meet such a contingency. In the event, no such attempt was made, and the full written orders were never put into force. The orders, however, served a useful purpose in that all concerned were fully aware of the C-in-C's intentions, and the task of intercepting those of the enemy who were bold enough to take to sea was made much easier in consequence. The codeword 'Retribution', . . . was adopted for use by the naval forces taking part.

4.   As the Armies began to close in on Bizerta and Tunis, night destroyer and motorboat patrols in the Sicilian Narrows were intensified, Mediterranean destroyers operating from Bône and Levant destroyers from Malta. In daylight the task of destroying any shipping that escaped our submarine patrols and offensive minefields was at this time undertaken by the air forces, since lack of fighter protection prevented our surface forces operating against the enemy supply routes by day.

5.   With the rapid advance of the Armies in the first week in May, however, our fighters were able to operate from more forward aerodromes and so cover the south west half of the Strait. By arranging with the Air C-in-C, therefore, daylight patrols by destroyers were instituted on 9 May. It was arranged that the air forces should continue to attack enemy shipping and small craft within five miles of the Tunisian shore (i.e., within range of enemy shore-based guns), and the surface forces should have complete freedom of action elsewhere. By night the inshore area was occupied by patrols of MGBs and MTBs of both the US Navy and the Royal Navy.

6.   This somewhat rigid dividing line between the responsibilities of the air and naval forces was necessitated by the fact that a large proportion of the pilots and air crews taking part had not hitherto been engaged in operations over the sea and were thus untrained in ship recognition.

7.   The degree of air support given to our light forces from 9 May onwards may best be judged by the almost complete freedom from enemy interference enjoyed by them. Only one incident marred the co-operation between air and naval forces – the bombing of HM Ships *Bicester* and *Zetland* on 9 May by our own fighter-bombers.[1] The

[1]*Bicester*: 'Hunt' cl, 1942.

incident was immediately and fully investigated and was due to the fact that the information as to the movements of the destroyers failed to reach some of the forward aerodromes before the aircraft took off early that day.

8.   The whole sea area in which the destroyers were required to operate had been heavily mined, both by the enemy and ourselves. Most of our mines, however, had been set to flood by the beginning of May, and it was judged that our intelligence of enemy minefields was good enough to allow a sharp distinction to be drawn between areas where the risk of mines was great and those where the risk could be accepted. In the event, this judgement proved correct, and no casualties from mines were suffered by the destroyers.

9.   The minefields had, however, a considerable effect on the operations, particularly the large field which extended north-eastward from Cape Blanc. The destroyers operating from Bône were forced to go a long way round the northern edge of this minefield when proceeding to and from patrol, and in doing so exposed themselves to air attack. This resulted in one casualty, when ORP *Blyskawica* was near-missed and slightly damaged and was unable to take any further part in the operations.[1]

10.   Minesweepers had been concentrated at Bône as soon as the fall of Bizerta seemed imminent, and by 11 May they had swept a channel through to Bizerta. This early success on their part was a forerunner to the excellent work they performed in the succeeding weeks, and it contributed materially to the successful work of the destroyer patrols by saving the destroyers a great deal of unnecessary steaming.

11.   From 11 May onwards, 10–12 destroyers were on constant patrol of the Cape Bon peninsula, with a similar number of coastal craft in the inshore area by night, until all attempts by the enemy to evacuate had ceased. The patrols resulted in the capture of some 700 prisoners and in the complete denial to the enemy of any chance of evacuating by sea any important part of his forces.

12.   To maintain the patrols at the strengths required meant a special effort on the part of the destroyers, coastal craft, and maintenance staffs alike. That this effort would be forthcoming was only to be expected; all concerned met the demands that were made on them with the same cheerful spirit with which they faced the not inconsiderable risks that had to be run.

---

[1]ORP *Blyskawica* (Polish): destroyer, 1936, 2011t, 39k, 8×4in, 6×21in tt.

107. *Diary*

9 July 1945

... Harwood came in with rather a bleat because in his valedictory
letter from the Admiralty they omitted anything that had been done
during the time he had been C-in-C, Mediterranean. Perhaps not – but
he had been kicked out, unjustly as I thought, and maybe the Secretariat thought the least said soonest mended.

SECTION B

'HUSKY':

THE LANDINGS IN SICILY
MARCH 1943–APRIL 1944

Long before 'Husky' took place on 10 July 1943, the Allies had decided that Sicily should be the next amphibious target. The decision was not arrived at easily, with a repetition of many of the arguments about 'Torch'. Furthermore, the Americans were reluctant to persist with Mediterranean operations for three reasons. In the first place, they regarded the Mediterranean as a strategic dead end. Secondly, they thought that subsequent Mediterranean landings would serve only to boost Britain's post-war position in the region. Thirdly, they were worried that further adventures in the Mediterranean would delay a cross-Channel invasion by a year. In the event, they were persuaded of the advantages of saving precious shipping by reopening the short route to the Far East and the prospect of precipitating an Italian surrender. Moreover, the British still held the cards of experience in war, intimate knowledge of the Mediterranean and superior military planning. The JCS went to the conference in Casablanca at the end of January 1943 without the slick organisation of the COS and came off second best.

Sicily was agreed to, with American grumbles. Apart from cutting the ground from under Mussolini and saving a million tons of shipping, the COS argued, it would use troops and landing craft who otherwise would have stood idle until the invasion of north west Europe took place – at the earliest in 1944.[1] Cunningham and the 'Torch' command were marginal influences in the decision, Cunningham actually preferring a descent on Sardinia as it was less well defended; it was, however, beyond the range of the all-important shore-based fighters. The planning for Sicily was just as hasty as that for 'Torch', as the commanders slated for it were engaged in the latter stages of 'Torch'. When Tunis surrendered in May 1943, the planning for 'Husky' was further bedevilled by squabbles over where and when to land. The decision was ultimately one for the soldiers, but their operational convenience was served at the expense of the seamen and airmen, both alarmed that the

[1]Benito Mussolini (1883–1945): teacher, journalist, former socialist, WWI soldier; founded Fascist movement 1919; PM 1922; dictator – 'Il Duce' – 1925; dismissal July 1943 followed by imprisonment; spirited away by German paratroops Sept 1943; head of puppet govt N Italy 1943–5; caught by partisans and executed April 1945.

army left vital airfields in the enemy's hands and landed in early morning light. Cunningham and Tedder made their protests but were overruled; in any case, Cunningham thought afterwards that the Allies would have succeeded no matter where they landed. As with 'Torch', however, Cunningham was rather dismissive of ideas other than his own and appears not to have examined the plans closely; this high-handedness brought him into conflict with that conscientious but temperamental planner, Bertie Ramsay [108–21].

The landings passed off with little opposition, despite a rough voyage and an extremely complicated series of approaches, due to the forces setting out from several different locations, inside and outside the Mediterranean [124]. The armada, even greater than that for 'Torch', was directed by Cunningham from the historic fleet base at Malta, though the sandy caves in the Lascaris Bastion were not the healthiest of headquarters.[1] Resistance increased once the troops were ashore and the Germans fought their usual skilful and determined retreat, Sicily not being cleared until 17 August. The invasion fleet, though suffering a handful of casualties, was largely untouched by U-boats, E-boats or bombers, amazing to Mediterranean veterans like Cunningham, as it lay close offshore for days. Naval bombardment was highly effective, notably in repelling a German counter attack at Gela [125]. Cunningham was critical, however, of the relative failure to exploit the Allies' marked maritime supremacy by staging substantial landings behind enemy lines [122–3].

When Cunningham came to make his report on 'Husky', it was drafted for him by his chief planning officer, Captain Manley Power, who had served on Mediterranean Fleet staff between 1939 and 1941. Though Cunningham acknowledged Power's role, he probably did no more than cast a cursory glance over the report, tweaking the odd phrase here and there. That is, of course, what chief executives do – but it does raise issues of authorship; no doubt Power, knowing 'ABC' well, would take care to become 'His Master's Voice' [127].

Cunningham aired his complaints forcibly, notably lack of time for planning and training, the wide dispersal of commanders, the use of men and ships for other duties up to the eve of D-day, and 'Husky's' unfortunate timing. He was free in his praise for the crews of the landing craft, the COPP parties (who suffered heavy casualties), the overcoming of difficulties of organisation in the voyage to Sicily, and in particular the successful mastery of steep seas on the way there.

---

[1]Lascaris Bastion, Valletta, Malta: underground Allied HQ, with scale model of Sicily; plagued by sandflies, causing a fever.

Once ashore, the value of the new American amphibious DUKWs became evident. The rest of the battle was largely an army and air matter but Cunningham came under censure for allowing many enemy troops and much equipment to flee the island, virtually unhindered. He pleaded that there was little the naval forces could do, since the channel was only two miles wide, bristling with defensive artillery, AA batteries and motor torpedo boats, and the evacuations were largely conducted at night. Both Italian and German evacuations were highly organised; over 100,000 troops were saved. Allied destroyers and larger craft were considered highly vulnerable in such waters and thus were not risked. Most of the Allied effort was by air, backed up by coastal forces. Although Cunningham claimed that little could be done in the circumstances, the Allied attempt at interdiction appears lame and an afterthought; eyes were on the mainland [126].

108. *To Pound*

Algiers,
15 March 1943

F. With regard to the covering force for 'Husky' I am not clear if it was ever intended to ask the US to provide a second force if it became necessary owing to the location of the Italian Fleet or other reasons.

On the basis that it was intended the UK supplies the entire covering force or forces required, you will find I have asked for two extra ships to be in reserve somewhere nearer than the UK – I thought Algiers.

109. *Ramsay to his wife*

Algiers,
19 March 1943

... it is never very satisfactory living in someone else's sphere of action, especially with someone so dominating as Andrew Cunningham, charming though he be. Everybody must play his tune and fall in with his ideas. . . .

110. *Ramsay to his wife*

Cairo,
7 April 1943

... I am not awfully happy about the way things are taking shape between ABC and his party and myself and mine. I found him most unsympathetic towards suggestions put up to him, making it appear as though he was at pains to find an excuse to knock them down instead of a way of meeting them. The fact is that he wants to keep everything very tight in his own hands and doesn't welcome suggestions or anything that doesn't emanate from himself or his staff. It will lead to a cleavage sooner or later, which is most undesirable. It seems that he regards anything to do with combined operations as anathema and that the RN must keep well clear and see to themselves. I on the other hand hold diametrically opposite views and consider the Army and Navy as one for thinking, planning action. He is of the 'true blue' school and I suppose I am not. I hope for the avoidance of trouble but am afraid it is going to be difficult. . . .

111. *Ramsay to his wife*

Cairo,
14 April 1943

. . . I've been having rather a difficult time lately owing to ABC running the show and allowing the Army to make plans without consultation with the Navy and in particular accepting plans which I should have to carry out, without me knowing anything about it. . . . I was confronted a few days' back with a plan which had been concocted which had been approved right up to the highest plane; in fact a *fait accompli*. I was horrified at its implications and protested to ABC who replied that it had received his full approval (meaning that he had not gone properly into it), but at the end of a long message he added grudgingly that if I liked to try and persuade a certain person and change it I might do so![1] I did try and got his immediate and hearty consent (and almost thanks) and have just had the great satisfaction of telling him so. But the work entailed in changing the plan is almost heartbreaking to the wretched staffs. If only I had been consulted at the right time, or if ABC's staff had done their job properly, the necessity would never have arisen. But anyhow this is going to count as a great step forward in putting things in the proper perspective and should put me and my staff in a greatly improved position.

I only hope that ABC will not resent it. He is not very helpful and dislikes suggestions and his staff are terrified of him and have to play up. It's a pity as I like him so much; he is the soul of kindness and the most able commander we possess from the purely naval point of view.
. . .

112. *Ramsay to his wife*

Algiers,
28 April 1943

. . . B[ernard] L[aw]M[ontgomery] upset plans; he made himself even more unpopular but neither knows nor cares about it; B[ertram]H[ome] R[amsay] has to be tactful though on good terms. I can however foresee that he will ever be putting one in the midst of most difficult circumstances which, with someone like ABC produces difficulties I would prefer to avoid. It is all a great pity because Montgomery is a great

---

[1]Probably Montgomery.

general. The trouble is that he adopts the attitude that he is now omnipotent. . . .

113. *To Pound*

Algiers,
28 April 1943

We are arriving at a state of deadlock out here over 'Husky'. As you know about 14 days ago the outline plan was produced by us after big difficulties had been overcome to meet Montgomery's objection that the assault on the south-eastern beaches was not in great enough force, and Malta was induced to accept a complete division for about 21 days. Four days ago Montgomery went to Cairo and re-examined the approved plan, pronounced it militarily unsound and has now produced one of his own and ordered his planners to work on it.

Shortly, it does away altogether with the assaults on the south-western beaches – those whose object was to take the south-western group of aerodromes – and concentrates all the assaults on the south-eastern beaches.

Personally, I think his plan is unsound as it leaves three aerodromes in the occupation of the enemy, except for such force as the RAF can put on to them, and we are landing from a mass of shipping a mere 30 miles off. It also seems to surrender our greatest asset – that of being able to assault the island in numerous places at once at will.

I am afraid Montgomery is a bit of a nuisance; he seems to think all he has to do is say what has to be done and everyone will dance to the tune of his piping. Alexander appears quite unable to keep him in order. Tedder is also absolutely opposed to this new plan.

But the seriousness of it all is that here we are with no fixed agreed plan, just over two months off D-Day and the commanders all at sixes and sevens, and even if we do get final agreement, someone will be operating a plan he doesn't fully agree with. Not the way to make a success of a difficult operation. Alexander has just arrived here and I am meeting him tonight and tomorrow we have a fairly representative party to discuss the question. It is certainly on the cards that, if Montgomery's plan is turned down, he will refuse the job of conducting the operation. . . .

114. *Ramsay to his wife*

Cairo,
6 May 1943

... ABC was charming as ever but the air was a bit tense owing to certain major modifications suggested by us and my army friends, which they were opposed to. ... We managed to get our way, however, in Algiers which has simplified things though causing us and everyone else an immense amount of work.

115. *To Pound*

Algiers,
8 May 1943

A. I think it is well that you should know of the atmosphere here after the acceptance of the final 'Husky' plan.

The Admiral and the General of the Western Task Force are very sore about it.[1] They feel they have been made to dance to Montgomery's tune and have been given rather a raw deal. There is no doubt that the maintenance of three American divisions in the south-western assaults is a very tricky problem, involving the supply over beaches and perhaps one small port for some six weeks, 3000 tons a day and no one really knows whether it can be done or not.

Hewitt has told Patton definitely that he does not think it can but Patton has taken up the attitude that he has been ordered to land there and he will do it.

I think myself that, barring accidents, it can be done and I have assured them of all the assistance we can give them.

But if you are discussing 'Husky' with the US Chiefs of Staff it might be as well to go delicately.

By the way COMINCH has categorically ordered *all* American units out of the Mediterranean as soon as possible after the landing. ... [2]

[1] Adm Hewitt.
Gen George C. Patton, US Army (1885–1945): cavalry 1909; Mexico 1916; Capt, AEF 1917–18; Maj Gen April 1941; Cdr I Arm Corps Jan 1942; Casablanca landgs Nov 1942; II Corps March 1943; Lt Gen, 7 Army July 1943; 3 Army, NW France June 1944; Gen April 1945; controversy surrounded his career and he was relieved Sept 1945; d in car accident Dec 1945.
[2] COMINCH: Adm King.

116.   *Ramsay to his wife*

Cairo,
10 May 1943

... ABC and I have been disagreeing rather seriously the last week or so, mostly due to misunderstanding and the lag of communications. ...

117.   *Ramsay to his wife*

Cairo,
11 May 1943

... We've been busy and the wires are red hot but generally speaking things are easier and more hopeful between us and ABC. There's nothing personal in it. ...

118.   *Ramsay to his wife*

Cairo,
28 May 1943

... Things are not easy between ABC and myself which makes it difficult. When we meet all is apparently 'as sweet as a [?] ...' but when apart he doesn't answer my letters, doesn't answer my telegrams and gives a prompt 'no' to every request or proposal put to him. The fact is he can't bear anyone whom he considers to be in competition with him and I suppose it is a sort of self-imposed jealousy. Some of his telegrams have been worded most rudely ... Two of my fellows have just returned from Algiers and they say they were taken apart and told how much they [Cunningham's staff] regretted the wording of these telegrams and the general attitude of ABC towards us. It has happened because of his invariable rule of saying 'no' without consulting his staff and giving due consideration to my proposals [but] he has on every occasion eventually had to agree. ... The fact is that he has outstayed his usefulness and it's time he was put on the beach. ... *nothing* will induce me to accept further employment in any role under him ...

119.   *From Pound*

30 May 1943

(b)   If there is any attempt to withdraw the American naval units from the Mediterranean before you can spare them after 'Husky' please let me know and I will tackle King.

(d)   Ward Price has confirmed what I expected and that is the sudden collapse of the Huns in Tunisia was due to the fact that with your destroyers and other craft all round Cape Bon peninsula they saw that any chance of getting away was out of the question.[1] I suppose that they had been told that the Italian Navy would come and take them off.

(f)   My feelings at present are in agreement with yours that ultimately we shall revert to the single Mediterranean command, but I do not think the time has arrived for that yet. . . .

120.   *To Pound*

Algiers,
25 June 1943

A.   I think myself that there is a good deal of unqualified optimism with regard to 'Husky', particularly in army circles. The soldiers seem to think that they will be landed at the exact spot they expect to be, that the weather will necessarily be perfect and that naval gunfire will silence all opposition.

Although most optimistic myself I have been uttering a few words of warning.

The weather does not appear to be settling down as it ought to at this time of year. We have just had a four-day blow in the Malta Channel which would have made any operation impossible.

The thought of having, perhaps at short notice, to turn back and delay all those ships and landing craft, over 2000 in all, is a bit hair raising. However, we have plans for it and we reckon up to 24 hours before H-Hour it can be done without much confusion.

Against these somewhat pessimistic reflections we can however get some favourable facts. I was at the big rehearsal of the 'Dime' assault (American) this morning and a feature was the exceptionally good handling of the assault craft, although of course mistakes of timing were made.

---

[1]G. Ward Price: British war correspondent, both world wars.

I only hope the crews of our landing craft are as well trained.

We seem to be getting on top of our troubles with regard to having the landing craft fit for the operation. But it has taken every repair facility in the theatre and practically everything else has had to be laid aside. So I have every hope that in spite of all delays we shall come up to the starting gate in good condition.

B.   I am sure you are right that [A. J.] Power should not remain VA, Malta, any longer than is necessary and that he should be off to sea again.[1]

He is, of course, doing splendidly and there is a real live spirit in affairs there at present.

Dorling was in here this morning and said his job in the States had really become a matter of routine and asked if he couldn't be considered for Malta.

... since he was Captain (D) under me I have had a very high opinion of him. He has brains, unrivalled technical knowledge and is a live wire, and taking it all in all, I would not at all mind seeing him VA, Malta.[2]

D.   HM's visit to Malta was a great success and I should think has been well worthwhile. He received ovations wherever he went and the entry of the *Aurora* into Malta flying the Royal Standard (painted in *Howe*) with the Barracas and battlements black with Maltese was an unforgettable sight. . . .[3]

121.   *From Pound*

3 July 1943

A.   This is just a line to wish you all the best of luck in your great endeavour. . . . It is certainly disturbing to realise how much dependence is put on naval gunfire and people are so prone to forget the lessons of the past. . . .

---

[1]Adm Sir Arthur J. Power (1889–1960): ent RN 1904; Lt 1910; gun spist; Dardanelles & Grand F 1914–18; Capt 1929; *Dorsetshire* 1931–3; IDC 1933–5; *Excellent* i/c 1935–7; *Ark Royal* 1938–9; RA & ACNS (H) May 1940; 15CS, Med F Aug 1942; A/VA & VA Malta May 1943; 2-in-C Med F; 2-in-C EF & VA 1BS Jan 1944; C-in-C E Indies Nov 1944–6; Adm & 2SL 1946–8; C-in-C Med 1948–50; C-in-C Portsmouth 1950–2; AoF 1952.

[2]VAdm J. W. S. Dorling: Dir N Eqpt Aug 1939; RA Sept 1939; *Sultan* June 1941; A/VA *Saker* (BAD) April 1942; VA ret, & FOIC *Eaglet* (Liverpool) Aug 1944.

[3]Visit of King George VI to Malta: see previous section.
Howe: battleship, 1941, 35000t, 28k, 10x14in, 16x5.25in.

122.   *To Aunt Doodles*

Malta,
14 August 1943

... I spent two days ... just clearing up things in Algiers and cheering up Eisenhower who gets a little down being left back at Algiers. These French political squabbles cause him a lot of trouble. ...

Things are going well in Sicily. ... On the whole I think the Americans have done rather better than our own Eighth Army. They have fought with more imagination and used their sea power to greater effect. Our people have just gone in for slogging matches and I think the casualties may have been heavy. ...

123.   *To Ramsay*

Bizerta,
20 September 1943

I have been very remiss in not replying before to your very nice letter. It was grand being with you in Malta especially in such a successful operation – the success being largely due to your organisation and careful preparation.

The campaign went according to plan. I think it is thought in some places now that it was a mistake to be so concentrated in the south-east corner and that the previous plan which if you remembered landed the Canadians on the Catania plain on D+3/4 would have produced quicker results.

As it was there is no doubt honours went to the Yanks who used their sea power in landing behind the enemy. Nothing would induce Montgomery to do the same till the last day when he wasn't bold enough and landed in front of the enemy.

It was greatly due to this failure to blow the Taormina road behind him that the fleeing enemy got away. I fear that Montgomery has not profited by the lectures on sea power which I'm sure you gave him. ...

124.   *Combined Operations HQ*

October 1943

Digest of some notes and reports from Operation 'Husky'

... 'Husky' enjoyed tideless waters, fine weather, moderate defences and a surprised and half-hearted Italian garrison. . . .

125.   *To the Admiralty*

14 November 1943

3.   The accuracy and effectiveness of these Cruiser bombardments in this Operation gave great satisfaction and fully restored the confidence of the Army in Naval supporting gunfire generally.

126.   *Report on Operation 'Husky'*

1 January 1944

Planning
4.   It is essential, if much time is not to be wasted and much confusion caused, that the responsible Cs-in-C, together with the Task Force commanders who will be responsible for the tactical control of the battle, should meet at the outset for the discussion and evolution of a sound basic plan which should not thereafter be changed except for reasons of exceptional urgency, such as a complete change of the enemy's dispositions or a major strategic upheaval.
5.   In the case of 'Husky' this was not done since General Alexander and General Montgomery were absorbed in the Tunisian battle. In consequence, although the operation was authorized on 27 January, the final firm plan was not evolved until 12 May. Thus, although five months were available for perfecting plans for the operation, all detailed planning had in fact to be compressed into two months, resulting in some confusion and considerable unnecessary duplication in the issuing of orders.
6.   It cannot be too clearly recognised that a combined operation is but the opening, under particular circumstances, of a purely army battle. It is the function of the navy and of the air to help the army to establish a base or bases on the hostile coast from which the military tactical battle to gain the object must be developed. It is upon the army tactical plan for the fulfilment of its object that the combined plan must depend. The naval and the air commanders must join with the army commander to

ensure that the base or bases selected for seizure are capable of achievement without prohibitive loss in their respective elements, and that, when seized, they will fulfil the requirements of the force; but is of no use to plan on the seizure of the bases unrelated to the realities of the military situation when ashore.

7. It was upon this point that the initial planning of 'Husky' broke down. . . .

8. . . . in the initial planning great weight was lent to the value of airborne troops for the softening of beach defences. The conditions of light required for the employment of paratroops was inimical to the security and undetected approach of naval forces. . . . the navies, for no advantage, had to accept a disadvantageous light for approach, and a consequent period of moonlit nights off the beaches which could have been avoided.

9. . . . airborne troops should be considered as a useful auxiliary rather than as a governing factor which may react to the disadvantage of other services involved.

10. . . . a dominating factor must always be a soldier's dislike of meeting aimed machine gun fire. Unless it can be guaranteed to the Army that the enemy beach defences can be neutralised by naval gunfire or air attack or both – or by smoke – it is felt that darkness will always be chosen for the first waves to reach the beach. . . . had the enemy been resolute and alert, it would have required more than the gun support actually available if the soldiers were to be landed in daylight without heavy casualties. . . .

Preparation, Training and Mounting

11. The training and mounting of 'Husky' proceeded under difficulties, particularly in the case of Force B of the Eastern Task Force, and to a lesser extent of the Western Task Force. Both these forces had to establish their base facilities in captured ports which had been considerably demolished, namely Sfax and Sousse for Force B, and Bizerta and Tunis for the Western Task Force. . . . Force B was faced at short notice with the task of capturing Pantelleria but the task was taken in its stride and successfully accomplished without prejudice to 'Husky', of which operation it was an essential preliminary.

12. The reception and absorption in the station of the great number of Landing Ships and Craft, and the establishment of their bases, presented a heavy problem to both navies. The probable performance of these craft, manned as they were by new and inexperienced officers and men but recently enrolled in their respective services, gave cause for some anxiety. . . .

13.   Another cause of anxiety at this stage was the large demand for the movement of troops, airmen and vehicles to their staging points or bases for the attack. This involved heavy and continuous running by the Landing Craft at times when they should have been training, and fear was felt, not only that their training would be inadequate, but that their engines would not stand the strain. These fears were happily disproved, and in fact the sea training provided by these voyages must have stood them in good stead. That the craft themselves withstood the extra wear and tear is a tribute to those who designed and built them.

14.   Additional difficulties in the way of training and mounting arose from the late arrival of craft and material. This was particularly so in the case of Force A of the Eastern Task Force, which received its LSTs extremely late and had little or no opportunity of trying and practising with pontoons. This portion of the force was also separated by 900 miles from the LSTs which were to form a part of its assault. A high standard of staff work was required to knit these scattered components into an operational whole.

15.   The Western Task Force was more fortunate in that opportunities for training and mounting were undisturbed, . . . the US warships came into the Mediterranean for the specific purpose of the operations, . . . in the case of the Eastern Task Force, all ships, belonging as they did to the normal naval forces of the station, were heavily and continuously employed right up to the date of sailing for the operation, and in but few cases took part in any rehearsal or training. . . .

Collection of Beach Evidence

16.   Much credit is due to the officers and men of the COPP beach reconnaissance parties for their arduous and hazardous efforts to obtain details of the beach gradients and sand bars. Credit is also due to the submarines of the 8th and 10th Flotillas which worked on the beach reconnaissance in company with the COPPs.[1]

   The estimation of beach conditions and gradients by air photography and the study of wave velocities have now reached a fine pitch of efficiency; but where sandbars exist there is at present no substitute for swimming reconnaissance, so the services of these gallant parties will continue to be necessary. Their casualties in this Operation were unfortunately heavy; apart from the natural dislike of such losses, the possibility of capture always gives rise to anxiety on the grounds of security.

[1] 8 (Gibraltar) & 10 (Malta) (S) Flotillas.

Location of HQ

17.   . . . communications problems, and to a lesser extent, lack of suitable accommodation caused an undesirable dispersion in that though the navy and army moved to Malta from Algiers, the AOC-in-C found himself unable to move from his existing HQ at Marsa, where he was in close touch with his main forces.[1]

I am sure Malta was a wise choice from both naval and army view-point, and apart from an unexpected assault of sandflies which devastated my staff, the arrangements were in all respects excellent.

18.   The separation of the Commanders did not in the end have a serious reaction, but was manifestly undesirable and might have proved extremely awkward had things begun to go awry. In particular the navy and the air are closely inter-related in a sea assault, and with the exception of the coastal air component, the air plans had all along appeared to be somewhat nebulous, and the day-to-day exposition was necessary to make the picture clear. . . .

The Approach and Assault

19.   The co-ordination and timing necessary to ensure the punctual concentration of this vast force in the assault areas, presented a prob-lem of some complexity. The problem was to some degree complicated by the great distance over which the forces were initially disposed, by the need for deceptive routeing to avoid disclosure of intention, by the bottleneck presented by the Tunisian war channel, and, finally by the requirement for topping up the fuel of escort vessels before their arrival in the assault area.

. . . everything depended, as always, on the seamanship and good sense of individual commanding officers and of the smooth working of the berthing and fuelling organisations of the ports concerned.

My confidence in their abilities was not misplaced. The operation ran like a well-oiled clock.

20.   . . . The passage of the convoys was covered most effectively by the operations of the North African Coastal Air Force and 201 Naval Co-operation Group. Their problem was one of complexity equal to our own. It was solved with conspicuous success, since no bomb was dropped on any convoy – the majority were not sighted by enemy aircraft – and all reports showed that the fighter cover was excellent.

21.   An aspect of the approach which caused me concern was the slow speed of the LCT convoys . . . it became clear that not more than $5\frac{1}{2}$ knots could be counted upon in safety, even in calm weather.

[1]Tedder.

It is, I suggest, a matter of urgency that some means be devised of landing supporting arms at an early stage from craft whose speed is at least in the region of that of the average infantry assault ship, if tactical surprise is to be aimed at.

Attainment of Surprise

23.   This little blow [a severe storm] had various effects but the most noteworthy was its contribution to our unexpected success in gaining complete surprise. The very efficient cover plan and the deceptive routeing of the convoys both played their parts. In addition the vigilance of the enemy was undoubtedly relaxed owing to the unfavourable phase of the moon to which we had been so unwillingly subjected. Finally came this wind which indeed came close at one time to making some, if not all, of the landings impracticable. These last two, to us, apparently unfavourable factors had actually the effect of making the weary Italians, who had been alert for many nights, turn thankfully in their beds saying, 'Tonight at any rate they cannot come!'
   But they came.

The Landings

24.   In consequence of the wind not all assault waves reached the beach at H-hour, but none was seriously late. . . . The performance of the small craft of both nations in this period was most creditable. They made valiant efforts to keep their rendezvous and in large measure were successful.

25.   The assaults were landed in all sectors in the right place, nearly at the right time and with negligible opposition. In some areas some interference was encountered after daylight from coast defence and shore batteries, but in most cases they were readily silenced by ships' gunfire. . . .
   The Western Task Force, on their exposed western beaches, bore the brunt of opposition both by gunfire and surf, the latter particularly at 'Cent' beaches which were most nearly a lee shore. Losses of craft by broaching in this area were considerable. That the surf was in no wise allowed to interfere with the smooth progress of the landing reflects highly on the determination, resource and sound training of the Western Task Force. . . .

26.   After the landings the troops moved steadily inland on both fronts, apparently encountering but little active opposition except inland of Gela in the 'Dime' area of the Western Task Force, where the floating reserve (Koolforce) was ordered to be landed in support. A determined counter attack by the Herman Göring Panzer Division started to develop in this

area from 0900 on D-Day and had some success, reaching almost to the beaches on the evening of D+1. Naval gunfire played a prominent and praiseworthy part in stopping this attack, being notably effective against tanks. By 2330 on D+1 the situation had been restored. . . .

Air Action during the Assault

27.   The degree of air opposition encountered in the assault and later could by no means be described as serious, but caused some casualties among shipping and had some nuisance value.

In this respect the Western Task Force was less fortunate than the Eastern Task Force and was somewhat bothered, particularly by fighter-bomber aircraft coming in over the hills from inland in such a manner as to evade detection by radar.

The Air Command had to strike a balance in the allotment of their resources between the value of defensive patrols and offensive action at the enemy airfields – both having the same object – the security of the assault from enemy air interference. . . .

29.   By results I consider that the air appreciation was proved sound. To one who had to fight through the Mediterranean campaign from the beginning it appeared almost magical that great fleets of ships could remain anchored on the enemy's coast, within 40 miles of his main aerodromes, . . .

. . . Nevertheless there was palpably room for improvement in the close air cover of the assault areas, and in particular, in the effectiveness of the liaison between the Naval Force Commanders and the fighter forces . . . This improvement was in fact effected in the next major amphibious operation . . .

Lessons of the Landings

30.   The following sums up, to my mind, the major lessons of the landings:

(a)   The need for a faster and more seaworthy craft for the landing of supporting arms.

(b)   The enormous value of the LSTs as a means of a rapid landing of reinforcements.

(c)   The importance of the 'water gap' and the need for a means of crossing it. The best means so far devised is the US 'side-centred' pontoon, but it is only suitable for calm seas.

(d)   The profound effect that DUKWs have had in amphibious warfare.

(e)   The importance of early hydrographic survey of the bars to find the gaps which usually existed.

(f)   The need for augmentation of labour in beach groups and steve-
dore gangs in merchant ships to ensure rapid unloading over beaches.
(g)   The importance of senior Air Officers with executive powers
and a full knowledge of the plan, to accompany the naval commanders in the assault.
(h)   The importance of AA fire discipline particularly in minor craft.

Routeing of Troop-Carrying Aircraft

32.   ... owing to heavy ground AA fire and possibly due to bad
navigation, large numbers of aircraft forsook the route and flew over
the Western Task Force assault areas coinciding with an enemy air
attack. Considerable losses resulted. . . .[1]

Naval Forces other than Assault Forces

34.   ... Force H was faced with the prospect of steady patrolling in
waters within easy reach of the enemy's air bases, in conditions of
moonlight and weather particularly suited to air attack and with a
growing U-boat threat.
... *Indomitable* had, not unexpectedly, been torpedoed and severely
damaged. Force H achieved its object.[2]
38.   The operation of coastal forces, and, at a later stage, of the American PT boats in the Strait of Messina were most gallant and determined.
They nightly faced an unpleasant volume of gunfire and inflicted losses
on the enemy. . . .
39.   The anti-U-boat operations, both air and surface, which were
instituted as soon as U-boat concentrations on the east coast of Sicily
became apparent, did not succeed in making any kills. But the U-boat
activity achieved little, and that this was the case was probably in no
small measure due to the active measures which were taken to discour-
age their presence. . . .

Lessons of Operations subsequent to the Assault

43.   The following sums up the major lessons of operations subsequent to an assault:
(a)   The importance of a means of identifying positions of our forward troops from the sea. (This has cropped up in every Mediterranean
campaign this war and is still unsolved).

[1]The paratroop drops were notably unsuccessful, as some aircraft were routed over
the invasion convoy, happening to arrive during an air raid and many planes were shot
down. Other gliders landed in the sea, and of those troops who did reach land, many
were dropped far from their target areas.
[2]*Indomitable*: carrier, 1941, 23000t, 31k, 54 a/c, 16×4.5in.

(b)   The need of first class officers to superintend the initial opening of captured ports.

(c)   The need to form, in advance, an ample force for the exploitation of outflanking opportunities and its existence and value to be firmly indicated in the plan.

(d)   The difficulties of airborne troop operations . . .

(e)   The importance of obtaining firm requirements from the Army regarding the movement of their 'tail'. That of the 7th and 8th Armies was endless and was still in motion long after the final capture of the island, thereby hindering the inception and mounting of subsequent operations by continuing demand for ferry by landing craft.

(f)   The need, as I suspected, for vigorous pruning by the Army of the elements of this 'tail'. Is it all really necessary?

(g)   The importance of early supply of tugs and lighters in captured areas, to release and conserve the life of LCTs.

Conclusion

48.   Of the Navies, I can only say that I never wish to command better, and I count it a great honour that, through the person of Vice Admiral Hewitt, I was privileged to command so large and efficient a force of the US Navy. Both the Western Task Force, under Admiral Hewitt, and the Eastern Task Force, under Admiral Ramsay, performed their unaccustomed tasks in a manner befitting the best tradition of any fighting service.

127.   *Diary*

17 April 1944

. . . Lofty Power came in and we discussed the 'Husky' report, which he wrote. Very good and will reveal just criticisms which unfortunately will not penetrate outside the Admiralty. Power just off to command a Home Fleet Destroyer Flotilla. I am sure he will do well. . . .

SECTION C

'BAYTOWN' AND 'AVALANCHE':

THE LANDINGS IN ITALY
AUGUST 1943–JANUARY 1945

The British case for invading the Italian mainland was really a repetition of the arguments they had put forward for 'Torch' and 'Husky'. Added to those, Churchill and Brooke advocated seizing on Mussolini's fall and the desire of the Italians for a speedy armistice. The Americans, though sceptical, were tempted both by that prospect and by the opportunity to acquire bomber bases in the southern regions from which it would be possible to bomb those parts of the Third Reich that other attacks could not reach. Roosevelt and Churchill were also swayed by the opportunity to draw German land and air forces away from the Soviet front, thus helping an increasingly sarcastic Stalin pending a landing in north west Europe.

Cunningham, who had spent a large part of his career in the Mediterranean and was an advocate of adventures there, was nevertheless somewhat reserved about a campaign in Italy, preferring the easier options of Sardinia or Corsica. He sensed Italy was good defensive country, difficult to supply, and that the operation had no real aims apart from a lodgement for airfields in the southern half. Moreover, Italy would be certain to descend rapidly into a backwater as the campaign to land in north west Europe developed, calling home troops and other resources, notably landing craft. For Cunningham, however, his connection with the Italian campaign was both brief and at one remove. The real responsibility lay with the American Admiral H. Kent Hewitt and after about a month, Cunningham, who as C-in-C, Mediterranean, was responsible for many other matters, left the scene of his triumphs for the post of First Sea Lord.

In the planning, done quickly, he had his disputes with both Alexander and the rather bumptious Montgomery and there were some showdowns, with Cunningham evidently proving as awkward as his military colleagues [94, 128–9, 134].

The initial assaults on 3 and 8/9 September 1943 were virtually unopposed – 'it looked more like Henley Regatta than anything else', wrote Cunningham – but these romps were soon overshadowed by the deadly intensity of the fighting round Salerno, where the 'Avalanche' landings, also on 8/9 September, had gone 'like clockwork' [134].

Within hours of securing a lodgement ashore, the troops found themselves facing the fury of a fierce and rapid German counter-attack, driving them back to the beaches. An evacuation seemed likely but the situation was saved by resolve and instant action on the part of Cunningham, Troubridge and other commanders and the effective application of much bombing and bombardment. Salerno was where the naval gun definitely earned the approbation of the armies. It was, however, a tense few days until the *Panzers* were repulsed [132–4,136,139,140].

Cunningham's main concern was the fate of the Italian fleet, still a formidable fighting force. He took no chances and retained battleships and carriers to deal with it if it emerged in defence of its homeland. It was, however, intent on surrender. Following the Italian Armistice of 8 September, Cunningham hastened to add a naval codicil to it. After the Italian fleet's formal surrender at Malta on 10 September, Cunningham sent the Admiralty his most famous signal, in appropriately Nelsonian language: 'Be pleased to inform Their Lordships that the Italian Battle fleet now lies at anchor under the guns of the fortress of Malta' [130–1]. On 22 September he journeyed to Taranto and there signed an agreement with the Italian Admiral de Courten providing for the Italian Navy's surrender, the fate of the warships and the allocation of the Mercantile Marine to the Allied shipping pool [135, 137].[1] Cunningham was especially concerned to secure light craft for escort and minesweeping duties and the intact Italian dockyards to relieve the pressure on those of Britain. He was, however, suspicious of Italian integrity and feared a second 'Scapa Flow' in the Great Bitter Lake, its Egyptian 'gaol' [132, 134]. This Cunningham-de Courten Agreement (later subject to minor changes) carefully made no provision for the disposition of the fleet after the war. The Italians, however, fondly imagined that by handing it over to British supervision and co-operating fully with the Allies it would be restored to them in full after hostilities. The President then unwisely let the cat out of the bag by blithely promising a third of it to Stalin, causing some embarrassment to Cunningham; eventually the Russians were loaned some over-age American and British warships pending the end of the war and the overhaul of Italian warships, some of which went to the Soviet Navy.[2] The shock of discovering their fate was most disconcerting to the Italian naval command [138].

---

[1]VAdm Raffaello de Courten: VCNS 1943; signed agreement with Cunningham on immediate fate of Italian Navy; see documents 135, 137.
[2]Marshal Josef Stalin (1879–1953): Comm pol commissar 1918–20; unquestioned dictator of Soviet Union by 1927–8; effectively C-in-C.

As Cunningham, appointed Pound's successor as First Sea Lord, had to return home in mid-October, the Italian episode remained nominally in the hands of his successor as C-in-C, Mediterranean, Admiral Sir John Cunningham (no relation but highly recommended by Sir Andrew) and more immediately in those of the very capable Admiral Kent Hewitt, US Navy, who produced the final report on the landings. Hewitt painted a picture of smooth disembarkation followed by German exploitation of their speed, skill, experience, formidable firepower and possession of the heights above Salerno. 'German tank elements drove to the water's edge', reported Hewitt, and 'it was touch and go whether a foothold would be established'. Fortunately, 'The weight of sea power determined the issue'[140]. By 17 September, when Cunningham visited the scene, the crisis was over and shortly after that he ceased to have any direct contact with a hastily planned, quickly launched and imprecise operation which was to lead to a draining slogging match of eighteen months' duration and which produced few of the benefits originally advocated [134].

128.   *To General Alexander*

Algiers,
26 August 1943

2.   You will recollect that on 28 July 1943 you despatched a message to General Eisenhower, with a copy to myself, in which you laid down a series of conditions, all of which were matters of purely naval concerns and internal organisation. You further stated that unless these conditions were fulfilled the 'Baytown' operation could not be undertaken, you further stated that, even if they were, the earliest probable date for the operation was 4/5 September.[1]

3.   Leaving aside the fact that this was entering into the sphere of responsibility which is exclusively mine, I trust you realise the effect of dealing directly with the Allied C-in-C on this matter when your HQ was within less than an hour's flight of Malta where, doubtless, any difficulties could have been resolved in five minutes' conversation. The impression that must have been left with the Allied C-in-C can only have been that our relations were such that it was necessary to refer to a higher authority to settle what must have appeared to him to be a dispute.

3.   . . . The whole matter was, however, reopened in exaggerated form by the statement by General Montgomery at the C-in-C's meeting on 23 August. At that meeting he stated that the Army was ready to execute the 'Baytown' operation on 1 September but that they were held up by the Navy which refused to do it until 4/5 and furthermore that the Navy was unwilling to do the operation by night. . . . I find that, not only were the statements incorrect, but that General Montgomery had at no time been in direct touch with the SNO of the Expedition and that his statements were, in fact, completely unfounded.[2]

6.   The Naval Commander had been informed by the Corps Commander, Lt-Gen Dempsey, that 4/5 September was the selected date but [he] was actually working to the 3 September . . .[3]

7.   With the full concurrence of the Naval Commander I gave orders to advance the date to the 2/3 in view of the Allied C-in-C's known wishes in the matter. Had I or Admiral McGrigor been made aware some days previously that the Army could be ready on 1 September I have no doubt another valuable day could have been saved.

---

[1] 'Baytown' was the landing of troops in the vicinity of Reggio on 3 Sept 1943.
[2] RAdm McGrigor, who became NOIC, S Italy and Liaison Officer with Italian Navy.
[3] Gen Sir Miles Dempsey (1896–1969): R Berks R, W Front 1915–19; Ireland 1919–20; Lt Col, R Berks R 1939; cmdg XIII Corps, ME 1942–4; 2 Army 1944–5; 14 Army, Burma 1945–6; Gen 1946; C-in-C ME 1946–7.

8. I found that the Naval Commander had very properly represented the naval disadvantages of a night landing to General Dempsey but had at the same time informed him that, after knowing what the Naval opinion was, the final decision must rest with the Army; again a complete contradiction to General Montgomery's statement that the Navy insisted on a day assault.

9. Another statement by General Montgomery to which exception could be taken and not only by me, was to the effect that the sole reason for 'Baytown' was to assure the use of the Strait of Messina for the Navy. This, it is true, *is* one of the reasons for laying on Operation 'Baytown' but as is well known to you not the only one. . . .

10. The object of this letter is to bring matters out into the open. I must make it clear that I cannot continue to accept conditions in which communications are made directly to the Allied C-in-C on matters of our mutual concern when our HQ are in close reach of one another. Nor can I accept that subordinate commanders, however high their standing, should be allowed to make statements of so exaggerated a nature as those to which I have taken exception. In short our continued relations must, for the good of the prosecution of the war, be based on mutual understanding and confidence and I should be glad of some assurance from you that steps will be taken to make quite sure that these incidents, or similar ones, will not recur. The effect between our own services is lamentable and in relation to the Americans, deplorable.

129. *Montgomery to Ramsay*

Sicily,
26 August 1943

We missed you sadly when you had gone, and 'The Old Man of the Sea' got very troublesome. In the end he really became beyond a joke, and refused to produce what was necessary for our next business. I appealed to Alex[ander] and he got on to Eisenhower, who ticked the 'Old Man' off – at which he said he would resign.[1]

But he did *not* in the end.

I went over and attended the meeting of C's-in-C which was summoned, and I gave all the facts. He could not refute them. Finally Eisenhower told him to get into an aeroplane, fly off to Sicily, see McGrigor and go into the whole matter – the point being that we

---

[1] 'The Old Man of the Sea', a term first used by Tedder in 1941 to describe Cunningham, subsequently adopted by Montgomery, whose testimony is somewhat dubious.

wanted to do our next business on 30/31 August and Cunningham wouldn't give us the necessary naval resources. It was made clear to him that he must play properly.

In the end he came over and was perfectly charming to everyone, and produced everything.

I think this showdown has really done some good. The Navy as a whole are delighted and everyone is now cracking along 100% and very harmoniously. You can't help liking old Cunningham but he can be maddening at times, his staff are not allowed to do anything, and everyone is frightened of him.

Eisenhower really ought to have you as C-in-C, Mediterranean. You understand us soldiers and you know more about the land battle than any other sailor.

130. *To the Admiralty*

Malta,
11 September 1943

Be pleased to inform Their Lordships that the Italian Battle fleet now lies at anchor under the guns of the fortress of Malta.

131. *To Aunt Doodles*

Algiers,
12 September 1943

. . . I went out in Gordon McKendrick's destroyer to see the big battle-ships pass Bizerta on their way to Malta and took Eisenhower with me.[1]
. . . All led by my old *Warspite*.[2]

I flew to Malta yesterday and saw the others that had come from Taranto.

The Italian admiral came ashore to see me, a nice enough man who spoke English well but felt his position terribly. . . . there was little spirit left in this poor man.[3]

---

[1]Lt Cdr G. W. McKendrick: Lt June 1934; *Britannia* July 1937; Lt Cdr June 1942; *Hambledon* Oct 1942; *Caprice* March 1944.

[2]*Warspite* was Cunningham's flagship in Med F.

[3]VAdm Alberto da Zara: Cdr *D'Aosta* 1937; A/S Sch Aug 1941; 7C Div June 1942; Cdr Taranto section, It F, surrendering at Malta, 11 Sept 1943.

132. *To Admiral Willis*

Algiers,
14 September 1943

[The Italian Fleet] is alright at the moment but I smell trouble coming. I am quite convinced that all the ships are prepared to scuttle should things not be to their liking.

. . . 'Avalanche' is giving me great anxiety and I am hoping we are not to have an evacuation on our hands. Unseasoned troops were landed and as you say Malta has been slow and I can't get Taranto reinforced.

I don't want the battleships to do monitors' work but I had an SOS from Hewitt tonight and if they can smash up this breakthrough to the sea it will have been worth the risk.

. . . A well-handled battle fleet can still effectively defend itself I am sure. . . .

133. *To Aunt Doodles*

Bizerta,
19 September 1943

. . . I just sit in my cabin reading signals and have hardly been out of the ship.

I took a trip in a destroyer to see the Salerno beaches and spent a very interesting forenoon there. Not much going on except men working like ants on the beaches unloading stores[,] ammunition[,] etc. for the army. Rumbling artillery fire on the shore and a few British and American men-of-war helping with their fire. Rather impressive [–] in fact the most impressive I have yet seen and an air raid in the middle just to keep us awake. . . .

. . . I wonder if any admiral has flown as much as I have. . . .

134. *To Ramsay*

Bizerta,
20 September 1943

. . .How long ago it seems and how far we have advanced since then. 'Baytown' was a yachting trip across the narrows and looked more like Henley Regatta than anything else. But we had trouble; Montgomery did not want to do 'Baytown' unless they landed three more divisions for 'Buttress' and neither he nor Alexander wanted to do 'Avalanche'. They were forced into it by the Quebecians who then proceeded to think all was over bar the shouting and moved squadrons of H/C, landing ships, etc., etc., which were required to make the operation a good gamble.[1] It got so bad that I had to make a signal to Dudley Pound warning him that if this removal business went on they were heading straight for failure. As a matter of fact I don't think it could have been a success except for the Italian crack up.

The landing went like clockwork but they found a Hun division waiting for them on the beaches. It was curious that they made little attempt to stop the landing but fought like tigers after our chaps got ashore.

I think one lesson wants rubbing in as a result of our experiences in 'Husky' and 'Avalanche'. One can't get surprise if one has to come some way over the sea if one uses an 8/9 knot landing craft as the LCT which of necessity is within 40 miles of the beach at dusk. They were designed for Channel landings but for ocean work I prefer something faster.

As it was after we had been ashore three days things began to go wrong and we had a crisis one afternoon when the enemy counter-attack nearly fetched up on the beaches between the British and US forces.

Fine work by the air force and our ships' gunfire saved the day and now Montgomery is coming along things are looking good. But I had to throw in *Valiant* and *Warspite* and well they did, but even if they hit nothing it was the great heart they put into the troops hearing the 15-inch bricks go hurtling over their heads.[2]

But it nearly cost us *Warspite*. Those rocket bombs are the devil and very, very dangerous.

Bringing in the Italian fleet was a fine show but they are giving me lots of headaches at my busiest time too. I suspect we shall use the little ones if they show signs of wanting to fight.

. . . I hope a good job awaits you. CCO would be suitable for you now that it is vacant. I thought the Supreme Commander racket was a big fine to pay to get Mountbatten off the COS Committee!!!

---

[1]Quebecians: There was a summit meeting at Quebec, 17–24 June 1943 ('Quadrant'), involving Churchill, Roosevelt, the CCS and aides.

[2]*Valiant*, like *Warspite*, had been present at Matapan.

135. *Memorandum of Agreement on the Employment and Disposition of the Italian Fleet and Mercantile Marine between the Allied Naval C-in-C, acting on behalf of the Allied C-in-C, and the Italian Minister of Marine*

23 September 1943

The armistice having been signed by the Head of the Italian Government and the Allied C-in-C under which all Italian warships and the Italian Mercantile Marine were placed unconditionally at the disposal of the United Nations, and HM the King of Italy and the Italian Government having since expressed their wish that the Fleet and the Mercantile Marine should be employed in the Allied efforts to assist in the prosecution of the war with the Axis powers, the following principles are established on which the Italian Navy and Mercantile Marine will be disposed.[1]

It is understood and agreed that the provisions of this Agreement as to immediate employment and disposition of Italian warships and merchant ships do not affect the right of the United Nations to make such other dispositions of any or all Italian ships as they may think fit. Their decisions in this respect will be notified to the Italian Government from time to time.

A. Such ships as can be employed to assist actively in the Allied effort will be kept in commission and will be used under the orders of the C-in-C, Mediterranean, as may be arranged between the Allied C-in-C and the Italian Government.

B. Ships which cannot be so employed will be reduced to a care and maintenance basis and placed in designated ports, measures of disarmament being undertaken as may be necessary.

C. The Government of Italy will decide the names and whereabouts of

(i) Warships

(ii) Merchant Ships

now in their possession which previously belonged to any of the United Nations. These vessels are to be returned forthwith as may be directed by the Allied C-in-C. This will be without prejudice to

[1]Italian M of Marine: VAdm de Courten.

PM: Marshal Pietro Badolgio (1871–1956): Gen 1917; Chief Sup Gen Staff 1925; Govr Libya 1928; Cdr It forces, Abyssinia 1935; Duke of Addis Ababa; res Dec 1940, opposed to Greek fiasco; negotiated It Arm smr 1943; PM July 1943–June 1944.

Victor Emanuel II, King of Italy (1869–1947): king 1900–46; replaced by son Umberto II (regent to 1946) June 1944; abdicated May 1946.

negotiations between the Governments which may subsequently be made in connection with replacing losses of ships of the UN caused by Italian action.

D.   The Allied Naval C-in-C will act as the agent of the Allied C-in-C in all matters concerning the employment of the Italian Fleet or Merchant Navy, their disposition and related matters.

E.   It should be clearly understood that the extent to which the terms of the armistice are modified to allow of the arrangements outlined above and which follow, are dependent upon the extent and effectiveness of Italian co-operation.

2.   *Method of Operation*

The C-in-C, Mediterranean, will place at the disposal of the Italian Ministry of Marine a high ranking Naval officer with the appropriate staff who will be responsible to the C-in-C, Mediterranean, for all matters in connection with the operation of the Italian Fleet, and be the medium through which dealings will be carried out in connection with the Italian Merchant Marine. The Flag Officer acting for these duties (FO Liaison Officer) will keep the Italian Ministry of Marine informed of the requirements of the C-in-C, Mediterranean, and will act in close co-operation as regards issue of orders to the Italian Fleet.[1]

3.   *Proposed Disposition of the Italian Fleet*

(a)   All battleships will be placed on a care and maintenance basis in ports to be designated and will have such measures of disarmament applied as may be directed. These measures of disarmament will be such that the ships can be brought into operation again if it so seems desirable. Each ship will have on board a proportion of Italian Naval personnel to keep the ships in proper condition and the C-in-C, Mediterranean, will have the right of inspection at any time.

(b)   Cruisers. Such cruisers as can be of immediate assistance will be kept in commission. At present it is visualised that one squadron of four cruisers will suffice and the remainder will be kept in care and maintenance as for the battleships but at a rather greater degree of readiness to be brought into service if required.

(c)   Destroyers and Torpedo Boats. It is proposed to keep these in commission and to use them on escort and similar duties as may be requisite. It is proposed that they should be divided into escort groups working as units and that they should be based on Italian ports.

[1]RAdm McGrigor.

(d)   Small craft. MAS [boats], minesweepers, auxiliaries and similar small craft will be employed to the full, detailed arrangements being made with the FO (Liaison) by the Italian Ministry of Marine for their best employment.

(e)   Submarines. In the first instance submarines will be immobilised in ports to be designated and at a later date these may be brought into service as may be required to assist the Allied effort.

4.   *Status of the Italian Navy.* Under this modification of the armistice terms, all Italian ships will continue to fly their flags. A large proportion of the Italian Navy will thus remain in active commission operating their own ships and fighting alongside the forces of the UN against the Axis powers.

The requisite Liaison Officers will be supplied to facilitate the working of the Italian ships in co-operation with Allied forces. A small Italian liaison mission will be attached to the HQ of the C-in-C, Mediterranean, to deal with matters affecting the Italian Fleet.

5.   *Mercantile Marine.* It is the intention that the Italian Mercantile Marine should operate under the same conditions as the merchant ships of the Allied Nations. That is to say, all merchant shipping of the UN is formed into a pool which is employed as may be considered necessary for the benefit of all the UN. In this will naturally be included the requirements for the supply and maintenance of Italy. The system will be analogous to that used in North Africa, where the North African Shipping Board controls all US, British and French shipping under certain agreements which will have to be arranged in detail in so far as Italian ships are concerned. While it may be expected that a proportion of Italian ships will be working within the Mediterranean and to and from Italian ports, it must be appreciated that this will not always necessarily be the case and ships flying the Italian flag may be expected to be used elsewhere as is done with the merchant ships of the UN. Italian ships employed as outlined in this paragraph will be manned as far as possible by crews provided by the Italian Ministry of Marine and will fly the Italian flag.

136.   *To Commodore G. N. Oliver*

Bizerta,
September 1943

I am carefully watching the situation. Everything possible is being done to send reinforcements into the area at once. You will have to hold

on like HELL. I am reconstituting Force V and furbishing up the Fleet
Fighters in case they are again required. Good luck.[1]

137.   *A. V. Alexander and Cunningham to Admiral Sir Percy Noble*[2]

7 October 1943

2.   Battleships:

(a)   *Littorios* to be steamed by their own crews to an American port
for complete examination and overhaul with a view to employment in
the Pacific manned by Americans or British.[3]

(b)   *Cavours* to remain demilitarised in British or Egyptian Mediterranean port except for one which may be kept in partial commission
at Taranto as a symbol of the Italian Fleet. Balance of crews to be
repatriated.[4]

3.   Cruisers:

The four remaining 6-inch cruisers to be used if practicable as fast
transports or minelayers under [British] Admiralty control, the necessary conversion work being carried out at Taranto. Thus employed
they would not be unduly exposed to air attack and could therefore be
used without any modernisation of AA armament and with Italian
crews.[5]

4.   Submarines:

Until the submarines have been inspected it is not possible to decide
on their employment. The [British] Admiralty is arranging for a detailed inspection to be carried out by the C-in-C, Mediterranean. The

[1]Force V: RAdm Sir Philip Vian in *Euryalus*: csr, 1940, 5450t, 33k, 10×5.25in, 6×21in
tt. *Unicorn*: a/c repair carrier, 1943, 14750t, 24k, 35 a/c, 8×4.5in. *Hunter, Attacker,
Battler, Stalker*: escort carriers, 1942–3, 10200t, 16k, 15–20 a/c.

[2]Albert V. Alexander was the First Lord.
    Adm Sir Percy Noble, head of BAD.

[3]*Littorio* (now *Italia*), *Vittorio Veneto*: battleships, 1940, 41377t, 30k, 9×15in, 12×6in,
4×4.7in, 12×3.5in; *Roma*: 1942, 41650t, was sunk by rocket bomb, 9 Sept 1943, en
route to surrender. *Impero*: not completed.

[4]*Conti di Cavour, Giulio Cesare*: battleships, 1914–15 (modernised 1933–7), 26140t,
27k, 10×12.6in, 12×4.7in, 8×3.9in. *Cavour* sunk at Taranto 11 Nov 1940. *Cesare* to
Soviet N.
    Andrea Doria, Caio Duilio: battleships, 1915–16 (modernised 1937–40), 26000t,
27k, 10×12.6in, 12×5.3in, 10×3.5in. Training.

[5]The surviving 6in cruisers were: *Luigi Cadorna*: 1933, 5400t, 37k, 8×6in, 6×3.9in,
4×21in tt. *Raimondo Montecuccoli*: 1935, 7550, 37k, 8×6in, 6×3.9in, 4×21in tt. *Duca
D'Aosta, Eugenio di Savoia*: 1935–6, 8662–8997t, 36.5k, 8×6in, 6×3.9in, 6×21in tt.
Aosta to Soviet N, *Savoia* to Greece. *Duca Degli Abruzzi, Giuseppi Garibaldi*: 1937,
9959–9387t, 10×6in, 8×3.9in, 6×21in tt.

Cagni which is at present at Durban could also be inspected by the C-in-C, South Atlantic.[1]

5.   *Miraglia*:

Aircraft transport under [British] Admiralty orders using Italian crew.[2]

6.   Transport *Saturnia*:

This important ship is to be removed from the danger zone and brought into service as soon as possible. She should therefore proceed at once with Italian crew to Gibraltar to be taken over by a British crew and sailed to the UK. Her future operation would be a matter for subsequent discussion between the Ministry of War Transport and the War Shipping Authority.[3]

7.   *Eritrea* at Colombo:

Base ship for small craft in Indian Ocean at discretion of Supreme Commander, South East Asia. To be reduced to care and maintenance pending decision and crew repatriation.[4]

8.   The above proposals if approved would form an interim policy. Such a decision is urgently needed if we are to avoid trouble with idle Italian crews.

9.   Agreement between the UN as to the ultimate or post-war disposal of the whole Italian Fleet will be needed at a future date. This probably will be settled separately but we strongly recommend that it should not be allowed to delay promulgation of an interim policy which is urgently needed.

10.   Above is sent with approval of COS and you are requested to consult Admiral King with a view to CCS directive being issued at once to General Eisenhower. This will enable us to deal with some of the most urgent problems.

---

[1]*Ammiraglio Cagni*: s/m, 1941, 1680/2170t, 16.9/9.14k, 2×3.9in, 14×17.7in tt. Surrendered Durban 20 Sept 1943; employed as training boat. VAdm W. E. C. Tait (1886–1946): ent RN 1902; Jutland; Capt 1926; NAt WI; DDNID; China; *Shropshire* 1934–7; RA 1938; VA Oct 1941; C-in-C South Atlantic Feb 1942; ret 1944; Gov-Gen, S Rhodesia.

[2]*Giuseppe Miraglia*: s/plane carrier, 1927, 4880t, 21k, 20 a/c. Employed as depot ship.

[3]*Saturnia*: Italia Line, 1927, 24470gt, 19.5k.

[4]*Eritrea*: colonial sloop, 1937, 2165t, 20k, 4×4.7in. Surrendered Colombo; tfd to France.

138.   *To C-in-C, Mediterranean, etc.*[1]

The Admiralty,
3 March 1944

You will have heard disclosure by President of USA on disposal of Italian Fleet. This is as much of a surprise to us as doubtless it is to you. Urgent enquiries are being made. In the meantime you should be entirely non-committal and express ignorance.

139.   *From Admiral H. R. Stark, US Navy*

HQ, US Naval Forces in European Waters,
20 Grosvenor Square, London, W1,
5 April 1944

I am just in receipt of a letter from Connolly and I think you would be interested in the following extract from it:[2]
   'My service in the Mediterranean was always interesting and I will remember my first flag assignment with pleasure. Admiral Cunningham was an inspiration to every naval officer serving in the Mediterranean. He was always more than fair to the Americans and, what we appreciated most, gave us full opportunity for action against the enemy. The British are faithful, dependable allies in action. I recall that in all instances, the British forces under me or next to me vied with the Americans in doing their part and I believe it was stimulating to both to fight together.' . . .

140.   *Admiral H. K. Hewitt, US Navy: Report on 'Avalanche'*

11 January 1945

2.   In the early phases of the landings it became apparent that the enterprise was a gamble, and that the narrowest of margins governed its success. The German artillery, armored force, infantry and air force met the 5th Army at the shoreline.[3] On some beaches the early waves were

---

[1]Adm Sir John Cunningham.
   [2]Adm Richard L. Connolly, US Navy (1892–1962): N Acad 1914; *Smith*, Brest 1917–18; elec engr, destroyers, engr; CO, *Case, Dupont* 1929–30; War Coll; Instr, N Acad, 1936–9; CO, DDivs 6 & 7, 1939–April 1942; N Dept; RA & CO Landg Craft & Bases, NW Af; TF, Sicily; amph ops, Pac F 1945; DCNO 1945; CO, US N Fcs Eur 1946; Pres, N War Coll 1950; ret 1953; Pres, Long I U, 1953–62.
   [3]5th [US] Army: Cdr Gen M. Clark.

permitted to land and were then pinned down on the narrow beaches by artillery, mortars and machine guns which also took under barrage fire succeeding waves of landing craft bringing ashore later waves of troops and equipment. The well-placed strong points, which the Germans had established behind the beaches during the fortnight preceding the landing, brought a withering fire against the soldiers debarking from the boats and craft, and the numerous formidable 'Tiger' tanks, deployed to cover the strong points, greatly increased the scale of the opposition thrown against the incoming waves.[1] During D-Day several beaches were denied our forces and German tank elements drove us to the water's edge, notably at 'Uncle' Green Beach and VI Corps Blue Beach, pocketing small groups of Allied soldiers. Thus it was touch and go whether a foothold would be established. The weight of sea power determined the issue. Monitors, cruisers, destroyers, and support craft were manoeuvred into position with dexterity and the weight of naval artillery, accurately placed in support of troops hemmed-in ashore, forced the retirement of all German formations which were not annihilated by the murderous fire delivered from the sea. Allied forces then advanced and deepened the bridgehead by capturing Salerno, Battipaglia, Altavilla and Albanella.

Although the initial opposition had been surmounted on D-Day, the crisis had by no means passed. German artillery was well established on the higher ground dominating the beaches and the valley in which the Allied troops were endeavouring to regroup. Reinforcing divisions were quickly moved in by Kesselring from north and south.[2] ... On 11 September the flanks of X and VI Corps had not yet been consolidated but Kesselring had concentrated sufficient forces to begin a series of counter-attacks which were destined to mount in fury over the next four days. The towns of Battipaglia, Altavilla and Albanella were retaken and the Allied troops driven back several miles. Salerno, though still held by the Allies, was taken under heavy bombardment thus denying this port to Allied shipping, and isolated the Rangers from the left flank of the X Corps.[3] ... By 13 September the enemy thrust continued to gain ground and drove a deep wedge between the Allied corps to within three miles of the beaches. The Allied formations were thus enveloped

[1]'Tiger' tank: the most formidable German tank, with 88mm gun; (Mk I) 56t; (Mk II) 68t.

[2]FM Albert Kesselring, German A (1885–1960): Gen Staff 1914–18; Col 1932; Maj Gen & CoS Luftwaffe June 1936; Lt Gen 1937; C-in-C, 1 Air F 1938; Poland; C-in-C, 2 Air F, France, May 1940; FM July 1940; Russia June 1941; C-in-C, South, SW, & Army Grp C, Dec 1941; C-in-C, W Eur March 1945; sentenced to d, commuted to life 1945; released 1952.

[3]Rangers: US Army commandos. 1, 3 & 4 Bns at Salerno.

in two small, low level detached areas and everywhere under artillery fire of German batteries sited on the dominating heights. The continued arrival of supporting units, vehicles and equipment, according to the planned build-up, with densely packed dumps and roads, thus became an embarrassment in the confined beachheads where movement was severely restricted. On 14 September the Allies were forced to give ground once more under renewed ferocity of the German assault, and the Commanding General, 5th Army, formulated plans for the evacuation of one or other of the narrow beachheads separated by the Sele River. The entire military line was in jeopardy.

Once again the decisive feature was the application of sea power augmented by air power. My request for these reinforcements was promptly granted by the C-in-C, Mediterranean. Under the gruelling fire of long range naval guns the German penetration was sealed off and rendered an immobile target for heavy strikes by Allied bombers. Day and night the weight of concentrated naval artillery pounded the German formations without respite and on the 15th the surviving German elements withdrew to escape this accurately placed curtain of death. Thus the Germans once more were defeated by the timely application of sea and air power, and an Allied Army, doggedly clinging to a narrow strip of beach, narrowly saved from being thrown back into the sea. On the 16th advanced elements of the 8th Army had reached Sapri and contact was gained with patrols sent out by the 5th Army, as Kesselring swung his line northward to Avellino. The Allies were now able to regroup and consolidate and to occupy favourable terrain preparatory to undertaking the offensive. . . .

Strategic Concept

87. Unfavorable Military Situation: On D+5 a grave view was taken of the naval situation. The unfavorable character of the critical military situation and the resulting new demands and requirements made upon naval ships and craft, the serious naval losses sustained as a result of direct enemy action were factors which threatened to introduce a major difference between the actual and the anticipated situations. . . .

PART III

FIRST SEA LORD

SECTION A

APPOINTMENT

SEPTEMBER 1943–MARCH 1944

It might be thought that Cunningham succeeded to the First Sea Lord's post by divine right and with the smoothness of a calm sea; that, it seems, is what the Navy as a whole expected and wanted. The actual transfer of power from the fading Pound, who was effectively out of the frame in September 1943, eventually dying on Trafalgar Day (21 October 1943), to the new man was, however, protracted because of Churchill's disinclination to accept Cunningham [150–1, 153]. He raised a smokescreen of reasons not to have him and actually summoned to London Admiral Sir Bruce Fraser, C-in-C, Home Fleet, who had become well known to the Prime Minister while serving at the Admiralty as Controller and Third Sea Lord.[1] He offered Fraser the post but the latter, in an act of magnanimity rarely paralleled, declined in favour of Cunningham [152]. Churchill had no choice but to interview Cunningham, whom he said was in accord with his own aims; that was surely an attempt to put the best possible construction on the appointment of someone he feared would prove obstructive and out of sympathy with his grandiose strategic vision. He had to take the advice of the First Lord, A. V. Alexander, in turn advised by the Naval Secretary, Rear Admiral Freddy Dalrymple-Hamilton, who put the case for Cunningham deftly, while Alexander showed unusual force and persistence in favouring the C-in-C, Mediterranean [141–6].[2]

Fraser would have proved a suitable candidate, for he was an officer of wide experience and, as a result of serving as Controller, knew his way round the Whitehall jungle and was adept at inter-service politics. He was relatively young, pleasant and sharp, technically proficient,

---

[1]AoF Lord (Sir Bruce) Fraser of North Cape (1888–1981): ent RN 1902; Lt *Excellent* 1911; Indian O & E Med 1915–16; Gun O *Resolution* 1916–19; imprisoned by Bolsheviks, S Russia 1920; Capt & AD, Tac Div 1926–9; *Effingham* EI 1929–32; DNO 1933–5; *Glorious* 1935–7; RA Jan 1938 & CoS to C-in-C Med; 3SL & Contrlr March 1939–June 1942; VA 1940; 2-in-C Home F June 1942–May 1943; C-in-C Home F May 1943–June 1944; Adm 1943; C-in-C Eastern F & BPF June 1944–June 1946; C-in-C Portsmouth May 1947; AoF & FSL Sept 1948–April 1952. See R. Humble, *Fraser of North Cape* (London, 1983).
[2]Adm Sir F. Dalrymple-Hamilton (1890–1974): ent RN 1905; Capt Dec 1931; *Britannia* 1938–9; *Rodney* Nov 1939–41; RA 1941; NOIC Iceland 1941–2; NS to FL Oct 1942; VA June 1944; 10CS & 2-in-C Home F 1944–5; VA Malta 1945–6; FO Scotland & N Ireland 1946–8; Adm 1948; JSM 1948–50; ret 1950.

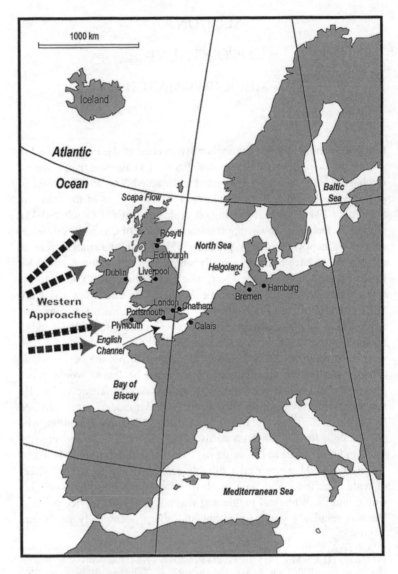

The North Sea and Western Approaches

open to new ideas, and had spent a year with the Home Fleet, gaining its confidence. The other possible contenders received hardly a mention by anyone. Sir John Tovey, Fraser's predecessor as C-in-C, Home Fleet, and now C-in-C, The Nore, had crossed swords with Churchill on several occasions, while Sir Max Horton, C-in-C, Western Approaches, and Sir James Somerville, C-in-C, Eastern Fleet, though spoken of occasionally elsewhere, seem not to have entered Whitehall discussions [141].[1]

Cunningham was viewed by Churchill as a dinosaur of the battleship age, unable and unwilling to adapt to aviation-led and small ship naval warfare. In any case, argued the Prime Minister, he was still needed in the Mediterranean, though this was now a theatre of dwindling importance for the Royal Navy. Cunningham seemed to Churchill to lack the patience and attention to paperwork necessary in a First Sea Lord; he was unfamiliar with the Admiralty and Whitehall and, as an inarticulate old sea dog, unused to tedious policy wrangles, would be at a disadvantage at the Chiefs of Staff Sub-Committee. The war was also entering its final phase, most of the key strategic decisions had been taken, many of the battles won, and all that was required at the Admiralty was a steady hand on the tiller – a job that could have been done by a shore-based admiral who was used to deskbound life, shuffling paper and attending endless committees [142, 144].

To the British public, Cunningham was the Royal Navy's best known figure. Moreover, though he often greeted new ideas with a firm 'No!', he generally accepted them after sleeping on them. He had been well tried in maritime air warfare and had presided over a small-ship armada in the three great landings, the great ships of the line mostly grey shadows lying beyond the horizon. He was sceptical and frequently scathing about modern technology but skilful at exploiting it, for example 'Ultra' at Matapan and the new concept of headquarters ships in the Mediterranean landings. He was an irascible and forceful admiral, but respected those who persisted in arguing their cases. He possessed unexpected depths of diplomatic skill, seen famously in defusing the fraught atmosphere between the French and the British at Alexandria in July 1940.[2] This patience, sagacity and native shrewdness, together with an observed modesty was evident when he went to Washington in June 1942, endearing him to the Americans so completely that there was a chorus for him to be ANCXF for 'Torch', a post to which he was appointed as a matter of course when it came to 'Husky', assuming a

[1]Adm Sir Max Horton (1883–1951): ent RN 1898; s/m spist; great success in *E9* 1914; *J6* 1915; *M1* 1917; CO, S/M Flo, Baltic 119–20; Capt 1920; 'K' boat flo 1922; CoS to Adm Keyes, C-in-C, Portsmouth; *Resolution* Med F; RA 1932; 2-in-C Home F 1934–5; 1CS, Med F 1935; VA 1936; Res F 1937–9; N Patrol 1939; FO S/M Jan 1940; refused C-in-C Home F because he wanted control of RAF Cstl Cmd Oct 1940; C-in-C W Apps 1942–5. See W. S. Chalmers, *Max Horton and the Western Approaches* (London, 1954).

[2]See M. A. Simpson (ed.), *The Cunningham Papers*, vol I, *The Mediterranean Fleet 1939–1942* (Aldershot, 1999), pp. 55–8, 86–97.

supervisory role in the invasions of Italy almost by right. He gained the admiration of Americans for the determined way in which he promoted inter-Allied relations and had frequently sat in council with his fellow commanders for over three years. While a brilliant tactician, he was adept at using a staff (one suspects it was because of his dislike for detailed deskwork) and had a broad and deep strategic vision which saw the fundamentals of the war with great clarity, such as realising that Germany had to be defeated on land after a substantial invasion. Though demanding on his staff, his inherent modesty would allow him to feel his way on the Chiefs of Staff Sub-Committee [141, 143, 147–9, 152].

Cunningham did not seek the post, abhorring desk work and a shore posting while feeling inadequate politically and inarticulate in committee meetings, as well as being bored by mountains of files. He did have a great sense of duty and was persuaded by many friends that he should fill the post. He was as apprehensive as Churchill about their relationship but was determined to offer firm resistance to the Prime Minister's often far-fetched ideas on strategy and tactics. With the First Lord, the genial Albert Alexander, devoted to the Royal Navy and a firm believer in Cunningham, he had a relationship in which their spheres were clearly defined, allowing them to respect each other, though they were otherwise as different as chalk from cheese [154]. Apart from prestige and celebrity, what told in his favour was his warm rapport with the Americans, now the senior partner in the western alliance, truly 'the arsenal of democracy' and who increasingly shored up the Royal Navy with ships, planes and equipment.[1] He needed all his skill and experience to extract what the Royal Navy needed from that cornucopia.

After a week or so of wrangling, Cunningham was finally appointed to the top post on 5 October and assumed duty on 17 October, after an emotional farewell in the Mediterranean. The Admiralty suffered no other change of personnel and it would have been impractical in wartime to reverse his predecessor's policies; nevertheless, Cunningham, who suspected the Admiralty had fallen into a rut, insisted on keeping his subordinates on their toes. There was a brisker step in Admiralty corridors after his arrival. He profited from longstanding acquaintance with many of those who served there and was able to slip into office without any major hiccup. Beginning his day at 0900, he conducted interviews until 1000 or 1030, when he attended the daily COS meeting. After lunch, there were further interviews, papers to be mastered

---

[1]'The Arsenal of Democracy' was a famous phrase used by President Franklin D. Roosevelt, 29 Dec 1940, while the USA was still neutral.

and a round of meetings. After dinner, the work continued, frequently ending in a drawn-out meeting of the COS with the 'Minister of Defence', starting at 2200 but finishing after midnight because of Churchill's long-winded soliloquies – hard going for Cunningham, who liked to be in bed by 2300. At least he could escape to wife, home and garden at The Palace House at Bishop's Waltham in Hampshire, the house they had acquired in 1938 but scarcely knew until late 1943.

141. *Rear Admiral Dalrymple-Hamilton to A. V. Alexander*

14 September 1943

If and when this question arises there appear to be three outstanding Flag Officers to choose from:

1.   Sir Andrew Cunningham (60.5 yrs)
2.   Sir John Tovey (58.5 yrs)
3.   Sir B. Fraser (57.5 yrs).

2.   Sir Andrew B. Cunningham seems the obvious choice on account of his outstanding pre-eminence in the eyes of the Service and the British public not to mention the Americans. The possible objections to his appointment, if they are objections, seem to be:

(A)   Whether his services can be spared from the Mediterranean.

(B)   Whether with his forceful personality he would be a difficult colleague to work with the PM and on the COS Committee.

(C)   The fact that he has only once served in the Admiralty for a comparatively short period.

As regards (A) I am not in a position to say but it appears to me that having spent three out of the four years of the war in the Mediterranean he might well be ready for a change and that a change would do him good.

The Italian Fleet having surrendered it is possible that there will shortly be a considerable reduction of Naval forces in that area and that the command might well devolve on a less Senior Officer.

As regards (B) this does not seem sufficient reason to deter the Navy's most distinguished Flag Officer from the post of First Sea Lord until it has been tried. If he had not a forceful personality he would not be where he is now.

As regards (C) Sir Andrew having a very quick and shrewd brain will make light of this disadvantage where a lesser man might fail. To me it does not appear that the objections can possibly outweigh the advantages and I feel it would be very difficult to explain to the Service and the public why he had not been chosen.

3.   Sir John Tovey also has a forceful personality but though well known would probably not command the confidence of the British public to the same extent as Sir Andrew. He has not had the same opportunities and his exploits are less known. He might have even more difficulty with the Prime Minister than Sir Andrew judging from past experience. He does however see things very clearly, is absolutely fearless in putting forward what he feels to be right and commands the confidence of the whole Service.

4. Sir Bruce Fraser having been ashore as Controller for the first three years of the war is, from no fault of his own, not quite as well known to the younger officers in the Service or the British public. He is younger than the other two Officers and has lately taken over command of the Home Fleet from which it would be a great pity to move him just as he has obtained the confidence of all the Commanding Officers, Officers and Men in that Fleet. He has great Admiralty experience and is of course well-known to all those in high places with whom he would have to deal. He has a first class brain and a delightful personality. I don't know how well known he is in America but imagine not particularly.

Many Officers I have spoken to seem to regard him as the obvious choice but I feel he should be regarded as the next First Sea Lord but one rather than come in now. This because I feel it important not to upset the personnel of the Home Fleet by two quick changes in command and that he would benefit by further time in high command at sea. All our First Sea Lords of recent years have spent two or three years as Commanders-in-Chief of the Main Fleets.

142. *Prime Minister's Personal Minute*

25 September 1943

First Lord

1. I have most carefully considered the question of filling Pound's vacancy, and I have no doubt whatever that we should offer it to Admiral Fraser. Admiral Cunningham has a great Command in the Mediterranean, and it would be wrong to remove him from the scene of action. He is an officer of the old school and of the pre-air age. This epoch finishes with Pound's four years of splendid service. We must move forward to younger men. Fraser is five years younger than Cunningham. These five years are very important.

2. We have not only to think of appointing a First Sea Lord but also a Chief of Naval Staff. The matter is therefore not one which concerns the Admiralty or Navy aspect alone. I doubt very much whether Admiral Cunningham for all his great qualities as a Commander, would be well suited to the prolonged, ceaseless work of the COS Committee which is the mainspring of our war-making machine. Fraser, on the other hand, I know will do all this very well. He is highly versed in the scientific and technical sides; he is patient on paper and in discussion; he was selected to command the Home

Fleet which contains our principal units; and he has been a year
with it as Second-in-Command and as Commander-in-Chief. He
therefore combines in a special manner the administrative and operational qualities.

3.   I should be glad therefore if it were possible for Admiral Fraser to
come up to London on Monday next in order that we may both have
talks with him.

143.   *A. V. Alexander to Churchill*

25 September 1943

I have your Minute No. M599/3 [above]. As you desire I am asking
Admiral Fraser to be here on Monday for consultation. The principal
argument in favour of the view you express is the five years' difference
in age. Before any final offer to Fraser is made I would ask you to
consider the following points.

1.   I asked Admiral Cunningham to go to Washington early in 1942 so
that he might work directly with the Combined Chiefs of Staff, get a
grip of the world strategy that you have to deal with, and incidentally
see whether he worked in harmony on such important staff matters. I
have heard nothing but praise from both the American and British
authorities for the manner in which Admiral Cunningham worked out
there. Moreover the result was the complete confidence of the Americans in his appointment as Allied Naval Commander-in-Chief for 'Torch'
and subsequent operations, all of which required the utmost concentration on the intricate and detailed methods of modern amphibious warfare
including the Air.

2.   Admiral Cunningham may have done his earlier naval service before the air had reached the stage of profound influence it occupies
today in sea as well as land operations but no Admiral in the whole of
the Royal Navy has had more experience of air operations over the sea
in this War. He was in command of the fleet which carried out the first
major attack on an enemy Fleet by ship-borne aircraft, at Taranto, used
aircraft carriers thereafter in many operations at sea and with the first of
our modern carriers the *Illustrious* and *Formidable*. Now, in 'Torch',
'Husky' and 'Avalanche', Cunningham has been in command of tremendous operations which in each case has involved the most carefully
prepared use of the Air, both by land and carrier-borne aircraft, and in
'Avalanche' for the first time the use of auxiliary carriers equipped with
fighters in support of the landing of assault forces. Nor do I suppose
any other Flag Officer has had to control an evacuation such as that

from Crete, or who better understands what air attack meant under such circumstances.[1]

3. I fully understand what you have in mind in your paragraph 2 and the need for a CNS who is not only competent to advise on detailed staff preparations for great operations and on general strategy but who is also likely to be *persona grata* with his colleagues. I can only say that no officer in the Navy today has so wide an experience of modern naval operations in this war as Admiral Cunningham. I have had no complaint from staff officers who have worked with him of any failure to get on with him and all those I have met who have worked under him, while admitting he works them hard, speak of him not only with respect but affection.

4. I agree with almost all you say about Admiral Fraser's qualities and competence. Moreover he is a great personal friend, can be 'hail-fellow-well-met' as well as any man I have known, but I should not describe him as one likely to be amenable on a matter on which he felt strongly. I had many battles with him when he was Controller, but we always remained friends.

5. Finally, let me say I have written at some length because the appointment to be made is of such supreme importance at this stage of the War. Experience in battle, achievements in the War and respect of the Fleet stand out strongly in support of Admiral Cunningham. Admiral Fraser is younger, well qualified professionally, has commanded an Aircraft Carrier as a Captain, but has only been at sea for fourteen months in the War and little more than six months as Commander-in-Chief. I shall be grateful if you will weigh up in your mind all the points I have put down as I feel I may not have put all of them adequately in my talk with you the other evening. We can only have one object in view, getting the best man to help secure the triumphant end of all our labours.

144. *Selection of new First Sea Lord:*

Note of Conversation between First Lord and Prime Minister

26 September [1943]

The Prime Minister said that he had carefully considered the First Lord's minute of the previous evening but remained convinced that the right course was to give the appointment to Admiral Fraser. Some

---

[1]See *Cunningham Papers*, I, esp. pp. 229–446.

discussion ensued on the relative merits of Admiral of the Fleet Sir Andrew Cunningham and Admiral Sir Bruce Fraser. One of the objections raised by the Prime Minister to the former was that he doubted whether Sir Andrew Cunningham possessed the temperament for amicable collaboration with the other members of the COS Committee. First Lord replied that he had never heard of any complaint that Admiral Cunningham was unco-operative: on the other hand his record both in Washington and still more in 'Torch', 'Husky' and 'Avalanche' suggested that he had considerable ability for working not only with the other Services but with high officers of other nationalities.

Continuing First Lord indicated that if the Prime Minister was fully satisfied that his preference was right, he had little more to say. He did, however, wish to emphasise two aspects of the matter.

(i)   He regarded it as essential that no risk should be run of creating a fresh division into two camps similar to the Beatty-Jellicoe schools.[1] The Prime Minister doubted whether there was any clear similarity between the circumstances of the present selection and those which led to the Beatty-Jellicoe factions.

(ii)   Supposing Admiral Fraser were the final selection First Lord felt that the Prime Minister would have a very difficult task in explaining to public opinion the passing over of Admiral Cunningham who, in his operational record, was bound in the public eye to be the natural successor to the highest professional post in the service. If of course Admiral Cunningham were offered the job and turned it down, that would be a different matter.

The Prime Minister undertook to consider what First Lord had said and to communicate with him again when he had done so, though his first reaction was to remain of the opinion that the appointment should go to Admiral Fraser.

145. *Draft Signal: from Churchill*

27 September 1943

Pound is unable to continue as First Sea Lord. In normal circumstances we should have no doubt having regard to your service record and fighting experience that you should succeed Pound. The situation in the

---

[1]The subordinates of Admirals of the Fleet Jellicoe and Beatty were divided sharply in their views of Jutland, at which both admirals were present. Much ink was spilt upon the controversy.

Mediterranean and the extent to which operations may develop there make it extremely difficult to decide whether to ask you to return or to remain in that important sphere. Without prejudice to the final decision I would be grateful for your frank view observing that your co-operation with the American and French Authorities has been most valuable to us.

146.   *Prime Minister to the King*

4 October 1943

Mr Churchill with his humble duty to Your Majesty has deeply considered what advice he should give about a new First Sea Lord. Having resolved various alternatives, he has no doubt whatsoever that Admiral of the Fleet Sir Andrew Cunningham, GCB, DSO and bar, is the outstanding naval figure who should fill that Office now. He has had long conversations with Sir Andrew, and has been more than ever impressed with his grasp of the naval situation and with his many qualities. He is sure that the Admiral is in full sympathy and accord with the broad lines of policy and strategy which are now being pursued, not without success, in many theatres.

Should Your Majesty be pleased to accept this advice the First Lord of the Admiralty, who as Your Majesty knows is in entire accord with it, will take the necessary steps to submit a new Patent for the Board of Admiralty.

147.   *From Noble*

BAD,
British Naval Staff,
CCS Building,
Washington, DC,
1 October 1943

. . . In the words of Winston, when he was out here the other day, 'we are in the position of a man who has suddenly succeeded to two fortunes, the Italian Fleet and the British Fleet which has been containing it so long'! . . .

Now I see that Dudley Pound has gone sick and as I saw him out here only a few weeks ago, I of course know that he is far from well – he has had a long bout in a most trying position and if he should be unable to go on, I assume that you will, in due course, take his place.

That is what the whole Navy would like to see, but I know that you personally would view the suggestion with some distaste! All the same, for the good of everyone, you ought to do it if it comes your way.

148. *From Tovey*

Admiralty House,
Chatham,
5 October 1943

. . . I have been dreading that the blinking politicians would find some excuse for not putting you where you should have been long ago, and I had my plans all ready for leading a mutiny.

As you know I have crossed swords with D[udley] P[ound] more than once but never have I wished him a sad end. I am terribly sorry for him, though he would wish nothing better than to wear himself out in the service of the Navy. He is truly a most gallant man.

. . . you take up your new appointment with the complete trust and deep affection of every officer and man in the Service.

For goodness sake don't overwork or let the PM persuade you to keep his own unnatural hours. . . .

149. *From Dill*

British Joint Services Mission,
Washington,
18 October 1943

. . . Of course added to your vast sea experience and knowledge, your understanding of the Americans, . . . will stand you in good stead as First Sea Lord. It is odd but a fact that the Americans know and I think understand Britain better than Britain understands America.

In council with – shall I call him the Minister of Defence? – you will have great difficulty in controlling your hackles! Perhaps it will be best if you don't attempt to control them entirely. King fortunately will take more from you than from any other British Sea Officer. He does not get any easier as time goes on and the strength of the American Navy grows. Percy Noble handles King well but cannot really make a friend of him – who could? And yet in a great many ways I like King and have a great deal of respect for his ability. However as long as he remains in his present position he is going to give us a lot of trouble. . . .

150. *To Aunt Doodles*

En route from Algiers,
23 October 1943

... We are going to be very occupied with Dudley Pound's funeral next week ... Poor man[,] it was a good thing the end came so soon and very appropriate that he should have passed out on Trafalgar Day. He did a great work for the country and kept things steady during the dark days.

151. *To Aunt Doodles*

Bishop's Waltham,
1 November 1943

... we had the Abbey service. Procession from the Admiralty. A fine misty day and the old Abbey looked wonderful in the half light. A fine service of about an hour.

At Portsmouth the procession was from the *Victory* to the Southern Railway jetty where the cruiser *Glasgow* was lying[,] then on board and to sea about 30 miles out where there was a committal service. Lady Pound's ashes were committed with his, very appropriate – she had worked hard for the sailors and their wives.[1]

152. *To Somerville*

19 December 1943

... I have the feeling that the former [Churchill] bitterly regrets his choice (it wasn't his really, he chose Bruce Fraser) of CNS. ....

153. *From Noble*

BAD, Washington,
23 December 1943

... It may interest you to know that Pound actually gave up the unequal contest here with me at Washington. ....

[1]*Glasgow*: csr, 1937, 9100t, 32k, 12×6in, 8×4in, 6×21in tt. There are hardly any Pound papers, as under his will they were destroyed by his executors, Cunningham and Dalrymple-Hamilton, but see R. Brodhurst, *Churchill's Anchor* (Barnsley, Yorks., 2000).

I got him to go and see the PM immediately . . .

. . . I had heard something of what you told me regarding the arguments pro and con you being made First Sea Lord, and in a way I am not surprised – a strong man is not always greatly welcomed in these days! . . .

154. *To Aunt Doodles*

Admiralty,
15 March 1944

We had Alexander the First Lord to lunch in the [First Sea Lord's] flat on Thursday and Willis my old Chief of Staff who is now Second Sea Lord. Alexander is a queer fish rather a rough diamond but his little wife is very nice. . . .

SECTION B

CHURCHILL, THE CHIEFS OF STAFF
AND THE COMBINED CHIEFS OF STAFF
OCTOBER 1943–MAY 1946

Churchill's and Cunningham's mutual misgivings about working together were reinforced during the years 1943–45. Cunningham shared
the general military exasperation with the Prime Minister's romantic
strategic verbiage, impractical notions, absurd prejudices and ignorant interference [155, 158, 160–1, 163–4, 170, 173–4, 187–8].
Cunningham vented his ire in letters to close friends like Somerville
or in his diary and it seems that he (and his service associates) never
had a good word to say for Churchill. The ultimate truth, however,
was in Cunningham's admission (echoed by other service chiefs) that
'With all his faults (and he is the most infuriating man) he has done a
great job for the country *and besides there is no one else*' [editor's
italics] [162].

Cunningham and his colleagues disagreed with the 'Minister of Defence' about almost everything. Many examples of their battles will
occur later but temper, childishness, lack of trust, wilful ignorance,
irrelevance, time wasting, dictatorial behaviour, bad advice and schoolboy fantasies are just a sample of the faults of which the Prime Minister
stood accused. There were specific disputes, too, over appointments,
manpower, the nature of the war against Japan, naval support for the
Normandy landings, anti-submarine devices and maritime air power.
Cunningham proved a more obdurate if less wily opponent than Dudley
Pound and his response to the Prime Minister's 'prayers' was always
likely to be a blunt 'No'.

Despite Cunningham's (and the Prime Minister's) apprehensions over
the new First Sea Lord's relationship with his colleagues on the Chiefs
of Staff Sub-Committee (COS), Field Marshal Sir Alan Brooke, the
chairman and CIGS, and Marshal of the Royal Air Force Sir Charles
Portal, CAS, the partnership proved a smooth one – not least because
all three were united in frequent opposition to the Prime Minister[189].[1]

[1]FM Viscount (Sir Alan Brooke) Alanbrooke (1883–1963): R Art; Lt Col 1918; Maj
Gen 1935; Mobile Div 1937; Lt Gen 1938, AA Cmd; C-in-C, S Cmd Aug 1939; cdr 2
Corps, BEF Sept 1939; C-in-C, Home Forces July 1940; CIGS Dec 1941–Jan 1946;
FM1944. A. Danchev & D. Todman (eds), *War Diaries, 1939–1945: Field Marshal Lord
Alanbrooke* (London, 2001); D. Fraser, *Alanbrooke* (London, 1982).

Service on the COS carried with it attendance at the CCS and brought Cunningham into contact – and conflict – with his old sparring partner, Admiral Ernest J. King, Chief of Naval Operations of the US Navy and, by the time of Cunningham's appointment as First Sea Lord, the 'senior partner' in the maritime alliance. Not only was the US Navy now larger than the Royal Navy, it was continuing to expand at a geometric rate. Moreover, its equipment, from ships to air conditioning, from aircraft to soda fountains was often better and more ample. Its officers increasingly dubbed the Royal Navy second class, outdated, and unwilling and incapable of fighting in the Pacific. They had lost any pre-war awe and jealousy of Britannia's navy and now, bolstered by their burgeoning strength and their emphatic victories again the Imperial Japanese Navy, were becoming mightily confident. King himself said little about the relationship and there were many instances of co-operation and offers to help – but there were also examples of arbitrary action [156–9, 167–9, 186]. King was not a man to be liked, even by his fellow Americans – and it hardly bothered him. Cunningham did his best to work with him, but was unable to form a friendship with him; dealing with his 'oppo' was one of the two crosses that came with the post of First Sea Lord, living with the Prime Minister being the other burden.

Cunningham attended the wartime conferences of Churchill, Roosevelt and Stalin held at Cairo, Tehran, Quebec, Yalta and Potsdam. Most of the great strategic questions had been settled by this time and those that were not, such as the decisions to invade Normandy and southern France, were decided against Churchill's wishes; the two emerging super-powers now set the agenda and the timetable. Much of the time at these meetings was spent tackling post-war diplomatic and political issues; the military men became virtual spectators [163–70, 172, 180–6].

Mshl of RAF Viscount (Sir Charles) Portal (1893–1971): RFC 1914–18; RAF 1918; AVM, Air Mem Personnel 1939; A/AM Sept 1939; C-in-C, Bbr Cmd April 1940; ACM & CAS Oct 1940; M of RAF Jan 1944; ret 1945. D. Richards, *Portal of Hungerford* (London, 1977).

155. *To Somerville*

19 December 1943

P.S.: Life is not a bed of roses here. The COS and high ups are at complete loggerheads about the Pacific v. SEAC strategy.

The 'Axiom' team were accepted as heaven-sent by the PM and his chorus of yes men and there has been some pretty good tripe talked.[1]

156. *To Noble*

3 January 1944

... As you say, there are some good men there [in the Navy Department] but the man at the top is, in my opinion, impossible. . . .

157. *To Blake*

18 January 1944

... My oppo gets more and more difficult. There is no question he dislikes us and does not want us in the Pacific although as you know that was a 'Sextant' decision.[2] But he is stalling as long as possible when going through that intelligent process of biting off his nose to spite his face.

158. *Diary*

29 May 1944

... Found another memorandum from the PM refusing to let James Somerville be relieved, such stupid reasons – he is quite childish sometimes. However we must return to the charge.

---

[1]'Axiom': mission devised by Mountbatten and led by his deputy, Gen Albert C. Wedemeyer, US Army, attempting to persuade London & Washington to back major operations in SE Asia, to no avail.

[2]'Sextant': summit conf, Cairo Nov 1943.

159. *Diary*

9 June 1944

. . . Went to Euston to meet the 1940 train from Holyhead bringing the US COS. Marshall as charming as ever and King as saturnine. I can't bring myself to like that man. . . .

160. *Diary*

6 July 1944

. . . Meeting with the PM to discuss Alexander's operations in Italy and strategy for the war against Japan. There is no doubt the PM was in no state to discuss anything. Very tired and too much alcohol. Meeting started unpropitiously by Brooke calling him to order by undermining generals in command at Cabinet meetings by his criticisms. This obviously hurt him badly. But he was in a terrible mood. Rude and sarcastic. I had a couple of blow-ups with him about the Far East. The net result was that we sat from 2200 to 0145 listening to him mostly talking nonsense and got nowhere. . . .

161. *Diary*

14 August 1944

. . . Cabinet meeting at 1730. Such a change with Attlee in the chair.[1] Everyone who wished gave his opinion and yet business was expeditiously accomplished.

162. *Diary*

29 August 1944

. . . Went to Northolt at 1745 to meet PM. . . . He certainly looked ill. The First Lord who went over to Downing Street after dinner said he saw Moran still there and two nurses and a specialist has been sent for.[2] I hope it is only wise precaution. It would be tragedy if anything

[1]Earl (Clement) Attlee (1883–1967): Maj 1914–18; Lab MP London (Limehouse) 1922; Ldr Lab Pty 1935; Dep PM, Lord Privy Seal, Lord Pres of Cncl & Sec St for Doms 1940–5; Lab PM 1945–51; Earl 1955.
[2]Lord Moran (Charles Wilson) (1882–1977): MO, R Fus 1914–17; Dean, St Mary's

should happen to him now. With all his faults (and he is the most infuriating man) he has done a great job for the country and besides there is no one else.

163. *Diary*

RMS *Queen Mary*,
5 September 1944

Talk with PM in his saloon [en route to Greenock] from about 1100 to 1230. If he keeps up his present attitude things should go well in Quebec and it will be what the Americans call a 'love feast'. But it takes little to rouse his vengeful temper and he will do anything then to get the better of our allies. . . .

164. *Diary*

RMS *Queen Mary*,
8 September 1944

. . . COS meeting at 1030 followed by one with the PM at 1215. He was in his worst mood. Accusing the COS of ganging up against him and keeping papers from him and so on. Would not see that Italy after Kesselring is again defeated becomes a secondary front and the real work is on the Russian and Western fronts. Wants at all costs to keep armies up to full strength even though there are more divisions than the Army can use. Is determined to have an amphibious operation to take Istria though it is of no military consequence and so on and so on. The worst of it is his feeling against the Americans whom he accuses of doing the most awful things against the British. There is no question he is not well and is feeling this hot sticky weather.

A peaceful afternoon and evening.

Hosp, 1920–45; personal physician to PM May 1940; Lord 1943. Churchill was seriously ill several times in the war – mostly, as here, from pneumonia. L. Rose, *Churchill: An Unruly Life* (London, 1994).

165. *Diary*

Quebec,
12 September 1944

COS meeting at 1030 and a first meeting with the US COS at noon. Found them in a most accommodating mood and had no disputes. . . . Continued the meeting after lunch and again had a successful meeting. The outcome of the day's work being that we got an undertaking that the four US divisions would be left under Alexander well after the present operations and the amphibious lift would be left in the Mediterranean for an attack on Istria.

Had a meeting with the PM at 1830 and found him in a mood of sweet reasonableness.

166. *Diary*

Quebec,
13 September 1944

. . . Plenary meeting at 1130. PM led off and gave quite a good review. He offered the British main fleet for operations against Japan in the central Pacific and it was at once accepted by the President. . . . Meeting with the US COS in the afternoon very friendly.

167. *Diary*

Quebec,
14 September 1944

. . . CCOS meeting at 1030. All went well till the use of the British Navy in the central Pacific was raised. King flew into a temper. It couldn't be allowed there. He wouldn't have it and so on. I called his attention to the President's acceptance of the PM's offer. He tried to make out that the acceptance did not mean what it said. Then he fell foul of Marshall on the Task Force in the South West Pacific proposal and they nearly had words. In fact King made an ass of himself and having the rest of the US COS against him had to give way to the fact that the fleet would operate in the central Pacific but with such a bad grace. . . .

168. *Diary*

Quebec,
15 September 1944

COS meeting at 0930 followed by CCOS at 1030. Everything went sweetly. Americans had some good news from Admiral Halsey in the Pacific and are advancing the date of [their] attack on the Philippines.[1]

A quiet day until a meeting with Admiral King and his staff at 1630. But things went smoothly and we had a very useful exchange of ideas. He was more or less resigned to having the British Fleet in the Pacific. We exchanged ideas on landing craft, escort carriers, bases in Australia and zones of occupation in Germany and American participation in the naval disarmament.

169. *Meeting between Admiral Ernest J. King, US Navy, and Cunningham*

Quebec,
15 September 1944

1. *Naval Facilities in Australia and Forward Areas*

(a) *Main Bases*

Admiral Cunningham stated British requirements in Australia for the fleet.

In the discussion which followed it was clear that the US Navy used Sydney chiefly for battle repair, but had larger interests in Brisbane, where General MacArthur's HQ were located. It was not known in Washington to what extent Commander 7th Fleet still required all the facilities which had been established in Australia; a great deal of the covered storages which have been built were occupied by the USAAF.[2]

---

[1]F Adm William F ('Bull') Halsey, jr, US Navy (1882–1959): grad N Acad 1904; Gt White F 1907–9; Lt 1909; destroyer cmds, inc Queenstown force 1918; Capt 1927; N & A War Colls 1932–4; pilot 1935; *Saratoga* 1935–7; Cdt Pensacola NAS 1937–8; RA 1938; carrier sqdn cmds, Pac F 1938–43; Adm Nov 1942; C-in-C , S Pac 1943; 3rd F June 1944; F Adm Dec 1945; ret 1947. E. B. Potter, *Bull Halsey* (Annapolis, MD, 1985).

[2]Gen Douglas MacArthur, US Army (1880–1964): W Point 1899–1903; engr; svd Philippines; Gen Staff 1913–17; Col 1917; Brig Gen, AEF 1917–18; Supt W Point 1919; Philippines 1922–30; Maj Gen 1925; COS Nov 1930–Oct 1934; Mil Advsr, Philippines Govt 1935; Cdr US army in FE July 1941; SAC, SWPA March 1942–April 1945; Gen of A Dec 1944; Sup Cdr, Allied Powers in Japan 1945–51; UN C-in-C, Korea 1950–1; relieved of all cmds by Pres Truman April 1951 following disputes over policy & strategy. (fn concludes overleaf)

Admiral King said he would make enquiries as to the release and availability of storage and facilities and would also act as agent in any problems arising in connection with airfields and storage at present used by the USAAF.

(b) *Forward Bases*

Forward bases in the Pacific for the British Fleet were then discussed. This presented a difficult problem. Espiritu Santo was still in use but to a decreasing extent; Majuro was a good anchorage but had few facilities. These and other anchorages might be used by the British Fleet, though the exact locality would depend on the area in which operations were being carried out.

(c) *Landing Craft Bases*

Moreton Bay, near Brisbane, and Cairns had been used as training bases, but had probably been closed down. These should be available if required.

(d) *Darwin*

This port was now used as an advanced fuelling base for submarines. Stocks of torpedoes were also maintained; otherwise, there were no US naval facilities there.

(e) *The Torres Strait*

Admiral King stated that considerable progress had been made in surveying and improving the passages north of Australia. On his return to the UK, Admiral Crutchley had given the opinion that battleships could now use the Torres Strait.[1]

2. *Use of American Aircraft in British Carriers*

Admiral Cunningham stated that it had been decided to equip the four fleet carriers in the Eastern Fleet with Avenger aircraft and that it was hoped to equip still more. The Barracuda was excellent for torpedo

---

Cdr 7th Fleet: Adm T. C. Kinkaid, US Navy (1888–1972): battleships 1907–13; ordnce engr 1913–17; Lt att Ady 1917–18; N War Coll 1929–30; *Indianapolis* 1937–8; NA Rome 1938–March 1941; Des Sqdn 8 June–Nov 1941; RA Cru Div 6, Pac F; Coral Sea, Midway; Cdr TF 16, *Enterprise*; Guadalcanal Aug–Nov 1942; Cdr N Pac Force Jan 1943; Aleutians; VA June 1943; Cdr Allied N Forces, SWPA & 7 F Nov 1943; Philippines 1944; Adm April 1945; E Sea Fr Jan–June 1946; Atl Res F Jan 1947–May 1950; ret 1950.

[1]Adm Sir Victor Crutchley (1893–1976): *Centurion* Jutland 1916; *Vindictive* Zeebrugge 1918 & VC; *Diomede* NZ; m/s & fishy protn 1935–7; *Warspite* 1937–40; Cdre Devonport RN Barracks 1940–2; RA Australian Sqdn 1942–4; VA & FO Gibraltar 1945–7; Adm & ret 1947.

attack but lacked speed and radius of action. Admiral King explained that Avenger aircraft were in short supply and that there were not enough to meet all the needs of the US Fleet. He understood that British requirements had been lodged in Washington and promised to give such requests most careful consideration.[1]

3. *LSTs*

The present employment of LSTs in 'Overlord' was discussed. Admiral King stated that the US LSTs already promised would be turned over, but he was not certain whether these particular LSTs would still be required by SCAEF. It was agreed that all the LSTs required by SCAEF might not be fully employed, especially with the advent of winter weather and the opening of extra ports. It was undesirable that a considerable reserve should be kept for contingencies.

The US and British Senior Planners were instructed to draft a telegram for examination by the CCS the following day, pointing out the urgency of release for accelerated operations in the Pacific, and prospective plans in SEAC and requesting SCAEF to forward a report on this matter.

4. *CVEs*

Admiral Cunningham said that three British CVEs required extensive repair and that the remainder were fully employed operationally or on ferrying duties. It was considered that the shipping of naval aircraft to the Far East was likely to be a major commitment for some time to come. He promised that Admiral King should be informed immediately if any British CVEs could be spared. In these circumstances British crews could not be made available. Admiral King said that the difficulty could be overcome when the time comes.

5. *Special Mosquito Aircraft*

. . . Admiral Cunningham said that he would arrange for the film of these aircraft to be sent to Admiral Noble who would arrange for it to be shown to the US Chiefs of Staff.[2]

---

[1]Fairey Barracuda: TBR, 1943–5, 1640hp, 686m, 228mph, 3 crew, 1500lbs/1620lb t, 2mg.

Grumman Avenger: TBR, 1942–5, 1850hp, 1020m, 271mph, 3 crew, 2000lbs/1920lb t, 5mg.

As can be seen, the Avenger had a far better range. It was also a more heavily armed, faster and more versatile plane.

[2]De Havilland Mosquito: F/B, 1941–5, 2×1290hp, 2 crew, 1370m, 408mph, 4000lbs.

6. Bonaventure *and X-craft*

In discussions it was decided that opportunities for the employment of X-craft might arise and Admiral King suggested that the flotilla should proceed to the Pacific with the British Fleet. Admiral Cunningham said he would make the necessary arrangements.[1]

7. *Occupation of Germany*

Admiral Cunningham described the system of control which it was proposed to establish in Berlin for the disarmament of Germany. He was of the opinion that the tripartite military committee in Berlin should consist of nine officers – the senior officers of the land, sea and air forces of the US, UK and the Soviet. Each admiral on the committee would be responsible for naval disarmament in his zone. Whatever the decision as to allocation of zones, it had never been the British intention to exclude the US Navy from taking part in the naval disarmament of Germany. Admiral King stated that he considered these proposals entirely appropriate.

Admiral Cunningham then gave brief details as to how he considered the German ports should be administered. He suggested that Flag Officers should be established at Kiel and Wilhelmshaven, who could conveniently control the ports in the vicinity.

Admiral King stated that he did not wish to establish any elaborate organisation in Germany which would be difficult to liquidate at a later stage. He wanted the US Navy to take part in the disarmament of German naval installations and also to take over such ports as were necessary for supplying the US forces of occupation. He would provide the necessary port parties for this purpose.

Admiral King stated that there were two distinct requirements – disarmament which the US Navy would carry out in conjunction with British forces under the zonal organisation; and the operation of ports for the purposes of supply, which was purely an American administrative matter. Admiral Cunningham was in entire agreement and added that the Belgian and Dutch authorities were being encouraged to open up and operate their own ports to the greatest extent practicable and that this would result in considerable saving in the provision of port parties. It was accepted that this was most desirable.

[1]*Bonaventure*: X-craft depot ship, 1943, 10423t, 10k, 2×4in. X-craft (actually XE, for svc in FE): midget s/m, 4 crew.

170. *Diary*

16 September 1944

Final CCOS conference at 1100 where we tied up loose ends and everything went very happily. Then to the Citadel for the final plenary meeting. We first had a meeting with the PM when he read out a document he was putting in about Burma. Very inaccurate and rather off the point. The President looked very frail and hardly looked to be taking in what was going on. . . .

171. *Diary*

3 October 1944

. . . Betty Stark came in at 1600. I was rather firm with him about COMINCH's suggestion of having a separate zone of responsibility for US squadrons employed on A/S operations, the US idea being that they should work under Kirk from France and not in Coastal [Command]. I told Betty I would firmly resist any such idea. . . .[1]

172. *Diary*

3 November 1944

. . . The President has arranged with Stalin for a meeting between 15 November and 15 December, Stalin refuses to go [on] a long journey so President suggests, without liking it, that we should go in battleships to a Crimean or a Black Sea port.

I have sent a minute to him [the Prime Minister] deprecating the Black Sea or the Aegean on account of mines and weather. . . .

173. *Diary*

4 November 1944

. . . CIGS told us that the PM had now completely changed round and decided to send Jumbo Wilson to relieve Dill.[1] Of course the only

---

[1] Adm Alan G. Kirk: Capt & NA, UK 1939–40; N Dept 1941; RA & cdr WNTF, Normandy June 1944; Cdr, US N Forces, France Sept 1944.

[2] FM Sir H. M. Wilson ('Jumbo') (1881–1964): Lt Gen, Br Troops in Egypt Sept 1939; Mil Govr, Cyrenaica 1940–1; GOC Greece 1941; GOC Palestine & Transjordan

reason for this is to get Wilson out of the way and appoint Alexander Supreme Commander, Mediterranean, a post for which he is totally unfitted. We balked this in Cairo last year but it looks as if CIGS and the PM have agreed on this together. I may however be maligning Brooke.

This is a good example of the way things are run now. The COS are just told what to do. In this case where it is proposed to put a man in command of the air and naval forces as well as the army I hold that the CAS and CNS should be consulted and heard.

174. *Diary*

7 November 1944

... Staff meeting with PM at 2230. I put forward my objections to Alexander as Supreme Commander, Mediterranean. These were received calmly by the PM who merely said he recognised my right through knowledge of the personalities to criticise the appointment but that he disagreed with me. He was not to be moved though I rubbed it in again later. The tragedy is that CAS and CIGS agree with me but decided to take the line of least resistance. The upshot was the PM had his way. ...

PM wants Ramsay away from SHAEF. Why?[1]

175. *Diary*

4 December 1944

... Dinner in Admiralty House. The Board of Admiralty dining the Prime Minister in recognition of his 70th birthday. PM sat between First Lord and myself. He was very cheerful and amusing. First Lord spoke well and PM replied and gave us a hopeful outlook for the Navy's future but warned that we must take the air into account. ... I thanked him for the encouraging things he had said about the Navy's future and assured him that in spite of his sometimes bad remarks I had always known that he was basically sound. I also assured him that we did take

May 1941; Syria June–Aug 1941; Gen Dec 1941; 9 Army, Levant; Persia-Iraq Cmd Aug 1942; C-in-C ME Jan 1943; SAC Med Jan 1944; Head, JSM Dec 1944–7; FM Jan 1945. Dill had died in Washington in Nov 1944.
[1]Probably because the PM considered the post redundant. Cunningham had a dispute with him over this after Ramsay's death.

the air into account. That we looked on it as our future principal weapon and would demand our share of it. . . .

176. *Diary*

10 December 1944

Found that Ernie King had brought off one of his best by ordering that the American LSTs in the Mediterranean cease taking British troops and supplies to Greece. This signal was later cancelled by the intervention of Harry Hopkins.[1] The PM had sent him a message.

177. *Diary*

11 December 1944

COS meeting at 1030. We discussed COMINCH's unilateral signal. Hopkins had asked the PM that there should be no recriminations and the PM had agreed. I pointed out however that this action of King's had made the whole system of command in the Mediterranean illusory so it was decided to send a message to this effect to Somerville for him to use as ammunition if it ever became necessary. . . .

178. *Diary*

13 December 1944

. . . A letter from James Somerville. He *is* getting under Ernie King's skin. He says there is genuine anxiety over these suicide bombers and there was some talk about our armoured carriers being able to stand up to them.

179. *Diary*

16 January 1945

. . . Betty Stark came in at 1800 chiefly to gather information to send to King. King likes to get information but refuses to part with it.

---

[1]Harry L. Hopkins (1890–1946): soc wkr, New York City; headed New Deal relief programmes 1933–8; Sec Commerce 1938–40; pers asst & roving amb for Roosevelt 1940–5; head, Lend-Lease 1941.

180. *Diary*

30 January 1945

... [PM] has a temperature and went straight on board the cruiser *Orion* where I gather he has made himself fairly comfortable.[1] COS meeting at 1030 and meeting with the US COS at 1200. ... Further meeting with US COS at 1430. We had no serious differences. I gave a short disquisition on the U-boat war. ...

181. *Diary*

Yalta, Crimea,
4 February 1945

... Plenary meeting at the US villa, which is the Czar's, at 1700. The President was asked to take the chair. ... I dotted the 'I's' and crossed the 't's' of Marshall's U-boat statement and was complimented by the PM on its clarity. ... Stalin was good and clear in his points, the PM also very good but the President does not appear to know what he is talking about, and hangs on to one idea.

182. *Diary*

Yalta, Crimea,
5 February 1945

... Meeting at the Soviet villa (Usopoff's, the man who killed Rasputin). ... Had a long talk with Kusnetsieff, the Chief of the Soviet Naval Staff.[2] He was very anxious to learn about the Hun U-boats so I gave him a good account and also about the midgets, etc., operating off Antwerp. ...

---

[1]*Orion*; csr, 1934, 7215t, 32.5k, 8×6in, 8×4in, 8×21in tt; a veteran of the Med Fleet, 1940–1.
[2]Adm Kuznetsiev, Soviet N. [no further information available]

183. *Diary*

Yalta, Crimea,
6 February 1945

Held a meeting with US COS at 1000. . . . The oil question was also discussed and General Somervell out of the blue produced new proposals cutting the British Admiralty oil and the RAF aviation spirit.[1] Portal indignantly rejected the proposals and I backed him on behalf of the Admiralty. It was agreed that a committee of three on either side should examine the matter and report. We chose Leathers, James Somerville and an RAF planner.[2]

We went to a meeting at the Soviet villa of the three staffs. . . . King gave a short account of the war in the Pacific. . . .

Discussed the oil situation with James [Somerville] after lunch . . .

In the meantime the big three appear to be getting on pretty well.

184. *Diary*

Yalta, Crimea,
8 February 1945

COS meeting at 1100. I had two brushes with Leathers, one about oil and the other about the fleet train being included in the shipping paper with no corresponding entry against the USA. Some slippery work as usual.

Met the US COS at noon and everything went as merrily as a bell. Complete agreement on all matters on the agenda.

Had a talk with King and he informed me it was not his intention to assign the British [Pacific] fleet to the first phase of the operation against the islands south of Japan. This starts on 15 March. His reason is that he is uncertain of what MacArthur is going to do. I [don't] doubt he is up to his usual game of trying to keep us out of it. Spruance has apparently asked for our fleet. . . .[3]

[1]Gen Brehon B. Somervell, US Army: engr; Brig, Gen Staff Nov 1941; Chief, Army Service Force, 1942–5.

[2]Lord (Frederick J.) Leathers (1883–1965): self-made coal & shipowner; known to Churchill pre-war; adviser on shipping in both wars; Baron & M War Tpt May 1941; S St Tpt, Fuel & Power 1951–3; Visct 1954.

[3]Adm Raymond A. Spruance, US Navy; grad N Acad 1907; CO *Bainbridge* 1913; Asst Engnrg O, New York NY 1917–18; CO *Mississippi* 1938; Cdr, 10 N Dist (San Juan) 1940–1; RA, Cru Div, TF 16, Pac F; CoS & DC-in-C, Pac F; C-in-C, 5 F 1943–5.

185. *Diary*

Yalta, Crimea,
9 February 1945

Meeting with King at 1000. Discussed and reached agreement on various points. Rather disappointing that he will not assign the BPF to the first stage of 'Iceberg' (the capture of the Bonin and Rykuyu Islands). I mistrust him rather. . .

186. *Full Account of a Meeting between Admiral King and the First Sea Lord*

Livadia Palace,
Yalta, Crimea,
9 February 1945

Heavy Repair Ships
The First Sea Lord explained the position from the British point of view, pointing out the need for the last three ships which had now been assigned to the Americans.

Admiral King pointed out that if these ships were built to British requirements they were not altogether interchangeable. The controlling factor, however, was the damage being sustained by the American Fleet in the Pacific which made it essential for him to retain the three ships in question.

The First Sea Lord said he fully understood the American difficulties but the fact remained that the BPF would now be short of three Heavy Repair ships. It seemed to him that the needs of the two Fleets should be weighed against each other. The First Sea Lord then asked whether Admiral King intended converting any further hulls. Admiral King replied that no further conversions were intended or contemplated. So many conversions, already done and in hand, had made serious inroads into cargo shipping and further conversions were not possible. In reply to a question, Admiral King said it took about nine months to convert a hull into an HR ship.

Admiral King then said that to help the British [Pacific] Fleet, he would carry out an immediate investigation to see whether, by squeezing American resources, he would be able to transfer any HR ships. When the American base was completed in Samar about July, the additional repair facilities on shore should make it possible to transfer at least one ship.

The First Sea Lord thanked Admiral King and said that this would coincide with the completion of the deployment of the BPF.

Information Concerning Fleet Operations in the Pacific

The First Sea Lord explained the need for the Admiralty to have full information concerning Fleet operations in the Pacific, now that the BPF was to operate in that area.

Admiral King fully understood the Admiralty wishes and undertook to send a daily signal to the Admiralty giving the information required by the First Sea Lord. . . . Admiral King further explained that it would be impracticable to transmit certain detailed information by signal, in which case he would pass it to Admiral Somerville.

Anti-Submarine Support Forces in the Atlantic

The First Sea Lord explained that British A/S forces could compete with the present scale of U-boat attack without American help in the Atlantic, but he would be grateful if Admiral King would confirm his offer, signalled last October, to make three support groups available for operations in the Atlantic. If the need should arise, owing to an increase in U-boat activity, he would suggest that the C-in-C, Western Approaches, and Admiral Ingram (CINCLANT) should deal directly with each other in deciding the best way to employ the American support groups.[1] He himself felt that it would probably be best if they relieved British ships engaged on ocean convoy escort duties.

Admiral King fully agreed and confirmed that Admiral Ingram was ready at any moment to implement Admiral King's offer. This he could do at the request of the C-in-C, Western Approaches, without further reference to Washington.

The First Sea Lord thanked Admiral King for what he had said.

A short discussion then followed on the U-boat situation in which Admiral King expressed the view that the training of A/S forces was of the greatest importance. Captain Grantham pointed out that training was being hampered by the insistence of the U-boats in operating in our training areas.[2]

---

[1] C-in-C WA: Adm Sir Max Horton.

Adm Jonas Ingram, US Navy: grad N Acad 1907; *New York* 1917–18; cded destroyers & sqdns 1924–36; CO *Tennessee* 1940; RA csr div 1941; VA Feb 1942; Cdr S Atl Force; C-in-C Atl Nov 1944–Sept 1945; ret 1947.

[2] Adm Sir Guy Grantham: Capt 1937; Ady 1939; NA to FL 1940; *Phoebe* June 1940; Capt & CSO 15CS, *Cleopatra* March 1942; *Indomitable* & CoS, Home F Carriers Aug 1943; DPD April 1944; VCNS 1954; C-in-C Med 1955.

It was agreed that the Russian advance along the Baltic coast would lessen the possibility of the scale of the U-boat attack becoming serious.

Richelieu[1]

The First Sea Lord explained his intention of sailing the *Richelieu* to the Indian Ocean as soon as she had completed her refit and had worked up in the Mediterranean.

Admiral King expressed his full agreement with this move, but said he could not yet agree to the *Richelieu* being employed in the Pacific Theatre.

The First Sea Lord said that this was not his intention at this stage but that he might wish to discuss the *Richelieu's* future employment later on if it became desirable to transfer her to the Pacific. She was a fine ship and her Radar efficiency had been considerably improved during her present refit.

Admiral King was agreeable to the First Sea Lord's suggestion and gave his views on the political aspect of French participation in the war in the Pacific. These he did not wish recorded (but his description of a certain American senior officer merits special mention. He referred to him as a man who was 'nobody's Watch but everybody's Mess').[2]

Assignment of Fleet Fighters

The First Sea Lord said he did not wish to discuss this matter fully as he did not have the necessary detailed information available. He would, however, like to say that he was most disappointed to hear that Admiral King was contemplating reducing or suspending agreed assignments of Fleet Fighters to the British. He would like to send the Fifth Sea Lord to Washington for a full discussion of American and British assignments.[3]

Admiral King explained that the number of fighters in each Fleet Carrier had greatly increased. Starting at 36, the number had first risen to 54, and finally last November, Admiral King had agreed to Admiral Nimitz's suggestion that it should be further increased to 72. This fact was responsible for the present shortage. The increase in fighters was made necessary as the American Fleet moved forward to areas where many Japanese airfields existed. It would be fully three months before the American Carriers were equipped with the increased numbers. Admiral King pointed out that the offensive power of the carrier was little affected by carrying extra fighters.

[1]*Richelieu*: Fr b/ship, 1940, 35000t, 30k, 8×15in, 9×6in, 12×3.9in. Incomplete at time of Fr surrender, towed to Dakar, completed in US.
[2]Probably Gen MacArthur, who was as unloved by all as Adm King, though that would have bothered neither.
[3]5SL: VAdm Boyd, succ by VAdm Troubridge, May 1945.

The Group bomb load was only reduced from 144,000lbs to 132,000lbs, and many of the fighters would be operating offensively against Japanese airfields. The Americans were more concerned in destroying Japanese aircraft than in bombing ships or targets on shore. Admiral King ended by saying he would welcome a visit by the Fifth Sea Lord.

Assignment of the BPF

The First Sea Lord asked Admiral King what his intentions were on assigning the BPF to specific operations. He was most anxious that the BPF should not lie idle once it was ready to operate.

Admiral King assured the First Sea Lord that he was not the man to allow ships to lie idle when there was work to be done. He considered the BPF formed a most useful and valuable Task Force. He did not, however, wish to commit the British ships just at present. He was awaiting an appreciation by General MacArthur on future operations in the SWPA and did not wish to make any decision on the employment of the BPF until he had time to study it. He was as yet undecided as to whether operations towards the capture of Hainan or North Borneo would pay the better dividend. Dependent on General MacArthur's appreciation, it seemed probable that the BPF would take part in the second phase of Operation 'Iceberg'. This would mean their active employment early in May. In the meantime the British ships could be usefully employed in accustoming themselves to American procedure.

The First Sea Lord ended by giving certain reasons, which he did not wish recorded, why he was particularly anxious that the BPF should start operating as soon as possible.

AEW Sets

Admiral Somerville asked that provision should be made for fitting receiver sets in the ships of the BPF, even if the special aircraft were not immediately available.

Admiral King directed that this should be done.

Russian Naval Crews

After the meeting, Admiral King explained to the First Sea Lord that he intended to turn over certain warships, at present on the west Coast of America, to the Russians. The necessary crews, totalling some 3000, were ready in North Russian ports. Admiral King asked the First Sea Lord if he would arrange for the shipment of the Russian crews during the next three months from Northern Estonia. He particularly asked that any transit arrangements which might prove necessary in the UK should be designed to avoid any publicity.

187. *Diary*

12 April 1945

... A violent memorandum directed against Tedder by the PM was considered at the COS today in private session. It is curious that with all his great qualities when he deals with personalities he gets childish. He is such a bad picker too. Most he has fairly well sized up but he is completely bluffed by Alexander.

188. *Diary*

13 April 1945

Heavy news in the morning papers – the death of Roosevelt. A sad blow for the Allies. On the whole it was by me not unexpected, he was a very sick man at Yalta. A difficult man to size up – a bit of an actor but charming and approachable. Possibly I saw him at his best. I wrote to Betty Stark. ...

The First Lord being away I had an interview by myself with the PM on the subject of his minute ordering trawlers to be given up. ... I was quite firm with him but persuasive and refused to give an undertaking other than that I would do my best to release 40 in May. As usual when one gets alongside him on a subject he knows little about I had my way. I was glad the First Lord was not there, he rather gets the PM's back up and he enjoys bullying him. ...

189. *From Field Marshal Viscount Alanbrooke*

7 June 1946

... I was always certain that after we had reached agreement at a COS I had your full support, no matter what turn the discussion took with Winston and that in itself was worth everything. We went through some very difficult days with Winston together and I could never have got through them without all your help and staunch support.

Then I should like to thank you for the wonderful cordial and friendly atmosphere which you engendered at all our meetings, your patience when listening to points of view you did not agree with, and your constructive help throughout.

SECTION C

COMMAND AND MANPOWER

OCTOBER 1943–JANUARY 1946

When Cunningham assumed control of the Admiralty in October 1943 the Royal Navy was engaged in important operations round the world – the defence of convoys in the Atlantic, great amphibious operations in the Mediterranean, preparation for the largest combined operation ever seen, gearing up for the final thrust against Japan, Arctic convoys to Russia, and the containment of Germany's surface warships. These were all major headaches for Cunningham and the Admiralty, though by the autumn of 1943 many of them were well on the way to solution. The most intractable problem, however (and one that is rarely mentioned by historians), was manpower [190–1, 203]. By the time Cunningham arrived in Whitehall, the Second Sea Lord, Cunningham's friend Jock Whitworth, and his assistants, had just about scraped the personnel barrel dry. Between September 1942 and September 1943 the Navy (including the Royal Marines) expanded from 529,000 men and 60,400 women to 710,000 men and 74,000 women, together with the nurses of Queen Alexandra's Royal Naval Nursing Service. The looming problem was: how much more could the Navy expand? Its commitments, especially naval aviation, the rise of a substantial shore-based 'tail' to support an increasingly technical service, the increase in ships' companies because of these technical advances and enhanced AA and A/S armament, the manning of landing craft, and of new construction arriving in increasing amounts from Canada and the United States, were growing. It faced greater competition from the Army and the RAF as their remits also grew [211, 218]. Civilian war work, and later the need to re-position the labour force for post-war reconstruction, were also great threats [201, 207, 209, 214–15]. The pool of male and female labour coming into the market place was also shrinking, victim of the progressively lower birth rate since 1921. Strength was scheduled to peak about the end of 1943 (at about 820,000 men and women); thereafter, casualties and the emphasis on a continental army and a longer term switch to civilian employment were likely to take their toll [192]. Naval requests for fresh recruits were slashed markedly – 288,000 were asked for in 1944 and only 50,000 were allowed [192].

Cunningham was aware of the difficulty, as Whitworth had drawn his attention to it several times in 1941 and 1942 and had persuaded him to accept WRNS personnel in lieu of sailors.[1] The issue was so acute, however, that he was faced with it from his first days as First Sea Lord, the Deputy First Sea Lord (Kennedy-Purvis) greeting his arrival with the remark that 'all our worst problems come back to manpower' [190]. It was a problem that Cunningham, A. V. Alexander, Willis (the new Second Sea Lord), the Controller and Third Sea Lord (Admiral Wake Walker), and others, had to wrestle with throughout their time [194–5, 200–1, 203–4, 210–12, 215, 218].[2]

Several expedients were mooted to counter the growing shortage. Older ships and those likely to be in dockyard hands for a long while were paid off. Commands were continually combed for surplus manpower. The Canadians and the Australians were invited to man more ships [191, 197]. Even new construction arriving from across the Atlantic was moored pending crews [191–2]. Cunningham, always exercised by the difficulty, was sure that coastal forces, the Fleet Air Arm and other elements of the service were over-manned and he observed, too, that the barracks were overflowing. Despite these convictions, however, the Royal Navy faced the acute and urgent necessity of having to choose between operations [200, 202, 204, 207–9, 215]. Even 'Neptune', the greatest of all amphibious landings, was under threat [191]. Escort vessels could not be sent east in 1943–45, partly because of a renewed U-boat threat, but also because there was a shortage of seamen, especially engine room personnel [191, 193, 215].The intensified prosecution of the war against Japan produced more difficulties, including those of sustaining morale and raising pay [194, 198–9, 200–1, 207–9, 212]. Of equal concern were the dilution of quality and the reconciliation of improved rates of pay with incentives for ratings to rise [192, 196]. By various stratagems, the Navy managed to meet its wartime commitments, but the problem was never solved. Even the outbreak of peace offered no respite, for there was a general shortage of labour, the RAF and the Army were maintained at strengths above their pre-war totals, and in any case the country could no longer afford to support inflated forces [221–2].

Of great moment to the Royal Navy was to make it an attractive service after the war. Before the war it could rely on history, seniority,

---

[1]See *Cunningham Papers*, I, p. 460.
[2]Adm Sir Frederick Wake-Walker (1888–1945): ent RN 1903; t spist; RNC, Ady & Tac Sch 1920–5; *Castor* 1928–30; DD, DTSD; *Dragon* 1932–5; *Revenge* 1938–9; RA 12CS 1939; RA (M) 1939; Dunkirk 1940; 1 M/L Sqdn 1940; Force K & 1CS 1940–2; shadowed *Bismarck* May 1941; VA, 3SL & Cntrlr 1942–5; apptd C-in-C Med but died before taking it up.

patriotism, tradition ('naval' families – officers, warrant officers and ratings – serving for long periods and several generations), the effects of the Great Depression and a regular supply of orphans. After a second world war social attitudes and economic circumstances were likely to change markedly and these factors were of diminishing appeal. The RAF and the Army had overtaken the Navy as recruiters of service personnel and post-war diplomatic, political and military changes were likely to exacerbate their competition. There was also an all-party commitment to use government leverage to maintain full civilian employment. In the circumstances, the Navy had to offer competitive rates of pay and conditions and market its appeal. While Cunningham was alive to pay and conditions, he dismissed rather abruptly gentle chiding from the press baron Lord Camrose that the Navy needed to publicize itself more aggressively, as the RAF, the junior service anxious to cement its existence, had always done [206, 219, 513–14]. As so often, Cunningham, after rejecting a novel idea, came round to embracing it [206, 219, 242, 513–14].[1]

Much more congenial to Cunningham was the promotion of officers and their appointment to posts of consequence. He had no clear purpose in mind, beyond selecting men on the basis of aptitude for the appointments in question, but in the assignment of senior officers to important commands, one detects a tendency to favour those whom he knew and who had served extensively and successfully in theatres of war. This was natural and moreover it did not seem unfair or productive of unfortunate outcomes [195, 205, 212–13, 216–17, 220].

[1]Visct Camrose (W. E. Berry) (1879–1954): jnlst & newspaper owner; Visct 1941.

190. *From Admiral Sir Charles Kennedy-Purvis*

15 October 1943

. . . As shown by the Second Sea Lord's and Controller's papers, all our worst troubles come back to manpower. . . .

191. *From Captain E. J. P. Brind*[1]

24 October 1943

I have been in constant touch with the difficulties of the manning situation and have long been anxious; . . .

2.   I am convinced that drastic measures are necessary at once and I make certain proposals below. . . .

3.   We have been definitely warned that we cannot commission the 'Overlord' bases and man all our new construction. If the 'Overlord' bases are skimped we shall pay seriously in the efficiency of the operation. . . . We can afford to take no risk in this matter, but at present we are taking a number of great risks because of a lack of suitable officers and administrative ratings.[2]

4.   It seems that we have already manned sufficient escorts just to manage 'Buccaneer' and to leave a little over to relieve old ships without reinforcing Western Approaches or Mediterranean. The proposals I make below should not therefore prevent 'Buccaneer', but this is not to say that this operation can be mounted from the manning point of view because there are commitments other than the ships concerned.[3]

5.   The position is that we have the following ships waiting to complete their ships' companies, mostly due to lack of ERA and Senior ER ratings, and there is constant danger that at short notice our dockyard space will be congested by ships awaiting men:

Black Prince, Amethyst, Kenilworth Castle, Pickle, Chesterfield, Tenacious, Bellona.[4]

---

[1]Adm Sir Patrick Brind (1892–1963): Capt 1933; *Orion, Birmingham, Excellent*; CoS, Home F 1940–2; RA & ACNS (H) 1942–4; VA & 4CS, BPF 1945; Pres, RNC Greenwich 1946–8; Adm & C-in-C FE 1949–51; C-in-C Allied Forces, N Eur 1951–3; ret 1953.

[2]'Overlord' was the invasion of Normandy, taking place on 6 June 1944; 'Neptune' was the maritime operation making it possible.

[3]'Buccaneer': a proposed descent on the Andaman islands.

[4]*Black Prince, Bellona*: lt csrs, 1943, 5770t, 33k, 8×5.25in, 6×21in tt. To RNZN 1948. *Tenacious*: 'T' cl destroyer, 1943.

Amethyst: sloop, 1943, 1430t, 20k, 6×4in. Earned fame escaping down Yangtze in 1949.

6. We are committed to commission the following ships during the next two months:

9 cruisers, 2 Fleet carriers, 9 escort carriers, 19 destroyers and about 60 escort ships, etc.

I am informed it will not be possible to commission *Indefatigable* without leaving a number of escorts, which I cannot yet estimate, unmanned, and it is clear that 'Overlord' commitments cannot be met.

7. In order to meet these commitments it is essential that we should establish a drafting margin, and I propose the following as an immediate measure pending the result of Admiral Kinahan's investigation:[1]

(a)   From 15 November 50% of the escort vessels completing in the USA to proceed direct to UK without working up at Bermuda. Their crews to be used as runner crews to fetch other escort vessels from the US.

(b)   50% of these new ships which have thus been ferried across would be manned with crews provided in this country.

(c)   The result would be that 50% of the escort vessels completing in USA would proceed to Bermuda and work up, 50% would be ferried to the UK and half of those ferried across would be commissioned immediately. We would thus have 25% of the new ships from USA waiting to commission as opportunity occurs (i.e., about 14 escort vessels by 1 March [1944]).

(d)   Pay off old ships and ships refitting. In addition to the normal procedure by which ships refitting for longer than a certain period are paid off, we should accept the following special measures for a limited number of ships:

New ships to be allocated to C's-in-C at Home who are to propose which ships they will pay off in exchange.

The ships' companies would change from the old to the new ships, subject to the minimum drafting adjustment required by RNB.

Note: The new ships allotted would be taken from the 25% referred to in para. 7(c), which would otherwise have to be manned by RNB on arrival in UK.

(e)   We should examine the implications of delaying commissioning, say, two cruisers.

(f)   We should ask N[ova] S[cotia] HQ to form runner crews to

---

Chesterfield: 'Town' cl destroyer, ex-US, 1920, tfd 1940, 1×4in, 3×21in tt.

Kenilworth Castle: 'Castle' cl corvette, 1943, 1010t, 16.5k, 1×4in.

Pickle: m/s, 1943, 950t, 16.5k, 1×4in. Sri Lanka 1959, *Parakrama*.

[1] Adm Sir Harold Kinahan (1893–1980): ent RN 1906; Capt 1934; RA 1943; DPS 1944–6; 1CS 1946–7; VA 1947; VP & Pres, Ordc Bd 1947–50; Adm 1950; Pres, RNC Greenwich 1950–2; ret 1952.

relieve those provided by us under para. 7(a). It will be necessary to obtain agreement of USA.

(g)   Inform Canada that we can no longer afford to man the British-manned ships in Western Local Escort Force. Request NSHQ adjust his distribution of escort vessels so that British-manned ships can return to the UK to pay off. We should thus gain nine crews.

(h)   Establish an organisation akin to that of Admiral Commanding Reserves to administer ships laid up.

(i)   Inform USA and NSHQ frankly what we are trying to do.

192.   *General Review of Present Manpower Situation*[1]

16 November 1943

5.   The general conclusion is that whereas we can probably meet quantitatively the remaining commitments envisaged for the current financial year, it is clear that we cannot do so qualitatively as regards either officers or ratings. . . .

6.   *Causes leading to present situation. . .*

(a)   urgent operational commitments which had not been fully budgeted for have had to be met. These are mainly the requirements for amphibious operations. . . .

(b)   the framing of operational requirements, without full regard to the manpower involved. This must be expected when striving to gain the initiative. . . .

(c)   the large intake in the years 1941, 1942 and 1943 compared with 1939 have upset our peacetime proportions of higher and lower ratings. . . .

(d)   the cream of the new entry ratings had had to be taken for officer material.

(e)   the natural reluctance of officers in the Fleet and in establishments to surrender their experienced men. . . .

(f)   the practice of retaining on the station officers and ratings from ship casualties and other sources. . . .

(g)   the difficulty of obtaining passages for men who could be released. . . .

(h)   increase in ships' complements due to increased armaments, and the fitting of new equipment. . . .

---

[1]Kinahan was the chairman.

The manning situation in 1944

... For 1944 the Navy has asked for a total of 247,000 men as new entries. ... It is understood that we cannot be allocated anything like this number. By 31 December this year the Navy will be approaching its manpower peak, ... its estimated strength will be 62,000 officers, 690,000 ratings and 62,700 women. Thereafter unless an allocation is made numbers will decline owing to wastage. ...

193.   *To Somerville*

19 December 1943

... Our principal preoccupation here at the moment is saving manpower. I do not know if you are fully acquainted with the position which has arisen from the fact that out of next year's intake, which is only 350,000 all told, the Navy asked for 288,000 and was granted only 50,000. Personally I am of the opinion that we put our demands too high, but there is no question that we are now in most straitened circumstances, particularly for the mechanic class. We are paying off something in the neighbourhood of six battleships, 13 or 14 cruisers, the old four-stacker destroyers and any escort vessels which are requiring so much upkeep that they are not worth running. Even with all this we are having to bring new construction over from America and place it in reserve at ports all over the country while the crews are collected to put the ships into commission. ...

194.   *Diary*

13 April 1944

... A Cabinet at 1830 chiefly on the manpower question. It was agreed that the COS should examine into the question of whether they could do with less than they have asked for. Fortunately it seems generally accepted that the Navy must be at full strength for the Japanese war.

195.   *Diary*

17 April 1944

... The war has now been going on for nearly five years and we are still employing officers who were Flag Officers or captains in the last war[,] all credit to them. But I think we should gradually pass them and use this war's vintage. . . .

196.   *To A. V. Alexander*

18 April 1944

I have today examined the Draft White Paper outlining the proposals resulting from the Review of Service Pay and Allowances.

2.   The general effect of the proposed alterations of pay to the junior ratings and decreasing scale of state contribution to the marriage allowances to wives with children, is to close the gap between successive grades. I am concerned with this effect on the higher ratings in the reduced incentive in future to seek advancement.

3.   To minimise this effect, I consider it to be essential that the pay of the Ordinary Seaman should remain at three shillings until he is rated Able Seaman, i.e., that he does not receive any automatic increase at the end of six months. I think that it should be emphasised that an OS of ability can be, and often is, advanced to AB, at the end of nine months. Assuming a *minimum* of one shilling between the rates of pay of an OS and AB, I notice that this gap will in fact close to sixpence a day if both these ratings are married and have children.

4.   I consider it equally important that there should be a reasonable gap between the pay of an AB and Leading Seaman and, to provide this, the latter's pay will require an upward adjustment.

5.   The Service requires a high standard of knowledge and ability for the higher rates. Those that have achieved this rate will not appreciate the higher relative rates of pay of those junior to them, and the junior ratings will not be encouraged to undertake the additional training for, and responsibility of, the higher rating. Even now we are not finding it easy to obtain candidates for advancement. The White Paper states that no general increase in basic pay is considered necessary. It is proposed that the words 'at present' should be added, in order to cover the Admiralty's views on the need for an increase of pay at the end of the European war.

197.   *Manning of Additional Ships by the RAN*

26 May 1944

With regard to the manning of extra HM Ships by the RAN, the Admiralty would welcome any such offer by the Australian Government.

This would be a real contribution to our manpower problem and could provide a foundation of modern ships on which to build up Australia's post-war fleet. However, this important contribution to the Royal Navy's manpower situation would not be effective if it were necessary to withdraw the RAN crews from the six Royal Navy destroyers and 20 Fleet minesweepers which Australia already mans.

2.   On an unofficial basis the Admiralty has understood that the Australian authorities might offer to find the crews for one small carrier, one or two cruisers. It is considered that the most suitable types would be a Light Fleet Carrier of the *Colossus* Class or one or two cruisers of the *Tiger* Class. . . .

. . . It is suggested that the *Venerable* (December 1944), *Defence* (September 1945) and *Blake* (October 1945) would be suitable ships to offer to the Australian Government.[1] . . .

4.   Until the Light Fleet Carriers become available, it would be practicable to lend an Escort Carrier to the RAN to enable the necessary experience to be gained. A number of Australian flying and maintenance personnel are now serving in the FAA. It would be possible to withdraw these gradually to form the nucleus of an Australian Naval Air Arm.

198. *Diary*

31 May 1944

. . . A long and good Sea Lords' meeting on manpower and the Japanese war. A very good paper by DPS discoursed on various measures to make the sailors go cheerfully into this second war.[2] The problem is difficult as though many men will be released from the Army and RAF comparatively few will be able to leave the Navy. This will undoubtedly cause some discontent. While realising that[,] it will I think be a mistake to make too much of it[,] though it may be necessary to persuade the Government to give bonus and/or rises of pay.

---

[1]*Colossus, Venerable*: lt F carriers, 1944–5, 13190t, 25k, 39–44 a/c. *Colossus* to Fr 1945 as *Arromanches*. *Venerable* became Dutch *Karel Doorman* 1948. The RAN got *Terrible* (1949) in 1948 (*Sydney*) and *Majestic* (1955) in 1955 (*Melbourne*); both were larger ships: 14000t, 26k, 37 a/c.

Tiger, Defence, Blake: 1959–61, csrs, 8885t, 31.5k, 9×6in, 10×4in, 6×21in tt. Completion long delayed; none tfd.

[2]DPS: Kinahan.

199. *Diary*

30 June 1944

... Board meeting at 1530. Promotions and retirements. I raised the question of the bonus to men going to the Far East and also reassurance on the question of their jobs when they return. With these large numbers in carriers and battleships that have sailed and are about to sail the situation is upon us. I urged for very early action to make an announcement to set these men's minds at rest.

200. *Diary*

18 July 1944

... Meeting after dinner on manpower and the PM's latest minute saying that the Navy should be able to run the Japanese war on 400,000 on Vote A. I pointed out that there was waste of manpower giving FAA, Coastal Forces and Landing Craft bases as instances. Further I advocated letting the Cabinet have a statement of what we considered the functions of the Navy in the Japanese war with the number of men required. And then letting them say what they were prepared to do without and putting the responsibility on them. I doubt we have a heavy fight before us. The Cabinet as usual wish to have their cake and eat it, i.e., deploy the best force possible against Japan and yet save a lot of men.

201. *Diary*

26 July 1944

... Meeting with the First Lord on manpower. The same ground traversed again.

1830 War Cabinet meeting on manpower. The PM first told the COS that their manpower requirements for the war against Japan were ridiculous. The attack on the Services was then taken up by the Minister of Production and Cherwell.[1] Both wished to ration the Services for the Japanese war in the interests of (a) getting exports going; (b) raising the

---

[1]M of Prodn: Oliver Lyttelton: M of St, ME 1941–2; M of Prodn 1942–5; Pres, BoT 1945; Visct Chandos 1954.

Lord Cherwell (Sir Frederick Lindemann): Prof of Physics, Oxford U; long-term friend of PM; chief of Ady stats secn; Lord 1941; Pay Gen 1942.

standard of living of the civilian population; (c) rebuilding the knocked down edifices and houses. Some doubt if America would yield any further long-term supplies. PM suggested we must come to an agreement with America as to the assistance she required from us in the Japanese war. A rather dangerous policy I thought. The fact is we are pledged to America and the Dominions to fight the war against Japan with all our power. The COS have produced their figures on this assumption. Ministers are now trying to get out of this and fight the war on a limited liability basis so as to get the above three activities going. Will the Americans see through this? I rather think so. PM eventually defended the COS and said they must be given more data. Much to the disgust of the Ministers he did not allow a decision to be reached but said he would write a paper. . . .

202. *Diary*

31 July 1944

. . . very informal talk with VCNS and Second Sea Lord on the waste of manpower.[1] My trouble is that I can't see why we are so short with the barracks so full that they can take no more. . . .

203. *Diary*

4 August 1944

. . . Started manpower meeting with Second Sea Lord, VCNS, ACNS (H) and others interested[,] made some progress over manning priorities when I had to attend the Cabinet meeting on manpower in the absence of the First Lord.[2] The PM handed out his directive which was to the effect that the Navy and Air were to be cut by 200,000 and the Army by 300,000 for the Japanese war. . . .

[1]VCNS: Syfret.
2SL: Willis.
[2]ACNS (H): RAdm Brind

204. *Diary*

10 August 1944

... Manpower meeting at 1500 with Second Sea Lord, VCNS, ACNS (H), DPS, DoP, etc., present.[1] Chiefly concerned with closing down unnecessary bases. I can't get a change of heart. Depots are still approving commitments which fritter away the men. ...

205. *Diary*

11 August 1944

... Then we settled the Rear Admirals to go on. As the three for decision were McGrigor, Vian and Moody there was little trouble.[2] ...

206. *Diary*

30 August 1944

... Had slight disagreement with Camrose at lunch. He asked me what is the Navy doing, to which I replied 'Nothing of course'. He tried to argue that we did not advertise ourselves enough. I told him I was not disposed to enter into an advertising competition with anyone and that the greatest compliment that could be paid to the Navy was that it should be taken for granted and that so long as those that mattered knew the truth I was quite content.

---

[1]DoP: Lambe.

[2]AoF Sir Philip Vian (1894–1968): Lt 1916; Jutland; gun spist; Capt 1934; 1DF, Spain 1936; *Arethusa* 1937; 4DF 1940; in *Cossack*, rescued Br PoWs from *Altmark* Feb 1940; *Bismarck* May 1941: RA July 1941; Force K, Spitzbergen Aug 1941; actions off Norway; 15CS, Med F Oct 1941; Sicily ldgs 1943; E TF, Normandy June 1944; F carriers, BPF Nov 1944; VA 1945; 5SL 1946–8; C-in-C Home F 1950–2; Adm & AoF 1952. See his *Action This Day* (London, 1960); S. Howarth, 'AoF Sir P Vian', in Howarth (ed.), *Men of War: Great Naval Leaders of WWII* (London, 1992), pp. 491–505.

Adm Sir Clement Moody (1891–1960): Capt *Curacoa* 1935; IDC 1936; *Eagle* 1937–9; DNAD 1939–41; RA, NAS 1941; RA (Air) Home F 1943; VA & FO (Air) EIF 1944–6; C-in-C S Atl 1946–8; Adm & ret 1948.

207. *Diary*

31 August 1944

. . . Cabinet meeting at 1800. Question of the publication of the White Paper on reallocation of manpower discussed. Much pressed and with reason by the Minister of Labour. Admiralty and Air Ministry view is that some announcement of increase of pay in the Services after the German armistice should accompany publication. Secretary of State for Air stated this lucidly and I supported him. Chancellor of the Exchequer quoted Mountbatten at us as having said all the troops required was a gratuity not a rise of pay. I wish that young man would mind his own business.[1]

208. *Diary*

4 September 1944

. . . Parliamentary Secretary attended the Chancellor's meeting today on increased pay for men kept on after the armistice with Germany. They refuse to hear of 25% increase. Bevin apparently saying that the Labour Party could not stomach a captain getting a rise of 14/- and an OS only 1/-. The difference in their responsibilities does not seem to enter into it. The Treasury are now producing a scheme by which an improved bonus is paid which Bruntisfield says will mean much the same thing. We shall see.[2] . . .

209. *Diary*

21 September 1944

. . . A signal from the Cabinet to the PM saying that all is agreed about the pay question for those taking part in the Japanese war but also

[1]S St Air: Sir Archibald Sinclair (Visct Thurso) (1890–1975): Life Gds 1914–18; confidante and aide to W Churchill 1912–21; Lib MP Caithness & Sutherland 1922–45; Chf Whip 1930; S St Scotland 1931–2; Lib ldr 1935; S St for Air May 1940–May 1945; Visct 1950.

C Ex: Sir John Anderson (1882–1958): Permnt US, Home O 1922–32; Govr Bengal 1932–7; Lord Privy Seal 1938–9; Home S 1939; Lord Pres of Cncl 1940–3; C Ex 1943–5; Chm, Port of London Authy 1946; Visct Waverley 1952.

[2]Ernest Bevin (1881–1951): ldr Dockers' Un 1910–21; Gen Sec, Tpt & Gen Wkrs' Un 1921–40; M of Lab & Natnl Svc 1940–6; For S 1945–51.

Lord Bruntisfield (Sir Victor Warrender, Bt): Gren Gds, E Eur 1917–18; Con MP Grantham 1922–43; Lord 1942; Parly & Fin S Ady 1935; Fin S, WO 1935–40; Parl & Fin S Ady 1942–5.

saying that it is impossible at this stage to guarantee security of employment for the men taking part when they come home again. I am glad to say the PM has taken exception to this. . . .

210. *Diary*

24 November 1944

. . . and manpower. The latest computation amounted to 140,000, a quite impossible number. The staff department kept sweating up numbers. Had a talk later with First Lord; he is also much upset over the manpower and ship repairs.

211. *Diary*

5 December 1944

. . . Meeting with First Lord, SOCRM, Second Sea Lord, etc., to discuss manpower.[1] The point is that the PM wishes the other two services to try and release men for the army so as to keep it up to strength for the final round of the German war. A very desirable idea but it means that something must be sacrificed. We came to the conclusion that we will, if I can get the COS to agree, try and save on the 3rd Assault Force. This should release about 25,000 men at least. We wish to put them into the marines and lend formations to the Army. If we gave them men only they will be swallowed up and lost to the Navy. . . .

212. *Diary*

10 January 1945

. . . C's-in-C meeting at 1600. Discussions on manpower, U-boat threat, Pacific and eastern commitments also repairs and maintenance. A very friendly and cheerful meeting. There was no doubt Admiralty difficulties are recognised. . . .

Pridham-Wippell came into my office after tea. He said he fully agreed that Dover should be reduced and offered to retire on that happening if it would be a benefit. Very public spirited of him but I told

---

[1]SOCRM: Lt Gen Sir Thomas Hunton: Col Cdt Oct 1938; T/Brig, Portsmouth Sept 1939; RMO (staff) Jan 1940; Maj Gen Oct 1940; Adj Gen Jan 1943; GOC Jan 1943; Gen May 1945.

him that I thought his services merited being considered for a C-in-C Home Port.[1]

213. *Diary*

11 January 1945

... Admirals' appointments are getting into a mess. This year we may have to find two C's-in-C Home Ports, a Controller, a VCNS and perhaps a C-in-C, Mediterranean.

Harcourt goes to the light fleet carriers – a good appointment. Claude Barry comes in as Naval Secretary.[2] McGrigor is really the only good candidate for both VCNS and Controller. ...

214. *Diary*

12 January 1945

... Meeting with the First Lord who reported the result of his meeting with the Shipping Controller.[3] The latter is not anxious to include shipbuilding and repair in his proposed Ministry of Production. It was decided that the First Lord would support the retention of MAP if it became necessary but would try not to antagonise the Air Ministry.

215. *To Fraser*

19 January 1945

2.   At home things are relatively difficult, firstly because all departments have been working at too early a date for the conclusion of the German war, which, as you know, was put down as the end of last year. Consequently, supplies and industrial manpower were cut down and, though they were not serious, there have been shortages. We are now

---

[1]Adm Sir Henry Pridham-Wippell (1885–1952): ent RN 1900; Capt 1926; RA & DPS 1938; VA & 1BS, Med F 1941; A/C-in-C, Med F April 1942; FOC Dover Aug 1942–5; Adm June 1944; C-in-C Plymouth 1945–7; ret 1948.

[2]Adm Sir Claude Barry: ent RN 1908; s/m spist 1914–21; Capt 1933; N Asst 2SL 1939; *Queen Elizabeth* Oct 1940; A/RA & FO (S) Nov 1942–4; RA Jan 1943; planned X-craft attack on *Tirpitz* 1943; NS to FL Feb 1945–6; Adm 1950.

[3]M Shipping: Richard Law (1901–80): n/paper edr; MP (Con) Hull SW 1931–45; Fin S, WO 1941; Parly US, FO 1941–3; M Shipping 1943–5; M Educn 1945; Lord Coleraine 1954.

setting about producing a new date, which I think will be put at the end of September this year.

4.   Another of our headaches is manpower. . . .

216. *Diary*

8 March 1945

. . . We further discussed the reliefs of the C's-in-C Nore and Plymouth. I recommended that while the German war and other activities in the North Sea were on that Jack Tovey should be retained in his job and not relieved before 1 January 1946. Leatham can be relieved three months after his time is up. First Lord concurred.

217. *Diary*

13 March 1945

Jack Tovey came in to see me after lunch and we discussed the relief of Holland problems and many other things. I was pleased to find that he agreed with me on the suitability of Pridham-Wippell as a C-in-C Home Port.

218. *Diary*

29 May 1945

. . . My first interview with the new First Lord Brendan Bracken at 1600. I found nothing in what he said to take exception to. In fact he talked great sense. . . . We discussed the two great naval headaches, manpower and the fleet train. He will I think be useful in settling these questions. He has no illusions about the War Office attitude over the former.[1] . . .

---

[1]Brendan Bracken (1901–58): jnlst, publisher, adventurer; MP (Con) N Paddington, London 1929–45; PPS Ady 1940; PPS to PM 1940; M Info 1941; FL 1945; MP (Con) Bournemouth 1945; Visct 1952.

219. *Diary*

26 June 1945

. . . Had a meeting with the First Lord and James Somerville about publicity. If he is as good as his word all's well. Fourth Sea Lord and First Lord had the promised meeting with Minister of War Transport, Chancellor of the Exchequer arbitrating. Fourth Sea Lord told me First Lord was a passenger and left half way through the meeting. He is so occupied with electioneering that he pays no attention to Admiralty business.[1] . . .

220. *Diary*

24 September 1945

. . . Very bad news. Wake Walker died tonight at his flat from a cerebral haemorrhage. A sad blow to the Navy. The man who tackled the magnetic mine and I have heard it said the greatest Controller we have had for many years. The country owes him much. I hope they realise it. I thought he looked flushed today when he came in to see me and we talked about the Mediterranean.

221. *Diary*

5 October 1945

. . . Cabinet meeting at 1130 on number of men in the post-war forces. We wished to fix a rough number so that we could retain some good men who would turn over if they knew what the prospects were.

The Admiralty put forward a figure of 170,000, which was an optimistic figure. The War Office and Air Ministry 230,000 and 200,000 respectively which were minimum figures.

We were met with the usual arguments from the PM. 'Who are you going to fight?' and 'The country can't afford it'. He seems perfectly willing to count on the US strength as our own and be quite prepared to let the US flag be seen everywhere and ours nowhere.[2]

[1]M War Tpt: Lord Leathers.

4SL: Adm Sir Arthur Palliser: gun spist; Capt *Excellent* (Whale I) 1938; Capt *Malaya* May 1940; Force H 1941; RA Aug 1941; CoS EF Dec 1941; Dep N Cdr ABDA Jan 1942; RIN June 1943; HF csrs 1943–4; VA Feb 1944; 4SL March 1944; C-in-C EI Sept 1945.

[2]Lab had won the Gen Eln of 1945 with a huge maj and Attlee became PM in July 1945.

... The First Lord took him up strongly and pointed out that in two world wars the US had come in after we had been alone for two years.

Question was deferred until some estimate of cost could be produced. . . .

222. *Notes on a Meeting about Manpower held by the First Sea Lord*

28 January 1946

3.   The First Sea Lord said the fleet afloat was not to be reduced below the limits laid down for the post-war fleet, and that further reductions must come from closing down barracks, schools, etc.

4.   The First Sea Lord raised the question of the reduction of complements of ships at sea. The Second Sea Lord said a meeting was to be held tomorrow about this.

5.   Return of BPF ships. The First Sea Lord said the Foreign Secretary does not want to reduce the size of the fleet at the moment and suggested that *Implacable* should come home in May, and a ship in June, and a third in July, provided the situation was then stable.[1]

6.   The First Sea Lord queried the necessity for having three ships in the FAMG to look after *Implacable* and decided that two of the three were to return home now.[2]

7.   The First Sea Lord will discuss bringing home of light fleets from the Pacific with VCNS, and also a reduction in cruiser, destroyer, and escort strength.

8.   The First Sea Lord decided that only one cruiser was to go to the Cape and one to the West Indies. These numbers to be built up to the planned figures as soon as possible.

11.   The First Sea Lord urged further reductions in coastal forces and all degaussing arrangements.

18.   The First Sea Lord asked ACNS (Air) what contribution was being made by the FAA; he said a meeting was being held shortly. ACNS (Air) said the policy was to put the pilots through divisional course to make them into naval officers and then teach them to fly well without bothering about weapon training at the moment.[3]

19.   The First Sea Lord said that the officer complements of destroyers should be further reduced.

[1]*Implacable, Indefatigable*: F carriers, 1944, 26000t, 32k, 60 a/c, 16×4.5in.
[2]FAMG: a supply group to major vessels.
[3]ACNS (Air): Lambe.

SECTION D

NEPTUNE AND AFTER

DECEMBER 1943–MARCH 1945

'Neptune', the maritime partner of 'Overlord', the invasion of Normandy on 6 June 1944, was Ramsay's 'show'. He deserves the credit for masterminding this, the greatest amphibious operation in history, but Cunningham was intimately involved, if only indirectly.[1] This was because it was a largely British enterprise (for which Cunningham bore the ultimate responsibility), because it was within easy reach of both the Admiralty and Cunningham's home at Bishop's Waltham (near Southampton and Portsmouth), and because it absorbed much of the Royal Navy's resources, limiting for several months what could be done elsewhere. It was principally because of Ramsay, however, that Cunningham took such a keen interest. Ramsay may have been the master of combined operations but one has the feeling that it had become something of an obsession for him, blinding him to the Navy's other vital tasks [223]. He was also an inveterate worrier and of necessity operated during the preparatory stage, the first half of 1944, at full pace. He did not get on well with Americans in general (except for Eisenhower, who was so genial and such a good co-operator that no one could take exception to him) [263]. Cunningham was urged to keep a close eye on Ramsay by the Prime Minister, but he needed no bidding. He was aware of Ramsay's foibles and did his best to keep Ramsay's shopping list, volatile temperament, stress level and abrasive relations with Americans (notably his deputy, Rear Admiral Alan Kirk, US Navy) in check, using his fortuitously sited home as Ramsay's 'health farm' (Bishop's Waltham is within half an hour's drive of Ramsay's HQ at Southwick) [240, 264].[2] Cunningham maintained a keen interest in the preparations for 'Neptune', visiting embarkation sites, ensuring a sufficiency of bombarding ships, anti-submarine vessels and aircraft, and logistical support as the armies moved eastward towards the Low Countries. In particular, he oversaw the provision of

---

[1] C. Barnett, *Engage the Enemy More Closely: The Royal Navy in the Second World War* (London, 1991), chs 24–7, makes much of this enterprise.
[2] 'Bertie Ramsay and Kirk did not hit it off': Cunningham, notes, p. 115, BLAM 52581B. See also R. W. Love, jr, & J. Major (eds), *The Year of D-Day: the 1944 Diary of Admiral Sir Bertram Ramsay* (Hull, 1994).

artificial harbours ('Mulberries') and their accoutrements ('Bombardons', 'Whales', 'Phoenixes' and 'Gooseberries') [223, 225, 229–33, 236].

The launch of 'Neptune' was fraught with great anxiety. Apart from the fact that no one knew if all the plans were going to work, adverse weather in the Channel caused a 24-hour postponement [233–4]. On 6 June, however, the wind and rain abated sufficiently for the attempt to be made [235]. All went well, except for the American 'Omaha' beach at the western extremity. Here severe casualties were inflicted on the invading forces and their support vessels and the issue was in doubt for a couple of days [237]. When that anxiety had passed, a terrible gale wreaked havoc in the 'Mulberries', the American one being wrecked beyond use and the British one suffering some damage; although the British artificial harbour was repaired it was found that beaching was a more efficient way of carrying supplies to the armies, an expedient supplemented by small harbours, though sabotage had often first to be dealt with [249, 257, 270]. The navies and air forces successfully prevented effective interference by U-boats, E-boats, destroyers and aircraft. Bombardment was heavy and accurate, causing even Rommel to wince at its effect.[1] As the summer of 1944 wore on, the Royal Navy played its part, to Cunningham's satisfaction [237, 259]. Churchill was not so sure and prodded Cunningham on bombardment and anti-submarine precautions, to be answered firmly and with unaccustomed patience [229, 235, 238–9, 246–8, 253–5, 258–9, 270]. Churchill, like all the senior figures, military and civilian, was most anxious about the whole operation [232, 234]. Cunningham himself paid a visit to the area on 16 June [244].

As the armies pushed out of France in the early autumn, Ramsay and Cunningham became anxious about their continued supply. Lack of suitable harbours meant that the armies were likely to be held up for want of supplies. The situation seemed to be resolved with the early capture of a major port, Antwerp, thankfully undamaged but 55 miles from the sea up the twisting, mudflat-infested, mine-laden Scheldt, held firmly on both banks by the enemy, who also launched rocket attacks on Antwerp. In vain did Ramsay and Cunningham advise the soldiers that possession of Antwerp was of little use without clearance of the Scheldt and its banks, warning that the armies' advance into Germany would be stymied for want of its substantial port facilities

---

[1]'Up to 640 guns have been used. The effect is so immense that no operation of any kind is possible in the area commanded by this rapid-fire artillery, by either infantry or tanks': Rommel to Hitler, n.d., quoted in M. Muir, jr, 'The United States Navy', in J. J. Sadkovitch (ed.), *A Reevaluation of the Major Naval Combatants of World War II* (Westport, CT, 1990), p. 11.

[264–6, 268–9, 272–3]. Ramsay himself led an assault, spearheaded by Royal Marines, to clear the river's banks and have the port functioning by the end of November, eight weeks after its capture.[1] The security of Antwerp continued to exercise him and he planned to fly up to the region on 2 January 1945, his last letter to Cunningham on 1 January explaining his visit; the next day, his aircraft crashed on take-off, killing all on board [273–4]. Ramsay's death was a great tragedy, but Churchill had already begun to question whether his post as ANCXF was redundant, receiving an itemised reply from Cunningham, who had earmarked Ramsay (supported by Tovey at The Nore) as British naval commander in defeated Germany [271]. After initial resistance, Churchill readily agreed to the appointment of one of Cunningham's proven subordinates, Admiral Sir Harold Burrough, to carry on Ramsay's work with the follow-up to 'Neptune' and the disarmament of the German Navy [272, 275–6].

'Neptune/Overlord' were supplemented by 'Anvil', a landing in southern France in August 1944, near to Toulon and Marseille and directed by the C-in-C, Mediterranean, Admiral Sir John Cunningham and commanded by the American Admiral Hewitt. Churchill insisted on renaming the operation 'Dragoon' on the grounds that he had been dragooned into it. A landing there had been agreed, but in the spring of 1944 Churchill began to advocate two alternatives – a switch of 'Anvil' forces to western France (supported by Cunningham, probably as a way of closing down U-boat bases), and a strike by Alexander's armies north-eastward through northern Italy into Yugoslavia and Austria [228, 241]. The COS swung behind the Prime Minister, as they did not like 'Anvil', which seemed beset with delays and also took forces from Italy. The American JCS, however, exercised their increasing muscle and insisted on 'Anvil'; they were now the superior military power and could count on the support of the other emerging superpower, the USSR. As a result, 'Anvil/Dragoon' took place, too late to help 'Neptune/Overlord' significantly but mercifully meeting little opposition. The slim forces, chiefly French and American, advanced rapidly up the valley of the Rhône, forcing the Germans to look over their shoulders but serving the Allies mainly by exploiting the ports of Marseille and Toulon. Cunningham was in fact ambivalent about 'Anvil' as opposed to further adventures from Italy, but rather shamefacedly admitted that the COS came badly out of the argument [224, 226–8, 241, 243, 250–2, 256, 260–2].

Churchill, Eisenhower, Cunningham and other leaders became convinced that the European war would be over by the end of 1944 [263,

---

[1]Cunningham to Adm J. H. Godfrey, 27 November [1954?], GDFY.

267]. The delay in opening the port of Antwerp, the German counter-offensive around Bastogne in the dead of winter, and the difficulty of soldiering in the flooded Rhine and Low Countries all contrived to push the fighting into 1945. As the spring of 1945 came, Cunningham, gingering up naval units in the North Sea, urged a bolder campaign against enemy forces based on north-west European ports; he was anxious to switch forces and focus to the Far East [277–80].

223. *To Somerville*

19 December 1943

... 'Overlord' preparations go on apace. You never saw such Rolls-Royce demands put up by the naval staff of the Supreme Commander.[1] There won't be a fathom of water unoccupied by a bombarding ship. Still it will be all right providing it is a success but we shall lose a lot of ships and sailors I expect, more especially as the mines are so thick that that they [will] have to anchor while shooting. ...

224. *Diary*

1 April 1944

So many interesting things are happening that I think it behoves me to keep a diary.

Although we had intended not to we held a COS meeting in view of the latest telegram from Washington setting out the views of the US COS on 'Anvil'. We are very near agreement but they are quite inflexible as regards carrying out 'Anvil', though some of their phrases gave rise to hope of reaching agreement. We decided to send them a draft directive for General Wilson.[2]

225. *Diary*

7 April 1944

Got up a quarter of an hour earlier and was at 21 Army Group HQ before nine. Heard Monty expound 'Overlord' plan. Well done but could have been done in half the time just as well. Ramsay expounded the Naval plan very well. He certainly has plenty of difficulties to contend with but at the same time I thought he overdrew the dangers and difficulties. The Air plan followed.

Perhaps to me the most remarkable thing was the lip service paid to certain lessons learned in Sicily and Italy. Monty talked of withdrawing the parachutists immediately they had attacked their object, a thing practically never done in the Mediterranean. He further talked of amphibious and parachute operations to prevent the battle from becoming static. He was notoriously opposed to these types of operations. The Air

[1]Gen Eisenhower.
[2]At that time SAC, Med.

C-in-C told us also how he was going to bomb the beaches right up to
the moment of landing. A procedure often previously pressed for but
always turned down by the air.[1]

226. *Diary*

10 April 1944

. . . A COS meeting in the afternoon. The American COS has adopted
the British view and consent ungracefully to the abandonment of 'Anvil'. The PM however is trying once more to get agreement by a
personal signal to Marshall on the basis of the battle for joining the
bridgehead having first priority then a look round and a decision whether
to carry out 'Anvil' or to go on in Italy. The extra LSTs from the Pacific
to be sent to the Mediterranean in the meantime. . . .

227. *Diary*

14 April 1944

. . . A COS meeting with the PM to discuss Marshall's reply to him
about 'Anvil'. I hope we have convinced him that the only thing to do is
to make a clean cut and abandon 'Anvil'. . . .

228. *Diary*

24 April 1944

. . . Portal and I had to slip away to a staff meeting with the PM.
Discussed operation 'Caliph'. i.e., landing a force in the west or south
of France when the enemy is otherwise engaged in 'Overlord'. The
COS said they would look into it.

[1]Monty: Gen Montgomery.
  C-in-C Air: ACM Sir T. Leigh-Mallory (1892–1944): RFC; RAF 1919; AVM, 12 Ftr
Grp 1938; AM, C-in-C, Ftr Cmd Nov 1942; ACM, C-in-C Air, Dec 1943–Oct 1944;
apptd AOC-in-C, SE Asia but killed in air crash en route.

229. *Diary*

25 April 1944

. . . A meeting with the PM, Eisenhower, Bedell [Smith], Ramsay and the production and supply ministers about the delay in producing Mulberry ports. The ministers came under heavy fire and made a poor showing.[1]

The question of further naval bombardment then was raised. The PM asked me why *Malaya* and *Nelson* were not fully ready. I reminded him of his minute saying there were too many battleships in commission. This silenced him on that tack. However perhaps *Nelson* can be prepared as a spare though I am averse to using her if it can be avoided.[2] . . .

230. *Diary*

29 April 1944

Drove to Southampton and met Pipon and C-in-C, Portsmouth, at former's office on the docks. Southampton has had a bad doing. The main street above the Bargate mostly destroyed but it was well tidied up and looked prosperous. The docks were well cleared and showed little sign of damage. Walked round one of the LSI (4). A fine stout captain. The ship excellently fitted for the purpose. Watched the embarkation of the Green Howards and had some conversation with the Colonel who had been in 1 Armoured Division with O'Connor in Libya. A fine looking tough lot. Particularly struck with the look of the RM landing craft crews.

Then via two hards where embarkation for Fabrus was going on. We decided that a turntable fitted in the LST would quicken things by 100% enabling the lorries to drive in head first.

Then embarked in an MTB and went down the Southampton Water, Solent and Spithead. G. N. Oliver's fleet. It was like a Coronation Review. Landed at Stokes Bay pier and met Vian. Saw some of the Phoenix just launched. Everywhere landing craft and assault shipping.

---

[1]M. Production: O. Lyttelton.
M. Supply: not known.
[2]*Nelson* had been mined and was awaiting repair.
  Malaya: b/ship, 1916, 29150t, 24k, 8×15in, 12×6in, 8×4in; she had not been reconstructed.

Lunched in the *Victory* with C-in-C and Lady Little.[1] ...

231. *Diary*

4 May 1944

... Staff meeting in map room on Mulberries and beach defences. Minister of Production wriggling hard on the former topic. Some interesting discussion on the latter. Although the experiments in progress may show efficient methods of destruction I remain of the opinion that if we can we should land on a low enough tide to attack them dry shod. Always presupposing the enemy does not put them down to low water mark or even further.

232. *Diary*

2 June 1944

... First Lord and I were sent for to the PM's map room at 1245 when he announced that he had arranged with Bertie Ramsay to embark in *Belfast* for 'Overlord' and that he would be seriously angry with anyone who tried to prevent him. I told him I'd risk that and that it was absolutely wrong for him to do any such thing. I doubt if he really means to go but he is in a very worked up state.[2]

The King has written to him and told him that if he goes he is taking an unfair advantage of him the King. This appears to have moved him a bit from his purpose. ....

[1]Adm Sir Charles Little.
VAdm Sir James Pipon: Capt 1920; RA 1932; RA-in-C & Adm Supt Gibraltar 1935–7; ret 1936; SBNO, S Cent Australia 1940–1; FOIC Southampton 1942–4.
Lt Col H. Shaw: CO, The Green Howards, Sept 1943.
Gen Sir Richard O'Connor (1889–1981): Lt Gen cmdg W Desert Force 1940–1; capt March 1941; escpd Sept 1943; cmd VIII Corps, Normandy 1944; India Dec 1944; Gen 1945. O'Connor was a great friend and admirer of Cunningham.
Capt of LSI (4): unknown.
[2]*Belfast*: csr, 1939, 10260t, 32k, 12×6in, 12×4in, 6×21in tt; now a floating exhibit of IWM, R Thames, London.

233. *Diary*

4 June 1944

Admiralty told me that 'Overlord' was postponed 24 hours. I was not surprised as it was blowing 5–6. Bertie [Ramsay] rang me up and told me it was really because of low cloud on the French coast. He is quite right, our great advantage is the superiority of our air force and we must have it or there will be a great risk of failure. Moreover to keep the batteries quiet we must have supporting fire from the ships. . . . first to Ramsay's HQ at Southwick House where I discussed the situation with him. Force V is badly mixed up and it will certainly take 48 hours to reorganise it besides which the weather prospects are not good till then.[1] Visited his war room. Then on to C-in-C, Portsmouth's house on Portsdown Hill. Quite a nice house and lovely situation. I had long talk with him and tea with them and walked round his HQ burrowed into the hill under Fort Southwick. Met Bellairs, Pat McLaughlin, Andrew and Holland Martin. Then drove to Selsey to see the Phoenix and Whales. Some difficulty in finding Burgess Watson's HQ but eventually found him in a railway carriage bungy more comfortable than it sounds.[2] The *Abortius* aground offshore made an impressive sight.[3]

234. *Diary*

5 June 1944

Usual COS meeting, little important work. Ismay informed us that the PM had finally abandoned all idea of going afloat in 'Overlord'. The COS were summoned to lunch at 10 Downing Street. A good lunch and as usual lots of wine. PM very worked up about 'Overlord' and really in almost a hysterical state. Much conversation. He really is an

[1]Force V: probably Vian's cmd.
[2]RAdm R. M. Bellairs: RA ret 1932; Br N rep, Lge Natns.
RAdm F. Burgess Watson: RA ret Sept 1933; cmd LST sqdn, Med *Hamilcar* April 1943.
Capt P. V. McLaughlin: Capt Dec 1939; ADNO Jan 1941; *Spartan* May 1943; cmd Coastal Forces, Channel, *Hornet* March 1944; *Swiftsure* Aug 1945.
Adm Sir Deric Holland-Martin (1907–77): *Britannia* 1931–3; destroyer cmds 1939–45; Capt 1946; NA S America 1947–9; *Agincourt* 1949–50; IDC 1951; DP 1952–3; *Eagle* 1954; RA 1955; FO (Flotillas) Med F 1955–7; VA 1958; D Chief Pers 1957–9; FO (Air) Home F 1960–1; Adm & C-in-C Med & Allied Forces 1961–4; Cdt IDC 1964–6; ret 1966.
Andrew: not identified.
[3]*Abortius*: unknown.

incorrigible optimist. I always thought I was unduly so but he far outstrips me.

Cabinet meeting at 1830. Prima donna de Gaulle making a nuisance of himself. He arrived Sunday and met the PM and Eisenhower that night and was told the plans. He consented to broadcast. Now he says he objects to some items in Eisenhower's broadcast so he won't and also says he will not permit the French Liaison Officers to accompany the assault. The PM very worked up about him.

'Overlord' is off and the landing is timed for 0630 and 0730 tomorrow morning.

Spent until about 0100 in the lower War Room following the convoys. The weather is not too good in the Channel. Vian reported some of his units 40 minutes late and that four LSTs with self-propelled guns all had their engine rooms swamped. It looks as though the bad weather has lulled the Hun's suspicions as no alarm had been given at 0100.

235. *Diary*

6 June 1944

Up early and down to the War Room to follow the landings. We certainly seem to have achieved tactical surprise. Some casualties to destroyers and sweepers but surprisingly few as yet.

British landings a great success. Enemy battery fire not heavy and apparently kept under by ships' gunfire. RAF attacks on batteries must have been very successful. Usual COS meeting – no important work.

Everything appeared to be going well in the afternoon but some anxiety about the American 'Omaha' beach where they appear to be badly hung up.

The submarines in the Bay ports to the number of 19 have been ordered to sail five or six into the Channel.

C-in-C, Plymouth, appears to be afflicted with infirmity of purpose. The three 'Narviks' are bound for Brest and he had issued orders for them to be intercepted by a destroyer force. When the submarines were sailed through the same area roughly – to give the air a free hand he cancelled the operation. A most mistaken sense of values for which we may pay dearly. I will give him snuff in the morning though it's little to do with me.[1] . . .

---

[1]C-in-C Plymouth: Adm Sir Ralph Leatham.
'Narviks': It is unclear which ships are meant. The term 'Narvik' is in any case a misnomer. There were German destroyers of several types at western French harbours.

236.   *From General Montgomery*

6 June 1944

I cross over to France tonight and may not see you again for a bit.

Before leaving I would like to thank you for all that you, and the Navy, have done to help the Army during the period of preparation. The past five months have not been an easy time – for any of us; but I have always felt that you personally would see that everything was all right and this has been so.

Goodbye and I hope we may meet again soon.

237.   *Diary*

7 June 1944

An anxious day as the situation on 'Omaha' beach did not appear to be clearing up well.

. . . Had an audience of about an hour with HM [the King] and talked over the landing among other subjects. We laughed a good deal as usual. . . .

PM called me up this afternoon to ask if I had seen Dönitz's exhortation to his U-boats to take all risks and get at the 'Overlord' shipping.[1] I replied that I hope to supply plenty of risks for them to take. He stressed the necessity of the Admiralty retaining control. I fully concur with him. I was much exercised a week or two ago when I found out that the Admiralty had rather farmed out what I thought was their responsibility. In fact the 'directive' to ANXCF is badly drafted and does not retain the Admiralty right to interfere.

Situation much better on the beaches after dinner. All but the northern one linked up and troops some way inland. Heavy fighting and progress behind schedule but progress is being made. Landing of stores also behindhand due to weather and slow progress ashore. Severe casualties from mines and one LST torpedoed last night by an E-boat. The old *Warspite* sounds like doing good work against the batteries.

[1] Grand Admiral Karl Dönitz (1891–1980), German N: ent N 1910; U-boat cdr, 1914–18; Cdre & cdr, U-boats 1935; RA 1939; VA 1940; Adm 1942; GA & head *Kriegsmarine* Jan 1943; succ Hitler 30 April–22 May 1945; sent to 10 years at 1946 trial. See his *Memoirs: 10 Years and 20 Days* (London, 1990).

238. *Diary*

8 June 1944

A day of waiting for news. . . . Meeting between COS and PM at noon to discuss future operations. Like all commanders Alexander has sent in an appreciation setting out that if he is only left all the forces he has now he will push on to the Pô and help 'Overlord' much more by containing enemy divisions than if some of his forces are removed for a new landing in France. There is a good deal of force in what he says but the arguments for a new landing to help on the battle in France appear weightier as we really have not, even with all the US can send us, enough troops. . . .

Better weather on the beaches has improved matters and unloading going well. J Beach, Oliver's, seems to be doing best as was to be expected.

The 'Narviks' are expected to make a dash from Brest to Cherbourg tonight. DOD (H) explained the dispositions made by the C-in-C, Plymouth, to intercept them. I thought them poor and showed a lack of knowledge of destroyer night tactics. I feel the team at Plymouth is weak. . . . I also saw the Portsmouth ones. Did not think much of them either. Six destroyers split up into penny packets of two each six miles apart to intercept a division two of which [are] the most powerfully armed destroyers in existence. There is no question the C's-in-C Home Ports in wartime should be chosen from those with fleet experience. Rang up Bertie Ramsay and told him my views which I hope he passed on. He was fairly satisfied with the situation ashore.[1]

The submarine situation is interesting. About 12 moving up Channel and being harried by our support groups . . .

239. *Diary*

9 June 1944

An anxious night but I was called at 0130 to tell me that the *Tartar* had the enemy destroyers in sight. Then again at about 0600 to say that after a running fight *Tartar* reported two enemy blown up and one on shore on fire. This proved to be too optimistic and the final result appears to be one destroyer torpedoed by *Ashanti* blown up and one damaged by *Tartar* and again engaged by the two Canadians

---

[1]DOD (H): Capt C. T. M. Pizey: Capt June 1939; *Campbell* June 1940; FCapt & CSO to RA(D), Home F, *Tyne* July 1942; DOD(H) Jan 1944.

ashore on fire and abandoned. The other two got back to Brest [,] one heavily hit.[1]

... Situation on the bridgehead appears to be improving but heavy fighting continues. Heavy rain today which must be very much against the air. Tennant has just rung up and tells me that Gooseberries and Mulberries are going very well. The former are already providing a much needed lee. He also tells me that everyone is in great heart over there.[2]

240. *Diary*

10 June 1944

... Drove down to Bishop's Waltham. Bertie Ramsay and Creasy came to supper both in good heart and much more cheerful. We cracked a bottle of Turkish wine to celebrate the invasion.[3]

241. *Diary*

11 June 1944

... Long discussion [with US JCS, at Stanwell House, Staines] on what to do when Alex[ander] gets to the Pisa-Rimini line and on the alternative amphibious operations using the troops in the Mediterranean that will then become surplus to requirements. Decided to study an operation in the Sète region and alternatively one in the Biscay area. We did not favour the Marseilles project. Marshall drew a vision before our eyes of an airborne landing of five divisions in connection with a seaborne operation to seize a good port. Burma also discussed[;] no particular decision. Marshall had been at Chequers and had obviously been indoctrinated by the PM over this idiocy including seizing an island and bombing Singapore from it. I found King not too averse to

[1]*Tartar, Ashanti, Huron* (RCN), *Haida* (RCN): 'Tribals'.
    The German casualties were *ZH1*, an ex-Dutch destroyer, 1941, 1922t, 37.5k, 5×4.7in, 8×21in tt (sunk); and *Z32*, 1941, 2603t, 38.5k, 5×5.9in, 8×21in tt (driven ashore).
[2]Adm Sir William Tennant (1890–1963): ent RN 1905; navig spist; N Sea & Med 1914–18; Nav O, *Renown*; Nav Sch; Nav O, *Repulse*; Staff Coll; Capt 1932; IDC 1939; *Arethusa*; CSO to FSL; SNO Dunkirk, May–June 1940; *Repulse* May–Dec 1941; RA, 4CS, E F 1942; RA i/c Mulberry hbr 1944; A/VA & FO Levant & E Med Oct 1944; FO Egypt; C-in-C NA & WI 1946–9.
[3]AoF Sir George Creasy: ent RN 1908; t spist; N Sea 1914–18; Tac Sch; Capt 1935; ADP; 1DF 1938–40; Dunkirk; PA to FSL; DASD 1940–2; *Duke of York*, Home F 1942; RA 1943; CoS to ANCXF; FO (S) 1944–5; FO (Air), FE 1947; VA 1948; 5SL & DCNS, VCNS 1949–51; Adm 1951; C-in-C Home F 1952; C-in-C Portsmouth 1954; AoF 1955.

our doing the Middle Strategy with Borneo as ultimate goal. CIGS not too good this afternoon either on the Pacific or Mediterranean. In that latter he was definitely against CAS and myself.

242. *Diary*

12 June 1944

... Good progress is being made in Normandy by the army and the build up is going well. Quite a ridiculous number of ships are being retained for bombardment and the ammunition expenditure is very heavy and wasteful. The army are of course delighted to see the navy fire – it saved their own ammunition and it's quite probable that they have been firing at not worthwhile targets. ...

Cabinet meeting at 1800. ... some very exaggerated claims for destruction of E-boats and damage to destroyers. I said at once the Navy doings had appeared in the press but gave them some facts about numbers and tons landed, our losses and the progress of artificial harbours.

It was evident that there was much appreciation in the Cabinet over the Navy's effort particularly by Mr Fraser and Amery though Attlee was full of complaints.[1] The First Lord mildly chided me for understatement but I told him that the greatest compliment paid to the Navy was to take them for granted.

243. *Diary*

13 June 1944

... Met US COS at 1130 and had a long discussion on future operations to help 'Overlord'. It was decided that three alternative courses presented themselves after reaching the Pisa-Rimini line[:] (a) An amphibious operation in the Loire area or Bay of Biscay[;] (b) An amphibious operation in the south of France, Sète area preferred[;] (c) An amphibious operation in the north east Adriatic in conjunction with an advance from the Pisa-Rimini line ...

[1]Peter Fraser (1884–1950): NZ; Lab; Dep PM, Sept 1939; PM Mar 1940–9.
Leo Amery (1875–1955): jnlst, Boer War; Con; FL 1922–3; Col & Doms S 1924–9; S St for India 1940–5.

244. *Diary*

16 June 1944

Drove to Portsmouth and embarked in *Arethusa* at 0745. HM came on board at 0800 and we sailed for France. I had little opinion of *Arethusa*, so slow in getting going and very dirty.[1]

Wonderful sight going across and seeing all the convoys going and coming. Arrived off 'Juno' beach at about noon. Quite rough. HM went off ashore to see Monty and we transferred to *Scylla*, Vian's flagship and sailed for 'Gold' beach.[2] Lunch with Vian. [Manley] Power, Douglas-Pennant, Talbot at lunch.[3] My party was CAS, Ismay, Laycock and Grantham.[4] Landed after lunch and went to Ouistreham where we climbed the lighthouse, which was being used to spot for our ships, and looked down on the positions where it was reported the Hun was. I wondered that the Hun did not knock down the lighthouse and the paratroop boys spotting from there thought so too and did not welcome our presence.

Re-embarked in *Scylla* and went back to 'Juno' beach[,] arriving after HM had embarked in *Arethusa*. However he did not notice our lateness.

A most interesting visit accompanied by much acrobatic changes of ships and boats in the prevailing weather conditions. Arrived Spithead at 2045 and disembarked. I took Grantham to the Palace House for supper and then we drove to town. Tired but pleased with our day, the principal features appeared to be the great collection of ships, the good organisation for the maintenance of the small craft and the shocking waste of naval ammunition.

[1]*Arethusa*: lt csr, 1935, 5220t, 32.5k, 6×6in, 8×4in, 6×21in tt.

[2]*Scylla*: lt csr, 1942, 5450t, 33k, 8×4.5in, 6×21in tt.

[3]RAdm A. G. Talbot: Capt June 1934; *Furious* Dec 1940; *Formidable* Aug 1942; RA July 1943; *Lothian* July 1944.

Cdre C. E. Douglas-Pennant: Capt 1935; *Effingham* 1939; CSO, *Pyramus*, Kirkwall 1940; Cdre, W Indies, *Despatch* June 1940; N SO to C-in-C Home Forces April 1942; RA 1944; 'Neptune'; CNSO, SAC, SEAC Nov 1944.

[4]Gen Sir Robert Laycock (1907–68): R Hse Gds 1927; BEF; Lt Col & Layforce, Med Feb–Aug 1941; ME Cdos 1941; CO Spl Sve Bde 1942; Sicily, Salerno 1943; Maj Gen & CCO 1943–7; Govr Malta 1954–9.

245. *Diary*

21 June 1944

... Usual COS meeting. The PM has stepped in on King's removal of the US Naval forces without consultation with us. As usual without knowing so we had to curb him a bit. ...

The weather has been better today but the strong north-easterly winds these last two days have wreaked havoc on the beaches. The Mulberries have stood up to it but many whale tows have apparently been lost and two days' build up for the armies. The Bombardon has not stood up to it either and is in bits. ...

246. *Diary*

22 June 1944

... I had some firm exchanges with the PM about the bombarding ships. He must poke his nose into what doesn't concern him. However he got little change out of me. He suggested that I had made him complain to the President about Admiral King's unilateral action in removing his forces from 'Overlord'. I told him quite plainly that I had not wished or asked him to signal to the President.

247. *Churchill to A. V. Alexander*

22 June 1944

Please let me have without delay the measures you are taking to sustain the bombarding Fleet. *Warspite* should certainly be used as long as she can swim and her guns can fire. *Malaya* I presume is ready to take over gadgets from *Warspite* in good time, or is she properly equipped already? It is much better to rely on the 15-inch fire than the 16-inch because of the larger stocks of ammunition and replacement mountings and tubes. I understand you are using *Revenge* and *Resolution* as stoker training ships. These vessels should be put to a higher use. We have great need to sustain our bombarding Fleet, which may have to deal with Cherbourg and will certainly be required for the flanks of the Liberating Armies.[1]

4. ... I am quite ready to complain about Admiral King, but let us make sure that our own house is in order.

[1] *Revenge, Resolution*: b/ships, 1916, 29150t, 8×15in, 12×6in, 8×4in, 21k.

248.   *To Churchill*

22 June 1944

1.   . . . As the area occupied is enlarged, bombarding ships are progressively withdrawn, leaving those required in support of the seaward flanks; and to prevent interference with the unloading of ships and craft.

2.   The position in 'Overlord' is satisfactory and the Allied Naval Commander has estimated that as soon as the northern part of the Cotentin Peninsula is in our hands the greater part of the bombardment fleet will be released.

3.   In view of the possibility of further assaults in support of 'Overlord', measures are being taken to keep available an adequate bombarding force. . . .

4.   *Revenge* and *Resolution.*

These two ships had to be paid off in order to provide the men required for 'Overlord' and are usefully employed on essential work.

8.   In my opinion there should be no requirement for naval bombardment of Cherbourg. It is impracticable to give close support when firing towards our own troops, and the coastal defence guns cannot be used to fire inland. It is not desired to increase the damage to the port unnecessarily.

9.   In conclusion, I am satisfied about the bombardment position. The maximum British forces were provided for the assault. Losses and damage have been small. The operation has progressed to the point when substantial naval forces will be released. Certain long term planned movements have become possible, and we should be able to take our full share in whatever future assault prove necessary in direct or indirect support of 'Overlord'.

10.   The unilateral action taken by Admiral King amounted to ordering the withdrawal of the bulk of the American forces engaged in 'Overlord' and allocating them to 'Anvil' without consultation with the Admiralty or the CCS, and before the SAC, Mediterranean, had stated his requirements.[1]

[1] SAC Med: Gen Wilson.

249. *Diary*

23 June 1944

COS meeting at 1030. Mountbatten paper took some clearing. I must say the figures of those remaining in the UK compared to those fighting in the Far East require some explanation.

Lunched with Betty Stark. Fraser, Geoffrey Blake and US Admirals Davidson and John present. Betty Stark evidently terrified of King and tried to get me to say that I agreed to the US Navy battleships departing. I said that while I agreed that there didn't seem to be any use in them bombarding Cherbourg it was a matter for Ramsay and Eisenhower when they could go.[1]

PM rang up about the damage to the Mulberries. Davidson showed me a photograph of the US one and it certainly has had severe damage. The shell has broken in. Not unexpected in the weather we have had. But I was glad to find that the building of spares had already been put in hand. The loss of the Whale piers is serious in that they can't be replaced in any reasonable time. The damage to landing craft has been heavy and it is undoubtedly limiting operations on the beaches. Heard this morning that George Creasy had collapsed. Very bad luck. Overwork I expect. . . .

250. *Diary*

26 June 1944

COS meeting at 1100. Discussion on future policy in the Mediterranean. The planners backed 'Anvil' but the CIGS and the CAS backed the defeat of enemy forces in northern Italy and no 'Anvil'. I found the arguments so evenly balanced as to have difficulty in making up my mind. So allowed myself to be guided by the other two whose arguments are sound enough if a little specious in certain directions. . . .

[1]Adm Sir Geoffrey Blake (1882–1968): ent RN 1897; Lt 1904; gun spist; Grand F 1914–18; Capt 1918; NA, Washington 1919–20; *Queen Elizabeth* 1921–3; N War Coll 1932–5; DD & Dir, N Staff Coll 1925–9; Cdre, NZ Sta 1929–32; RA 1931; 4SL 1932; VA 1935; BCS 1935–7; ret 1938, after suffering 2 heart attacks; ACNS (F) 1940; FO Liaison, US N Forces, Eur 1942–5; Black Rod 1944. AoF Lord Chatfield had him earmarked for FSL about 1943. Pound considered him more of an all-rounder than Cunningham, who profited from his retirement. See Cunningham, *Sailor's Odyssey*, pp. 181–2, 187; Simpson, *Cunningham*, pp. 35–6.

RAdm L. A. Davidson, US Navy: i/c ldg cft, TF 37 July 1942; RA, TG 34.10, Safi, Morocco Nov 1942.

RAdm John, US Navy: unknown.

Further meeting with PM. Telegram in reply to the US COS drafted. We took a firm line turning down 'Anvil' and pressing for completion of the north Italian campaign. I fear US COS will have much to say. However we are in the position of the man in possession – the campaign is going on.

251. *Diary*

28 June 1944

... COS meeting at 1100[:] principal business drafting and discussing a reply to the rather tough US COS reply to our message suggesting that 'Anvil' should be cancelled and that we should concentrate on Italy with all the Mediterranean forces. Americans would have none of it. Our opinions much strengthened by 'Boniface' message saying Hitler had ordered Kesselring to fight south of the Appenines, on the Appenines and at all costs prevent the Allies breaking into the Pô valley. General agreement reached to send a pretty tough one back, sticking to our guns. It is easy to see that the Americans think we have changed our ground and so we have to some extent. We were not firm enough when they were here.

252. *Diary*

30 June 1944

COS meeting at 1100. Had to be firm with CAS about the Admiralty rocket bomb. It should now have top priority. Principal business [was] discussion about US COS and President's reply about 'Anvil'. Absolute refusal to consider Italian strategy and demanding 'Anvil'. President put forward some most unfair arguments, i.e., that he would have to refer to Stalin and that anything but 'Anvil' would damage him politically. It was decided that though militarily we were quite unshaken in our views that since the Americans appeared so set that we had better agree to carry out 'Anvil'. I feel myself that taking the long view we shall gain by this seeming surrender. . . .

253. *From Churchill*

10 July 1944

At one time in the last war we had a great development of Anti-U-boat nets of quite a light description which enwrapped the U-boat and towed a buoy on the surface. Can anything like this be adapted to the human torpedo? Surely these light webs could be spread about in the harbour, buoyed so as not to impede the navigation, and yet always giving a tell-tale buoy or flame for counter-attack.

254.   To Churchill

11 July 1944

Light indicator nets of the type you suggest are in use now as temporary defences for an anchorage, but inside the anchorage their use hampers the mobility of shipping and patrol craft.

These patrol craft are used extensively and successfully to intercept and destroy human torpedoes, and to be successful they need freedom of action.

Although a net of the above type forms an obstruction to a human torpedo, its value is limited since the crew has little difficulty in cutting it.

Its use is at present being considered as a means of catching drifting mines which the enemy are reported to be laying off the beaches.

255.   From Churchill

13 July 1944

Well do not say I did not tell you.

256.   Diary

12 July 1944

. . . A signal from King this morning refusing to provide anything else for 'Anvil' so I replied pretty firmly. I wonder, however, if my firm replies ever get to King. . . .

257.   Diary

15 July 1944

COS meeting at 1100. CIGS mentioned that Montgomery thought Cherbourg was not going fast enough. I was very firm with him and told him that Montgomery must learn to believe that the men entrusted with opening up the harbour, who are great experts, are doing their best – and that I wasn't going to have another Tripoli nonsense. CIGS took it very well.[1] . . .

258. *From Churchill*

4 August 1944

What are the Navy doing on the western flank of the Armies? I should have thought that they would be very lively all along the Atlantic shores of the Brest Peninsula, driving off all enemy vessels, isolating the Channel Islands from all food or the escape of the German garrison, being ready at Quiberon Bay or elsewhere to join hands with the advancing American columns. We shall soon be possessed of harbours or inlets at which bases for E-boats or destroyers could be established dominating the waters round the Brest Peninsula and greatly helping the movements of the land forces. As it is they seem to be doing very little except to fight on the north-eastern flank. There are plums to be picked in the Brest Peninsula. Admiral Ramsay must not weary of well-doing.

2.   When I have heard from you, I will address General Eisenhower on the subject. It is not the least use telling me that General Eisenhower has not asked for anything. He is very busy with the land battle and knows very little about the sea. I am convinced that opportunities are passing. . . .

259. *To Churchill*

7 August 1944

A close watch is being kept on the situation in the Channel Islands and on the coasts of Brittany and the Bay of Biscay to defeat any attempt by the enemy to reinforce or to evacuate stores and personnel.

2.   During the past week forces have been operated as follows:

  (a)   MTBs in the Channel Islands area;
  (b)   Destroyers off the N. Brittany coast;
  (c)   Cruisers and destroyers in the coastal routes between Belle Isle and the Gironde;
  (d)   A/S escort groups off Brest and Lorient.

---

[1]Tripoli: a ref to Monty's complaint about apparent RN dilatoriness in clearing it; claim vigorously denied by Harwood & Cunningham. See Part II, sec C.

3.   At Admiralty request Bomber Command has attacked the U-boat pens at Brest and laid mines in the U-boat ports.

4.   AOC-in-C, Coastal Command, is working in close contact with C-in-C, Plymouth, to keep pressure on the coasts of Brittany and the Bay of Biscay. He has moved 40 Beaufighters from the East Coast to reinforce his striking power in the west.[1]

5.   C-in-C, Plymouth, has been ordered to render to ANCXF every assistance within his resources.

6.   Three LSTs are loaded with ammunition and fuel for the US forces and are ready to sail with escort as soon as required.

7.   With regard to 2(a) above, five MTBs attacked a small convoy off St Malo a.m. 6 August, sinking one trawler and one TLC and damaging three TLCs.

8.   With regard to 2(c) above, *Bellona* and four 'Tribal' destroyers engaged a convoy off the Isle D'Yeu about midnight 5/6 August. They reported sinking the convoy and escort – some seven ships. Subsequently they engaged another convoy off St Nazaire, but though damage was inflicted it escaped into harbour.

9.   With regard to 2(d) above, the 2nd Escort Group sank a U-boat 40 miles SW of Lorient during the afternoon of 6 August.[2]

10.   I think you will see from the above that without advertising all its operations the Navy is playing a full part on the western flank of the Armies and will continue to do so.

260.   *Diary*

4 August 1944

. . . Staff meeting with PM at 2200. Discussion on putting 'Anvil' into a Biscay Bay port. PM said Eisenhower had already sent a telegram to Washington recommending it. The upshot was that the British COS sent a telegram recommending this change and a warning to Wilson that it might come off. All this due to the spectacular advances of the US armoured forces in Brittany.

---

[1]AOC-in-C, Coastal Cmd: ACM Sir Sholto Douglas (1893–1969): RFC, ftrs 1914–18; RAF 1920; AVM 1938; DCAS June 1940; AM & C-in-C Ftr Cmd Nov 1940; AOC, ME Jan 1943; AOC, Cstl Cmd Jan 1944; M of RAF Jan 1946.

[2]2EG was formerly under Capt F. J. Walker, most celebrated ASW proponent. *U-736* was sunk.

261. *Diary*

5 August 1944

... Drove to Eisenhower's HQ where we had an excellent lunch.
Discussed the changing of 'Anvil' to Brittany and to my surprise
found Eisenhower dead against it and had never sent a message putting
it forward. It was very apparent that the PM knowingly or not had
misled the COS and bounced them into sending their telegram to the
US COS. ...

262. *Diary*

7 August 1944

... The US COS turned down the suggestion to change over 'Anvil'
and in the meantime the PM has sent a telegram to Harry Hopkins. ...

263. *To Blake*

17 August 1944

The COS thought that after three days of undiluted PM they were also
entitled to some relaxation so I am off to Cape Wrath for a few days.

VCNS has handled the Ramsay-Wilkes situation.[1] I must say I don't
understand what Ramsay is up to. He certainly rubs the Americans up
the wrong way though, mind you, they are not blameless. Wilkes though
I believe efficient is more than difficult. I had a similar one in the
Mediterranean and got rid of him quickly.

Shall be pleased to have Betty [Stark] back as I have one or two
things to discuss with him. I don't suppose he will enjoy his visit if
Pearl Harbor was under investigation. ...

I am betting on November for the end of the Hun war if indeed an
end comes. Chaos and guerrilla fighting is most likely.

[1]VAdm John Wilkes, US Navy (1895–1957): grad N Acad 1916; s/m 1919–41; Capt,
S/M Sqdn 20, SW Pac 1941–2; *Birmingham* 1943, Sicily; cdr, Landing Craft & Bases,
Amphib Forces Eur Aug 1943–July 1944; RA & Cdr, Landing Bases, France July 1944–
March 1945; Cmdr Admin Cmd, Amphib Forces, Pac F 1945; Cdr S/M, Atl F 1945–7;
Cdr, N Forces Germany 1948–51; Cdr E Sea Fr 1951; VA & ret 1951.

264. *Diary*

2 September 1944

... Bertie Ramsay to supper [at Bishop's Waltham] and a cheery party. Bertie shares my anxiety about opening up ports for the supply of the Army. I am quite sure they will presently be hung up. Apparently the beach head ports are so crammed up they may not be able to land all that is delivered.

265. *Diary*

5 September 1944

... V[ery] G[ood] news from the front. We have occupied Antwerp and crossed the Netherlands border and taken Breda. I trust the soldiers will remember that Antwerp is 30 miles up the river and though it may be intact sweeping the channel before the entrance forts are destroyed is not a practicable proposition.

266. *Diary*

7 September 1944

... COS meeting at 1030. I again impressed on the COS that Antwerp though completely undamaged was as much good to us as Timbuktu unless the entrance and other forts were silenced and the banks of the Scheldt occupied. I fear this is being overlooked by our generals and the consequences will be slowing up of our advance.

267. *Diary*

20 September 1944

... The PM told us that Eisenhower had sent a message to the President telling him that he thought a German collapse was not far off.

268. *Diary*

4 October 1944

Bertie Ramsay left after breakfast. A very useful visit from our point of view. The fact appears to be that Monty has not given the clearing of the estuary of the Scheldt the attention it should have had and Ike though realising the urgency has not succeeded in compelling Monty. Well they will and are paying for it by the slowing up and even halting of the advance into Germany. An outstanding case of not putting first things first. . . .

269. *Diary*

6 October 1944

COS meeting at 1100. . . . CIGS back from France where he had attended a conference at which Bertie Ramsay did some straight talking about Montgomery's failure to clear the estuary of the Scheldt. Eisenhower apparently took the blame on himself. He would. But the fact remains that the whole army is stuck due to not having captured a port close enough to the front line, and will be stuck until Antwerp is opened up. It is extraordinary that the generals will pay no attention to our warnings, too close up to the fighting, I suppose, while the administration sits back, takes a broad view. . . . Jack Tovey on the same lay about clearing the Scheldt. He is rather pessimistic about it as he says it has been heavily mined. . . .

270. *To Churchill*

16 October 1944

Summary of Present Situation at Arromanches

After a week of northerly weather culminating in a gale of force 7–8 the situation at Arromanches was reported on 7 October, to be:
  (a) Detached mole – breached by the collapse of two units.
  (b) Gooseberry – apparently intact but some of the Blockships and Phoenixes had moved short distances.
  (c) Eastern shore arm – some Phoenixes had moved.
  (d) Boat Camber breached.
  (e) Western shore arm – one Phoenix damaged by collision.
  (f) Piers – some damage which put some of them temporarily out of action.
  (g) Moorings in Liberty Trots had dragged.
2.   The bottom of the deeper part of the harbour is now believed to be formed of smooth rock, the layer of sand having been scoured away.

There is increasing difficulty in preventing moorings and ships from dragging. Measures are in hand to improve this. Excessive tidal streams through the harbour exaggerate the difficulty of handling ships and cause delays.

3.   The situation as regards AX Phoenix at present is:

   (1)   5 have been planted for double banking the eastern end of the detached mole. (4 of these were planted after the gale and have filled in the most important breach).

   (2)   2 from Tees are weather-bound at Isle of Wight.

   (3)   3 on passage from Tees.

   (4)   2 on passage from Milford Haven.

   (5)   16 ready waiting towage.

   (6)   2 were sunk while in tow.

4.   There were 13 large and 13 small tugs on the job. Given suitable weather these can deliver Phoenixes to Arromanches as soon as they can be dealt with there.

5.   Three Blockships are being sailed in the middle of the week for reinforcing at the boat camber.

6.   The War Office states that the damage experienced to date has not restricted the present unloading requirements at the port.

How long the harbour lasts even when strengthened depends on the number and strength of northerly gales which may occur.

271.   *To Churchill*

15 November 1944

At the Staff Conference held on 7 November I undertook to consider whether the appointment of ANCXF had outrun its usefulness. I do not think this is so for the following reasons:

   (a)   Further operations in the 'Overlord' area, calling for active help from seaward, will probably be necessary before Germany is defeated. ANCXF will be required to co-ordinate their planning and execution.

   (b)   An Allied Naval C-in-C is an excellent institution for controlling the activities of the large number of Allied Navies represented in SCAEF's command.

   (c)   If there were no Allied Naval Commander, SCAEF would tend to seek naval advice from the Commander of the US Naval Forces in France whose HQ are in Paris. The tendency of the US Navy to settle questions in France without consulting British interests might also be increased.

(d)   Naval disarmament and control upon collapse of resistance require to be closely co-ordinated with the action of land and air forces. It is advantageous to have a British Admiral responsible at Supreme HQ for Anglo-US planning in this field who can also step into the senior British naval post in the Control Commission.

(e)   No other British naval authority could fill the place of ANCXF in meeting the above needs.

272. *Diary*

21 December 1944

... COS meeting at 1030. Directors of Plans present. They reported the results of the examination of the possibility of an amphibious operation to turn the line of the Rhine. They were not very hopeful. Possible floodings, lines of sand dunes and the fringe of islands made such an enterprise doubtful of success. We thought something might be staged against the Ymuiden area to gain control of the Ymuiden-Amsterdam canal and thus gain access to the Zuider Zee. . . .

273. *From Ramsay*

1 January 1945

I *do* congratulate you. To be a Knight of the Thistle must surely be the height of ambition of any Scotsman . . .

I am going up to Brussels and Holland tomorrow as I'm not at all happy about the military dispositions for the defence of the Islands north of the Scheldt and that part of Holland south of the Maas and north of Antwerp.

There are clear indications that the Boche have accumulated considerably greater forces north of our lines in the areas stated, than are required for defence; and information points to the fact that plans have been laid to stage a sudden attack destined to deny us freedom of approach to Antwerp, as well as the capture of Antwerp itself, if only temporarily. The Army are aware of all this but say that no more troops are available to reinforce our already too weak forces holding the line and the islands. They have therefore asked us to provide the necessary additional protection. It is possible that this attack will not now be launched as their main offensive has petered out, but it is not safe to count on this.

I've pointed out to SHAEF the dangers of the situation and said that the Navy can't in any circumstances be considered as a substitute for the Army in this matter and that in my opinion a great risk is being run unless additional forces are provided.

SHAEF are apprehensive themselves, and much more so since I've reminded them of the consequences, but as has always happened they are not taking any direct action about it, any more than they did when I used to point out the necessity of taking both sides of the Scheldt in order to free Antwerp. They hope that I can persuade Monty to do so and I may, but where they make their mistake is in not themselves issuing direct orders as to what is to be done to the Army Group concerned.

NC Force T has his HQ at Bergen-op-Zoom, in close touch with Canadian army and I Corps, and we are taking all the steps we can to assist the Army but they are quite inadequate to ensure the security which is so essential.[1]

I am making a tour of the area and meeting all the parties concerned, in the next few days, and I will bring all the pressure I can in the highest circles to make the Army provide adequate insurance!

The sinking of those two large Personnel Ships has shaken the Americans, who never seem to be alive to the dangers of this sort of affair until it happens.[2] We have been inordinately fortunate in respect of such incidents, so far, and I'm afraid it is too much to expect it will not recur, for those big ships are undoubtedly very vulnerable in such confined waters to the new submarine technique and the latest torpedoes.

I hope you will strengthen available escorts by every means possible, but even then I shall always dislike the use of these large ships, which are however a necessity I fear.

Very large Army reinforcements will be necessary from the USA if we are to conduct a really powerful offensive this year, or even if only to hold the Germans if they can scrape up additional forces with which to pursue an offensive. We have *no* strategical reserves at all which is a constant source of anxiety – at any rate it is to me.

It is not safe to express one's thoughts too openly on the matter of command, but no doubt Brooky keeps you well informed on this subject.[3]

---

[1]NC, Force T: probably Troubridge.
[2]Possibly *Samsip*, 7219t, & *Fort Maisonneuve*, 7128t, mined in Scheldt estuary, 7 & 15 Dec 1944.
[3]Gen Brooke.

274. *Diary*

2 January 1945

... the news was brought to me that Ramsay's aeroplane had crashed on taking off and that he was killed. A bad and sad business. A Hudson!! ...

275. *Diary*

6 January 1945

Informed by telephone that night that PM refused to agree to the appointment of Harold Burrough to relieve Ramsay on the grounds that the post should now be abolished and the staff saved. How he works in such complete ignorance and disregard for facts beats me.

276. *Diary*

7 January 1945

[To France for Ramsay's funeral]. . . . Ike asked about Ramsay's relief but I rode him off and suggested that Kirk working through ANCXF's staff should temporarily do the job. We told Kirk and Bedell [Smith] this when we arrived at Ramsay's HQ for the funeral. . . .

Went over and saw the PM. He consented at once to Burrough's appointment.

277. *Diary*

9 March 1945

. . . COS meeting at 1100. Principal business the frightful conditions of starvation in Holland . . . We can't allow four or five million of the Dutch people to die of starvation without raising a finger to help them. I spoke on this subject to Jack Tovey this morning, he thoroughly agrees and is planning to send over supplies by landing craft. . . .

278. *Diary*

21 March 1945

... I held much converse with the [Norwegian] Ministers of Justice and Foreign Affairs. .... it was obvious they did not think the British Navy was doing enough to help them. They stated that one and a half million tons of Swedish shipping and 300,000 tons of Norwegian shipping was immobilised in Swedish waters and asked why we did not open the Kattegat. It certainly wants looking into.[1]

279. *Diary*

23 April 1945

COS meeting at 1100. .... The negotiations for the neutralisation of the forces in Holland under keen discussion. I am all against letting the Germans sit unattacked in Holland and letting them use it as a middle U-boat and E-boat base to attack our convoys. The enemy's undertakings to be limited to not inundating the whole country. I am sure the PM is with me but the other two alas are against me. We decided to give Eisenhower what we thought ought to be the terms and leave it to him.

280. *Diary*

4 May 1945

Spent the time before the COS meeting gingering up all and sundry. They are all sitting back too much and not taking advantage of the situation. They should have been into Hamburg by sea and off the Danish coast already. Spoke to CoS to ANCXF on the phone and stuck a pin into him. Got a good move on.[2]
... Another ginger up of our people after dinner.

[1] For Minr: Trygve Lie, later 1st Sec Gen, UN. M Jus: probably Terje Wold.
[2] CoS to ANCXF: not identified.

SECTION E

THE GERMAN NAVY:

U-BOATS AND SURFACE WARSHIPS
JANUARY 1944–AUGUST 1945

It may seem odd but when Cunningham went to the Admiralty in October 1943, the primary concern with regard to the German Navy was not the U-boats, apparently defeated utterly in May 1943, but the surviving major warships of the surface fleet, notably *Tirpitz* and *Scharnhorst*, both of which, based in Norway, threatened Allied convoys to North Russia.[1] They were fast, well-armed, heavily protected and aided and abetted by U-boats, dive bombers, torpedo bombers and reconnaissance aircraft, and escorted by large, fast, powerfully armed destroyers. Sheltered in narrow, winding, high sided fiords, they could not be reached easily or by conventional means. They were guarded by numerous smoke canisters, heavy flak batteries and fighters. Aerial assault by land-based planes from Scotland was precluded by range while carrier attacks were made difficult by smoke and AA and aerial defences, as well as exposure to air and submarine attacks. Watching over their exit was a difficult task, given the frequent cloudy, drizzly or snowy conditions. Neutralising them by some means or other was a headache for the Admiralty from the middle of 1942, the time of their move to Norway. Something had to be done, for they threatened, and sometimes attempted (or, in the case of PQ 17, *appeared* to attempt) the savaging of convoys to Russia. The psychological menace was at least as great as the actual one. Taking measures against them could well expose a convoy (like PQ 17) to destruction from other enemies, the U-boats and the *Luftwaffe*. Laying the predators to rest was the Admiralty's concern, for Churchill, Roosevelt, Stalin and their political and military advisors were quick to criticise the suspension of convoys or serious losses [301–2]. Since their arrival in Norway in 1942, the apparently unsinkable *Tirpitz*, and the *Scharnhorst* which had dashed up the Channel, had exercised a hypnotic effect on the Admiralty – and Churchill. They caused a heavy concentration of Allied force not only as distant cover but also as close escort.

It was into this uncomfortable situation that Cunningham came, though a scheme was under way to attack *Tirpitz* with a novel form of attack –

---

[1]*Tirpitz*: German b/ship, 1941, 42900t, 29k, 8×15in, 12×5.9in, 16×4.1in, 6×21in tt.
Scharnhorst: German b/csr, 1939, 34841t, 32k, 9×11in, 12×5.9in, 14×4.1in.

charges attached to her hull by midget submarines, towed to their launching positions off the Norwegian coast by conventional boats. It was unlikely that all craft would survive the short but hazardous journey, coping with rocks, wind and mist as well as nets, patrols and depth charges. It was also unlikely that the charges would sink the unsinkable, but they might cripple her enough to prevent her going to sea and perhaps make repair impossible without going south to a German dockyard [289]. A successful strike would lessen also the increasing likelihood of a long range heavy bomber attack by RAF special forces, launched from a Soviet airfield. That might well finish off *Tirpitz*, but it would signal the Air's triumph over the impotent Senior Service. British and Admiralty prestige was as much at stake as the immobilisation of a key enemy unit.

In the event, the midget submarines, despite heavy casualties and the inability of several attackers to lay their charges, managed to put *Tirpitz* out of action for six months. Thereafter, although seen, anxiously, as a continuing threat, she was regarded by the Germans essentially as a floating battery, though they were no doubt pleased to see that she continued to tie up considerable forces and exercise operational constraints on the British. Following the X-craft assault in September 1943, the Fleet Air Arm had a go in April 1944. Barracuda bombers were flown off a variety of fleet and escort carriers but smoke, flak and fighter defences and the lack of heavy bombs meant that the attempt did no more than damage the ship's upperworks [286].[1] Cunningham wanted an almost immediate repeat of the attack, but was met with a firm refusal by Fraser, the C-in-C, Home Fleet, who cited aroused defences as his reason. Cunningham, no doubt feeling the pressure of the political and military leadership, stressed the Admiralty's right to direct the use of forces, Fraser the superior knowledge of the man on the spot. It was reminiscent of several occasions in the Mediterranean, when Pound had voiced Admiralty wishes and Cunningham, the station commander, had pointed out the local problems [287–8]. Bad weather and smoke frustrated subsequent attempts, despite Cunningham's unrelenting pressure for attacks [287–90, 294–6]. In the end, the RAF's specialist squadron, 617 flying Lancasters from a Russian base and using heavy armour-piercing bombs, caused *Tirpitz* finally to turn turtle in November 1944 [304–5]. The junior service had had the last laugh, though Cunningham stoutly maintained that the Royal Navy's X-craft and carrier planes

---

[1]Operation 'Tungsten', 3 April 1944, resulted in much structural damage to *Tirpitz*, putting her out of action for 3 months.

had already reduced her to a floating flak platform and removed her from operational considerations.[1]

Fortunately for the Navy's reputation, it did manage to dispose of *Scharnhorst*, Fraser and his subordinates skilfully exploiting the ineptitude of the German high command, adverse weather conditions, the superiority of British search and gunnery radar, and sheer sea-keeping grit to sink her on Boxing Day, 1943, a fitting end to Cunningham's settling-in period at the Admiralty [281].[2] After the loss of *Scharnhorst* and the effective removal of *Tirpitz*, the *Kriegsmarine* had no major surface warships in Atlantic waters; such as remained were either undergoing repair in Germany, disabled, or supporting the armies resisting the Red Army's advance in the Baltic.

The U-boats, effectively defeated in May 1943, had virtually withdrawn from the North Atlantic – and found few pickings in other seas – and were hastily re-equipping with new technology, shipping enhanced armament and devising novel tactics [282–4, 303]. Cunningham found a largely untroubled sea but conventional boats were re-equipped with the Dutch *Schnorkel*, a device for prolonging underwater endurance and increasing submerged speed. They had heavier flak armaments, more sensitive radar and torpedoes carried expressly for use against escort vessels [299, 303, 316].[3] The AA guns, acoustic torpedoes and improved radar made little difference but the *Schnorkel* device threatened to nullify the threat of air attack, searching aircraft having great difficulty in locating *Schnorkel*-fitted U-boats, which also returned to coastal waters, using tide rips, rocks, shallows, shoals of fish and wrecks as cover. That was enough headache for ASW practitioners, despite 'Hedgehogs', 'Foxers', 10cm radar, escort carriers, support groups, blanket air and surface ship coverage, hard-won experience, effective training, excellent command and organisation headed by Admiral Horton, and particularly the 'black magic' boffins who intercepted U-boat communications, plotted their whereabouts by HF/DF and analysed trends and situations. Cunningham, at first rather abruptly dismissive of this 'black magic', came to recognise its value.[4]

---

[1]No. 617 Squadron: RAF's specialist bombing unit, led originally by Wing Cdr Guy Gibson VC and then by Wing Cdr Leonard Cheshire VC; otherwise famous as the 'Dambusters'.

Avro Lancaster: bbr, 1941, 4×1640hp, 1660m, 287mph, 7 crew, 12000lbs 'Tallboy' bomb, 10mg.

[2]See R. Humble, *Fraser of North Cape* (London, 1983), pp. 187–224.

[3]*Snorkel* device was Dutch, acquired by Germans after conquest of Netherlands in May 1940.

[4]'Hedgehog': an ahead-throwing anti-submarine weapon, first used in 1942. 'Foxer': an anti-Gnat device, first used in 1943. 10cm radar: a short-wave set, first used in 1941.

Allied ships and planes had coped easily with attempts by U-boats, supplemented by bombers, mines, midget submarines, and E-boats, to disrupt the Normandy landings and their aftermath. Although there were warship and merchant vessel losses in the Channel and lower North Sea, these were mercifully minimal [284]. Cunningham was uncomfortably aware, however, of intelligence which warned him that new types of U-boat would spearhead a renewed offensive in the early part of 1945. They would be equipped with the latest arms and technology, but they were much more like true submarines than submersible torpedo boats. Both the Type XXI and Type XXIII could stay submerged for long periods, they enjoyed higher speeds on the surface and under water, they were extremely hard to detect and they could escape pursuit much more easily than the older boats. It was likely that they would enter the war in February 1945 and that by the spring there would be about 100 of the two types [303, 308, 315–16].[1]

Cunningham knew he faced a major problem. Getting it under control was likely to take time and might lead to greatly enhanced Allied casualties, perhaps holding up the armies on shore and requiring vessels to remain in home waters rather than reinforcing the fleets in the Indian and Pacific Oceans. Cunningham and the Admiralty were once again under intense political, military and international spotlights. It was the First Sea Lord's responsibility to deal firmly and quickly with this new threat. The trouble was that while new technology, the sufficiency of aircraft and escorts, better training, tactics, management and command, and vital intelligence, as well as raw courage had given the Allies the decisive edge in May 1943, there was no effective answer to the new German threat. The Air was '90% out of business', most of the escorts were too slow, and the scientists had no counter-measures to offer [313]. Cunningham, concerned and feeling the burden of duty, resorted to a variety of other expedients. Every escort vessel that could run was disposed to meet the renewed threat. Minelaying on a huge scale was ordered. The Air was exhorted to find new devices to locate U-boats, to hasten blockbuster bombs which could penetrate thick concrete U-boat shelters, to bomb assembly yards, and to mine coastal waters. There was little to be expected from the slow advance on the western front. Although American forces had driven the U-boats out of their Biscay bases, this was of little strategic consequence. The underwater war now centred round the British Isles and the new U-boats did

---

[1]Type XXI: U-boat, 1945, 1595/1790t, 15.6/17.2k, 6×21in tt (23 carried).
Type XXIII: U-boat, 1945, 230/254t, 15/22k, 2×21in tt (2 carried).
These figures differ slightly from those given in No. 315.
There were also 'Seehund' and 'Biber' midget submarines, extant 1944.

not suffer so much curtailment of their operations by going north-about into the Atlantic. Their bases were chiefly those of German, Dutch and Norwegian ports, mostly out of western soldiers' reach. Cunningham's great hope from ground operations was the Red Army's advance along the Baltic coast, the principal area for U-boats working up. He urged Soviet commanders to speed up their advance [292, 303, 306–19, 322–3, 325].

The European war ended in early May 1945. To Cunningham's and the Admiralty's great relief, the revived U-boat campaign petered out. It was true that U-boats were hard to find, but sinkings did not rise to the heights of early 1943. Many U-boats were destroyed in port or on the assembly slips, others fell to mines plastered thickly in the Channel, Irish Sea, North Sea and Skaggerak, while the Red Army duly rolled up the Baltic ports. The new U-boats were delayed partly by Allied measures and partly by teething troubles; almost none got to sea. It was, nevertheless, a close run thing; had the German war lasted into the summer, Cunningham's fears of a fleet of new type U-boats and a rash of merchant ship sinkings might well have come true. It was, after all, a situation over which the sailors exercised only limited control [320–2, 324, 329, 331]. More characteristically, Cunningham pushed commanders at sea for more aggressive measures in the Bay of Biscay, the Norwegian Leads and North Sea coasts, dismissing fears of bombing and other attacks [281, 294, 296, 329, 336].

With the end of the war, there arose the problem of what to do with the German Navy. There were relatively few major warships afloat or undamaged, but there were plenty of U-boats and, despite carpet bombing, ample installations, floating cranes, minor craft, barges, laboratories and other infrastructure and equipment [332, 334]. Cunningham had thought about the problem since becoming First Sea Lord and inherited an official Admiralty position: that the German Navy should not rise from the ashes, as it had in the 1930s [285, 297, 300, 326]. By the time the war ended, Cunningham and other members of the CCS had become deeply suspicious of the Russians, an attitude shared by Churchill, but, it seems, by precious few other British or American politicians or diplomats. A secondary principle was, therefore, that nothing advanced should be allowed to go to the USSR, which would be held tightly to the letter of shares and agreements and would be dealt with only on a strict *quid pro quo* basis. In particular, Cunningham made efforts to ensure that advanced U-boat technology – boats, equipment, laboratories and their scientists – should not go to the Soviets but remain firmly in British or American hands. He put in place a thorough scheme of Royal Navy administration of German naval bases and personnel, intent on destroying the *Kriegsmarine*, which had brought so much grief to Britain in particular in two world wars, except for the temporary retention of minesweeping services. Having overseen the naval scene in postwar Germany, it was time to turn Admiralty attention to the continuing Far Eastern war and to his 'home' sea, the Mediterranean [328, 330, 333–5].[1]

---

[1]See C. Madsen, *The Royal Navy and German Naval Disarmament, 1942–1947* (London & Portland, OR, 1998).

281. *To Aunt Doodles*

1 January 1944

. . . I did get to the Palace House for Christmas and the day after but spent most of the latter on the telephone watching the course of events in the sinking of the *Scharnhorst*.

Well we have finished our year well and I hope will keep it up this year. Did you see the new *Scorpion* took a large part in the battle[,] you should ring a peel on the old bell to celebrate it.[1]

The cruisers in the Bay did well too and altogether I don't think the Huns can have enjoyed their Christmas season.[2] . . .

282. *Meeting of Anti-U-boat Warfare Committee*[3]

12 January 1944

U-boat Trend

The First Sea Lord said that during the first three weeks of December [1943] the concentration of U-boats on the Gibraltar route had continued to move to the north-westward, where a straggler from a westbound convoy had been attacked at the end of the year, the only successful action by U-boats in this area during the course of the whole month. Towards the end of the month an American destroyer operating with an escort carrier and HMS's *Hurricane* and *Tweed* had been sunk about 600 miles west of Finisterre.[4] The U-boats operating on the Russian convoy route had no success whatsoever. In the Mediterranean two

---

[1]*Scorpion*: destroyer commanded by Cunningham, 1911–18: 1910, 950t, 27.5k, 1×4in, 2×18in tt; evidently Aunt Doodles received the ship's bell. The newer *Scorpion*: destroyer, 1943, 1710t, 36k, 4×4.7in, 8×21in tt.

[2]The cruisers *Glasgow* and *Enterprise* (1926, 7580t, 32k, 7×6in, 3×4in, 16×21in tt) intercepted 11 German destroyers, some of them large, in the Bay of Biscay on 28 December 1943, sinking 3 and damaging several.

[3]Churchill set up (and usually chaired) the Anti-U-boat Warfare Cttee on 31 December 1942. The CAS, the C-in-C, Western Approaches, the AOC-in-C, Coastal Cmd, ministers and other naval and air officers and scientists attended, along with Cunningham. See D. Syrett (ed.), *The Battle of the Atlantic and Signals Intelligence: U-boat Situations and Trends 1841–1945* (Aldershot, 1998) and *The Battle of the Atlantic and Signals Intelligence: U-boat Tracking Papers 1941–1947* (Aldershot, 2002); and E. J. Grove (ed.), *The Defeat of the Enemy Attack on Shipping, 1939–45* (Aldershot, 1997).

[4]*Hurricane*: destroyer, 1939, 1340t, 36k, 3×4.7in, 8×21in tt; ex-Brazil; sunk NE of Azores, 24 December 1943.

Tweed: 'River' cl frigate, 1943, 1370t, 19k, 2×4in; sunk by *U-305*, Atlantic, 7 January 1944.

US destroyer unidentified.

'Hunt' class destroyers had been sunk off Bougie and one merchant vessel off Oran. The two U-boats concerned in these attacks had been sunk.[1] As regards the distant areas, two or three U-boats had operated in the Caribbean area and three merchant vessels had been sunk off the West African coast.[2] In the Indian Ocean where about five Japanese and one German U-boats were operating, several ships had been torpedoed. In general the tactics adopted by the enemy were extremely timid. The number of U-boats sunk had decreased considerably. This was mainly due to this timidity, but also due to the use by the enemy of the acoustic torpedo. The necessary counter tactics to the latter necessarily delayed and hampered counter attacks, while the use of the device 'Foxer' reduced the asdic efficiency of hunting vessels. New methods to overcome the latter disadvantage were under trial. Operations by aircraft during December had been hampered by poor weather, but in the last eight days there had been an improvement and 10 attacks had taken place in the Bay [of Biscay].

283. *From Admiral Sir Harold Burrough*

FO Commanding Gibraltar and
Mediterranean Approaches,
31 January 1944

[visiting the Azores Islands]

3. . . . I could not have had a more friendly reception from the Portuguese . . .
4. So far as our general relations with the Portuguese are concerned they appear to be willing and anxious to carry out their side of the agreement to the full. There can be no doubt, I think, that they are greatly influenced in their dealings with us by the ancient alliance which exists between the two countries, and this is something which no other nation shares. While therefore they are prepared to give us every concession within the agreement they do not feel quite the same about the Americans. . .[3]

---

[1]'Hunts': *Holcombe* (1942, 1050t) and *Tynedale* (1940, 1000t), torpedoed by *U-593* on 12 Dec 1943; *U-593* and *U-73*, sunk on 13 and 16 Dec 1943.
[2]*Kingswood*: Constantine, 1929, 5080gt, 10.5k; 17 Dec 1943.
Phemius: A. Holt, 1921, 7406gt, 14.5k; 19 Dec 1943.
Dumana: Br India, 1932, 8427t, 12.5k; 24 Dec 1943.
[3]Portugal, allied with UK since 1374 but neutral.

284. *Meeting of Anti-U-boat Warfare Committee*

15 March 1944

U-boat Trend

The First Sea Lord said that during the last two months the number of U-boats in operational service had remained constant, and that the rate of killing had been satisfactory. The outflow of U-boats from the Baltic to offset sinkings had averaged the same rate as in 1943, but it appeared that a considerable proportion of these U-boats had joined the Arctic force, as the scale of effort against our Russian convoys had been higher. Of about 165 U-boats in operational service, some 115 were based on Biscay ports, about 15 in the Mediterranean, about 30 in the Arctic and about six in the Black Sea. We had suffered serious casualties in the Indian Ocean as a result of a campaign by six U-boats which sailed from Penang, but which were expected to return to Biscay ports. Some six 740-tonners outward bound from the Bay of Biscay might be intended to renew this eastern campaign. The outstanding feature in the Indian Ocean was the boldness with which U-boats operated in focal areas, in great contrast to the North Atlantic where the initiative had been retained by our surface and air forces to harry and subdue a far larger number of U-boats.

In early January the U-boat dispositions had been close to the North Channel but towards the end of the month they withdrew to about 25°W, probably as a result of the weight of air attack. There had been no pack attacks of the type familiar a year ago, and it was thought the dispositions employed spread the U-boats more sparsely and led to fast travel by night to bring together enough U-boats for attack on any convoy reported. Co-operation with enemy reconnaissance aircraft west of Ireland had been a feature of recent enemy attacks, but this co-operation was far less effective against homeward than outward convoys, and was therefore a poor method of attack against our military build-up. Two bold U-boats were operating in the West African coastal areas, and there was some danger that this comparatively soft spot might be exploited. There had been no activity off Brazil, probably due to the strategic air patrols encountered there last summer. The Caribbean and US seaboard had also been inactive. There had been no indications so far that the enemy had increased his U-boat forces to meet any military invasion.

Operation 'Overlord' (2).

The Prime Minister enquired about possible enemy U-boat activity during Operation 'Overlord'.

In the course of discussion on this point the following views were expressed:

(a)   The enemy was unlikely to attempt to operate more than 20 to 25 U-boats on the western Coastal Convoy route. Others might be operating on the main route, on the eastern Coastal Convoy route in the Bristol Channel and off the North Cornish coast.

(b)   The enemy might well stage diversionary attacks by U-boats both in the Northern Approaches and in the Atlantic, as he would judge that we would have withdrawn considerable escort forces from the Atlantic. It would be of greatest help if American escort carriers and their attendant destroyers could act as support groups in the Atlantic during the 'Overlord' period.

285.   *To Admiral Sir John Tovey and Admiral Sir Bertram Ramsay*

17 March 1944

I have had brought to my notice more than once, in connection with 'Rankin' Case 'C', the disadvantages resulting from the lack of a naval authority to co-ordinate post-hostilities planning.[1] ... Post-hostilities planning in the naval sphere must proceed because it is necessary to work out beforehand an outline policy on operational and administrative questions such as the following:

(a)   The surrender of the German Fleet and U-boats.
(b)   Despatch of a naval force to Kiel, Brest and, possibly, other ports.
(c)   Control of the Belts and Sounds.
(d)   Obtaining control of the German naval organisation and bases, with particular reference to division of responsibilities between the Royal Navy and land forces.
(e)   Control and employment of enemy minesweepers.
(f)   Organisation for the Naval Control Commission.

Many of the above questions require co-ordination of policy between the Services and co-ordination of detailed planning between the Services in the various commands.

3.   The Admiralty must undertake formulation of general naval policy for the post-hostilities period and co-ordination of this policy both with

[1]'Rankin': scheme to exploit a German collapse.

the other Services and with our Allies. They cannot, however, under-take responsibilities for co-ordinating the plans of naval authorities with Army and Air Force authorities in the individual commands. To undertake this co-ordination of planning in post-hostilities matters a superior naval authority outside the Admiralty is therefore essential.

5.   It has been proposed that a naval authority should therefore be designated and provided now with a CoS and staff to plan for the situation which will arise after a collapse or an Armistice. The staff would have to work in close touch with the staff of SCAEF and other post-hostilities planning authorities.

6.   An organisation such as the above is necessary if the Navy is not to be left behind when the requirements of the post-hostilities period are being discussed. The plans for the Army and RAF are already being advanced by the staff placed at the disposal of SCAEF.

7.   The authority designated would be appointed when the appropriate time arrives to put into effect the plans to be prepared now by his staff. He might become Allied Naval C-in-C after the Armistice and/or Brit-ish Naval Plenipotentiary under the Armistice. The C-in-C, Nore, upon whom will devolve the main work of securing enemy naval bases in the north west of Germany, would be the natural authority to designate.

8.   It does not seem necessary or indeed desirable for the arrange-ments to provide for the linking of naval planning for Norway to the SAC in the post-hostilities period. On the other hand, the relations of the American Naval authorities in Western France with the SAC, with the Home Commands, and the Admiralty, is a problem of some diffi-culty. The existence of an Allied Naval C-in-C would facilitate the solution of this problem, though it may be capable of solution in other ways.

286.   *Diary*

3 April 1944

Held the usual COS meeting. During the meeting the news of the attack by the FAA on *Tirpitz* in the Altenfiord came through and then after lunch the report from the Vice-Admiral (Moore) that the attack had been successful[,] several hits having been scored. It is of course doubt-ful if the aircraft were carrying heavy enough bombs to put her out of action but we can hope that her AA armament, controls and upper works are badly smashed up. . . .

287. *Diary*

13 April 1944

. . . Henry Moore came in and I talked to him about a repeat 'Tungsten'. There appear to be no objections from a personnel point of view and he was quite ready to do it.

I called up Bruce Fraser about a repeat 'Tungsten' and found him in a most truculent and obstinate mood. He had held a meeting with his admirals and captains and made the decision that 'Tungsten' was not to be repeated. I reasoned with him and pointed out that the C-in-C's decisions were not irrevocable and that the Admiralty must be allowed some voice in what operations were to be carried out. He did not admit this and said if we were not satisfied we must get another C-in-C and in fact indicated he would haul his flag down if ordered to repeat 'Tungsten'. I told him to sleep on it and call me up in the morning.

I do not know what the underlying reason for this attitude is; to me a most untenable position to take up, but it may be that he resented very much being practically bludgeoned into 'Tungsten' originally and is determined to resist further pressure. . . .

288. *Diary*

14 April 1944

Called up by Fraser at 9.45 and discussed the repeat 'Tungsten' operation. I understood him to acquiesce.

. . . VCNS informed me that far from Fraser agreeing in our morning's conversation he refused to carry out the repeat operation and if ordered to would haul down his flag. This of course could not be tolerated but I held up the Admiralty's signal ordering him to carry out the operation and drafted one to him to come to London and see me and discuss things. This to give him another chance.[1] . . .

On my return to the Admiralty I found wiser councils had prevailed in the Home Fleet and some manoeuvring on a lower level and made Fraser more tractable therefore sent off both signals.

[1]VAdm Syfret.

289. *Diary*

25 April 1944

... In the afternoon Claude Barry brought in the captain who commanded the X submarine who entered Bergen and torpedoed the big ship and also the CO of *Sceptre* who towed him there. ... He told a very interesting story and his exploit was a fine one.[1] ...

Heard that 'Planet' i.e. second attack on *Tirpitz* had had to be abandoned because of weather but the aircraft from *Furious* and *Victorious* had attacked a convoy off Bodö and destroyed four ships and an escort.

290. *Diary*

17 May 1944

... Very disappointing that the second attack on *Tirpitz* was baulked by the weather. Sent a signal to the C-in-C, Home Fleet, emphasising that we must persist and try again as soon as possible. ...

291. *Diary*

22 May 1944

Bruce Fraser came in. .. Had a long talk with him about morale in the escort carriers. I can't agree with him that publicity has a great bearing on morale. If he *is* right it is a poor state of affairs and should be dealt with. He thinks Moore should now be allowed to command the Home Fleet as it is fading out a bit. I agree with him and if the PM were not so obstinate that would work out well.

---

[1] *Sceptre*: s/m, 1943, 715/1000t, 14.5/10k, 1×3in, 6×21in tt.

CO: Lt I. S. McIntosh: Mid Jan 1939; *Sussex* Sept 1939; Sub Lt Dec 1939; course, Portsmouth Sept 1940; Lt April 1941; *Porpoise* July 1941; *Thrasher* March 1942; *Sceptre* Feb 1943; *Mercury II* (signal est) Nov 1944.

Capt, X-craft: probably Lt K. R. Hudspeth, RANVR, CO of *X-10*, which attacked *Scharnhorst* but foundered on return, in tow. The two X-craft which successfully attacked *Tirpitz*, putting her engines out of action, were sunk at the scene and their survivors taken prisoner.

292. *Diary*

14 July 1944

COS meeting at 1100. CAS put forward a suggestion for an examination of productive capacity (Admiralty's) so that a bigger and better Tallboy bomb (22,000 lbs.) could be made. I refused the joint examination and turned it over to the Controller who feels we can do something about it.[1] . . .

293. *Diary*

17 July 1944

. . . Heard this morning of failure of attack on *Tirpitz*. First wave unable to see ship on account of smoke and second wave recalled because of fog. No luck.

294. *Diary*

20 July 1944

. . . I held two meetings after five. The first to decide whether to go for the *Tirpitz* again. This would mean holding back *Formidable*. I put forward several ideas to make the smoke defences expend themselves and we decided to have one more try. I also told the meeting that we must now pursue a more active policy against enemy shipping. Why should shipping still go peacefully up the Norwegian and Biscay Coasts unattacked except by the air or submarines? We must put aside all thought of the enemy air and get after this shipping with surface craft.

295. *Diary*

24 July 1944

. . . Meeting at 1500 with the C-in-C, Home Fleet, VCNS, etc., on further attack on *Tirpitz*. Nothing will do for them but Mosquitoes flown off from a carrier so as to attack from another direction than from southward. They entirely neglected the fact that had the RAF decided

[1] Adm Wake-Walker

to attack the *Tirpitz* they could long ago have flown Mosquitoes to Russia and do it from there. . . .

He [Churchill] is much inclined to publicise the work of the escort groups and Coastal Command in keeping the invasion passage clear of submarine attack. The President has however rather forbidden it. I do not wish to speak ill of anyone but this is a noteworthy all-British success and I fear President's message has been put up by the Navy Department.

296. *Meeting held by the First Sea Lord*

24 July 1944

Attack on Tirpitz.

1.   Another attack should be carried out as soon as practicable. The attack, so far as possible, should be on different lines from those hitherto carried out.

The method favoured by the C-in-C, Home Fleet, involves the use of 15 Mosquitoes, flown off a carrier simultaneously with an attack on shipping near Bodö, Mosquitoes making a detour to attack *Tirpitz* from the eastward. Carrier force then to proceed to the northward for an attack on the lines of those previously carried out, if possible taking steps to exhaust the enemy's smoke supply before the attack.

2.   The First Sea Lord authorised steps to be taken to ask the Air Ministry for Mosquitoes (Assistant Director of Planning (Air) for action). He made it clear that we should endeavour to attack *Tirpitz* whether or not these Mosquitoes can be made available.[1]

It was estimated that the Mosquitoes would require about four weeks for training.

3.   C-in-C, Home Fleet, asked that the *Implacable* Wing should be made available, and ACNS (Air) reported that he understood that this would require four to five weeks. The First Sea Lord approved the use of the *Implacable* Wing but said this training must be reduced.[2]

4.   C-in-C, Home Fleet, asked for a detailed appreciation of the possibility of exhausting the smoke supply in the Kaa Fjord (Director of Local Defence for action).[3]

---

[1]ADP (Air): Capt B. L. Moore: Cdr June 1935; *Cumberland* Nov 1938; Capt June 1940; Asst Dir, NAD Feb 1941; ADP (Air) Feb 1943; *Slinger* June 1944; SBN Lia O, Philippines May 1945.

[2]ACNS (Air): RAdm R. A. Portal: Capt 1934; *York* Aug 1939; RA Aug 1943; ACNS (Air) Jan 1943; RA, NA Stas, Australia & Pacific, *Golden Hind*, Sydney 1945.

[3]DLD: VAdm A. L. Phillips: Capt 1932; RA & DLD March 1942; VA & ret 1945.

Attack on Shipping in the Leads

5.   C-in-C said it is unlikely that we shall be able to enter the Leads with destroyers without considerable risk of casualties from guns and/ or mines. He intended to examine the plan on the following lines:

6.   With carrier-borne aircraft lay mines in the Leads and thus force convoys into the open sea, and attack them with surface forces. He asked for an appreciation of the mine-laying problem (DDOD (Mining) for action).[1]

7.   The First Sea Lord emphasised the importance of bringing surface forces to bear in order to *sink* more ships rather than damage them; our present air operations are not sinking enough.

Operations by Surface Forces in the Bay [of Biscay]

8.   The First Sea Lord directed that a force should prepare at Plymouth for attacking enemy ships in the Bay and that it should consist of two small cruisers and destroyers. He considered a Flag Officer would be required and asked C-in-C, Home Fleet, if he could spare one.

9.   C-in-C, Home Fleet, thought he could spare CS10 provided he could be available at Scapa one week before the sailing of the North Russian convoy, and he could take *Diadem* and *Bellona*.[2]

10.   C-in-C, Home Fleet, said that CS10 should sail for Plymouth as soon as practicable to prepare a plan. A signal would be required to C-in-C, Plymouth, and C-in-C, Home Fleet (DOD (Home) for action).[3]

11.   The First Sea Lord directed that an escort carrier should be made available with about 12 fighters to give fighter support to the force when retiring.

297.   *Diary*

1 August 1944

. . . Meeting with C-in-C, Nore, ANXCF and others to decide on the responsibility for planning and execution of the plans to occupy the German ports on Germany's surrender. I blew some of the grandiose ideas about personnel to the winds. A very useful meeting which cleared the air a lot. . . .

---

[1]DDOD (Mining): Capt J. S. Cowie: Cdr June 1931; TSD Sept 1939; A/Capt & OD 1940; DDOD (M) Jan 1942.
[2]CS10: VAdm F. Dalrymple-Hamilton.
Diadem: lt csr, 1944, 5770t, 33k, 8×5.25in, 6×21in tt.
[3]Adm Leatham.
DOD (H): Capt Pizey.

298. *Diary*

4 August 1944

... Much discussion on the offer by Petersen, head of the Swedish Secret Service, to exchange full information on the V2, V3 and V4 secret Hun weapons for our plans for the occupation of Norway. The offer was made to the Naval Attaché and it was decided to see if he could get it for nothing by telling him that 'The First Sea Lord was inexpressibly shocked that he should try and bargain over information which had to do with the lives of innocent British women and children' and pointing out the bad effect it would have on Swedish-British relations if the story was ever disclosed, etc., etc. Should he persist in having his pound of flesh he will be given the Norway cover plan.[1]

299. *Diary*

11 August 1944

... A new wile of the Hun appears to be a slow running torpedo which goes a long way and either steers itself into a ship by some device or circles after it has gone some distance. Another nuisance but one should be able to meet it.

300. *Diary*

3 October 1944

COS meeting at 1030. ... we had an animated discussion on the Control Commission for Germany. I was much against the present suggestions in which to my mind the Army representation outweighs the Navy and Air ditto out of all proportion to the relevant disarmament tasks ... I got several amendments made which to some extent met my point of view. ...

---

[1]NA, Stockholm: T/Lt H. D. G. Harris, RNVR: Lt April 1940; A/NA by Aug 1944.
V-2: German bombardment rocket bomb. V-3: long-range gun. V-4: there was none; possibly this is mis-numbering, as V-1 was a pilotless jet bomb.

301. *From Churchill*

26 October 1944

I think it will be regarded as a very serious misfortune if the *Tirpitz* succeeds in returning to Germany. I consider that every effort should be made to attack this ship even if losses have to be incurred.

302. *To Churchill*

27 October 1944

I fully agree. . . . Co-ordinated plans have been arranged with the Air Ministry for action by the Home Fleet, Coastal Command and Bomber Command in the event of the *Tirpitz* attempting the passage to Germany.

2.   It is known that the [German] High Command wishes the ship to remain in North Norway to contain strong British forces. Her move from Kaafjord to Tromsö was evidently dictated by the advance of the Russians. The ship moved at seven knots for the passage.

3.   These facts taken in conjunction with her present damaged condition, lead to the conclusion that it is most improbable that the long passage southward to Germany will be attempted at present.

4.   Meanwhile Bomber Command has planned an attack on the ship in her present berth as soon as weather conditions are favourable. Further action will depend on the results of this attack.

303. *Meeting of Anti-U-boat Warfare Committee*

31 October 1944

U-boat Trend

Sir Andrew Cunningham said that in mid-August enemy U-boats had withdrawn from the Biscay ports, after which operations in the Atlantic had been on a reduced scale, culminating in the present month of October during which they had scored no success whatever. In more distant parts the last six months had been quiet and although losses had been experienced in the Indian Ocean during the summer, for the past six weeks no U-boat had operated successfully there.

Off the east coast of Canada one to three U-boats had been operating, but in the Mediterranean the U-boat threat had been practically eliminated. It was anticipated that U-boat activity would start again in the near future, and would probably include the eastern coasts of Canada and the USA, and the approaches to the Mediterranean. Intelligence and PoW reports pointed to this resumption of activity and also indicated that the enemy's production of the new fast large type U-boat would probably reach a peak output of 30 boats per month by the end of December. It was estimated that there would be 95 of these U-boats in operation by April 1945. By the 1 December it was estimated that the enemy would have 200 U-boats operational, including 15 of the new type and that his present building programme should enable him to maintain this scale of activity on both sides of the Atlantic and on important shipping routes. The underwater speed of the new U-boats was from 13 to 15 knots and they were fitted with improved Radar which enabled them to obtain early warning of aircraft and surface vessels searching with Radar. They were fitted with a form of double hull which should render them less vulnerable to damage and they were more streamlined and hence formed a difficult end-on target. They were fitted with very silent engines and had very considerably increased underwater endurance; a PoW report spoke of one having spent 30 days under water.

The Committee: Took note of this statement.

Counter-action against the new U-boat Threat: (2) The Prime Minister raised the question of counter-action against the enemy's new U-boats and asked in particular if bombing action was proposed against production centres for the pre-fabricated parts, against the three known assembly yards and against the depot ships and U-boat pens in Norwegian waters.

In the course of general discussion the following points were made:

(i)   Sir Charles Portal agreed that the enemy's U-boat threat by itself formed a very strong case for bombing action, and said that this problem would be considered inter-departmentally. He felt, however, that before any decision was taken the effect on other operations must be carefully assessed. For example, it had been estimated that only 10 days suitable for visual bombing by the heavy air forces would obtain over the next two months. It had been estimated that even if one such day was devoted to attacks on U-boat installations the effect on the present campaign of bombing the enemy's oil plants would be a gain to the enemy of 15,000 tons of oil per month, which figure represented the present monthly allotment of all the German Army Groups in the west. Judged in this light it might be unwise to make any diversion from the oil campaign until the extent of the new U-boat threat was more certain.

In reply to a suggestion that a small part of the heavy bomber force might be diverted to anti-U-boat targets, he pointed out that this would probably entail considerable complication regarding fighter escorts, as a small bomber force would be a very vulnerable target by day over Germany.

(ii)   Sir Max Horton said he anticipated that the principal danger would be from U-boat operations in the focal areas, particularly in the north-west and south-west approaches. The enemy had never previously operated close inshore except on a limited scale for very short periods. He felt that our hunting forces would be handicapped in the anticipated new campaign by three factors: firstly, the enemy's use of the 'Schnorkel', which would greatly reduce the effectiveness of our coastal air forces and surface forces; secondly, the enemy's new Radar which would enable him to evade air and sea hunting forces using Radar; and thirdly, the reduced efficiency of our Asdics due to temperature layers frequently experienced in the shallow waters where operations were expected and to the presence of wrecks in these waters. He gave an outline of probable enemy tactics, saying that he anticipated that U-boats would lie on the bottom near focal points, particularly in areas where wrecks were common, and would remain in this position listening for approaching convoys. On the approach of a convoy the U-boat would probably come to about 80 feet, carry out an attack and then return to the bottom. He pointed out, however, that such tactics would place a great strain on U-boat crews, particularly on the Captains, and that in view of the present state of the enemy's morale, it was likely that only a minority would prove really determined in such tactics.

He mentioned that we had modified one of our submarines to achieve 12 knots submerged and had been using this craft for exercises with escort groups. A particularly experienced group had had no success during the first week of such exercises, but had improved rapidly thereafter. As this was the only submarine so modified, the training programme was a difficult one.[1]

(iii)   Sir Andrew Cunningham mentioned that our anti-submarine forces were being increased to 21 escort groups of which 18 were already operational. He agreed that the threat, if the new U-boats operated inshore, would be serious. While agreeing that the cost must be carefully counted before diverting bombers from the present oil campaign, it must be remembered that the enemy's U-boat was his only remaining worthwhile weapon.

(iv)   Captain Howard-Johnston said that he had analysed a large number of attacks on wrecks carried out in the Channel during the invasion period. Provided the attacking forces when in contact with a

---

[1] *Seraph*: s/m, 1941, 715/990t; streamlined July 1944; 16.75/12.5k.

non-sub[marine] echo adopted the policy of three accurate attacks, the presence of wrecks should not serve to give a submarine immunity. The enemy's use of the 'Schnorkel' during the above operations had been a considerable handicap to our coastal air forces, but nevertheless he had achieved little during this period.[1]

(v) Sir Max Horton said that one of the great handicaps under which attacking forces were operating at present was the use of 'Foxer' and 'Cat' devices to defeat the 'Gnat' torpedo. These devices seriously affected 'Asdic' efficiency, but it might be possible to dispense with them by means of a new scheme to reduce the propeller noise of attacking craft. Another possibility was the use of an expendable 'noise maker' which was showing considerable promise and which should deflect the 'Gnat' torpedo without adverse effect to 'Asdic' efficiency.[2]

(vi) The First Lord mentioned the concrete piercing bomb for attack on U-boat pens as Bergen and Trondheim. Sir Charles Portal said that so far only Fortress aircraft could carry this weapon and that their range was insufficient to reach Trondheim.

(vii) In answer to the Prime Minister it was stated that considerable anti-U-boat mining had been carried out both in the north-west and south-west approaches and in the Channel and off the coast of Norway.

(viii) Admiral Stark suggested the possible use of blimps fitted with MAD equipment for locating U-boats resting on the seabed in coastal waters. He said that Admiral King had enquired regarding our estimate of the probable enemy tactics when the new U-boats were in service and had offered assistance if required.[3]

(ix) Dr Goodeve mentioned a form of underwater IFF which was under design and which might be of value for marking the position of well-known wrecks. The endurance of this device at present was about one week, but this might be increased to several months by modification.[4]

(x) Sir Robert Renwick (MAP) suggested that a Radar coast watch might be instituted in narrow waters where it was thought probable that new U-boats would operate. Although the range of ASV on 'Schnorkel' was only six miles from aircraft, it might be possible to increase this figure if the Radar set was mounted ashore.[5]

[1]Capt C. D. Howard-Johnston: Cdr June 1937; *Malcolm* Dec 1940; *Eaglet* (Liverpool) Dec 1942; Capt June 1943; DAUD Oct 1943.

[2]'Gnat': a German acoustic torpedo. 'Cat': Canadian noise-maker.

[3]MAD: Magnetic Anomaly Detector, an aircraft s/m location device, 1942.

[4]Dr (Sir Charles) Goodeve (1904–80): b Canada; chemist & metals; Cdr, RNVR (ret); DD, Misc Wpns Dev 1940–2; DCntrlr, R&D, 1942–5.

[5]Lord (Sir Robert) Renwick (1904–73): businessman; Cntrlr of Cmns, Air Min, 1942–5.

(xi) The Prime Minister, in summing up the discussion, said he was not alarmed by this new enemy U-boat threat, although it was perfectly proper to give urgent consideration to all possible counter-measures. While no major diversion of bombing attack from the main oil targets should be made at this stage, detailed plans should be made for attacking all elements of the U-boat organisation such as production centres, pre-fabrication yards, assembly shipyards, depot ships and U-boat pens. All other counter-measures and the development of all devices to meet this new threat should be pressed ahead with energy. He asked to be supplied with a chart of the north-west approaches showing the wrecks there and the most probable areas of U-boat operations, and to be kept informed of any important developments. The whole matter should be kept under review and should again be considered at a meeting on 28 November unless the Admiralty felt that any major changes in the situation in the meantime called for an earlier meeting.

304. *Diary*

12 November 1944

. . . Was rung up both by the Admiralty and CAS to tell me that Bomber Command had sunk the *Tirpitz*. A very good job though it actually makes little difference to the naval dispositions. *Tirpitz* had been written off as a fighting unit six months ago and one only had to look out that she did not make her way south.

305. *Diary*

13 November 1944

It looks as though *Tirpitz* had been sunk by close misses alongside and one hit as she heeled over and capsized. . . .

306. *Diary*

27 November 1944

. . . COS meeting at 1100. A fierce discussion with the CAS as to who was responsible for the removal of the A/S aircraft from the Azores. There is no doubt the Air Ministry are clothing a political object in A/S garb. . . .

307. *Diary*

19 December 1944

Anti-U-boat meeting at 1830. PM inclined to lash out at all and sundry and rather petulant. Declared that he couldn't understand the difficulties of finding a U-boat on the bottom. Why had the problem only just been encountered, etc., etc. Then we had a good discussion on bombing U-boat targets. The Air Ministry were on a bad wicket as they had bombed naval targets in Gdynia without any consultation with the Admiralty. CAS came a long way to meet us and Stafford Cripps did us a real service by saying that it was obvious that the liaison on bombing and targets required improving. Good results altogether and I think CAS will do as he said he would.[1]

308. *Meeting of Anti-U-boat Warfare Committee*

19 December 1944

[Statement by the First Sea Lord]

U-boat Trend

... in November only four merchant ships were sunk by U-boats, two in the North Atlantic and two in the Indian Ocean, but the number of U-boats had also been low and the number of operational U-boats was therefore increasing.[2] To date two ships had been sunk during December, one off Cape Cod and the other in the English Channel.[3] The enemy had concentrated his main effort in the focal areas around the British Isles with patrols in the Channel and South Western and North Western Approaches. The re-appearance of U-boats in the Channel pointed to the enemy's intention to interfere with our supply lines to the Continent. A frigate had been sunk off Cape Wrath and another damaged in the North Western Approaches; one merchant ship had been sunk off Fowey and another damaged off Cherbourg.[4] Surface

---

[1]Sir Stafford Cripps (1889–1952): barrister; Lab MP; Solr Gen 1929–31; Amb to USSR 1940–2; Ld Privy Seal & Ldr, HC 1942; MAP 1942–5; mission to India 1942; Pres, BoT 1945–7; C Ex 1947–50.

[2]The only UK loss was: N Atl: *Shirvan*: Baltic Trading, 1925, 6017gt.
Indian O: *Marion Möller*: (Danish), 3827gt.

[3]Neither ship identified.

[4]Sunk off Fowey, Cornwall: *Silverdale*: probably an S. & J. Thompson vessel. Cherbourg ship: unknown.

forces had made some promising attacks in coastal waters and a U-boat had run ashore on the Wolf Rock the previous day and foundered.[1] In the Atlantic three or four U-boats appeared to be patrolling the Canadian Coastal area, including the Gulf of St Lawrence. A merchant ship had been damaged and a Canadian frigate was presumed lost in this area.[2] No Atlantic convoys had been attacked. The Indian Ocean had been quiet apart from the two sinkings mentioned, and in that area a Liberator had heavily damaged a U-boat, probably Japanese. The average number of U-boats in the Atlantic and UK Coastal Waters was estimated at over 25 and the figure was tending to increase. 120 U-boats were thought to be available for operations, apart from some 40 in the Arctic and Baltic, while 150 boats of all types were working up in the Baltic. The Arctic Force of 25–30 U-boats was employed on attacking Russian[-bound] convoys but apart from damage to one destroyer, their efforts had so far been ineffective, and the escorts of a recent convoy claimed to have sunk one U-boat for certain and possibly three others. As regards the new type U-boat, there was no definite sign yet of their operational use but nearly 40 of the larger and 20 of the smaller type were believed to have been completed and in addition up to 90 large and 35 of the smaller type were building. It was thought that the enemy intended to withhold these new type U-boats until he had sufficient numbers to deliver a really telling attack and we might, therefore, have about two months' respite. The smaller type would probably operate against the East Coast and Continental traffic, and the larger type in focal areas and on Oceanic routes. In general U-boats at present appear to be feeling their way with new devices, particularly the 'Schnorkel' and when the fast U-boat campaign started it would have the experience of considerable 'Schnorkel' experience. This device, combined with the higher speeds would seriously reduce the power of surface craft and aircraft to take a toll of the attacking forces.

In the course of a general discussion on the First Sea Lord's statement the following points arose:

1.   Sir Sholto Douglas said that the targets were proving very elusive and that although about 35 U-boats were operating in Coastal Command's area, sightings other than smoke or swirls were rare.

C. Wrath frigate: *Bullen*: 'Captain' cl [US built], 1943, 1400t, 23.5k, 3×3in; sunk by *U-775*, 6 Dec 1944.
NW Apps frigate: unknown.
[1]*U-1209*.
[2]Unknown.

Aircraft were working in close collaboration with escort groups and homing them on to such sightings whenever possible.[1]

2. Sir Max Horton agreed that enemy's new tactics were proving very difficult to combat and said that he had concentrated the majority of his escort groups in the Approaches to give safe passage rather than to seek to attack the enemy in the transit area. The enemy's use of shallow water was proving a severe handicap to the Asdic.

3. In reply to a question by the Prime Minister as to why the enemy was not achieving more success, Sir Max Horton said the chief factor was the human element; the enemy did not appear to have recovered his morale and very long periods submerged or proceeding by 'Schnorkel', no doubt had a depressing effect on submarine crews.

4. Lord Cherwell pointed out that whereas between a third and half the number of U-boats were operational, compared with the height of the U-boat campaign, the sinkings were less than a tenth of those achieved at that time. Sir Andrew Cunningham thought that this was accounted for by the fact that the enemy had been taking up inshore patrolling positions. While he was not unduly disturbed by the present campaign, the enemy undoubtedly had it in his power to launch an intensive attack later which might be extremely difficult to counter.

5. It was explained that the enemy's use of shallow coastal waters handicapped surface forces using Asdics because of the presence of wrecks, the temperature gradations of the water and the reverberation suffered by Asdic under such conditions.

309. *Diary*

11 January 1945

. . . It was decided that the Joint Planners would investigate the implications of a successful submarine war and recommend measures. The CAS raised no objection to the bombing question being looked into. . . .

[1] ACM Sholto Douglas.

310. *Diary*

15 January 1945

... Meeting with the Controller, VCNS and ACNS (H) and (UT) to decide on mining policy in regard to this new attack of the U-boats in coastal waters.[1] Controller has at hand 35,000 mines but at present can only prepare 1500 a month. He was instructed to put measures in hand to increase output to 5,000. *Ariadne* to be recalled from Pacific to help to lay.[2] Immediately after came the news that *Thane* (escort carrier) and a tanker had been torpedoed in the Firth of Clyde. Also another off Holyhead.[3] We are having a bad time these last two days. ... First Lord getting very het up about the U-boats.

311. *Minutes of First Sea Lord's meeting to discuss methods of frustrating the U-boat campaign*

15 January 1945

The First Sea Lord opened the meeting by saying that our present counter measures to the U-boat campaign were not effective and that he had called this meeting to review the proposals for the future.

Minelaying

The probabilities of an extensive minelaying campaign in the Coastal Waters of the British Isles were then discussed. The Controller said that the present bottleneck was insufficient labour at the mine depots, but that he would take the necessary steps to remedy the situation. The First Sea Lord said he would speak to the Minister of Production and inform him of this requirement, and direct the Controller to examine the possibility of opening up an additional mine depot or depots. DDOD (M) said that the physical conditions were such that he doubted if a laying effort of more than 4,000 mines per month could be maintained.

The mining proposals received from C-in-C, Western Approaches, were examined in detail and discussion followed as to the best method

[1] ACNS (H): Adm Sir Desmond McCarthy (1893–1966): Capt 1935; RA 1944; ACNS (H) 1944–6; RA (D), Med 1946–7; VA 1948; C-in-C S Atl 1948–50; ret 1950; Adm 1952.
ACNS (UT): RAdm J. G. L. Dundas (1893–1952): Capt 1935; Cdre & CoS, Med F April 1942; RA & ACNS (UT) Oct 1944–March 1945; VA & ret 1948.
[2] *Ariadne*: minelayer, 1943, 2650t, 39.75k, 100–156 mines, 4×4in.
[3] *Thane*: escort carrier, 1943, 11420t, 16k, 2×5in, 20 a/c; torpedoed by *U-482*, 15 Jan 1945, irreparably damaged.
Tanker damaged in Clyde: unknown.
Tanker sunk off Holyhead: *Maja*, Anglo-Saxon Petrol, 1931, 8181gt; 15 Jan 1945.

of laying the fields. First Sea Lord said that the first thing to do was to mine the enemy out of the Irish Sea. C-in-C, Western Approaches' proposals appeared the best means of achieving this with the laying of the inner fields first. First Sea Lord also directed that a signal should be sent asking COMINCH to release *Ariadne* to take part in these minelaying operations. The depth of the fields was then discussed in the course of which the First Sea Lord said we did not want to incommode our own ships and that it was necessary to patrol as many deep minefields as possible. DDOD (M) said that from the technical point of view, a standard depth of 60 feet would have a favourable effect on the laying output.

First Sea Lord decided that the initial fields should be laid at a standard depth of 60 feet below chart datum, and experience may show later that a better comparative depth can be arrived at. The First Sea Lord said that this minelaying campaign was to have priority over minelaying by SHAEF and that he would mention this to Admiral Burrough. He also confirmed that the increase in defensive minefields was not to be at the expense of the defensive effort by Bomber Command.

The question of controlled minefields and indicator loops was finally discussed, and the possibility of their use is being further investigated by DAUD.[1]

Nets

The various types of net were then discussed and the advantages and disadvantages of each explained.

The First Sea Lord said that the OB (bottom net) and the O (Jackstay on surface) have value, and directed ACNS (UT) to work out a plan for their use with C-in-C, Western Approaches. The First Sea Lord also said that the OP (piano wire on floats) was a promising weapon and experiments were to be continued as fast as possible. ACNS (UT) was directed to report results.

Memorandum regarding Counter Measures taken and in hand

(a)   Improvement of Radar detection of Schnorkel. Certain types of aircraft and surface vessel radar sets modified. Investigations and trials continuing.
(b)   Automatic signalling wreck buoys. Designed and produced for purpose of assisting classification of contacts.
(c)   Extension of GEE and SS Loran chains. In north western and south western approaches to facilitate accurate fixing and the

---

[1]Capt Howard-Johnston.

plotting of wrecks and other non-subs. North west approaches completed; south west approaches in progress.[1]

(d)   Detection by infra-red. Investigations proceeding.

(e)   Provision of additional training submarines, converted to fast underwater speed and Schnorkel-fitted.

(f)   Provision of Schnorkel targets for training.

(g)   Investigation into possibility of improved H/E detection. Proceeding.

(h)   Laying of trap mines near convoy routes and in likely areas. Proceeding.

(i)   Laying of wire obstructions for damaging Schnorkels. Proceeding.

(j)   Re-institution of coastal convoys in Irish Sea.

(k)   Inclusion of U-boat building yards, pens and operational bases in weekly Naval Targets priority list.

(l)   Aircraft mining in Baltic, Kattegat and [off] Norwegian coast.

(m)   Pure tone anti-Gnat. A noise-maker tuned to home the Gnat. Being developed to take the place of the existing Foxer noise-maker. It will cause less interference with asdics.

(n)   Expendable noise-makers. Anti-Gnat, to reduce necessity for using Foxers. Being developed.

(o)   Provision of three-dimensional radio sono buoys.

312.   *Diary*

18 January 1945

. . . C-in-C, Coastal Command, Sholto Douglas, came in to see me. He is naturally very much against operations on the defensive against the U-boats. The truth of the whole matter is that his aircraft are for the moment out of business and asdics are not functioning very well in shallow waters. So until we can make our coastal waters prohibitive by minefields we must go on the principle that where the carcass is, there will be the eagles gathered together – and go into convoy.

[1]GEE: an electronic navigation system for aircraft, 1942.
SS Loran chains: long range navigational aid.

313. *To Fraser*[1]

19 January 1945

5.   We are having a difficult time with the U-boats. There is no doubt this schnorkel has given them a greater advantage than we first reckoned on. I believe some of them have done as much as six weeks at sea without surfacing. The scientists have not yet caught up and the air are about 90% out of business. The asdic is also failing us. The U-boat has found out that if he conducts his patrol close inshore or in confined waters where there is a good tidal stream, the tidal rips will to a great extent defeat the asdic – so it is about 50%, I imagine, out of business. As you probably know, they have been active and caused us losses in the last few weeks in the Channel, off Holyhead and one specially bold one penetrated into the Firth of Clyde. Science having failed us for the moment we are entering on an extensive deep minefield programme, starting by mining them out of the Irish Sea and the East Coast and then extending the minefields to the southward to try and keep them in deep water again – this of course will take time but we hope to finish in the early summer. . . .

314. *Diary*

22 January 1945

. . . It looks as though he [Churchill] is waking up to the U-boat threat. He talked [at Cabinet] of increased bombing of the assembly yards.

315. *To Admiral G. C. Jones, RCN*[2]

25 January 1945

Forecast of the U-boat Campaign during 1945

Present Situation

Since early 1944 the main U-boat effort has moved from the Atlantic to inshore waters particularly those of the UK including the English

---

[1]By this time, Adm Fraser was C-in-C, BPF.
[2]VAdm G. C. Jones, RCN: Capt Aug 1938; Ottawa, 1939; Cdre 1st Cl, Canadian DF, *Assiniboine* 1941; RA Dec 1941; *Strathcona* (RCN Barracks, Halifax, NS) 1942; VA & COS, Ottawa May 1944.

Channel and Irish Sea, where U-boats have recently achieved some measure of success.

2.   Although the enemy has generally operated in force against the Russian convoys, our percentage of kills has been favourable compared with our losses. Due to sinkings of U-boats and supply ships activity in the Indian Ocean has decreased.

3.   Since Operation 'Overlord', in which our losses were slight, the effectiveness of our aircraft and surface forces has been greatly reduced by the enemy's increasing experience in the use of Schnorkel, improved equipment and bottoming tactics in shallow waters where asdic conditions are in favour of the U-boat. Recently they have shown a more aggressive spirit and penetrated the focal areas of the UK where casualties have been more severe than in the summer.

New Offensive

4.   It is estimated that February or March of this year will see the advent of two new types of U-boat, large numbers of which are under construction and working up.

   (a)   Type XXI – a 1600-tonner carrying 26 torpedoes with a high surface speed and a submerged speed of 15 knots with increased underwater endurance.

   (b)   Type XXIII – 180 tons, 2 torpedoes, about 13 knots submerged and long endurance.

5.   It is estimated that about 30 Type XXI and 15 Type XXIII can be made ready for operations during February. It is possible that these numbers will be considered sufficient to start the campaign in strength. This is thought to be the enemy's intention.

Future U-boat Dispositions

6.   The old and new types will probably be used simultaneously and the most likely operating areas are considered to be:

   (a)   Type XXI – Western Approaches to UK but concentrating against ocean convoys using pack tactics in the Atlantic.

   (b)   Type XXIII – Coastal convoy routes and focal areas on the east and south east coasts of the British Isles.

   (c)   740-tonners and U-Kreuzers – Indian Ocean, Caribbean, off West Africa and North and South American coasts.[1]

   (d)   500-tonners – In UK coastal waters and between the UK and Gibraltar.

[1]U-kreuzers: cruiser s/m, probably larger s/m of c1500t.

Such dispositions would undoubtedly cause serious dispersal of our very limited A/S forces.

7.   On present estimates, by mid-February, the enemy will probably be able to maintain a total of 60 increasing to 80 boats *on patrol* compared with an average total of 30 at sea during the past three months.

Counter Measures

8.   The development of counter measures is proceeding at high priority. (Details are given in the Appendix.) Whether these will prove effective in time to prevent heavy losses of shipping remains to be seen.

Bombing

9.   The three main U-boat assembly and building yards are at Hamburg, Bremen and Danzig.

They are accorded the highest priority by the Admiralty. Danzig is now threatened by the Russian advance and it estimated that the capture of this port will reduce U-boat production by about 30% but that the effect will not be felt at sea for four to five months afterwards.

Morale

10.   Recent U-boat successes indicate improved morale of Commanders and, as their successes become more widely known by the U-boat arm, the offensive spirit generally will increase. On the other hand, morale will no doubt be influenced by:
   a.   the success or failure of land operations in Europe.
   b.   the ability of our A/S forces to kill and harry the U-boats.
   c.   the development of new allied technical equipment and counter measures.

Estimated Shipping Losses

11.   On the assumption that each U-boat during a patrol will sink one ship, it has been estimated that our shipping losses may rise to about 200 ships a quarter from the beginning of the main offensive, later increasing to 250, compared with 180 a quarter during the worst period in the spring of 1943.

These figures, being based on surmise, may vary greatly. Sinking by midget U-boats, which are now operating off the coast of the Low Countries, have not been taken into account.

Such high losses might well seriously interfere with the maintenance of our forces in Europe and the Far East.

Conclusions

12.   The new U-boat offensive could begin about mid-February. Experience and confidence in the Schnorkel and improved GSR have considerably reduced the effectiveness of our air and surface forces in combating this new threat which is severe and may result in high shipping losses.[1] Much depends, however, on the morale and offensive spirit of U-boat crews and the effectiveness of our counter measures.

Appendix

Counter Measures against U-boat Threat round British Isles

1.   Convoys in the Irish Sea.

Daily convoys on the principal routes have been instituted in the Irish Sea for all shipping excluding coasters of less than 1,000 tons.

2.   Mining

A large mining policy has been embarked on with the object of protecting our shipping in the Irish Sea and the English Channel, and eventually of driving the U-boats out of coastal areas. Lines of mines are being laid across the north and south approaches to the Irish Sea. In the English Channel, trap minefields near selected focal areas are being laid.

   All available resources, both as regards the production of the mines and vessels to lay them have been brought to bear.

3.   Escorts

A diversion of escorts from foreign waters has been ordered, which, together with new construction, by early next month will have added substantially to our resources at home.

4.   Inshore Patrols

A collection of various types of small patrol craft, capable of keeping the sea in our inshore focal areas, is being made in the Western Approaches Command, with the idea of flooding likely areas to the maximum density. These craft, few of which will be asdic-fitted, are more in the nature of an embarrassment to U-boats than of killing groups, but the great majority will mount lethal weapons.

---

[1]GSR: unknown.

5. Non-Lethal Traps

Devices to snare U-boats with wire obstructions and indicating devices, are being produced, and a first lay of 30 miles of wire across the U-boat route north-east of the Shetlands is already being laid.

Another device is floating lengths of piano wire, with indicating floats, to catch the Schnorkel and so disclose the submarine's presence. Experiments are proceeding.

6. Schnorkel Detection

Experiments are proceeding at highest priority to improve radar and Thermal detection of Schnorkel by aircraft and surface forces.

316. Meeting of Anti-U-boat Warfare Committee

26 January 1945

1. U-boat Trend

Sir Andrew Cunningham said that since 20 December [1944], 15 merchant ships and five warships had been lost as a result of U-boat activity. Of the merchant ships, 12 have been in the English Channel and the Irish Sea. Our successes compared unfavourably with our losses; subject to final assessment, three U-boats were known to have been sunk, two probably sunk and there had been only one promising attack. Only one of these successes took place in the inshore waters of the British Isles. With their growing experience in the use of Schnorkel and comparative immunity from attack by bottoming tactics, the enemy had shown a much more offensive spirit. About 12 U-boats have been operating in coastal waters round the UK, two or three in the Halifax area and one in the Western Approaches to the south of Gibraltar. In Arctic waters a convoy to Russia had made the return trip without loss. The extent of the U-boat offensive depended a good deal on the spirit of the U-boat commanders which will, no doubt, be influenced by the success or failure of land operations, upon our ability to destroy U-boats, and also upon the degree to which bombing of U-boat construction slips, repair yards and bases can be pursued. By mid-February the enemy should be able to maintain a total of 60, increasing during the spring to 80 boats on patrol. The possibility of Type XXIII boats operating on our East Coast at an even earlier date could not be ruled out.

2. *U-boat Campaign of 1945*

... Sir Andrew Cunningham warned the Committee that the enemy was achieving his present successes entirely with the older type of U-boat and that there was little doubt that the threatening offensive, with the new type U-boat, would shortly materialise. ...

317. *Diary*

26 January 1945

1130 Anti-U-boat [Committee] meeting, PM in the chair. Nothing much done but the problem laid bare. The scientists came in for a bottle for letting the Huns get ahead of them. I had given ours one the day before. ...

318. *CCS Directive*

2 February 1945

The CCS consider that the current German U-boat programme, if not countered, will present a serious threat to our North Atlantic shipping lanes.

It is therefore directed that the following counter measures be taken by all appropriate commanders:

(a) Build up as much as practicable the strength of surface hunting groups and anti-U-boat air squadrons.
(b) Maintain, and if possible increase, 'marginal' bomber effort on assembly yards, concentrated as far as is practicable against Hamburg and Bremen.
(c) Maintain 'marginal' effort against operating bases, be ready to increase this when bases become crowded beyond the capacity of concrete pens.
(d) Increase, by 100% if possible, the air mining effort against U-boats, including the training areas.
(e) Mine waters beyond the range of (d) above by using surface minelayers and carrier-borne aircraft.
(f) Intensify operations against enemy minesweepers.
(g) Maintain and intensify operations against the enemy shipping used to supply U-boat bases.

319. *Cunningham's comment on DAUD's Memorandum D353 (4 February 1945): Anti-U-boat Results*

22 February 1945

These excursions into statistic calculations mean just nothing. DAUD is back at his old habit of making didactic assertions on insufficient data.

320. *Diary*

26 February 1945

. . . The U-boat situation is also causing me some anxiety. In the last two or three days we have had sinkings off Land's End, south of the Lizard, off Berwick, off Ramsgate, and on the Thames-Flushing route. More U-boats are appearing from German ports than for some time. Added to this the small ones, Seehunds, Bibers, etc., and the E-boats at night are very active. We may be in for a difficult time. . . .

321. *Diary*

1 March 1945

. . . The losses on the Thames-Flushing channel are rather disquieting.

Held a meeting to discuss A/S measures and also anti-E-boat measures just to reassure myself that all steps that can be taken are being taken. I directed that no escort vessel that could run however badly was to be paid off and that new ones must be commissioned without paying off corresponding old ones. If necessary commitments to the Far East and East Indies must be deferred. It seems to me to be a case of putting our greatest effort into holding the U-boats for the next three months and everything must be sacrificed to that object.

As regards E-boats C-in-C, Nore, wants more destroyers and we must try and get them for him. Of course the chief reason for the E-boats' success is that our own MTBs are so slow that they can't overtake or even keep up with them.[1]

We also discussed the question of putting obstructions to the north of the Flushing-Thames channel.

---

[1] E-boat: various classes, 33–42.5k. MTB & MGB: various classes, 27.5–45k

322.   *Diary*

2 March 1945

. . . Two more ships sunk by U-boats in the Irish Sea. Have ordered six 'Hunts' home from the Mediterranean and am trying to make others available for C-in-C, Nore.[1]

323.   *From Captain J. G. L. Dundas[2]*

9 March 1945

Reasons for the failure of Coastal Command to follow up sightings with kills

I have discussed this with SNSO, Coastal Command.

2.   It is quite clear that the principal cause of successes during the last two years has been the U-boat policy of remaining on the surface to engage our aircraft. The great majority of engagements have resulted in a victory for Coastal Command. The U-boat was detected or sighted on the surface and remained on the surface to fight it out. Thus our target was never lost to view. Now the enemy, on becoming aware of the presence of aircraft either by periscope or search receiver, at once shuts off his Schnorkel smoke and submerges Schnorkel and periscope. The result is that the aircraft cannot get to close enough range for a good shot before the point of aim is lost.

3.   A minor contributory cause arises from the fact that the U-boat can submerge his Schnorkel from periscope depth very much quicker than he can submerge from the surface, and thus again the aircraft's point of aim is lost to view too early for accurate attack.

4.   On the other hand Coastal Command do claim that they have made a few promising attacks at night when they have come upon the Schnorkel unawares, and with progress in the latest detection devices, they hope to improve considerably on their present performance.

---

[1]*Oriskany*: 1644gt; 24 Feb 1945.
Norfolk Coast: Coast Lines, 1937, 646gt, 11k; 28 Feb 1945.
'Hunts': unknown.
[2]RAdm Dundas

324. *Diary*

13 March 1945

. . . Though fuel is not abundant, the requirement of enemy submarines can be met. . . .

325. *Diary*

28 March 1945

. . . I sent off a signal to Somerville pointing out the necessity of opening the German naval ports and capturing them to hinder the U-boat war, also the necessity clearing Holland from an E-boat and midget submarine point of view and again the desirability of opening up the Skaggerak and so releasing the one-and-a-half million tons of Swedish shipping lying idle in Swedish ports to say nothing of the Norwegian shipping. I told him to put these points to King. . . .

326. *Diary*

4 April 1945

COS meeting with Directors of Intelligence. In the paper they rather wrote down likelihood of the German fleet or what remains of it issuing from the ports and doing as much damage as possible before sinking. Well we shall see. . . .

Burrough came in and we had a long talk. I think he went away fairly happy. I talked to him of opening Bremen and Hamburg and the reduction of Heligoland and the islands at the mouths of the Elbe, Weser and Jade.

327. *Diary*

9 May 1945

. . . U-boats have started popping up so the signal has gone through.

The formal terms of surrender signed in Berlin last night. Tedder signed on behalf of the Anglo-US armies.

328.   *To Stark*

17 May 1945

I enclose . . . a copy of a signal which the British COS have sent to our JSM in Washington concerning the disposal of the German U-boats in Norwegian ports.

The policy set out therein has the approval of the Prime Minister. If you are in agreement perhaps you would support it with Admiral King. You will realise the urgency as the sooner we get these 100 or so U-boats under our control in ports in the British Isles before our Russian allies start to ask questions the better. Perhaps I should also point out that bringing them over here constitutes an infraction of the rules, but I think we can get away with that.

329.   *Cunningham's Minute on Operation 'Halfback'*

25 June 1945

Action with three German destroyers 27–28 January 1945:
HMS Diadem, *HMS* Mauritius

If it is really considered that two cruisers cannot fight a snap action against three destroyers without having a 'carefully considered and flexible tactical plan' (para. 9 of DSTD's minute), I despair of the future of the Navy.[1]

I also disagree with para. 5 of the same minute. The VAC 10 CS had just a few minutes to close the range, which he wisely used to that purpose, instead of messing about to avoid what might be imaginary torpedoes. Probably his gunfire benefited also thereby. He took the risk and though he failed to achieve decisive results, I see no way in which his actions could be bettered with the inadequate force under his command.[2]

---

[1]*Mauritius*: csr, 1940, 8525t, 33k, 12×6in, 8×4in, 6×21in tt.
DTSD: Capt H. P. K. Oram: Capt 1936; *Hawkins* May 1940; D Tac, Torpedo & Staff Duties Div, Sept 1942.
[2]VAdm Dalrymple-Hamilton.

330.   *COS Minutes*

9 July 1945

172: Relations with the Russians

The Prime Minister had agreed that the receipt of information or facilities from the Russians must be a pre-requisite of any exchange of information which might take place in the future, and that our attitude to the Russians must be determined by their attitude to us.

331.   *Diary*

10 July 1945

. . . I present the final bill for the U-boats.

1200 actually commissioned. 783 sunk. 151 in our hands, 6 in Japanese hands except one believed to be scuttled. The odd one I reported had fuel still to be able to be at sea. Curiously that night one surrendered at Mar de La Plata.[1] . . .

332.   *Diary*

22 July 1945

. . . Went all round Kiel harbour in the barge. A wonderful harbour with miles of wharfage. Of course there is no tide. The harbour full of all facilities. Floating cranes, lighters, tugs, docks, etc., etc. It looked as though one could comfortably have fitted out Portsmouth, Plymouth and Chatham.

The U-belt shelters were intact and we saw one with about 12 complete midget submarines and lots of parts. Every part of the yards appeared to have prefabricated bits of submarines.

We saw the *Hipper* in dock. Slightly damaged by our bombing but most by her crew with depth charges. Also the *Scheer* capsized and many other ships.[2] Plenty of merchant ships there. . . .

Then to one of the torpedo works at Eckernförde. . . .

---

[1]P. Kemp, *U-Boats Destroyed: German Submarine Losses in the World Wars* (London, 1997). Some U-boats were still unaccounted for, since the total here is 941.

This was probably *U-530*, arrived 10 July 1945. *U-977* also arrived 25 Aug 1945.

[2]*Hipper* heavy csr, 1939, 14050t, 32k, 8×8in, 12×4.1in, 12×21in tt.:

Scheer: pocket b/ship, 1934, 11700t, 28k, 6×11in, 8×5.9in, 6×4.1in, 8×21in tt.

We then saw Dr Walther himself who demonstrated his mixture
Eagelin. Some sort of Hydrogen Peroxide.[1] ...

333.   *Admiralty to Vice Admiral Miles and Rear Admiral Parry*[2]

13 August 1945

*Directive to British Representatives on the Tripartite Naval
Commission*

The UK, US and Soviet Governments decided at Potsdam that a Tripar-
tite Naval Commission should be established not later than 15 August
in Berlin, to give effect to the Naval clauses of the Protocols agreed at
Potsdam concerning the disposal of the German Navy and Mercantile
Marine. Each Government is to appoint two representatives to the
Commission. You are appointed the British Representatives.

2.   The task of the Commission is to agree and submit to the three
Governments recommendations for the progressive allocation of specific German warships, and to handle other detailed matters arising out
of the Naval clauses of the Protocol. ...

3.   ... You should co-ordinate your activities with [British Naval and
Military authorities in Germany] through British Naval C-in-C, Germany.[3]

5.   ... Paragraph 5 of the Protocol provides that the Representatives
of the three Governments shall have reciprocal rights to inspect German warships wherever located. You should therefore arrange for the
necessary facilities to be granted to the USA and USSR for the inspection of German warships under British control subject to full
reciprocation. In the case of the USSR, you should insist on full facilities being received for the inspection of the *Graf Zeppelin*, *Lützow*,
Gneisenau, *Schleswig-Holstein* and U-boats in Russian hands. Although
it is unlikely that the ships named will qualify under paragraph 2 of the
Protocol for inclusion among the ships for allocation, great importance

---

[1]Dr Hellmuth Walter.
'Eagelin': a hydrogen peroxide fuel.
[2]VAdm G. J. A. Miles: Capt 1931; Flag Capt *Nelson* Home F 1939; RA Aug 1941;
head of N Mission, Moscow Jan 1942; COHQ June 1942; N Rep, India HQ, Delhi June
1943; VA March 1944; FO W Med July 1944; RN reprv German Control Cmn May
1945; FOC R Indian N 1946.
    RAdm W. E. Parry: Capt Dec 1934; *Achilles* (RNZ Div) June 1939; R Plate battle Dec
1939; Cdr 2nd Cl & 1st NM, NZ June 1941; Cdre 1st Cl, *President* Oct 1942; *Renown* Jan
1943; RA Jan 1944; asst to Miles, Germany May 1945.
[3]Adm Burrough.

is attached to ascertaining their present condition and whether the USSR are making plans for their salvage.[1]

6.   ... It is, generally speaking, HMG's policy not to give the Russians technical or other information except on the basis of strict reciprocity, owing to the almost complete failure of the Russians heretofore to make information available to the UK. You are accordingly to interpret narrowly the right of inspection when applying it to the USSR ... In particular, the Russians are not in any circumstances to be allowed access to the research laboratory, establishments or equipment of the Walther Werke.

8.   *Surface Force*

The Royal Navy has no requirement for German combat vessels as operational units of the Fleet, but has important requirements for:
(a)   combat vessels for experimental and technical purposes;
(b)   naval auxiliaries, e.g., oilers, depot ships, repair ships, etc., both during the Japanese war and for retention in the post-war Fleet. ...

9.   The USSR may claim *Prinz Eugen*, but you are to insist on this ship being allocated to the UK for technical examination, or subject to the view of your US colleague, to the UK and USA jointly for technical examination. Possible courses for negotiating such an allocation are that:
(a)   The Russians should receive *Nürnberg* as equivalent to the half share of *Prinz Eugen* obtained by the UK or by the UK and USA;
(b)   In the last resort, it might be agreed that *Prinz Eugen* should, after full technical examination by the UK and USA, be delivered to the Soviet Navy.[2]

Precise directions cannot be given concerning the course of action to be taken in the allocation of the cruisers until it is known whether *Leipzig* and other major units are to be counted as available for disposal under paragraph 2 of the Protocol.[3]

---

[1]*Graf Zeppelin*: carrier, 1931–(never completed), 29090t, 35k, 16×5.9in, 12×4.1in, 41–43 a/c.
  Lützow (ex-*Deutschland*): pocket b/ship, 1933, 11700t, 28k, 6×11in, 8×5.9in, 6×4.1in, 8×21in. tt.
  Gneisenau: b/csr, 1938, 34841t, 32k, 9×11in, 12×5.9in, 14×4.1in.
  Schleswig-Holstein: b/ship, 1907, 12983t; ex-WWI, later cadet trng ship.
  [2]*Prinz Eugen*: csr, 1940, 16974t, 32.5k, 8×8in, 16×4.1in, 12×21in tt.
  Nürnberg: lt csr, 1935, 6250t, 32k, 9×5.9in, 12×21in tt; Soviet *Admiral Makarov*.
  [3]*Leipzig*: lt csr, 1931, 6515t, 32k, 9×5.9in, 12×21in tt.

10. *U-boats*

HMG's primary object, the destruction of the German U-boat fleet, has been secured by paragraph 3 of the Protocol, which provides that not more than 30 U-boats in all shall be preserved, and divided equally among the three Powers for technical and experimental purposes. A maximum of 10 U-boats is therefore to be allowed to each country and you are not, in any circumstances, to propose or entertain any proposal that this number should be increased.

11.   The disposal of the latest types of U-boat, fitted with hydrogen peroxide propulsion units, presents a problem of special importance and some difficulty. The most valuable boats are *U-1406* and *U-1407*, which are fitted with the unit type 18X, and are capable of being completed within a reasonably short time. Search for a third boat of the same type, No. *1405*, has been unsuccessful and has been abandoned. In addition, there are four badly damaged boats fitted with a smaller unit, type 17, namely *U-792, 793, 794, 795*. These boats are incapable of being completed within six months, and their propulsion units were all destroyed by sabotage. It has been previously agreed with the US Navy that *U-1406* should be allocated to them and *U-1407* to the Royal Navy. The US also hold *U-795*.[1]

12.   It is desired to exclude the Russians from acquiring any of these two special types of U-boat. The Russians are, however, almost certainly aware of the existence of one or both types, and have a right under the Protocol to inspect the boats. The exercise of this right, if a request is made, should be permitted, but inspection should be confined to the boats themselves and restricted to the minimum. You should report immediately any enquiries made by the Russians concerning these types, and pending further instructions your case should be:

(a)   to maintain that *U-1406* and *U-1407* are the only boats of this type available for disposal within paragraphs 2 and 3 of Protocol, and that remaining boats are excluded from consideration as being incapable of completion within six months.

(b)   to insist, in concert with your USA colleague, that *U-1406* and *U-1407* are to be allocated to the USA and UK respectively.

The refusal of any of the *U-792–5* class to the Russians may be a delicate matter, but has great importance, since the acquisition of one of these boats might lead the Russians to put forward a claim under

---

[1]*U-1405-7*: s/m, 1945, 307/332t, 8.5/21.5k, 2×21in tt (4 torpedoes). *U-1406* to USA; *U-1407* to RN as *Meteorite*. These had a Walter motor plus diesel & elec.
U-792–5: s/m, 1945, 232/289t, 9/25k, 2×21in tt (4 torpedoes). *U-792–3* to RN.

paragraph 3 of the Protocol to examine and take equipment in the Walther Werke establishments for the purpose of providing spares for the U-boats to be delivered to them. Further consideration is being given to the question of the disposal of these special types of U-boat and establishments in relation to the Russians. Meanwhile, you should, if possible, avoid discussing the subject with the Russians.

16. *Minesweepers*

HMG proposed at Potsdam that the German minesweepers should remain under the control of the International Minesweeping Board until the tasks of that Board had been completed. The Russians did not accept this proposal, but insisted on obtaining immediately one-third of the minesweepers for employment under their own control. British Naval C-in-C, Germany, has established a special German organisation entitled 'German Minesweeping Organisation' for the purpose of working German minesweeping forces after the disbandment of the German Navy. The withdrawal of one-third of the minesweepers, the crews of which may be unwilling to serve under Russian control, may give rise to complications. Your object should be to keep as many serviceable minesweepers as possible in useful employment, and to ensure that adequate numbers are allocated to clearance of the western entrances to the Baltic. . . .

17. *France*

HMG proposed at Potsdam that a small share of the German Fleet should be allocated to France, but received no support whatever from the USSR or the USA. The Protocol, in consequence, makes no provision for France. Nevertheless, it is HMG's desire that the French Navy should receive such ships as can be spared from the British share after satisfying essential British requirements. You should bear this consideration in mind particularly with reference to the allocation of destroyers and torpedo boats.[1]

20. In general, you should be aware that the Admiralty and other Departments of HMG have learnt by bitter experience that it is useless to negotiate with the Russians in a spirit of reasonable compromise. The Russian Delegation may be expected to drive the hardest possible bargain and concede nothing unless forced to do so. It is recommended that your tactics should be generally to hold out, so far as possible, on all points of importance to the Russians until essential British requirements have been met. Concessions made in advance by way of

[1]Fr N share: destroyers, submarines, light craft.

inducement have not, in the past, been found effective in obtaining countervailing concessions from the Russians.

334.   *From Vice Admiral Miles*

Tripartite Naval Commission,
Naval Division HQ,
Berlin Area, BAOR,
[n.d., 1945]

4.   ... There was little to see at Pillau. Three E-boat hulls and a few sunken submarines, trawlers and minesweepers. The town has few habitable houses left, but the port had apparently not suffered from demolition.

5.   In the afternoon we bumped our way over the 50 km of shell cratered road to Königsberg. This town is dead and completely demolished. No inhabitants to be seen at all. Again, the port area was not so badly damaged, and a large number of cranes appeared to be intact.

6.   We here looked over the *Seydlitz*, which to our surprise we found afloat, flying the Red Flag, and a Soviet Navy care and maintenance party living on board. ... The Germans were evidently contemplating turning her into some sort of carrier. ... there is a perfectly good hull and apparently efficient machinery, but she could not possibly be completed into anything within six months with the existing repair facilities.[1]

8.   At Danzig. .. In the course of a walk around the submarine assembly sheds and ships we came across about six prefabricated sections, intact, as were the sheds and ships. It was quite obvious that this wasn't the state of affairs found by the Russians on entry into the port. ... They [German workmen] confirmed that at the time of the Soviet occupation there were 11 completed submarine hulls, some with and some without engines, and that they had all subsequently been towed away. ...

9.   ... we flew to Swinemünde. On the way we circled over Gdynia and confirmed what our inspection party had seen the day before, namely –

(a)   The port has suffered considerable damage from demolition, but the town has many houses still standing.

(b)   The *Gneisenau*, minus her bows and guns, has been sunk as a blockship across the harbour entrance and is a complete write-off.

[1]*Seydlitz*: carrier, 1936–(not completed), 18000t, 32k, 10×4.1in, 18 a/c.

(c)   The *Schleswig-Holstein* is sunk alongside on an even keel, but
is considerably damaged and obviously could not be repaired in
six months.

We also sighted three wrecked destroyers on the shore and on sand-
banks nearby.

10.   I was met at Swinemünde by the Soviet NOIC – Captain 1ˢᵗ Rank
Guskov – a very live wire.[1] . . . we first of all went outside the harbour
to see the *Schlesien* aground with her back broken and very much
damaged from bombing.[2] We then returned and had a look at some
sunken submarines and then on to the *Lützow*. She is moored up alongside the west bank of the Oder, some miles away from the harbour. She
is aground with about three feet freeboard aft. A direct hit between the
bridge and her funnel has wrecked her engine-room, and before leaving
the Germans blew up each 11-inch turret (the after 11-inch particularly
looks a shambles) and the breeches of all secondary armament guns.
The Soviet Navy were still examining her with divers, but there is no
doubt she is of no further value.

11.   . . . a creek beyond Stettin where the *Graf Zeppelin* is moored
alongside the bank. From the outside she looked perfectly all right
except for a few shell holes in her side. Her interior is a different story.
The deck of the upper hangar was convex in section instead of flat, and
the three lifts (all on the centre line) had been wrecked by demolition.
The Germans must have effected a very large internal explosion to have
produced the damage and distortion in the hangars. The hull appears to
be intact as she was afloat. It would take a year or so in a properly
equipped dockyard to get her going again.

12.   There is an astonishing sight at Stettin, where we passed at least
1,000 barges (of several hundred tons each) moored up alongside the
banks in tiers of three or four for miles. Every barge was loaded to
capacity with loot, all labelled and marked for the USSR. . . .

335.   *Diary*

21 August 1945

. . . COS at 1030. . . . Another paper on the use of German scientists in
this country. There is no question that by bringing them over here we
prevent the Russians getting at them and also take advantage of their
brains and knowledge. There are however grave security risks. . . .

---

[1]Capt 1ˢᵗ Rank Guskov, Soviet N. [no further information available]
[2]*Schlesien*: b/ship, 1907, 12983t; ex-WWI, later cadet trng ship.

336. *Cunningham's Minute on Operation 'Foxchase'*

24 August 1945

Attack on Enemy Convoy, 3–4 April 1945

... A heaven sent opportunity of doing severe damage to the enemy was thrown away by the irresolution of Captain D17 who allowed himself to be influenced by every bogey that his imagination could conjure up.[1]

C-in-C, Home Fleet, should have his attention drawn to this failure to destroy the enemy in sight. Concern should also be expressed at the failure of most of the destroyers to fire torpedoes which appears to be due to lack of training.[2]

---

[1]Capt D17: Capt H. L. S. Browning: Cdr Dec 1937; OD Sept 1939; *Quiberon* Sept 1942; Capt Dec 1942; *Cochrane*, Rosyth Escort Force March 1943; Capt 17DF, *Onslow*, Sept 1944.
[2]Adm Moore.

SECTION F

THE MEDITERRANEAN

MARCH 1943–FEBRUARY 1946

By the time Cunningham left the Mediterranean in mid-October 1943, that sea, forever associated with Cunningham's high reputation, was becoming something of a naval backwater. Military vision was now fixed on the forthcoming invasion of Normandy, set for the late spring of 1944, and beyond that the climax of the war against Japan. With the Italian armistice, including Cunningham's agreement with de Courten on the surrender of the Italian fleet, and the completion of the landings at Salerno, there was no need to retain substantial naval forces in the Mediterranean. With the departure of Eisenhower and Tedder to head 'Overlord' and of Cunningham to lead the Admiralty, most of the commanders involved in Mediterranean operations from November 1942 to October 1943 had gone, to be followed shortly by substantial military and air as well as naval forces.

Andrew Cunningham made no bones about recommending his successor, plumping unhesitatingly for his namesake (but no relation). Admiral Sir John H. D. Cunningham. John Cunningham had not enjoyed a 'good' war. He had been involved marginally in the *Glorious* disaster and also in 1940 had commanded the abortive Dakar expedition.[1] Since that time he had served as Fourth Sea Lord, responsible for dockyards, bases and supplies. Andrew Cunningham, however, had formed a high regard for his abilities; he was a cerebral officer who had considerable political skill and high organising capacity. Though Churchill had reservations about his sea-going war, he accepted him readily enough, following Eisenhower's prompt lead [337, 339].

John Cunningham quickly based himself at Naples and kept the First Sea Lord in full touch with events in the Mediterranean. He yearned to re-establish British control over the sea and was somewhat suspicious of the Americans, who, he felt, were getting somewhat 'uppity' following their recent rise to strategic and military ascendancy [347, 349,

---

[1]*Glorious* (carrier, 1930, 22500t, 30k, 16×4.7in, 48 a/c) was sunk off Narvik, 8 June 1940, by *Scharnhorst* and *Gneisenau*. VAdm J. Cunningham, then commanding 1CS, was in *Devonshire* bringing the King of Norway to UK and dare not break radio silence. He commanded the Dakar expedition of Sept 1940, which was a fiasco, though not his fault; as usual, the responsibility was Churchill's.

355–6, 369]. Also in the Mediterranean were other old associates of Andrew Cunningham, notably Admiral Willis (succeeded by Admiral Rawlings) as C-in-C, Levant, charged with responsibility for carrying on the costly and ultimately abortive Aegean adventure, one of Churchill's pet schemes. It demonstrated that the Germans held local control of the air and were able to mount successful counter-attacks on Kos and Leros, while establishing a firm grip at once on Rhodes after the Italian armistice. Allied sea power was badly mauled by a virtually unopposed *Luftwaffe*; it was sadly reminiscent of Greece and Crete in April and May 1941 [338–41].[1]

Britain was able to exploit the benevolent neutrality of Turkey during these Aegean operations but, in truth, Churchill, Andrew Cunningham and other British leaders were rather disappointed with the Turks. They showed no inclination to get into the war, despite strong pressure since the 1930s, led during the war by the Prime Minister himself. It was hardly surprising that they did not bite, for there was little if anything to be gained and Germany and the Soviet Union were too close for Turkish comfort. Thus, Admiral Sir Howard Kelly, who had been in Ankara since 1940 in the hope that an alliance would be formed and there might be real naval advice and liaison work to do, left in 1944 with little to show for his considerable efforts [338, 341–3, 349–50].[2]

Greece, though one of the Allies, turned troublesome towards the end of the war, as rival Royalist and Communist camps jockeyed for position in the post-war world. This led to mutiny in several of the Greek ships and later a British naval and army presence in Piraeus, capped by a personal intervention by the Prime Minister at Christmas time in 1944. Cunningham counselled firm and immediate action against the mutineers; his 'strong disciplinarian' streak was evident [352–5, 357, 364, 369].

The amphibious operation at Anzio ('Shingle', 22 January 1944) was on a much smaller scale than the landings in North Africa, Sicily and southern Italy, but it was designed to fulfil a major strategic purpose – the early seizure of Rome. It is common to lay the blame on the soldiers for their timidity and for allowing Kesselring to box them in near the beaches, but the main fault was that the Anglo-American high command had taken away so much 'lift' and so many specialist and experienced troops that the operation was scarcely likely to succeed.

---

[1]This was another of Churchill's grand ideas. It was launched on 8 Sept 1943, with the intention of seizing Rhodes and other Italian Aegean islands. After a see-saw campaign, extremely costly to the RN, British forces withdrew or surrendered in Nov.

[2]For earlier dealings with Turkey, see *Cunningham Papers*, vol. I, *passim*. Turkey declared war on 23 February 1945.

The navies, nevertheless, carried out their role with almost complete success. Their complaint was that the stalling of the plan meant a long, unwelcome and unexpected supply commitment to the stranded land forces [344–9].

The second major landing passed off without undue difficulty. Commanded by Vice Admiral Hewitt and consisting entirely of French and American troops, the assault on the southern French coast in August 1944 met little opposition. It had been christened 'Anvil' but Churchill renamed it 'Dragoon', as the Americans had insisted upon it as back-door assistance to 'Overlord', the landing in Normandy in June, against most British political and military opinion. Cunningham, unusually, was undecided whether to support it or further major offensives in Italy. It was little help to 'Overlord', as it was delayed a couple of months, and it served mainly to give the Allies two major supply ports in Marseille and Toulon [344–5, 348–9, 357, 360–1].

John Cunningham was able to tidy up the Cunningham-de Courten agreement of 1943, tightening up several minor issues [357].

The Admirals Cunningham were further exercised by command in the Adriatic. Air Chief Marshal Sir John Slessor was proposed as the Allied commander in that sub-theatre, but, aside from the fact that the two admirals did not like or trust Slessor, they felt that the command should go to a naval officer. This was presumably on account of a long seaward flank and numerous islands off the coast; it had been a scene of naval, commando and special agent enterprise throughout the war [355, 357–9].

Much of their concern was now with post-war matters. They aimed to restore Britain's pre-war position of dominance and regarded the United States and France as rivals quite as much as the Soviet Union. John Cunningham seems to have accepted that Britain's historic position in Egypt was no longer tenable; the army could not guarantee to defend it against the rising tide of nationalism. Andrew Cunningham, a lifelong Mediterraneanist by conviction as well as by service, hoped to strengthen Britain's position in the area by acquiring the former Italian territories in North Africa as a UN mandate. He was also opposed adamantly to the historic Russian ambition to enter the Mediterranean via the Dardanelles. The French sought also to revive their pre-war dominance in Syria and Lebanon and de Gaulle sent ships and troops to regain them for France after the war, much to Andrew Cunningham's disgust [351, 360, 362, 368–9, 370–2]. He regarded Malta as the lynchpin of British control of the Mediterranean. He had lamented the poor state of the island's defences in 1940 and had much to do with the island's survival and offensive capability in 1941–42. At the earliest opportunity he made it his headquarters (in July 1943). With the war's finale just off stage, he turned to considering the future of the historic base of the Mediterranean Fleet. He recognised there would be little money to spare for improving airfields, providing adequate dock facilities and excavating submarine shelters, but he was determined to maintain the Royal Navy's prior claim to the island's resources and fought off the RAF, who also eyed the airfields [360–1, 366–9].[1]

It was ironic that the Mediterranean, so long associated with Cunningham and the scene of his greatest triumphs, was by this stage a secondary theatre and that the First Sea Lord was now more concerned with what was happening in the North Atlantic and home waters and was to take place shortly in the Indian and Pacific Oceans.

[1]For Malta's trials, see *Cunningham Papers*, vol. I, *passim.*

337. *From Admiral Sir John H. D. Cunningham*

The Admiralty,
23 March 1943

... I hope to call in on you on the way and get the low-down on the situation [in the Levant] and any special points you may wish to make. I did not – nor do I now – know anything of the circumstances behind H. H[arwood]'s relief and the offer of his job came as a surprise – most welcome of course – especially as there had previously been 'feelers' regarding the relief of James Somerville further on. Coming so shortly after WSC[hurchill]'s return I imagine that in some way his venom had been stirred up in which case my prospects look petty thin! Indeed both A. V. [Alexander] and D. P[ound] seemed to anticipate difficulty getting his agreement and seemed relieved when they did so. Now the position is again complicated by H. H.'s going sick – I hope not too seriously – it is bad luck on Leatham but just at this moment you will understand I could not leave this damned chair ...[1]

338. *From John Cunningham*

Levant,
19 September 1943

A. I was very glad to get the six ships of 8 DF and was, as you will have seen, able to turn them to good account immediately – the convoy which D8 sunk was most important to the Huns in Rhodes and as I expected, has caused an immediate and violent reaction on their part against the airfield at Kos, and will doubtless provoke air attempts against Leros despite the fact that the Kos affair cost them heavily for little real advantage.[2] Our policy now is to put some 4,000 more men into Leros, Kos and Samos to stiffen up the Italians in the smaller islands with British detachments. The supply problem will be difficult but I think can be managed by destroyers and air if the caique scheme does not do all we hope for.[3] The fleets with their higher speed and double carrying capacity are much more suitable than the 'Hunts' and I don't at present see quite how to sustain our effort without them so I

---

[1]VAdm J. Cunningham had been appointed C-in-C, Levant in the spring of 1943 but was tied to an office chair for a time, as he was 4SL. Leatham, Dep Govr, Malta, took tempy charge.
[2]D8: unidentified.
[3]A 2-masted Greek fishing & coasting vessel.

hope I may keep them for a bit. Had they left . . . 'Accolade' for a few days longer we could not have failed to take Rhodes and the situation would have been simple but unfortunately that was not to be.

B.   As it is the Italians in Leros are playing well – their dockyard and shops are reported to be quite good and I hope to use it as an advance base for the MTBs you are sending me and for an occasional anchorage for destroyers, etc., operating against the Salonika-Dardanelles-Athens shipping routes upon which the Hun must come to depend more and more as you strangle his Adriatic route. The worst of it is I can't send Greek ships to Italian ports without provoking a riot and probably causing the Italians to throw in their hand. . . .

C.   If we could supply through our Turkish ALLY the problem would be solved and I think the moment has come to put pressure on our gallant but reluctant ally to that end.

D.   . . . I can't see any employment for Italian ships in Levant ports. The flag alone is of course anathema to Greeks and French. . . I feel that Italian-manned ships under the Italian flag *must* be based on Italian ports such as Taranto. . . .

339.   *To the VCNS (for the Prime Minister)*[1]

9 October 1943

I have now had the opportunity of talking over with C-in-C, Levant, the events preceding the recapture of Kos by the enemy.

I am satisfied that small naval force available was used to best advantage. It is true they did not succeed in intercepting enemy convoy but it would have been much to expect of fortune for so small a force to make certainty [of] this. Even had they proceeded directly to Kos when landing was reported they would have been too late to interfere with disembarkation.

Since then naval forces have been handled boldly for the preservation of Leros. Risks have been taken and losses sustained which I think are no longer justified now that it is agreed that 'Accolade' cannot take place at the present time. I would urge strongly that Admiral Sir John Cunningham be appointed to relieve me as C-in-C, Mediterranean. I am convinced of his suitability for this important command which I am sure he will fill with great benefit to the Allied cause and credit to himself. General Eisenhower will gladly accept Admiral Cunningham as my relief.

[1]VAdm Syfret.

340.   *From Admiral Sir Algernon Willis*

19 October 1943

. . . The destroyers have been playing up extremely well and by going right into harbours and bays in Kalino and Kos, shooting up everything they have found, lighting up the coasts by searchlights and dropping various delay action devices about I think they have created quite a lot of alarm and despondency. . . .

The cruisers have been unlucky with the bombing but fortunate in the little damage done – except in the case of *Carlisle*. . .[1] In two cases at any rate there were our fighters in the vicinity but something went wrong with the fighter direction! I am having this chased up. I do not feel that cruisers ought to get clocked nowadays with fighter cover though admittedly the Beaufighters can't catch Ju88's.

I must now ease up a little with the destroyers to get some maintenance done, but will go on sending some up most nights with the primary object of getting reinforcements and stores in.

Of course if we can only get more aircraft to pound his aerodromes, for long-range fighter protection and especially for shipping strikes by day I believe we could deny the use of the sea routes to the Dodecanese to the enemy. I find it difficult to swallow the little support the Middle East is getting from Mediterranean Air Command when I remember the enormous preponderance of air power we have in the Central Mediterranean. I suppose the Air people know their business best but I can't help wondering sometimes.

As it is, it has been the case again of our Navy and the German Air Force and the conditions [are] not so very different to Greece and Tobruk. However I think we have won the first round and in any case will go all out to keep the enemy thinking more about supplying his own islands rather than attacking ours. . . .

341.   *From Willis*

27 October 1943

I am afraid I am going to write you a rather gloomy letter about the Aegean situation, but I know you would wish me to be quite frank about it and it is impossible to give the whole picture in a signal.

---

[1]*Carlisle*: AA csr, fmr lt csr, 1918, converted 1939–40, 8×4in; cnstrv tot loss 9 Oct 1943.

I am not at all happy about Leros itself. Rumours reach me through junior officers coming back that they are having a much more difficult time than either the SNO or the Brigadier, both being very stout hearts, would let on in signals.

. . . I suggested it would be a good thing to send a couple of high SO's to Leros, and I would send Commodore (D), to review the whole situation jointly. The Army sent the DMO, Brigadier Davy and a Brigadier 'Q' and the three of them went in *Eclipse* with the first flight of reinforcements. The two Brigadiers were saved, thank God, but I am grieved to say there is no news of the Commodore. . . .[1]

So far all the supplies I have put in by destroyer (I may say that J. H. D. C[unningham] would not use them on this and I think he was right, but I felt that the situation was so bad when I got here that I had to do so for a period) and what is going in by submarine and caique are not even keeping up stocks, much less building up. . .

I know very little about Samos. The Army view is that if attacked the garrison can retire to the hills and play guerrillas. Anyway the Navy cannot do much about it, it is so far away and at the extreme limit of 201 Group's best reconnaissance aircraft. . . .

You know the naval situation and what I have been trying to do. I have not had to expose the destroyers to day bombing outside some fighter cover lately but if there *is* an attempted invasion of Leros they will have to go for it, despite the combination of Ju 88's and Ju 87's, which is a very nasty menace.

But they have had a lot of night bombing running in supplies to Leros. The Hun spotted what was going on and just shadowed the ships up there with flares. Leros bluffed them for a time by changing the harbour for discharge but this was eventually discovered and one night the destroyers had a very nasty time, in fact they had to leave without discharging. This is one reason why I have taken the destroyers off supply running and have told the Army it cannot be done except in great emergency.

We have now got the rest of the reinforcing Battalion there, but it has been tricky work and the loss of so many in *Eclipse* with the CO and

[1]Cdre (D), Med F: Cdre P. Todd: Capt Dec 1936; Gun Sch, *Pembroke* (Chatham) May 1938; *Inglefield* Nov 1939; Cdre (D), Med F *Woolwich* Aug 1942.

Brig G. M. O. Davy (1898–1983): RFA & RHA, W Front 1914–18; Staff Coll 1932–3; Bde Maj 1935–6; RMC Sandhurst 1937; RNC Greenwich 1939; Fr & Bel 1939–40; W Dst 1941; Greece April 1941; armd bdes 1941; DMO, ME 1942–4; DACoS (O) SHAEF, Algiers 1944; Adriatic cmd 1944–5; Lia O, Polish A, WO 1945–7; ret 1948.

Brig (Q): unknown.

Eclipse: destroyer, 1934, 1405t, 35.5k, 4×4.7in, 8×21in tt; mined E of Kalymnos, 24 Oct 1943.

Battalion HQ seriously reduces their effectiveness. Just had a report that the enemy laid the mines which got her, *Hurworth* and *Adrias* by caique.[1] May well be true.

I am using Turkish territorial waters to the full but how long this can go on I do not know. I only trust the Germans will not mine these waters. Then we shall be sunk. As it is destroyer movements around the islands are severely restricted by mined areas and it is very difficult navigationally for them at night and will be a good deal more so in the winter when the visibility is not so good.

I fully appreciate the importance of hanging on to this island if we can and appreciate the enemy are very stretched too, but they have practically everything in their favour, distance, adjacent islands, good air reconnaissance and complete air supremacy. . . .

I mentioned in my personal signal 25/1651 October [not reproduced] that the destroyers were feeling the strain of these operations and this aspect is causing me a good deal of concern. . . . Nor can they understand why at this stage of the war they should not have better support from the air. . . .

A further feature is that they have done *so* well all through the Central Mediterranean campaigns and when the Italians gave in many of them felt that the Naval war in the Mediterranean was practically won. . . .

. . . The personnel of the Navy will stand up to anything if they think it is necessary. If they get into their heads that they are to be thrown away for what they consider is an inadequate object we may be in difficulties, . . .

342. *From Admiral Sir Howard Kelly*

Ankara,
4 December 1943

I daresay the C-in-C told you how very well the Turks have been behaving during the Dodecanese operations, they could not have done more, and in spite of their rigid views on the subject, they have broken every law of neutrality in our favour.

The people here are getting very restive; they feel that they may be driven into a war, that almost everybody wishes to avoid. . . .

---

[1]*Hurworth*: 'Hunt', mined 22 Oct 1943.
Adrias: Greek, 'Hunt' (ex-*Tanatside*); cnstrv tot loss 22 Oct 1943.

An Appreciation of the Situation in Turkey on 1 December 1943

2. Turkish foreign policy in recent years has been much influenced by the dread of the establishment of a Russian zone of influence in the Balkans, this fear has been strengthened by Russian opposition to the idea of a Balkan Federation, one of Turkey's most earnest desires.

7. The cession of bases without a declaration of war does not appeal to Turkey, but it is quite conceivable that the cession of bases, combined with mobilisation and the manning of the defences, might be all that Turkey would be called upon to undertake in [the] early stages of war.

18. The Navy, which depends entirely on the army and is ruled and directed by the General Staff, consists only of a few submarines and destroyers which could assist in patrol and convoy work. At present these vessels are reserved for work in the Black Sea but possibly in the event of war the method, at least, of their employment would come under our control, though no previous arrangements are possible.

343. *To Kelly*

17 December 1943

. . . I do not think the Turks are very wise if they stay out of the war now, particularly as they have been invited to come in by Russia. They would not be asked by us to do very much beyond giving us the necessary bases and perhaps attacking the Greek islands. Your paragraph 7 seems to sum it up exactly. . . .

I feel myself that the real reason the Turks are hanging back is the doubt held by the Government whether they can make the Turkish people see the necessity, or indeed any reason, for going to war. . . .

344. *From John Cunningham*

Naples,
27 January 1944

. . . I'm afraid I have not so far had any reason to modify my opinion of the Army's dilatory methods. I am sure that had they any guts they could have walked practically without any opposition to any 'feature' that they wanted. . . . I foresee . . . this venture [Anzio], which had all the makings of a brilliant success, developing into another Tobruk so far as the Navy's part is concerned. . . .

As was, perhaps, to be expected Admiral Lowery is very much overborne by the US Army . . . On the whole, however, Lowery and his staff did an excellent planning job and executed the plans with complete success.[1] The presence of Morse, Troubridge and Mansfield undoubtedly contributed vastly to both the material and moral preparations and execution . . .[2]

C.   The seizure of Anzio by the Rangers was an excellent bit of work on the part of both the troops and landing craft crews – timed for 0200 it took place at 0159, achieved absolute surprise and so prevented the demolition charges, which were all in place, being fired . . . The southern beaches are poor but workable with pontoons by LCTs. The LSTs have to unload either to LCTs or in Anzio. We have on the whole a good bit of luck with the weather and have already made two trips with the whole 82 LSTs and should I think get nearly another turn round before starting to pull out those for UK and refit. The result is that build up by the day before yesterday is ahead of schedule . . .

E.   I would, however, beg to impress on you that our chaps have done everything and very much more than was asked of the Navy originally or even as late as Marrakesh. I have no doubt we can make the grade still but it is sickening the way the Army has accepted this or that limitation and then completely ignored it . . .

The W/T controlled bombers and torpedo bombers have continued to be a nuisance and have caused deplorable losses but on the other hand the ships and the air have got quite a few and I hope they may be a wasting asset especially if the heavies have a good day against their nests today. We have had a good many lucky escapes so things might well have been much worse. I think the Air is on its toes and I find the new man is easier to deal with than his predecessor – Slessor also plays well – but nevertheless I feel that they might have done a bit better in view of their stupendous superiority in their new element.[3] The sneak raids by [Focke-Wulf] 190s are of course difficult to counter, but the ships have got quite a few of them and there can't be very many left; it is the dusk raids in force which have done most damage and they are the ones where something was rather lacking on the part of our fighters; I am, however, assured that things will now be much better as at last the south eastern fighters are to

[1]RAdm F. J. Lowry, US Navy: grad N Acad 1911; N War Coll 1925–6; Capt *Minneapolis* 1940–2; RA, Gt Lakes NTS 1942; Cdr Moroccan Sea Fr Feb 1943; Cdr 8 Amph Force Nov 1943; Cdr, amph force, Pac F; VA, ret 1950.
[2]VAdm J. M. Mansfield (1893–1949): ent RN 1906; s/m 1915–21; b/ships & csrs 1920s; RN Coll Greenwich 1931; Capt 1934; RN War Coll 1934–7; F Capt, *Norfolk*, E Indies 1937–9; CoS, NAWI 1941–3; RA 1943; 15CS 1944–5; ACNS (UT) March 1945; FO Ceylon 1945–6; VA & FO (S) 1946.
[3]It is unclear which air commanders are being referred to here.

be told they must stay up until the night fighters relieve them even if it means a night landing![1] Coastal had already learnt this lesson after many bitter comments upon their defence of the convoys against dusk attackers but it seems to have been a novel idea to 'Tactical'!

F.   I'm very pleased with my team . . .

345.   *To John Cunningham*

6 February 1944

A.   I share your disappointment in the poor results of the Nettuno [Anzio] landing. I do not think it has escaped anyone here what a great success the naval side of the operation was; I have had many congratulatory references.

Now we are faced with a long hard battle, and a fairly uncertain supply line. I do not, however, think it can be compared to Tobruk, as at Tobruk there was no air cover and at Anzio at least there should be ample though coming from a distance until the fighter strip is made. But the failure of the Army to take advantage of a wonderful opportunity is most irritating.

C.   The absence of a definite decision about 'Overlord' and 'Anvil' is making things very difficult. The present situation which has been recommended for acceptance by the CCS is that 'Anvil' should be reduced to its original conception of a diversion and that only a lift of one division should be retained in the Mediterranean, all the rest going to increase the lift for 'Overlord'.

It is further intended to bring home most of the Mediterranean cruisers for 'Overlord'. The demands for bombarding cruisers are very heavy and amount in all to 18; these cannot be provided without taking this step. Later when the definite instructions are sent I shall be glad if you will let me know whether you can spare Mansfield to come with his cruisers. The ones intended to come are, I believe, *Ajax*, *Orion*, *Penelope* and *Mauritius*. The move will be left as late as possible as the Mediterranean cruisers are past-masters at bombardment and should require only three or four days working up.[2]

F.   There is a suggestion in the Admiralty that four assault carriers and *Royalist*, fighter direction cruiser, should proceed to the Mediterranean. So far I have not approved as I fear it would very much complicate your

[1]Focke-Wulf Fw190: German ftr-bbr, 1939, 2100hp, 500m, 408mph, 4 can, 2mg.
[2]*Penelope*: lt csr, 1936, 5270t, 32.25k, 6×6in, 8×4in, 6×21in tt; sunk by *U-410*, Anzio, 16 Feb 1944.

escort problem, nor do I see that there is very much for fighter carriers to do in the Mediterranean at this moment though perhaps they could try and intercept the enemy bombers from the south of France that attack our convoys in the Oran area.

There are advantages, however. There has been much criticism in the US about the inactivity of our FAA – a criticism which, I regret to say, I feel to some extent is justified. Our auxiliary carriers have a habit of going to the Clyde and practically never emerge for months – a state of affairs I am anxious to put an end to. Moreover four assault carriers in the Mediterranean are well placed either to take part in operations in that area or move to the east. I believe they could exercise without escort in the northern part of the Red Sea.

Please give me your views as to whether you can usefully employ these vessels or if you consider they would be too much immobilised for the want of escorts. Bisset would come out in command of them in the *Royalist*.[1]

346. *From John Cunningham*

Naples,
11 February 1944

A.   The position at Anzio continues to stagnate. . . . It is Suvla all over again and has been from the very beginning, except that, so far as I can judge, the Navy cannot be blamed this time, even for the venial sin of landing the wrong kind of mules.[2] . . .

B.   My signal will have given you the number of trips made by LSTs, in addition I have sent in stores in LCIs and have used the LCTs for shuttling between Naples and Anzio and others (the USA smaller ones) for unloading the Liberty ships off the beaches; the 800 DUKWs have contributed materially to the latter task. . . . according to our estimates, I calculate that we had put ashore up to 1800 on 10 February:

(a)   65,240 tons of stores and ammunition.
(b)   between 130,000 and 150,000 officers and men.
(c)   over 25,000 wheeled vehicles out of which we have brought back some 5,000 for reloading. . . .

[1]*Royalist*: lt csr, 1943, 5450t, 33k, 8×5.25in, 6×21in tt.
Escort carriers unknown.
    RAdm A. W. LaT. Bisset: Capt 1932; *Shropshire* 1939; *Formidable* Aug 1940; RA July 1942; Ady; RA Force H 1943; RA Escort Carriers, *Royalist* Oct 1943; RA (Air) Home F March 1944; attack on *Tirpitz* April 1944; ret Jan 1945, ill health.
[2]Suvla, Gallipoli, invasion, 1915.

E.　The chance of an LST being hit in the entrance to Anzio is an abiding anxiety but it has not happened so far despite bombing and, now, quite considerable shell fire from 6-inch batteries which the Army do not deal with. It is almost impossible to make them realise that their very existence depends upon this little port and that to land, as we have done, an average of some 3,500 tons of goods and some 1300 vehicles a day through a port about the size of Bridport is a feat worthy of such help and support as they can give us.[1]

F.　... *Spartan* was a sad blow. .... *Spartan's* CBs and No. 32 fuses were an anxiety to me at first because her bilge was about four feet above water; there were some 600 projectiles to deal with and diving was impossible owing to bombing. However, she is now sinking so rapidly into the sea bottom that only some 200 feet of her length projects above the sand.[2] ...

... it is taking practically all my available forces (and playing merry hell with maintenance of ships) to secure the bridgehead and provide the Army with gun support on the flanks etc.

[Captain M. L.] Power has been a very great help to me and I hope you will let me keep him for a little longer without prejudicing his prospect of getting command of a Destroyer Flotilla – his knowledge of and relations with the various USA Army officers is invaluable to me ...

I am sure he [General Maitland Wilson] should take a lead in this affair... It's a thousand pities we didn't let Patton do the job!

347.　*From John Cunningham*

17 February 1944

4.　I was disappointed to learn that in addition to the ships you mention all the rest of the cruisers except the damaged *Aurora* and possibly *Penelope* were to go. The two French ships would be a poor substitute and the problem of command may be difficult, especially if you take Mansfield as I suppose you must. I would, however, very much like to keep him if any effective British cruisers remain so that I can leave to him the education of the French ships and avoid letting Davidson do so. I feel sure you will share my disinclination to allowing such preponderance of USA senior officers and ships as may result in tending to convert the Mediterranean into a USA sphere of influence. For that

[1]A small port in Dorset.
[2]*Spartan*: lt csr, 1943, 5770t, 33k, 8×5.25in; bbd Anzio 29 Jan 1944.

reason alone an adequate British representation seems desirable. Would you consider taking a couple of French cruisers in place of British for 'Overlord'? It would be some compensation for their disappointment about 'Anvil' and would avoid the preponderance of USA ships in the Mediterranean.

5. Mansfield is doing well and the ships have all gained most valuable additional bombardment experience and have earned high praise from the Armies.

7. I fear I can see no useful employment for the fighter-equipped assault carriers. . . They will be needed if 'Anvil' comes off . . . Long-range land-based fighters have already made one or two interceptions of South of France-based bombers en route to Oran convoys and are, I think, more suitable for the task. . . .

8. I will most certainly wish to have Troubridge, even for a one-divisional operation; I am anxious at all costs to avoid making any amphibious [operation] a purely US affair. Troubridge can do anything he likes with the US Army, while as you know the US Navy has an inferiority complex and always has trouble. They are also terribly Rolls-Royce in their requirements but do accept, grudgingly, Troubridge's recommendations in view of his great experience in these operations.

10. I do wish to keep Morse . . .

348. *From John Cunningham*

Naples,
4 March 1944

1. . . . the many signals you were getting about LSTs . . . unfortunately too much weight was given by the Allied Supreme Commander to the opinions expressed by Hewitt. The trouble is that without consulting me and during my absence, Hewitt was invited to attend C-in-C's meetings . . . He thus became aware of certain signals which it would have been better had he not seen [them] until I had a chance of educating him. . .

2. . . . there is no doubt that Hewitt's obsession regarding 'Anvil' has caused sight to be lost of the immediate object . . . I calculate that a force of 48 operational LSTs is essential to maintain the Anzio beach-head until the armies join forces. I have directed that Hewitt's attention should be drawn to this calculation. . . . I hope that we may now get rather clearer thinking.

4. . . . The great preponderance of US forces is liable to present me with an awkward problem. You know how terribly 'mission minded'

they are and how reluctant to take their share or help out in the hum-drum routine of the station. . . .

7. I assume that the 44 US escorts you threaten me with are sufficient to cover the agreed 'Anvil' bill including the carrier escorts. Otherwise the maintenance of the regular convoy cycle will become nigh impossi-ble, unless they go naked of escort.

10. The enemy shelling of Anzio is becoming rather more than a nuisance because the US Liberty ships often won't come within six or seven miles of the beach, which naturally plays merry hell with any unloading programme and also, of course, causes extra damage to LCTs alongside.[1] When they do come close enough, they weigh as soon as shells get near them and that is almost worse. A few LSTs have been damaged by shell fire but so far we have been lucky not to have a big explosion in the harbour.

349.   *To John Cunningham*

21 March 1944

. . . The Americans do not appear to be very clever on the subject of 'Anvil'. They appear determined to have it regardless of anything else that is going on in the Mediterranean. I see a large armada of American ships, including three battleships, is billed to appear in the Mediterra-nean by 3 May. Hewitt will have to be wheeled into line and made to understand that he is under your orders, but in the American idea operational control only works one way.

A.   . . . It appears fairly certain that 'Anvil' cannot take place and so, in addition to the 41 [landing craft] already billed to come home, Eisenhower will probably demand 26 more. . . .

You will have seen that we are trying to get two French cruisers home for 'Overlord' and leave you two in the Mediterranean.

B.   I thought I had already told you that Mansfield would stay in the Mediterranean. I realise that you cannot do without him.

The question of Troubridge is rather more difficult. I can probably leave him with you but we must have the *Bulolo*. . . .

D.   The question of the retention of Howard Kelly in Ankara has arisen. I very much doubt if he can do much more there. You remember that he was sent there as Head of the British Naval Mission if and when Turkey came into the war. This does not appear likely to happen now. . . .

---

[1]Liberty ship: 7126t, 11k, 1941–5; all-purpose cargo ship, 2710 blt in US, ess UK design.

350. *From Kelly*

3 April 1944

I quite agree that under existing circumstances there is no advantage in retaining my services in Turkey more especially as I am not in sympathy with our present policy, as no doubt you have guessed. . . .

Our recent action [the Aegean operations] I think has definitely put an end to the possibility of the entry of Turkey into the war under conditions such as they might be able to render us any efficient service, they would therefore be more of a liability than an asset.

351. *Diary*

5 April 1944

. . . A Cabinet meeting at 1830 at which the other two COS having salted [gone absent] I had to represent the views on American interest in Middle East oil. The COS from the strategic aspect were favourable so as to have US support should Russia in post-war days cast sheep's eyes at Iranian or Iraqi oilfields.

352. *Diary*

10 April 1944

They were rather losing their heads about the Greek subversive situation. The PM butting in and a disinclination to leave it to the man on the spot, Rawlings. John Cunningham is also in Cairo. Shortly a few ships of the Greek fleet have refused duty and there has been some minor violence to officers. On the other hand some of the destroyers and other ships are performing their duty as usual. The mutineer ships are isolated and I have no doubt will come to heel when a proper Greek Government is formed. The King of Greece left London for Cairo yesterday.[1] . . .

353. *Diary*

22 April 1944

. . . Things as regards the Greek mutineers are moving to a crisis. Both naval and army C's-in-C are contemplating the use of force. I am sure

[1]King George II (1890–1947): after war, forced to abdicate in favour of regency.

the Greek C-in-C will not produce the Greek forces to board the insub-
ordinate ships which means that the sailors will be shot at and perhaps
killed. This I am much averse to. I believe torpedoing of *Haephestos*[,]
the HQ of the mutineers[,] would bring them all to heel. In the meantime it is as well to be clear that FO and other authorities are approving
the use of British force against the Greeks.[1]

PM approved my signal to C-in-C suggesting torpedoing of the
Haephestos and at the same time sent me a very after lunchy minute
about what the C-in-C should do and what precautions he should take. I
did not signal any of it to C-in-C, Mediterranean, who I feel must be
left to do his own job.

354. *Diary*

23 April 1944

Heard over the phone that the loyal Greeks boarded and took one
destroyer [and] two corvettes in Alexandria last night.

355. *To John Cunningham*

6 May 1944

A.   . . . Hewitt is quite a good fellow but both he and his Chief of Staff
require keeping in their places. This unrest and attempt to assert independence is going on wherever British and American operations impinge.
. . .

B.   Wilson before the COS produced a suggested organisation for the
command in the Adriatic.

He said he was contemplating setting up one commander responsible
to him for all operations in that area and he said he thought an airman
should fill the post. As far as I could see he had been in close contact
with Slessor about it.

I do not know what your views are but I contested the idea of an
airman for the job and said it should be a sailor. I have long held the
view that all the Commandos should be under the Naval C-in-C. I
believe the commandos hold that view also. When they are under the
army they are seldom used for the proper job but generally as infantry.

---

[1]Adm Petros Voulgaris: C-in-C, April 1944.
Haephestos: this appears to be *Hifaistos*: repair ship, 1920, 4549t, 11.5k, 4×4in.

Incidentally the PM has suggested that all operations in Adriatic and Aegean should come directly under you. I do not see how this could work.

The upshot is that Wilson is to discuss it with you and Slessor and make proposals.

C.   This Greek business is rather a nuisance. I would like to know in due course how far the Greek ships can be relied upon. You know we stopped the *Avonvale* being turned over.[1]

D.   I hope this next offensive your way will meet with success. We have had much trouble with the American COS over cancelling 'Anvil' but there is a chance they may provide more LSTs in June to give you about a 2+ division lift.

E.   Things go fairly smoothly here but the demands for 'Overlord' are frightful. If we had demanded to be furnished on such a lavish scale no Mediterranean operation could have been carried out.

356.   *From John Cunningham*

Naples,
23 May 1944

2.   After investigation it is clear that a considerable measure of integration of US officers into the staff of the C-in-C, Mediterranean, would be possible but it is also quite clear that before such a step could be taken, there should be a complete integration of US and British naval forces in the whole Mediterranean theatre.

4.   I have recently had Hewitt staying in the house with me for four or five days and have talked the whole thing over with him. I gather that he felt that in the past, there were occasions where he was not as fully informed as he would have liked to be but that he now has no complaints on this score. . . .

7.   I fully agree that the problem of Deputy Naval Commander is not a particularly simple one, nor do I think, except on the score of prestige, that it is necessary. . . . I do suggest that someone more live-wire than Hewitt might be preferable. I have no personal objection to Hewitt but I certainly would not choose him as my deputy. . . as I do not consider that he is sufficiently widely informed . . .

---

[1]*Avon Vale*: 'Hunt'; never tfd.

357.   *From John Cunningham*

Naples,
26 May 1944

4.   *The Adriatic Command*

This business reeks to me of intrigue ... I saw no reason why the same organisation as Chiefs of Staff Committee, Middle East Command, . . ., etc., should not function equally successfully for the Adriatic operations, namely that all three commanders should be jointly responsible both for the co-ordination and execution of plans.

5.   I quite agree with you that at the present stage, unless I had a considerable increase in staff, the control of the Adriatic and Aegean operations would be very difficult to manage from my HQ.

7.   *The Greeks*

I was glad that you stopped the *Avonvale* being turned over and that you have now stopped *Cowdray*.[1] I very much doubt if we will ever be able fully to rely upon the Greek ships. As I forecast last month, there is undoubtedly a considerable element in the crews of the Greek ships who will never accept any government except a purely communist one and that among others who affect to accept a Pan-Hellenic government, there will be many who refuse duty (they do not call it mutiny) on the grounds that they disagree with this or that representative of one party or another in the set-up of the government.

8.   The sorting out of the Greek mutineers is proceeding slowly and in the end, I think about 50% of the original number will be labelled 'loyalists'. The quality of their loyalty will, however, not be very high but if I have time to 'sweat' them, I hope to get the majority of the ships back into operations in a state of moderate efficiency. Their defection has seriously handicapped me, especially coming at a time when it was necessary to withdraw so many British ships from this theatre.

9.   *'Anvil'*

I was glad to learn that we were getting the extra 19 American LSTs and that each of them would bring an LCT. Planning goes on apace and I am, of course, assuming that the various escort and support craft now gathered for the 'Overlord' bill will return to us in time for operations before the weather sours on us.

---

[1] *Cowdray*: 'Hunt'; never tfd.

13. *Disposition of Escorts*

I was a little hurt at receiving AM 1255 16 May [not reproduced] which seemed to suggest that I had failed to note that the U-boat threat was greater in the Western than in the Eastern Mediterranean. As a matter of fact I have skinned the Eastern Mediterranean almost to the bone. Furthermore, the results recently achieved against the U-boats confirm rather than otherwise the correctness of the dispositions of the much-reduced light forces in this theatre which have been made.

14.   A very marked feature and a very substantial contribution to the success of recent anti-U-boat operations has been the superior equipment of the US light craft. A further contributory feature to our success has been the very large escorts which COMINCH provides for the UGS convoys, as this enables a substantial hunting force to be detached from the convoy escort whenever a U-boat discloses its position by attacking the convoy or escorts.

15.   The loss of Armstrong and *Laforey* was a very serious blow and a great grief to me. Both Armstrong and his ship were absolutely outstanding. It was shocking bad luck that *Laforey* should have been hit by the one torpedo fired and that she went in 90 seconds. Armstrong was apparently taking anti-Gnat precautions and therefore going too slowly to dodge the ordinary torpedo which was fired at him. The enemy's Gnats have had success lately, especially against Americans whose Foxer is, I think, not very good.[1]

16. *Italian Affairs*

I have had a long interview with De Courten and, I hope, cleared up most of the difficulties. He is, I think, still fully prepared to play but needs an occasional jolt. The pathetic thing about him is that he believes, or affects to believe, the Italian Fleet will be reconstituted after the war on much the same scale as before. For that reason, he is inclined to ask for facilities sufficient to enable him to train the personnel needed to man a first-class fleet. So long as it suits our purpose, I have no intention of disillusioning his mind of this idea. I had a little difficulty with him over the appointment of Senior Officers but have now told him that I require his proposals for appointments of all Captains and above, but will leave to his discretion the appoint-

---

[1]*Laforey*: flotilla leader, 1941, 1935t, 36.5k, 6×4.7, 1×4in, 4×21in tt; sunk by *U-223*, 30 Sept 1944.

Capt H. T. Armstrong: Cdr June 1937; *Maori* May 1940; Capt June 1941; *Onslow* Aug 1941; Capt, Cstl Forces, *Pembroke* Jan 1943; *Laforey* March 1943; d 30 Sept 1944.

ments of lower rank, even though they might be in command of small craft.[1]

358. *Diary*

2 June 1944

Usual COS meeting. Good fight with CAS about the new Adriatic set up suggestion. CAS produced or tried to all John Cunningham's arguments which had been signalled to him by Slessor. John Cunningham himself had not favoured me with them so I had to fight unbriefed. I rather mistrust Slessor and on the whole question it appears to me quite wrong to have two authorities running each a small show in the Adriatic. The upshot was that Admiralty should prepare a paper setting out their objections to be signalled to Wilson. . . .

359. *Diary*

9 June 1944

. . . COS meeting at 1100. Discussion on command in the Adriatic. Finally signal sent to Wilson telling him to clarify his directive. Undoubtedly an attempt by Slessor to get an RAF command over the other two Services . . .

360. *To John Cunningham*

1 September 1944

2. . . . I also talked to him [the First Lord] at considerable length about the development of Malta. I do not think there will ever be money enough for anything but essentials which I put down as a graving dock and submarine shelters on a long term, airfields for the FAA which can be turned over to the RAF in wartime, and rehabilitation of the dockyard.
4. We very much hope that you will be able to take on the refit of *Richelieu*. I would suggest a refit at Malta and docking at Taranto. . . . It is essential that more work is undertaken in the Mediterranean. Every port and dock in Great Britain has a long waiting list of ships to be repaired or refitted and overhaul of landing craft, the aftermath of

[1]Cunningham-de Courten Agreement, No. 135.

'Overlord', and there is no prospect of improvement in the near future. Have you considered that in the Mediterranean area you have 37 dry docks, nearly as many as there are in the UK?

5.   My experts are not sympathetic to your request for more sweepers. They state, with what truth I know not, that you have 257 already in the Mediterranean, as against 381 in the UK. I expect that they counted some of yours two times over. I note in the list that they have included French, Italian, Greek, Yugoslav and American. However, you will get the modest reinforcement in September that we have promised.

8.   'Dragoon' [formerly 'Anvil'] appears to have been a great success but did not have quite the effect which was expected of it. ... But though it is still decried at home here, I think myself that it has been well worthwhile in causing the abandonment of South West France. . . .

361.   *From John Cunningham*

Naples,
25 September 1944

... I put to him [the First Lord], in connection with the future development of Malta, my view that we will in any future war, as in the past, require a Fleet Base in the Eastern Mediterranean in addition to Malta and that with the unfortunate experience of Ireland to guide us, we should develop such eastern base in territory likely to be permanently under our control, and preferably, on an island. For this reason I am most strongly of the opinion that the formerly projected naval base at Famagusta in Cyprus should be put in hand as early as possible and that development of Malta should be reviewed in the light of what we intend to do in Cyprus. . . .

2.   ... There is no doubt that we are beginning to feel the effects of five years of war and that it is manifesting itself in the shape of mental fatigue on the part of rather unexpected people and more especially in some of the Captains, some of whom have had a very strenuous five years. I spoke to Harcourt about this and was glad to find that this matter was fully appreciated at your end.

4.   You will by now have seen that we are quite prepared to take on the refit of *Richelieu* at Casablanca and her docking at Gibraltar. . . .

5.   You may be assured . . . that the Mediterranean repair and docking facilities will be required in future to play a large part in maintaining the ships operating in the Far East and that I am planning accordingly. . . .

6.   . . . [with regard to minesweepers] if I exclude the foreign manned, damaged and paid off minesweepers on the station, I only make the

number likely to be available to me as 169, together with a few dan layers, and many even of these are in an advanced state of decrepitude.[1] However, you may be assured that we will do our best and undoubtedly I am fortunate in having many very keen and experienced officers and men on the station for this important job.

8.   I agree with you that despite the way it has been cried down in some circles, 'Dragoon' has paid a pretty good dividend ... In the Southern French area there is the usual bickering between the US Army and Navy, but despite this we are getting on well with the opening of Marseille, which the Hun actually made a most frightful mess of as he had also of Toulon. I think the latter will require almost complete reconstruction when the French have the time and inclination to undertake such a vast job.

9.   ... I was very grateful that I was allowed to retain the escort carriers; their use in the Aegean has certainly paid a good dividend and I hope almost completely disrupted the Hun's plan for the evacuation of the islands. It took, of course, a few days to get them going and into position as they were all much over their boiler hours when released from 'Dragoon'. They did a magnificent job in 'Dragoon' under conditions (no wind on most days) which might well have greatly curtailed their operations and caused considerable losses in aircraft. Under Troubridge's inspiration they flew an incredible number of sorties and incurred, in the circumstances, a very small number of casualties. ...

P.S.: Eighth Army seem, as you know, to regard it as the Navy's sole job in life to be the answer to their prayer 'give us this day our daily bread – and see that there is lots of jam on it'. They seem to lose all power of movement as soon as they get away from the sea and to be disinclined to move at all unless they have got a reserve of at least 60 days' supplies within a couple of miles of the front line! I fear you spoiled them and robbed them of their self-reliance!

362.   Diary

1 September 1944

COS meeting at 1100. In closed session I brought up and spoke strongly about PM's private telegram to Alexander asking him if he was getting proper naval support. The CIGS [Brooke] is so nice and friendly about these things that it is difficult to be offensive about these Army affairs.

---

[1]Dan layer: minesweeping buoy vessel.

He will I think take action if Alexander is so foolish as to comply with PM's request. . . .

363. *From Admiral Sir Bernard Rawlings*

Flag Officer, Levant
and Eastern Mediterranean,
27 September 1944

When the First Lord was out here he told me that subject to whatever conclusion Quebec came to, would I like to consider myself a starter for eastern adventures in due course. That is of course a most attractive idea – thank you very much indeed. . . .

I'm hoping to enjoy things up in the Aegean – now we've got some-thing to do it with. It's very much of a Jimmy-round-the ruddy-orchard game with these little craft and barges and things popping in and out of the islands – there aren't any decent targets left – and the whole place a mass of minefields. I'm hoping to get a lane swept through the main barrier in a day or two and get at them from the side they haven't catered for – the north. It's the first time I've had anything to do with modern aircraft – carrier aircraft that is. Give me the old '40/41 vintage – they weren't so fussy and finicky and brittle. They always seem to have the wrong something or to lack this and that – the truth is I believe we're too Rolls-Royce these days. Lord knows what the Combined Operation ships are like – they seem to want incessant mending and pulling to bits. Someone was saying the other day that an LC(B), for Brothel, was the only marine speciality we hadn't yet got. . . . I think it's an awful pity we must have three of everything . . . Or perhaps I'm being archaic. But I do dislike Private Navies – it seems to me to strike right at the root of all the poor RN stands for. Besides being so grossly extravagant that the taxpayer will rebel in peacetime – and the surface ships, old fashioned type, lose thereby. For I fear I still believe in the Battle Fleet as the last and final word. What a good time your old *Warspite* has had this war – I'm very angry indeed about my old ship and the dock.[1] It's monstrous. . . . What have you been doing to the First Lord? He looks so much fitter and more cheerful and happier than two years' ago. My guess is that you have stopped the PM bullying him!

[1] A dock collapsed under *Valiant*, 8 Aug 1944, Trincomalee, Sri Lanka; she was never fully repaired.

364. *Diary*

10 October 1944

COS meeting. Principal item being the further operations in the Mediterranean. Joint Planners in attendance. They provided a paper deprecating the allocation of more resources to Italy. Pointing out that the north west front is the decisive one, that the divisions there are tired and that Eisenhower can absorb all the divisions he can lay his hands on. They also suggested that the retention of the American assault lift in the Mediterranean is unjustified. There is no question but they are right all through. It will possibly cause a storm when the PM sees it. . . .

Both the airborne and seaborne troops have arrived in Athens. Some losses of minesweepers sweeping the channel to the Piraeus. It does one good to see the old names *Dido* and *Ajax* among the arrivals there. *Ajax's* last departure was just after the ammunition ship blew up.[1]

365. *Diary*

20 November 1944

COS meeting at 1100. . . . Some discussion on US COS message about operations in the Mediterranean. They pointed out that there were not sufficient troops for extensive operations in both Italy and Yugoslavia and suggested landing only light forces on the Balkan side. We had come to much the same opinion ourselves so were able to agree.

Good meeting with C-in-C, Mediterranean, after lunch at which we resolved all our difficulties. There was little difference of opinion. . . .

366. *Diary*

1 December 1944

. . . Governor of Malta's letter pointing out that there were conflicting claims between the Navy and RAF for the airfields in Malta and how dependent the Maltese were on the services[,] the Navy in particular.[2] I spoke a few straight words to the CAS on the Air Ministry's attitude.

[1]*Dido*: lt csr, 1940, 5450t, 33k, 10×5.25in, 6×21in tt.
For the explosion at Piraeus, 6–7 April 1941, see *Cunningham Papers*, vol. I, pp. 330–1.

[2]Govr Malta: Lt Gen E. C. A. Schreiber (1890–1972): RA; Eur 1914–18; staff posts 1930s; Col 1938; Maj Gen 1940; 45 Div 1941; 5 Corps 1942; Lt Gen & Govr & C-in-C Malta Sept 1944–6.

The situation is that while the Navy are perfectly prepared to state their post-war requirements the Air Ministry refuse to do so until the principles of Imperial Defence after the war are established. It is in fact fairly well known that they think of ousting the Navy from Malta by claiming all the airfields and that they are occupied in trying to establish posts for Air Marshals after the war. John Cunningham was very outspoken about it when he was here. . . .

367. *Diary*

18 December 1944

COS meeting at 1100. Governor of Malta attended. CAS tried to make out that the airfield question could be dealt with by itself and so could be left until after the war. I disputed this and pointed out that the Admiralty were planning to make full use of Malta. Any fleet stationed there would include carriers and airfields would be required. . . .

368. *Diary*

28 May 1945

. . . Trouble has broken out in Levant. The result of de Gaulle's insane personal policy. He will have the whole Middle East aflame unless we watch it. . . .

369.   *From John Cunningham*

Naples,
7 June 1945

I feel I owe you some explanation of my reasons for asking Glassford whether US ships would be available for the Levant Area in case of necessity. I had in mind the possibility that the Syrian incident might drag on for weeks and that the working up ships might then have gone on their way to the East. . . . In view of our experiences in Greece last year I would be most reluctant to use US ships without previous decision having been communicated from Washington.[1]

---

[1]VAdm William A. Glassford, US Navy (1886–1958): grad N Acad 1906; destroyers 1918–24; ONO 1924–7; Capt & *Maryland* 1937–9; RA & Cdr Yangtze Patrol 1939–41; A/VA, TF 5, Asiatic F 1941–2; Cdr US N Forces, SW Pac Jan–May 1942; head, US Mil Mission, Dakar Dec 1942; Cdt, 6 N Dist 1943; VA & French W Africa appts June 1943–

2.   Hitherto my policy has been to bring in US ships as much as possible when we break new ground, not only to show the Flag, but also to emphasise the accord between the great Allies. Provided they were free agents both Hewitt and Glassford agree. A further advantage of this policy was that if, as I understand, there was at one time some reluctance on the part of the US Authorities to accept full participation by British Naval Forces in the Pacific theatre, it might help if it could be pointed out that American participation was not only accepted but welcomed in this theatre. . . .

8.   I had a very interesting trip to Greece in April for the handing over of *Vengeful*. The atmosphere there is extensively pro-British and Admiral Voulgaris is doing, I think, a very good job as Prime Minister and First Lord.[1] . . .

370.   *Diary*

15 September 1945

. . . When asked I said that the major military interest was in keeping any powerful potential enemy state away from the shores of the Mediterranean, that the COS were more interested in preventing others from having bases there than in acquiring them themselves and that consequently the entry of Russia into the Mediterranean on any terms would in the opinion of the COS be most undesirable. Decided to refer the US proposal [for international trusteeships run by staff from the great powers] to the Deputies [DCOS] committee.

371.   *From John Cunningham*

25 October 1945

I have written officially today reporting my audience with King Farouk and the desire of the Egyptians to buy some ships from us with which to start their Navy and of their wish to send up to about two dozen young officers to do specialist courses in England. As we seem to owe them a lot of money this seems to me to be an excellent way of getting

---

July 1944; US N Forces Eur July 1944–April 1945; Cdr 8 F & Cdr, US N Forces, NW Africa; Cdr, US N Forces Germany Dec 1945–Jan 1946; ret 1947.

On Greece, 9 Dec 1944, see R. E. Sherwood (ed.), *The White House Papers of Harry L. Hopkins*, vol. II (1942–45) (London, 1949), pp. 831–5.

[1]*Vengeful*: s/m, 1944, 545/740t, 12.75/9k, 1×3in, 4×21in tt; tfd as *Delphin*.

some of it back and I have asked for Their Lordships' policy in this matter.[1]

I have been struck by the very friendly attitude of the King and the Egyptian Navy as well as some of the present government and am sure that if we don't delay or haggle too violently over prices we will be able to secure for ourselves a much more favourable position than I had anticipated. Both Tennant and Creighton are very popular with the Egyptians and have done a really excellent job.[2] . . .

372. *Diary*

16 February 1946

. . . Attlee's attitude to the Mediterranean question is past belief. He doesn't seem to realise what the passage throughout the Mediterranean means to us. He seems to think it is an idea maintained for the benefit of the Navy.[3] . . .

---

[1]King Farouk (1920–65): acceded 1940; abdicated 1952.

[2]RAdm K. E. L. Creighton (1883–1963): ent RN 1907; navig spist; Navig Sch 1910; navigr, *New Zealand* 1914–18; Mr of F, Grand F 1918; Capt 1921; RNC Greenwich 1928–9; Dir Navig 1929–31; Capt *Royal Sovereign* 1932–3; RA ret 1934; Cdre, convoys 1939–43; DG, Ports & Lights Admin, Egypt 1943–6.

[3]Clement R. Attlee: As a consequence of the Labour victory in the 1945 General Election, Attlee had now become PM.

SECTION G

THE BRITISH PACIFIC FLEET AND THE EAST INDIES FLEET

NOVEMBER 1943–MARCH 1946

At the time of Cunningham's appointment as First Sea Lord, the British did not have a very substantial or offensive record in the Far East. There were significant naval losses in 1941–42, notably the *Prince of Wales* and *Repulse* but also including a carrier, three cruisers, several destroyers and numerous light craft. The Royal Navy's principal bases at Singapore and Hong Kong were occupied by the Japanese and bases in the Indian Ocean were insecure. For most of 1942 and 1943, therefore, Admiral Somerville, Cunningham's term-mate at *Britannia* in 1897 and a life-long friend, in command of the Eastern Fleet, was driven back to Kilindini in Kenya and had mostly elderly ships – and not many of them. He was confined to convoy escort, anti-raider patrols and hunting down German supply tankers.[1]

By the autumn of 1943 matters were changing for the better, for the defeat of Italy meant that Somerville received a steady stream of re-inforcements, including battleships and fleet carriers, so that in 1944 he could contemplate offensive operations. Nothing better exemplifies the fact that the Royal Navy was a two-ocean fleet trying to fight a three-ocean war than the release of substantial forces from the Mediterranean to permit offensives in the east. Somerville prosecuted the offensive in the Indian Ocean so vigorously in the first half of 1944 that Churchill was impressed by the 'fighting admiral' and was averse to his impending move to Washington to head the BAD. Somerville was the right man in the right place at the right time, however, for his exuberant personality, flair for good personal relations, reputation as a 'fighting admiral' and recent knowledge of the war in the east fitted him well for the Washington scene.[2] He used a mixture of cajole, humour and firm-ness in dealing with King on Cunningham's behalf [373, 381, 383, 388, 392, 395, 399, 407, 413, 443, 450, 463, 500].

For Cunningham, however, the Indian Ocean and South East Asia remained a secondary theatre. His strategic calculation was that, if

---

[1]For fuller information on Somerville's time as C-in-C, Eastern Fleet, see M. A. Simpson (ed.), *Somerville Papers*, pp. 349–585.
[2]See M. A. Simpson (ed.), *Somerville Papers*, pp. 589–657.

The Far East

Japan was tackled in her home waters and islands and defeated there, the territories that she had conquered in China and South East Asia would fall into the hands of their pre-war owners without them firing a shot. Britain's main effort against Japan, just getting under way when he became First Sea Lord, would be led by a British Pacific Fleet, fighting alongside the Americans. This would serve several functions: It would demonstrate to the sceptical Americans that Britain was in earnest about finishing the Far Eastern war; It would enable Britain to regain her pre-war position in the Orient, notably trade with China; It would help Britain to claim a voice in the post-war settlement in Japan. It would lead to the return of former colonies; and it would give the Royal Navy valuable experience in a somewhat neglected theatre of war, enable it to learn new techniques, and endow it with much-needed prestige ahead of the expected post-war competition with the other services for a share of the defence budget, an undoubtedly shrunken one.[1]

There were several major obstacles to Cunningham's strategic dream. The first was the formidable opposition of the Prime Minister. Churchill remained sceptical of the wisdom of fighting Japan on her front doorstep and, apologist for empire as he was, preferred to set about liberating the colonies, which would have meant major operations in the Indian Ocean, led by his protégé, Admiral Mountbatten, appointed Supreme Allied Commander of the newly-created South East Asia Command in the autumn of 1943. Churchill was opposed resolutely by all of the Chiefs of Staff, led by Cunningham, for the fleet was the only instrument which could be made available in strength in 1945, the earliest date at which Britain could envisage a major contribution to the defeat of Japan. For a long time in 1943–44 there was stalemate between the Prime Minister and his service chiefs. The quarrel became so deep and bitter that the chiefs contemplated resignation. In time, Churchill's political allies came to see the wisdom of the chiefs' proposals and eventually the old imperialist, isolated, was driven to agree with them [381, 385, 389, 397, 399–402, 426, 467].

The end of Churchill's opposition was signalled with dramatic suddenness when, at the Quebec conference of September 1944, he offered a British fleet in the Pacific. President Roosevelt took up the offer without hesitation, both to humour Churchill and to prepare the ground for later policies not to Churchill's liking. There arose at once a second barrier. The Chief of Naval Operations, Admiral Ernest J. King, as crusty as Churchill, was wrong-footed by the President's airy accept-

[1]See H. P. Willmott, *Grave of a Dozen Schemes* (Annapolis, MD, 1995).

ance of a British Pacific Fleet. By the following day, at a meeting of the Combined Chiefs of Staff, King, recovering his wits, pranced and snorted, alleging that the President had not meant what he had said, it could not be allowed, and he would not have it. Receiving no support from the other members of the American Joint Chiefs of Staff and faced with his Commander-in-Chief's clear decision, King had to accept that there would be a British Pacific Fleet alongside the American one. Most American reaction was, in fact, favourable. [379, 381, 387, 394, 397, 401–2, 405, 414, 417, 451, 459, 462, 464–5, 477, 480]. Cunningham suspected, however, that King and his subordinates dragged their feet and tried to divert the fleet to operations against other targets. The probability is that King did not know what forces would be required, or in which direction they would go, until early in 1945 and moreover he was concerned that a British fleet should be logistically self-support-ing, as he felt that American supply facilities were already stretched [376, 379, 394, 396, 412, 422–3, 443, 450, 453, 459, 463, 480].

No sooner had King accepted, grudgingly, a British presence off Japan than a further hurdle loomed. It was not about warships, for by then there were more than enough, all of them modern vessels. The problem lay in logistics. Where would the British find a rear base and one nearer the operational zone, and could they find enough ships of the right types to service the fleet at sea, far from even an advanced base, for distances were vast in the Pacific? In 1944–45 Cunningham wrestled with these questions. None of them were settled satisfactorily, though a comfortable and well-equipped rear base was established in Sydney and a forward base, much less comfortable and more primitive, at Manus in the Admi-ralty Islands. The major headache was the Fleet Train, a body of merchantmen designed to accompany the warships, meeting their needs for oil, supplies, replacements, repairs and hospitalisation. The Ameri-cans had a large, modern, speedy, largely purpose-built fleet train. In three years of Pacific warfare, they had perfected it, meeting most of the task forces' needs on the high seas. This development was new to the Royal Navy, still essentially short-legged and tied to shore bases. These were either a long distance away from the front line or they were held by the enemy.

It was not only the lack of fast, modern ships, especially tankers, that was the problem, for the Admiralty had to compete for shipping with the needs of large armies in Italy and Germany, occupation forces once the fighting was over, and a civilian population and industries restless after a long and exhausting war for more abundant foodstuffs and raw materials – and the exports to pay for them. The Minister of War Transport, Lord Leathers, was jealous of his shipping and most reluctant to let the Admiralty have any of it. Cunningham, who disliked Leathers, whom he dubbed 'slippery', had many fights with him. He obtained a fleet train, partly with the Prime Minister's aid, but Leathers continued to snipe. In any case, Britain simply did not have the types of ships necessary. They were often old, war-worn, slow and otherwise deficient, and always too few. The shortcomings in the fleet train exercised a major influence on the size of warship fleet that could be sent and hamstrung its operations. The British Pacific Fleet, the greatest force assembled by this nation since Jutland, consisting almost entirely of ships built during the war (some of them fresh from working up), was serviced by a fleet train that performed wonders but often did so with a silent prayer [380, 382, 409, 415, 430, 440, 452, 473].

Cunningham had his difficulties with the Australian Government, always somewhat spiky, now feeling the weight of three years of war, during which it had raised substantial forces and also hosted General MacArthur's South West Pacific Area. The Government in Canberra had now to summon up its spirit and resources, and those of its people, to provide a home for the BPF. By late 1944 there was little spare capacity left in Australia – either in labour, supplies or industry. Admiral Fraser, C-in-C of the BPF, found the Australian Government (and the strong unions) no easier once he arrived there [378, 381, 383, 385, 391–4, 410, 413, 415–16, 422, 451, 470, 478].[1] MacArthur, who initially had cast covetous eyes over the BPF, mercifully proved relatively unconcerned over its disposition when it arrived [378, 381, 389, 410, 413, 443, 451, 488, 491].

Fraser, though the obvious choice for the appointment after his victory in the Battle of North Cape, had a prickly relationship with Cunningham. A man of immense abilities, normally quite affable, at home in the political world, he was also rather petulant and quick to take offence, lacking sound judgement. Cunningham and Alexander had their doubts about him on occasion and there were several clashes with the First Sea Lord, himself an obdurate and stubborn figure but one with the shrewdness to realise the demands of his position for tact, patience and vision [381, 383, 389, 392, 403, 413, 415–16, 421, 424–5, 427, 437, 443, 447, 449, 451, 476–8, 486, 488, 494, 495].

Neither Cunningham, Fraser nor the C-in-C's senior officers were pleased with the BPF's advanced base at Manus. It was quite well equipped – by the Americans, and it was owing largely to their generosity and capacity for turning a blind eye to Washington's strict instructions to let

---

[1]For the RAN's effort in the Second World War, see D. Stevens (ed.), *The RAN in World War II* (St Leonards, NSW, 1996).

the British fend for themselves that the BPF was able to function from there. Its drawbacks were its spread out geography and its horrendous, humid climate [451, 471, 490]. In vain Cunningham, and Somerville at BAD, tried to find a base nearer the front line, but the Americans were reluctant to let the British into their own imperial possession, the Philippines (shortly to be given their independence), and the negotiations, often explosive, were fruitless [459, 463–4, 471, 476–8].

On a happier note, Fraser enjoyed excellent relations with Admiral Chester Nimitz, C-in-C of the American Pacific Fleet, based at Pearl Harbor (seen as an ideal HQ for Fraser but unacceptable to King). While Cunningham and King circled each other warily, Fraser and Nimitz cooperated happily and much of the success of the BPF can be put down to this warm relationship, which extended to the commanders of the great American Task Forces, Spruance and Halsey [412, 428, 431].

Though the BPF was impressive, it was dwarfed by the Americans, becoming no more than a Task Group in their vast forces; Neptune's trident truly had shifted. The Americans enjoyed not only numerical but frequently also qualitative supremacy and, for half a century primarily a Pacific-oriented navy, they had become smooth operators in the immense island-punctuated wilderness. The Royal Navy came, saw, and was impressed. It was important that the BPF came to see the future of maritime warfare and adjust the Royal Navy's own post-war organisation [374–5, 388, 403, 408, 417, 432, 435–7, 464, 470].

The BPF had a preliminary strike at the Palembang oil refineries in January 1945, carried out at Nimitz's behest. It was successful but of doubtful strategic value, though it gave the BPF useful operational training. Its main operations took place from March 1945, when it tackled Japanese planes and airfields to the south of Nimitz's chief strike against Okinawa [376, 378, 361, 405, 410, 412, 427, 450, 460]. Thereafter it bombed, strafed and bombarded Japanese cities and airfields. It cannot be said that it was a decisive weight in the final struggle – probably, the Americans could have accomplished Japan's surrender in 1945 by themselves. Nimitz, Halsey and Spruance were all grateful for its help, however, for it relieved the Americans of specific tasks and performed well, both in the new style of sea-keeping and in the operational sense. Much was achieved with American *matériel*, notably many of the aircraft, some of the communications equipment and the signal code. The Americans, however, were impressed by the ability of British armoured carriers to shrug off Japanese *kamikaze* hits.[1] One detects, nevertheless, a note of desperately trying to keep up

---

[1]See M. A. Simpson (ed.), *Somerville Papers*, pp. 623, 637, 640, 643, 647.

the White Ensign's reputation in a subordinate, strange situation [443, 451, 453, 455, 460, 462, 478–9, 490–1].

Relations with Australia and New Zealand, both of whom supplied ships and other resources to the BPF, were somewhat frayed. During the inter-war period, Britain had focused on the Japanese threat, built a major fleet base at Singapore, and assured Australia and New Zealand that on the threat of war in the Far East, the 'main fleet' would be despatched hither. In the later 1930s, as it became clear that Italy would become a third opponent, the Royal Navy (led by Cunningham) made plans to fight a major fleet campaign in the Mediterranean. When war threatened in the east in the autumn of 1941, the Royal Navy was heavily committed in the Atlantic and Mediterranean; there was no 'main fleet' to spare for Singapore, for most of its earmarked ships were sunk or damaged – many of them during Cunningham's days as C-in-C, Mediterranean – and only *Prince of Wales* and *Repulse* could be sent, with disastrous results. In consequence, Australia and New Zealand were left exposed to attack and scuttled under the American umbrella, bitter at Britain's pre-war equivocation and lamentable war-time failure to defend her dominions; it was a Gallipoli of the Pacific. Cunningham, who had never served east of Suez, did not fully grasp the significance of 1941–42, or the extent or speed of the Empire's disintegration – nor did most British political and military leaders. Thus, Cunningham and the Royal Navy officers who headed the Royal Australian and Royal New Zealand Navies contemplated a post-war Empire fleet, to which the RAN and RNZN would contribute sizeable forces. Though the RAN did take on two of Britain's surplus light fleet carriers, independence, autonomy and economy, together with the ANZUS pact of 1951, ensured that an imperial fleet was nothing more than a dream [378, 390, 481–2].

The main focus of the period 1944–45, inevitably, is on the BPF, but there was another substantial, vigorous fleet in the Indian Ocean, where, with the Army and RAF, and largely British and Commonwealth forces, it pursued Imperial objectives, as much a 'forgotten fleet' as Slim's Fourteenth Army was the 'forgotten army'. This was the Eastern Fleet, under Admiral Somerville, which had been created in February 1942. Somerville was succeeded by Fraser in August 1944 but the latter soon passed on to Sydney. Vice Admiral Sir Arthur Power, who had been deputy to both of them, inherited a new command, dubbed the East Indies Fleet [373, 375, 388, 390, 400, 417, 434, 439, 475]. Power was a trusted favourite of Cunningham, under whom he had done well in the Mediterranean; their correspondence had a natural intimacy about it which cannot be detected in the Cunningham-Fraser exchanges. Power was effectively captain of the Second XI; most of his ships were super-annuated, or if they were war-built, consisted of escort carriers [417, 419–20, 424, 426, 429, 432–3]. Power was also short of amphibious vessels and had to become adaptable in order to keep pace with the Army's advance southward along the coasts of Burma and Malaya [377, 381, 426, 429, 433, 439, 441–2, 444, 457, 466, 469, 472, 474, 484]. Power worked in close concert with Mountbatten, but Cunningham was frequently exasperated with the Supreme Commander's grandiose plans, interference in matters not his concern, and ploys to gain control of ships and even the whole fleet [373, 381, 390, 394–5, 398–9, 403–4, 407, 411–12, 414, 426, 432, 445–8, 454, 456, 458, 461, 468, 483, 489].

The end of the war against Japan came with the dropping of the two atomic bombs. For that sudden end, without the heavy cost in Allied and Japanese lives which would have ensued from an invasion of the Japanese home islands, Cunningham and the rest of the CCS were profoundly thankful. For Cunningham, the immediate issues were re-gaining Hong Kong (he suspected that the Americans wished to hand it to the Chinese Nationalists) and reducing the fleet in line with the country's parlous financial situation [485–9, 492–3, 496–9, 501]. The coming of the nuclear age had implications for navies, however, and Cunningham had to begin reconstructing the post-war navy with the mushroom cloud hanging over him.

373.   *From Admiral Sir Geoffrey Layton*[1]

Office of C-in-C, Ceylon,
Sector Buildings, Colombo,
10 November 1943

... You will know of course all about the set up here which I was detailed to start in March 1942. It has worked very well on the whole, and co-operation in the three Services in Ceylon could not have been better. I have had difficult times off and on getting the Civil side to play up and also to keep their keenness and interest alive. The lack of further attacks (and bombs) has had an enervating effect on the local population, who regard the war at any time as a ruddy nuisance. ...

James [Somerville] has now arrived with his colossal Staff (and still bigger army of WRNS) – but no ships. It has not been easy to find accommodation for them all. They have now got settled down more or less, but some of them have not got very much to do to keep them busy, especially over Trincomalee way. That will be cured no doubt as soon as the ships arrive.

In the meantime, James is as usual busy trying to do everyone else's job for them! He came back from Delhi about a week ago with the project of finding somewhere in Ceylon for Mountbatten to set up his HQ, and a Reconnaissance Party arrives this week by air for that purpose.

I have told James that Ceylon is suffering from 'Services Indigestion' already. ...

Regarding my own job, I feel someone must hold it until Ceylon is no longer in the front line, and we have made some substantial progress towards recovering Burma and Malaya. ...

... I think it [the post of C-in-C, Ceylon] should be held by a sailor. The main problems all come back to the sea, and it wants someone who can make up his mind and stick to it and is not afraid of speaking his mind to Ministers or anyone else!

---

[1]Adm Sir Geoffrey Layton (1884–1964): Lt 1905; Capt 1922; *Renown* 1933–4; Cdre, Portsmouth Barracks 1934–6; RA 1935; DPS 1936–8; VA & BCS 1938; 2-in-C, Med F & 1BS 1939; 2-in-C, Home F & 18CS 1939–40; C-in-C, EF Dec 1941–March 1942; C-in-C Ceylon March 1942–Aug 1944; C-in-C Portsmouth Aug 1944–7.

374. *To Churchill*

24 November 1943

The following table will show you the build up of the Eastern Fleet in 1944 and early 1945.

MAIN UNITS

Date of arrival	Battleships	Fleet Carriers
1944		
February	Queen Elizabeth	Illustrious
	Valiant	Unicorn
	Renown	
March		Victorious
June	Howe	
July		Indefatigable
		Indomitable
		Formidable
August	King George V	
1945		
January	Anson	
April	Duke of York	

OTHER FLEET UNITS

Escort Carriers: Eight in middle of February 1944, rising to 16 by 1 January 1945, provided they can be manned.
Cruisers: 18 by end of February 1944.
Fleet Destroyers: 28 by end of February 1944.[1]

375. *To Layton*

1 January 1944

... We have now started some of the major units of the Eastern Fleet out to you and I hope you will be able to tuck them away somewhere. You will not probably have them very long – at least not all of them – as you will have seen that the 'Sextant' decisions remove the greater part of the British Eastern Fleet to the Pacific. You will always, how-

[1]*Renown*: b/csr, 1916, 32100t, 29k, 6×15in, 20×4.5in, 8×21in tt; extvsly mod 1930s.
Anson: b/ship, 1942, 35000t, 28k, 10×14in, 16×5.25in.

ever, have some major units. On the whole I think that the new strategy
is the best; the Pacific theatre and the South East Asia theatre are really
so far apart that the doings in one have little effect on the other.

I can quite understand that Ceylon is becoming overcrowded and if
Mountbatten arrives it seems to me there will be too many Big Noises
all together in one small island and I cannot see how there will be work
for everybody to do, especially the large staffs which, I now understand, run into some thousands. . . .

376. *From Admiral Sir Percy Noble*

BAD, Washington, DC,
29 February 1944

. . . Nimitz always helps our people in every way that he can. . . .

. . . There is no doubt that with the successes in the Pacific, King is
getting more and more powerful and is taking into his own hands many
things which he never touched before. For example he stopped our
AMCs from coming over to be converted into troop carriers for the
reason that the MWT had, in his opinion, exceeded their responsibilities by dealing direct with the similar body over here. He is taking such
an active interest in what we call the 'Fleet Train' for British Naval
Forces destined for the Pacific, that nothing can be approved or even
recommended without his approval.

. . . King, in giving us the *Saratoga* rather spoilt the magnificence of
the loan by including in his letter the demand that the ship be returned
on 1 May [1944] – I think he might at least have left that open until we
know more of what was going to happen in the Bay of Bengal, etc.[1]

377. *To Churchill*

18 March 1944

In reply to your unnumbered minute of 17 March [not reproduced], my
first reactions on SEACOS 115 are as follows:

(a)   In the light of the now accelerated American programme for the
      Pacific, the Japanese will probably consider their vital interests
      threatened after the capture of the Marianas in June 1944 and
      certainly after the Pellews have been captured in September 1944.
      Japan, Formosa and the Philippines will then be exposed to at-

[1]*Saratoga*: US carrier, 1925, 33000t, 34k, 8×8in, 12×5in, 90 a/c.

tack. It appears therefore likely that the Japanese Fleet will withdraw from Singapore in the summer or autumn of this year.

(b)   The period for which it will be necessary to retain increased naval strength in the Indian Ocean for defensive purposes is therefore likely to end sometime during this autumn. In any case, since the move of the Japanese Fleet is probably basically *defensive* the threat to the Indian Ocean can be countered by our shore-based aircraft in conjunction with a *small* fleet.

(c)   There should therefore be little difficulty in providing the necessary fleet component for any fleet-amphibious forces intended for the Pacific from autumn 1944 onwards. Indeed, the fleet component is still likely to be ready before any amphibious forces which are more dependent on the defeat of Germany.

(d)   In the light of the timing described above, any threat which we can impose against the Malay Barrier by 'Culverin' in the spring of 1945, will be negligible as far as the movements of the Japanese Fleet are concerned, since it will almost certainly have moved back into the Pacific by then.[1]

(e)   If, due to a hold-up in the Pacific advance the Japanese Fleet *should* still be at Singapore in the spring of 1945, the greatly increased naval strength, over and above our defensive commitments, required in the Indian Ocean for operation 'Culverin', would be a serious diversion if the main Allied effort was to be made in the Pacific.

378.   *From Admiral Sir Guy Royle*[2]

Navy Office,
Melbourne,
25 March 1944

... I venture to offer a few possible lines of approach to our Prime Minister, John Curtin, who is shortly paying you a visit.[3] ...

---

[1]The Japanese Fleet moved to Singapore, Feb 1944, to escape US bombing in the Pacific, a purely defensive move.
'Culverin': operation planned against N Sumatra, a PM favourite.
[2]Adm Sir Guy Royle (1885–1954): ent RN 1900; gun spist; Grand F, Jutland & Cdr 1916; FGO Atl F 1919–20; Capt & N Ordc Dept 1923; NA Tokyo 1924–7; *Canterbury* 1927–9; *Excellent* 1929–31; *Glorious* 1932–4; NS to FL 1934–7; RA 1935; RA (Air) 1937; NS to FL Sept 1939; 5SL Nov 1939; VA 1939; 1st NM, Australia 1941–5; Adm Oct 1942.
[3]John Curtin (1885–1945): journalist, TU ldr; Australian Labor MP 1928; leader 1935; PM 1941–5.

Crutchley's Relief

Curtin and his party are naturally inclined to be parochially minded and being very proud of Australia would prefer to rely on their own people than on such imports as myself, Crutchley, etc., and hence they preferred to promote John Collins to Commodore 1st Class and put him in command of the squadron.[1] . . .

You know John Collins and have reported very highly on him so I don't think any serious harm will result, and there is every chance of him making the grade. One of the snags of this arrangement which, however, the Government accepted, was that owing to Collins's lack of seniority it will automatically place the squadron under a more senior American Flag Officer who is already commanding a part of it under Crutchley.

Naval Set Up in S. W. Pacific

. . . Everything works very smoothly and our staff and the Americans work in very well together. Crutchley has commanded the squadron with great skill and tact and was a most admirable choice; no one could have hit it off better with the Americans than he did.

Relief of First Naval Member

. . . anything you can say to Curtin to impress on him the desirability of having fresh war experience from the UK for a job like this will be a great help. . . . We should want a good man for this job as it will be a big fight for the Navy after this war.

My idea would be for Collins to complete his two years in command of [the] squadron, i.e., till June 1946 and then go to the UK for some administrative post as Rear Admiral for two years and take on First Naval Member out here in June 1948. So we have to fill in a three year gap, June 1945–1948, with an import.

Post-War Problems

. . . Australia will not readily forget the position in which she found herself after Pearl Harbor, open to invasion with nothing with which to defend herself or even delay the blow. . . . She realises that with her own resources she cannot hope to prevent an invasion by powerful sea and land forces, including carriers. She would wish, however, to be able to delay such an attack until help could arrive.

I am afraid this Government is very Air and Army minded, . . . the Navy is rarely seen or heard of, . . .

---

[1]VAdm Sir John Collins RAN: Capt 1939; DNI 1939; *Sydney* Nov 1939; *Shropshire* 1943; Cdre 1st Cl 1944; *Penguin* 1945; RA 1947; VA & 1st N Member 1950.

Naval Building Programme

I am pushing very hard to start a building programme of cruisers and destroyers out here now, . . . they are far more likely to become Naval minded if they build their own ships. . . .

Post War Fleet

. . . My main object is to try and persuade them to maintain a Task Force of such a composition, that, while it is at large it would form such a serious threat to the enemy's line of communications that he would not be prepared to risk an overseas operation involving a large movement of troops and supplies. . . . I have in mind a force consisting of – one Battleship, two Carriers, six Cruisers and about 15 Destroyers. . . .

The Battleship and Carriers would, of course, be obtained from the UK under some sort of agreement. . . .

Pacific Command

On purely strategical grounds the whole of the Naval forces in the Pacific should be under Nimitz, who should allocate the forces required for any particular operation in whatever area it may be required. Unfortunately the SWPA was given a Supreme Commander and there has been a feeling of rivalry between our man and Nimitz, and we have been left very much on our own. I think the situation is probably improving as Nimitz and Halsey are over here today discussing future plans with MacArthur. I feel sure that the correct disposal of any British Task Force in the Pacific should be under Nimitz. . . .

379.   *From Noble*

2 April 1944

. . . Last Friday, Dill and I got Marshall and King to meet us to discuss generally the Pacific situation. . . .

There is no doubt about it that complete agreement between the four of us was reached regarding the necessity of having a 'back-base' in Australia, as it appeared obvious that a back-base of sorts is the best situation there for all operations excepting 'Culverin' which is, of course, far nearer Ceylon.

King quite frankly gave his opinion that he will soon have so heavy a naval force in the Pacific as to make the logistics for it very difficult – indeed, he further said that an addition of the British naval units would be more of an embarrassment than a help. With this in view, therefore, he gave his opinion that there would be productive targets for our naval forces in the South West Pacific or the Indian Ocean.

King urged that the logistic arrangements for our naval forces should be most flexible and he also urged that no decision should be taken as to the exact operations we should undertake until things had developed further generally. As you know the march of events has been more rapid in the Pacific generally than was expected – at this moment they are almost within touch of the Philippines.

General Marshall pointed out that experience gained up to date against an enemy who are lodged on a great many islands, points to the advantage of avoiding those islands where the enemy are known to be strong and establishing ourselves where they are known to be weak – this at any rate is the first step. . . .

I think there is great sense in Marshall's arguments and I only stress them to you because reading between the lines there seems to be some difference of opinion as to the advantages or disadvantages of attacking the north end of Sumatra.

Finally, it was understood that nothing very much could be done from a purely British Naval point of view until Germany had been beaten as our force would be so small.

I hope this is all right and understandable.

I wonder what your reactions are to King's suggestion to me of yesterday re[garding] a diversionary operation to be carried out [in] mid-April. I am wondering whether James Somerville is sufficiently ready for that and, of course, the *Saratoga* will only just have joined up.

380.   *Diary*

3 April 1944

. . . Another [Cabinet] meeting at 2230 to discuss the provision of LSTs for the Eastern War next year and the provision of the Fleet Train. The PM agreed to send a message to the President to ask him to continue the production at peak level so that we could have the balance.

A fine exhibition of slipperiness by the Minister of War Transport over the Fleet Train ably helped by the Paymaster-General (Cherwell) the upshot being that the Controller and Leathers are to settle it between them and that the Admiralty are to release equivalent shipping as the Fleet Train ships come along.[1]

---

[1] Adm Wake-Walker.

381. *To Noble*

8 April 1944

A.   The situation as regards your relief is very unsatisfactory. As you know, Fraser was suggested as Somerville's relief but as a result of Somerville's telling Dickie Mountbatten that he rather approved of Operation 'Culverin', the PM is now very unwilling that Somerville should be relieved. However, we hope to clear up this situation soon and get Fraser out to relieve him in June. This looks as though your relief may not take place till August.

B.   Thank you for your account of your discussion on the Pacific situation. There appear to be two competing strategies – the Pacific and the Indian Ocean. As you probably know the British COS are firmly of the opinion that 'Culverin' would be a mistake and would only be tapping at the outdoor ring of the Japanese sphere and that we should put in our major effort in the Pacific on the left of the American forces.

The PM takes diametrically the opposite view and from what you say it appears that the American COS are half-hearted about having the British in the Pacific. On the other hand, Porter tells me that on the planning level it is considered improbable that the Americans will have sufficient forces in the Pacific to do without our help and that this will appear as soon as Nimitz has had an opportunity of thoroughly working out the plans. There is, of course, also opposition by MacArthur and this has appeared in the answer sent by Curtin in reply to our request to send reconnaissance parties to Australia.

In the meantime a third course has been suggested and that is that the British, using northern Australia as a base, should fight their way into the China Sea. The PM is favourably inclined to this suggestion as he says his objection to the Pacific strategy was the long haul round Australia. We are now going into the question of these operations. Personally I find them quite attractive and we should be in a position to move into the Pacific to the assistance of the Americans if it proves necessary.[1] My own feeling is that their programme, with the forces they have at present available, is on the optimistic side and I should put the dates for the various operations at six months later than is at present intended.

It is in any case essential, in my opinion, that Daniel and his mission should go to Australia. The naval information is not available here and

---

[1] The 'Middle Strategy', of a Commonwealth advance from Australia through the SW Pacific, appeared likely to unite the PM and the COS but was found to be impracticable. Porter was probably a member of BAD visiting the Ady.

he will have to examine carefully in the north and west. I hope to get permission for him to go on shortly.

With reference to King's suggestion of a diversionary operation in the Indian Ocean, Somerville points out that all the Japanese forces have already moved back to where they were before and, in fact, stronger than ever there but I hope he will carry out some type of operation, if only a fleet sweep which can be turned into a diversionary effort if the Japanese forces move east. At present I agree with him that the shore-based air is too strong to make the risks worthwhile. . . .

382. *Diary*

10 April 1944

. . . The PM is sound on the Fleet Train. This guarantee cannot be given but it was accepted in principle. Actually I am sure Admiralty departments if they tried could release some shipping and by economy use less shipping.

383. *Diary*

19 April 1944

. . . it transpired that the PM is still holding up signal to Australia about naval mission until he hears who is in charge. Daniel to whom he objects is in charge and I have no intention of changing him.[1] . . .

A memorandum from PM arrived today about Fraser's appointment to the Eastern Fleet and Somerville to relieve Noble in Washington. It appears that a C-in-C's views on the strategy to be followed in the theatre he is intended to command must be tested before he is appointed. Presumably if his strategical views do not coincide with those of the PM he does not get the job. This appears to be nearing a relapse to the time when an admiral's correct political views were a better reason for his employment rather than his ability.[2]

---

[1]VAdm Charles S. Daniel: Capt 1934; Capt (D), 8DF, *Faulkner* 1938; DP 1940–1; Flag Capt & CSO, 2BS *Renown* Aug 1941; RA Jan 1943; COHQ June 1943; A/VA (Q), BPF, Australia 1944–5; 1BS June 1945; 3SL & Cntrlr Sept 1945.

[2]For the influence of politics on sea power, see N. Rodger, *The Command of the Ocean: A Naval History of Britain, 1649–1815* (London, 2004).

384. *Diary*

20 April 1944

... I succeeded in getting First Lord to send a minute to PM questioning the procedure of submitting Fraser to a strategical means test before being appointed C-in-C, Eastern Fleet. ...

385. *Diary*

5 May 1944

COS meeting as usual. ...

General Blamey attended at 1130 and we had a good discussion on Australia as a base assuming that the Pacific strategy was adopted.[1]

Australia is determined on a minimum of six divisions of fighting men and about 70 squadrons RAAF[,] the naval forces remaining at present strength and the question is what extra forces can she support with the production of the rest of her manpower. We gave the maximum British forces that would be required to be based on Australia as six British divisions, 60 squadrons RAF, four battleships, five fleet and other carriers and the necessary cruisers and destroyers. ...

386. *Diary*

8 May 1944

... a meeting with the PM at 2300. The Simalur project trotted out and at last I had to say quite plainly that I did not agree with it. PM took it well but moaned about there being apparently nothing for the British forces to do against Japan this year. I agreed with him on this and suggested to Brooke that the whole thing should be re-examined.

---

[1]FM Sir Thomas Blamey (1884–1951): staff, 1914–18; Australian Impl Forces; police chief, 1920s/1930s; cmdg Australian Corps Feb 1940; C-in-C Australian Mil Forces March 1942; Allied army, SW Pacific Area; FM 1950.

387. *Diary*

16 May 1944

Usual COS meeting. The desirability of getting agreement on *some* strategy for the war against Japan stressed and realised by all. We are quite hung up for want of decision. . . .

388. *Diary*

17 May 1944

. . . A big meeting to discuss the allocation of cruisers, destroyers and escort vessels after 'Overlord'. I made it pretty clear that it was essential to reinforce the Eastern Fleet yet it wasn't good sending out more ships than there were maintenance facilities for.

Another instalment of James Somerville's diary. Very interesting but Dickie Mountbatten is not playing the game. That disgusting communiqué from his HQ after Sabang which I thought had been done without his consent was apparently sent out after full consideration.[1]

389. *Diary*

18 May 1944

COS meeting as usual. Discussed Pacific strategy with Joint Planners. Generally agreed in order to reach agreement to plump for Central Strategy. Empire force, i.e., Australian Divisions and British Fleet to go for Amboina late 1944 or early 1945. Some discussion on command[,] generally agreed it would have to be under MacArthur in first instance.

390. *From Layton*

20 May 1944

. . . we have been having a great deal of difficulty in finding sufficient labour and plant to progress all the undertakings we have in hand for the FAA and the RAF. . . .

I was not satisfied myself that the Navy were making the best use of the labour and plant provided on the various works, ... I therefore got

---

[1]For controversy over Sabang and other communiqués, see M. A. Simpson (ed.), *Somerville Papers*, pp. 486–92, 499, 502–9, 557–9.

the services of an expert American engineer . . . he goes so far as to say
. . . that only 50% output is being obtained from available labour. . . .

I have experienced considerable difficulty in dealing with the vast
flood of stores and materials which are now arriving in the Port of
Colombo. . . .

The SEAC party have settled down very well at Kandy, they are
certainly providing a good deal of extra work for all concerned. . . .

391. Diary

26 May 1944

. . . Meeting in Map Room with PM, Mr Curtin, Blamey, Shedden,
Ministers of Production, War Transport, Deputy Prime Minister, and
Foreign Secretary.[1] General discussion on Middle Strategy. Curtin not
wishful to commit himself but inclined to relate everything to what
was required of Australia in the way of maintenance. He made the
statement that the Admiralty was asking him to man more ships, and
asked for a reply to his query made last October to the effect that he
wanted back the men already manning RN ships. I put him right on
the first question by pointing out that it had been the Australian
authorities who had raised the question of manning more ships and
told him that the Admiralty would welcome an offer from Australia to
man a carrier and one or two cruisers and would gladly provide the
ships.

392. Diary

2 June 1944

. . . He [Churchill] told us that he had seen Pownall and that Mountbatten
was not against James Somerville's relief by Fraser so he the PM was
prepared to agree to it.[2] This [is] all to the good but if Mountbatten
thinks that Fraser is going to be easier than Somerville to deal with he
will have a rude awakening. . . .

---

[1]Sir Frederick Shedden: Sec to Australian War Cabinet 1939–46 & Sec to Dept of
Defence 1937–56.
[2]Lt Gen Sir Henry Pownall (1887–1961): RFA 1906; W Front 1914–19; Staff Coll
1926–9; NW Fr 1931; CID 1933–6; Brig & Cdt Sch Arty 1936; DMO & I 1938; CoS to
Gort; Inspr Gen, Home Guard; C-in-C N Ireland 1940–1; VCIGS 1941; CoS, ABDA
1941–2; Lt Gen & GOC Ceylon 1942–3; GOC Persia & Iraq; CoS to SACSEA Oct
1943; ret 1945.

Pownall came to see me at 1630 and we had a long discussion on the SEA[C] set up. Half the trouble is due to the staffs fighting and the long distances between C's-in-C. . . .

393. *Diary*

7 June 1944

COS meeting at 1100. Pownall attended and presented his memorandum of what was wanted in the command set up in SEAC. I had made it clear that nothing was to be altered in respect of the fleet.

394. *Diary*

14 June 1944

COS meeting at 1100. JIC present[;] very optimistic on the conclusion of the war which they expect before 1945 . . .

Meeting with US COS at 1430 and discussed Pacific strategy. They have very big ideas about the speed of their advance in the Pacific. They may be right but they have not yet encountered stiff opposition. They are not averse to our advance from Darwin but would prefer an attack on Surabaya, Java, in preference to one on Amboina[,] either attack to be a prelude for an attack on Borneo.

I got King to admit the US Navy would not require the repair facilities of the East Coast ports of Australia and so they would be available for the British Fleet. Meeting closed by the US COS asking us to put forward a paper setting out our views.

395. *Diary*

21 June 1944

. . . A signal from Mountbatten showing that he and James Somerville have had a royal row. I am afraid it was bound to happen that way. . . .

396. *Diary*

7 July 1944

. . . COS meeting at 1000. . . . I also raised the question of COMINCH's request for the loan of six LSI (L) for the Pacific. There are obvious advantages in letting them go but manning them as White Ensign ships will be difficult . . .

397. *Diary*

14 July 1944

. . . 1130 COS met the PM with Foreign Secretary, Minister of Production and Deputy Prime Minister. We had hoped to get some decision on Far East strategy but we were treated to the same old monologue of how much better it was to take the tip of Sumatra and then the Malay Peninsula and finally Singapore than it was to join with the Americans and fight Japan close at home in the Pacific.

The attitude of mind about this question is astonishing. They are obviously afraid of the Americans laying down the law as to what is to happen when Japan is defeated to the various islands, ports and other territories. This appears to be quite likely if the Americans are left to fight the Japanese by themselves. But they will not lift a finger to get a force into the Pacific; they prefer to hang about outside and recapture our own rubber trees. No decision of course though there are indications that the three ministers are starting to disagree with the PM. . . .

398. *Diary*

7 August 1944

. . . COS meeting at 1100. . . . Mountbatten and Wedemeyer then explained the plans for the proposed operation in Burma in the next interval between monsoons.[1] Plan 'Y' an advance from north Burma to a sort of Mandalay line. Plan 'Z' the capture of Rangoon. There is no doubt that Mountbatten in his desire to have something to do in his command is inclined to underestimate the difficulties and attempt to carry out operations with insufficient forces. A case in point the ad-

---

[1]Gen Albert Wedemeyer, US Army: China 1930s; War Plans 1941; Maj Gen & DCoS, SACSEA Oct 1943; Allied CoS, China, Oct 1944–April 1946; Lt Gen Jan 1945; ret 1951; Gen 1954.

vance up-river from the sea to Rangoon, which was just wishful thinking. He said James Somerville agreed with the plan but I can't believe it. . . .

399. *Diary*

8 August 1944

. . . Further staff meeting at 1800. The ugly head of 'Culverin' reared itself up and we got no further. Lots of useless discussion.

Further meeting at 2230. . . . Ministers definitely turning against the PM, Attlee notably batting with the COS.

I had two tit-ups with the PM, one when he said no information had been procured about northern Australia to [which] I replied that we had plenty of information and that the delay in receiving it was entirely due to his want of decision on sending the party to collect it. The other he tried to compare the casualties of the FAA with those of the Bomber Command which he said were 7,000 out of 10,000. I disputed this figure which of course is entirely fallacious. It is more like 7,000 out of 40–50,000.

No decisions were reached[,] in fact a thoroughly wasted day. What a drag on the wheel of war this man is. Everything is centralised in him with consequent indecision and waste of time before anything can be done.

400. *Diary*

9 August 1944

COS meeting at 1030 when we drafted a paper setting out how we thought the strategy for the Japan war should go. Meeting with the PM at 1230. He also had produced a paper on the same subject. Curiously they were not very different. To Ismay was given the task of producing a paper for the night's meeting combining the two views.[1] . . .

Ismay produced the combined paper at 2230. It had been ready at 2000 but the PM had given orders that he was not to circulate it to the COS before the meeting. Thus we are governed!! I presume he himself has such a crooked mind that he is suspicious of the COS.

A breeze at the start when Brooke backed by me asked for time to consider it. However we sat down and produced a paper of conclusions.

[1]Lt Gen Ismay.

The first four paragraphs devoted to the subjects on which we were to approach the US COS and the way it was to be done and the fifth arranged to double cross them. I often wonder how we expect the US COS to have any respect for us. We allow our opinions to be over-ridden and ourselves persuaded against our own common sense at every turn.

Poor news from the Eastern Fleet. The floating dock broke up under her while *Valiant* was being docked and she is badly damaged – three 'A' brackets broken. It might indeed have been worse as there was no loss of life. I feel there is something wrong about it. The dock was built by us in Bombay and was supposed to be the same as the Singapore dock.

401. *Diary*

10 August 1944

. . . Message to US COS drafted this morning came back after dinner as amended by the PM.

As usual full of inaccuracies, hot air and political points. Not the sort of businesslike message we should send to our opposite numbers. One good political point he wishes to make. He wants to be able to leave on record that the US refused the assistance of the British Fleet in the Pacific. He will be bitterly disappointed if they don't refuse!!!

402. *Diary*

11 August 1944

. . . COS meeting at 1100. We discussed PM's amendments to our telegram to [US] COS. In a closed session Ismay told us that he was just raving last night and absolutely unbalanced. He can't get over not having had his own way over 'Anvil'. To my surprise it was Portal that suggested we should have to have a showdown with him before long if he went on as he is now. I have long thought it. He tries now to dictate to the COS what they should say to the US COS. We decided to alter the message to some extent to meet his views and hold it up for 24 hours to let him recover his balance a bit. He left last night for the Mediterranean and arrived Algiers this morning.

403. *Diary*

14 August 1944

... COS meeting at 1100. Nothing of moment except Mountbatten and Wedemeyer before the latter's departure for Washington. Dickie Mountbatten had written two letters to General Marshall both of which we suppressed.

Spent the afternoon talking to Fraser about eastern affairs. Boyd came later and we decided to equip large carriers with Avengers in lieu of Barracudas. Purely for tactical reasons. The Barracuda though it can dive-bomb and is an excellent torpedo machine is 50 miles short of the Avenger in range. ...

404. *Diary*

18 August 1944

... COS meeting at 1100. Mountbatten in attendance running in blinkers – no ideas except his own there. The First Lord told me yesterday that Mountbatten had interviewed the Chancellor and the Secretary of State for War about increased emoluments for the forces in SEAC and incidentally had made proposals at variance with those of the Admiralty.[1] I dragged it out of him in front of the COS and I hope made him see that he was interfering with what did not concern him. He can't keep his finger out of any pie. ...

405. *Diary*

29 August 1944

... Cdr Hopkins came in later. He is our liaison officer with Nimitz. Had a good talk on Pacific operations and American ideas generally. Their ideas of command are very strange.[2] ...

---

[1]S St War: Sir James Grigg (1890–1964): civil servt 1915–18; Army, E Eur; Chf Sec, Treasy & India; USec, WO 1939; S St War 1942–5; Con MP Cardiff E 1942–5.

C Ex: Sir John Anderson.

[2]Cdr F. H. E. Hopkins: Lt 1933; Lt (O), *Peregrine* (Ford, Sussex) May 1939; *Formidable* Nov 1940; Lt Cdr Nov 1941; *Saker* (BAD) July 1942; A/Cdr; Cdr June 1945; NLO, US Pacific F Jan 1945.

406. *Diary*

31 August 1944

COS meeting at 1030. Joint Planners present. Discussion on their paper on the second stage of the war against Japan, i.e., after the US have captured Formosa or Luzon. A very timely paper bringing out the difficulties still before us – a trifle pessimistic perhaps but useful to dispel the illusions in some quarters that the Japanese war can be run as a sideshow. . . .

407. *Diary*

2 September 1944

. . . James Somerville came to bath and breakfast straight from Eastern Fleet. He looks fit and well. As I thought Mountbatten's approach to the Chancellor of the Exchequer on the subject of increased emoluments was entirely unauthorised. Somerville considers an increase of pay essential. . . .

408. *To the Chief of the Air Staff*

4 September 1944

Requesting Mosquitoes

. . . we had it in mind to use the Mosquitoes afloat for long range strikes against Japanese targets.

3. We are limited by circumstances to operating a relatively small Naval force in the Pacific and we must make up in quality what is lacking in quantity. It is also desirable that we should be able to do things from our carriers which the Americans cannot do from theirs.

4. The advantage of the Mosquito over other carrier types which could be immediately available lies in its great range, combined with really high performance. Deck landing trials were successfully completed in May and we know that Mosquito squadrons could be operating in a normal way from *Indefatigable* and *Implacable* and, of course, later fleet carriers. De Havilland have prepared designs of a folding-wing version of the Mosquito FB Mark VI. The firm say they could start production of the Naval type nine to twelve months from the time they were given the contract.

5.   At first I should like to be able to introduce some hooked fixed wing Mosquitoes into the Naval service early in 1945 with a view to getting experience with the type and sending them out as alternative armament squadrons for special carrier operations, re-equipping them with folding Mosquitoes later on.

6.   Our requirements are relatively very modest. We would need some 200 Mosquitoes in 1945 and 250 more in 1946. Towards the first 200 we could accept up to about 120 of earlier Marks for training and working up squadrons.[1] . . .

409.   *Diary*

20 September 1944

. . . Leathers, Ismay, PM and myself talked till 1600. He [Churchill] told Leathers that the fleet train must be done on a handsome scale and that if we wanted 30–40 more ships we must have them!! . . .

410.   *To Churchill*

26 September 1944

British Participation in Operations in the Pacific

2.   I feel it is essential that there is no doubt in Mr Curtin's mind, nor General MacArthurs's, that the British Fleet will take part in the main operations against Japan under Admiral Nimitz, and that this force has been accepted by the President and the US COS. This is certainly not incompatible with a force being detached when it can be spared to assist General MacArthur's operations on the left flank of the main Pacific advance. The telegrams quoted above [not reproduced] leave me with the impression that both Mr Curtin and General MacArthur will consider that a permanent British Naval Force will be available to operate in the South West Pacific Area.

3.   Perhaps you would consider sending a telegram to Mr Curtin making these points quite clear and amending your telegram to General MacArthur, of 25 September [not reproduced], in the same sense.

---

[1]These do not seem to have been supplied.

411. *Diary*

2 October 1944

COS meeting at 1100. Somewhat occupied with ways and means for 'Dracula'. It looks as though landing craft will not be available. Owing to the failure to capture ports they can't be spared from 'Overlord'. . . .

Meeting with the PM after dinner on the subject of 'Dracula'. Conclusion was reached regretfully that it must be postponed as we could not at this stage withdraw the necessary troops from France and Italy.[1]
. . .

412. *Minutes of Meeting held in the First Sea Lord's room*

5 October 1944

Command of British Naval Forces in the Pacific and South East Asia Commands

1.   It was agreed that one C-in-C could not command both stations.

2.   As it was unlikely that Admiral King would allow the British C-in-C to make his HQ at Pearl Harbor alongside Admiral Nimitz, it was considered that he should proceed in the first instance with the BPF to Sydney, and set up his HQ there temporarily. Later he would probably transfer his HQ to a forward base. At all times he should be at liberty to proceed to sea with the Fleet.

3.   The C-in-C would have at Melbourne a Vice Admiral, Administration, who would be responsible to him for ensuring that all necessary administrative action was taken in Australia for the operation of the Fleet. To this end, the Vice Admiral, Administration, should have power to communicate directly with the Admiralty and the [Australian] Minister of the Navy.[2]

4.   It was considered that the C-in-C should have direct approach to the Prime Minister of Australia, through the Navy Minister.

5.   It was decided that a Flag Officer, Naval Air Stations, Australia and Pacific, would be required.[3]

6.   It seems more than likely that a Senior Flag Officer will be required as a liaison officer with the C-in-C, US [Pacific] Fleet at Pearl

[1] 'Dracula': operation to seize Rangoon by sea.
[2] VAdm Daniel.
M Navy: N. J. O. Makin.
[3] RAdm R. H. Portal.

Harbor, and furthermore another Flag Officer may be required as liaison officer with General MacArthur.[1]. . .

413. *Diary*

5 October 1944

. . . Meeting at 1730 to discuss chain of command in the Pacific. DFSL, James Somerville, VCNS, Harcourt and DoP (Q).[2] General opinion that Fraser will in the first instance set up in Australia. Some difficulty will undoubtedly be experienced in dealings with the ACNB and the Australian Government. MacArthur may be difficult too. Daniel will have to be head of the administration. Fleet will be parted from the East Indies Squadron.

414. *Diary*

23 October 1944

COS meeting at 1100. Among other things CIGS gave us a review of his conferences with Mountbatten and Wilson.[3] I do not much care for Mountbatten's new plan. It seems to be sticking your neck out six months before you can bring forces to support. Fraser came in after lunch. He supports Mountbatten but without good reasons I thought. The real trouble is going to be the landing craft; we can't get SHAEF to release any.

Philip Vian came in looking well. Highly pleased with his appointment I think.[4] . . .

Americans are going strong in the Pacific but heard that both *Canberra* and *Australia* had been hit.[5] . . .

[1]No appts made.
[2]DFSL: Adm Kennedy-Purvis.
VCNS: VAdm Syfret.
DP (Q): Capt W. H. D. Friedburger: Cdr Dec 1931; PD Sept 1939; *Menestheus* April 1940; *Welshman* May 1941; DP (Q) Dec 1943.
[3]FM Wilson.
[4]RAdm Vian was RA Aircraft Carriers in *Indomitable*.
[5]*Canberra*: US hvy csr (named in honour of HMAS *Canberra*, sunk at Savo I, 1942), 1943, 13600t, 33k, 9×8in, 12×5in.
Australia: RAN hvy csr, 1928, 9750t, 31.5k, 8×8in, 8×4in, 8×21in tt.

415.   *Meeting in the First Sea Lord's room*

24 October 1944

Command and Administration of the BPF

1.   The operations to be carried out could [not?] be decided before Admiral Fraser has visited Admiral Nimitz at Pearl Harbor. The First Sea Lord stated that it would be important, when talking to Admiral Nimitz, to stress that the War Cabinet would insist on the BPF taking part in the main operations against the islands of Japan. Subject to this requirement, it would probably be as well for the fleet to operate initially in the South West Pacific theatre. Admiral Fraser said he was still in doubt as to where he should establish his HQ.

Build Up of the Fleet in the Pacific
3.   The First Sea Lord stressed the importance of building up the Fleet in the Pacific as rapidly as possible and taking all steps to supply adequate resources and repair facilities, rather than allowing the existing resources to govern the size of the Fleet.

Timing of Move of the Fleet to Australian Waters
9.   It was agreed that Admiral Fraser should sail in the *King George V* about the 20 November and arrive Sydney about the 6 December. He would call on Mr Curtin, the Australian Government and Service Authorities, and investigate preparations being made for the reception of the Fleet. About 15 December he would fly to Pearl Harbor for discussion with Admiral Nimitz, returning to Sydney, if possible, before the arrival of the Fleet at the end of December.

416.   *Diary*

24 October 1944

. . . Very good meeting with Fraser and Admiralty staff about the move of the fleet to the Pacific. Very much talk about staffs and administration and finally I had to point out it was going to fight in the Pacific and that the administration must be fitted to the fleet and not the fleet to the administration.

. . . The main body of the fleet to arrive Australia the end of December. Rawlings and Vian to arrive Ceylon early in December to take up their respective commands.[1] . . .

---

[1]Adm Sir Bernard Rawlings (1889–1962): ent RN 1904; Mil Mission to Poland

417. *A. V. Alexander to Churchill*

25 October 1944

Command and Redeployment of the Fleet in Far Eastern Waters

4.   The remainder of the Fleet under the Flag Officer, Second-in-Command, consisting of:
   1 Fast Battleship
   4 Fleet Carriers
   6 Cruisers
   21 Destroyers
   and a number of Escorts
will leave Ceylon in time to reach Sydney towards the end of December. Thereafter the Fleet will operate as arranged between Admiral Nimitz and Admiral Fraser.

5.   The strength of the BPF will be built up as rapidly as possible, and by July 1945 the Fleet should consist of:
   4 Fast Battleships
   6 Fleet Carriers
   4 Light Fleet Carriers
   16 Cruisers
   40 Fleet Destroyers
   90 Escorts.

These units will be supported by a Fleet Train, minesweepers and ancillary craft, to maintain its lines of communication from Eastern Australia and to defend its bases.

8.   . . . a new command will be formed in the Indian Ocean and the present Second-in-Command, Eastern Fleet – Vice Admiral Sir [Arthur] John Power – will be appointed C-in-C, East Indies Station.

9.   The East Indies Squadron will consist of:
   2 old Battleships
   6 Cruisers
   Up to 20 Assault and GP Auxiliary Carriers
   22 Destroyers
   About 120 Escorts.

1918–21; Capt 1930; *Active, Curacoa, Delhi*; NA Tokyo 1936–9; *Valiant* 1939; RA & 1BS Jan 1941; 7CS 1941; ACNS (F) 1942; A/VA & FO W Africa 1943; VA Nov 1943; FOIC, E Med Dec 1943; 2-in-C & 1BS, BPF Dec 1944; Adm & ret 1946.

418. *Diary*

26 October 1944

. . . Tonight it looks as though the Japanese fleet had really taken a knock and there has been some surface action too. I trust some will be left for us to sweep up.

419. *Churchill to A. V. Alexander*

29 October 1944

2. I have not the pleasure of knowing Vice Admiral Sir [Arthur] John Power and I should like to have more information about his record and qualifications before I approve his selection. It is important that this appointment should be filled by an officer who will work in the closest harmony with C-in-C SEAC, and also that he has the qualities needed for a theatre in which audacity and the powers of improvization are essential. I consider this to be one of the most important appointments that has to be made. . . .

420. *[Cunningham] to A. V. Alexander*

30 October 1944

. . . Vice Admiral Sir [Arthur] John Power is an officer of great ability and forceful character and who has my complete confidence.
2. As will be seen from the record of his most recent services, he left the command of the 15 CS at my express wish to become Vice Admiral, Malta and take charge of the multifarious and very considerable naval activities in Malta preparatory to and during the invasion of Sicily. His organising powers and drive materially contributed to the success of this operation.
3. During the Salerno operations his contribution was equally important.
4. I specially selected him to command the operation which resulted in the seizure of Taranto.
5. He has now been second in command of the Eastern Fleet for nearly a year and has participated in all the operations off the enemy coasts that have taken place during that period.
6. I have no reason to suppose that he will not work in closest harmony with the Supreme Commander, South East Asia.

421. *Diary*

30 October 1944

... Fraser came in to tea. Still concerned about his staff. I fear he is very staff minded. ...

422. *Diary*

13 November 1944

... Daniel came in to say goodbye. I don't envy him his job. There is a sort of passive resistance about the Australian Government's attitude. Perhaps these difficulties will pass away when he gets out there and deals on a lower level.

Rather a nasty signal from Ernie King which I fear foreshadows trouble. It is on the command question in the Pacific and is an attempt to put Fraser under any old American admiral. ...

423. *Diary*

18 November 1944

... Telegram from Ernie King. He agrees almost entirely to our views which is a great relief. He has not however confirmed the date of Fraser's visit to Nimitz.

424. *From Fraser*

Colombo,
14 November 1944

... On arrival had a long talk with A. J. Power who prior to my arrival had sent a signal gratefully accepting his appointment but without optimism! I cursed him for this and told him he had got to make up his mind 'Yes' or 'No' and there could be no qualifications.

His gloom was caused by the apparent lack of support for the Eastern Fleet on which I reassured him.

We discussed at length the second-in-command and both came to the conclusion that Walker had insufficient experience yet to take complete charge of the sea-going fleet and therefore in looking for an officer senior could only think of Turtle Hamilton who is longing to get away from Melbourne.[1]

Whilst the big units of the Fleet are likely to be somewhat less the number of officers and men out here will increase, if the ships proposed ever arise and although the operations envisaged may be smaller, they are infinitely more difficult on account of the distances, the lack of facilities and inferior staff.

Therefore if I may be perfectly frank your signal 1323/11/11 [not reproduced] summarily turning down all the proposals of VAEF and myself has reacted most unfavourably.[2]

I had hoped to leave the Station in fine fettle both from my own point of view and from the fellows I leave behind, but the constant reverses one gets when I ask for things makes one mistrust one's own judgement. One can't bicker with the Admiralty and it is obvious that I must now go and start things off in the Pacific, but I can't continue as C-in-C unless one's inferiors think he carries some weight (which I do perhaps I'm afraid!). I would be very grateful therefore if as soon as possible you would select someone whose judgement you would trust and advice you would follow, to relieve me and will undertake any other task you desire.

I would not for a moment criticise the Admiralty for taking any line they wish but if it is consistently different to the C-in-C then the only answer is to get another one.

You will I hope forgive me for being quite frank especially after your readiness to see me and hospitality at home, and the fact that it is too far distant to have personal discussion on these matters, but when one begins to see the effect of constant rebuffs on subordinates, I realize it was time someone else was chosen for the C-in-C's job.

425. *Diary*

20 November 1944

. . . An unpleasant letter from Fraser complaining that the Admiralty consistently turned down all his proposals and saying if we couldn't trust his judgement we had better appoint someone else as C-in-C, BPF. I am in doubt myself if he is the man for the job the way he has behaved recently. He seems to think he has only to put something forward and the Admiralty must agree. I decline to accept this idea of how things should work.

[1]VAdm Sir Louis Hamilton.
[2]VAEF: VAdm Sir Arthur Power.

426.   *To Vice Admiral Sir Arthur J. Power*

19 November 1944

I am very sorry that you are depressed at your appointment, but I see no necessity for it. You should read Mounttbatten's directive. Your destinies are not entirely controlled by the Kandy set-up. I see no reason why you should remain on shore all the time, there appears every reason for you to go to sea with the Fleet periodically, like Somerville did. Your selection as C-in-C, East Indies Station, was obviously owing to your knowledge of the conditions there. . . .

You know, I expect, that it is intended that *Nelson* proceeds to the East Indies Station. She will make a very good full-back.[1]

With regard to the operations that are being proposed by SACSEA, I am personally dead against the Kra Isthmus. Not only if it succeeds will we be left for some eight to nine months with the supply question, but also an unlimited commitment as regards reinforcements. The use of the troops for this purpose may also make all the difference between carrying out 'Dracula' or not in the end of 1945. Once they are ashore in the Kra Isthmus, they cannot be taken off and used for anything else. On the other hand I am much in favour of having a go at the Andamans. This gives a very limited commitment and the troops used for this operation, less a small garrison, could be used again at the end of the year. The supply commitment would also be simple.

427.   *Diary*

29 November 1944

. . . Message from Fraser in the course of the day giving various alternatives all delaying the fleet's arrival in the Pacific. The principal reason given being that Nimitz wishes Palembang attacked and it can't be done in December. I confess I do not understand Fraser. It may be the climate but there has been dilatoriness in all his dealings particularly changing the carriers over to Avenger squadrons, since he has been in charge of Eastern Fleet.

[1]*Nelson* did not appear to take part in operations.

428.   *To Churchill*

1 December 1944

Although Admiral Fraser has not yet been able to visit Pearl Harbor, he has been in direct touch with Admiral Nimitz regarding operations to be carried out by the BPF. Admiral Nimitz has made it clear that he regards the destruction of the Sumatran oil refineries of primary importance, and that this would form the best initial means of assisting Pacific strategy.

Weather conditions preclude successful attacks being launched by naval aircraft in December.

2.   Although I am most reluctant to accept any delay in the arrival of the Fleet at Sydney, I have in the interest of furthering the close co-operation between Fraser and Nimitz which is so essential in the later employment of the Fleet, agreed to attacks by the main carrier force in the first week of January. The passage to Sydney would then be completed at the best possible speed. . . .

429.   *From A. J. Power*

Naval HQ,
Colombo,
1 December 1944

. . . I have signalled you today asking for Walker to be appointed in command of the battleships and for a Rear Admiral to be appointed to command the cruisers.[1] . . .

. . . It will be a very nice command as seven cruisers are allocated to this squadron.

At Kandy in the three days that I was there, I think I attended seven conferences, to which there must be added a number of meals each of which developed into a conference. . . . Supreme [Commander] overworks himself to an almost alarming extent, and one evening after dinner Leese, with my support, made a frontal attack, as the result of which Supreme has promised to give up fiddling about with details and only to attend conferences on things that really matter.[2]

---

[1]VAdm H. T. C. ('Hooky') Walker (a one-handed officer): Capt Dec 1931; Flag Capt & CSO to Layton, *Barham* Med F Jan 1939; Cdre Portsmouth Barracks April 1940; RA Aug 1941; DPS Nov 1941; 5CS *London* EF May 1944; VA, 2-in-C, EIF & 3BS, Dec 1944; C-in-C Germany 1946.

[2]Lt Gen Sir Oliver Leese (1894–1978): Eur war 1914–18; Adjt, 3Bn, Coldstream Guards 1920–2; GSO2, WO 1935–6; GSO1, Quetta 1938–40; DCGS, BEF 1940; CO,

We discussed 'Talon' in some detail . . . I think it will be quite a nice operation. . . . I very much hope 'Talon' will go on.[1]

I opposed any landing on the Kra Isthmus and was very glad to see in your letter that I had reflected your opinion. On the other hand I advocated seizing Hastings Harbour. This place is virtually undefended. It is a fine anchorage and if we could become established there it would be a tremendous achievement and a good roadhouse on our way south.

I believe we could take Hastings Harbour with the Marines of the Fleet . . . I don't think the Japanese could allow us to become established at Hastings without fighting . . . I think, however, a fight would be all to the good . . . Eventually it was decided to go on planning for an operation against Hastings, so that if 'Talon' went well and things in the Pacific progressed, we should be ready (on paper) to meet the necessary forces. . . .

The *Indefatigable* is in trouble and wants to land all her aircraft for training, as they are apparently so backward they can't fly at sea. *Victorious* has this bad rudder. Floating birdcages, though invaluable, can be very disappointing properties.

I am exceedingly cheerful again, and realise how much there is to be done in this job . . .

430. *Diary*

13 December 1944

. . . COS meeting at 1100. . . . We then discussed the shipping shortage. Leathers attended and gave us his usual lecture about the great shortage. He is a slippery customer. It was decided to press the US COS to consent to a resources paper. There appears to be no doubt that much shipping is being sucked into the Pacific.

431. *Diary*

22 December 1944

. . . A very good signal from Fraser giving results of his meeting with Nimitz. He is of course bitten with the US logistic bug. I hope things will now go well.

Guards Armd Div 1941; XXX Corps 1942; cmded 8 Army 1944; C-in-C, Allied Land Forces, SEAC 1945–6.

[1]'Talon': seaborne attack on Akyab.

432. *From A. J. Power*

3 January 1945

... Mount B does everything possible to keep me in the Kandy picture and not to slip off his mat; ... Mount B is easy, and we shall hit it off well, I am quite sure. From reading some ancient dockets he has not always had an easy time.

We have been doing everything possible with our resources to get Philip Vian's party in good order; he is, I think, fully conscious of this and very grateful.

H. B. Rawlings is not in very good health and lies up for a bit. I am very pleased that Patterson is coming this way. Moody is getting the air stations into good order and C. Rawlings left him a good foundation on which to build.[1]

433. *From A. J. Power*

11 January 1945

... When it was obvious that we were not following up the Japanese withdrawal quickly enough, I offered [the Fleet Royal Marines] to capture Ramree Island ... [on 19 January].

... if the Marines are used on this operation they will learn a lot themselves, and we shall have started an enterprising raiding force capable of running about at 25 knots ...

We must open Akyab as an advanced base immediately ... My own private opinion is that a much bigger jump down the coast will be possible in the immediate future. And I don't think it is over-optimistic to hope that we shall be off Rangoon before the monsoon breaks. ...

Admiral Layton left yesterday, and Wetherall is installed as C-in-C, Ceylon. We all like him very much, ...[2]

We are all trying to cut down in every direction. ...

[1]VAdm Patterson.

VAdm Sir Clement Moody (1891–1960): Capt *Curacoa* 1935; IDC 1936; *Eagle* 1937–9; DNAD 1939–41; RA, NAS 1941; RA (Air) Home F 1943; EF 1944; VA 1944; FO (Air) EI 1944–6; C-in-C S Africa 1946–8; Adm & ret 1948.

RAdm C. Rawlings (1883–1965): Jutland 1916; Capt, *Devonshire* 1929–31; DNAD 1932–4; *Glorious* 1935–6; RA ret 1936; convoy cdre Sept 1939–May 1940; RA, staff, Nore 1940–2; convoy cdre 1942–3; RA, NAS, Indian O 1944–5; Head, Ady Tech Mission, Canada, 1945–6.

[2]Lt Gen Sir Edward Wetherall (1889–1979): Glos R; Eur 1914–18; Maj 1927; GSO, Scot Cmd 1930–4; Lt Col, 1Bn York & Lancaster R 1936–8; CO 19 Inf Bde 1938–40; CO 11 African Div, Abyssinia 1941; GOC, E Africa 1941; GOC Ceylon 1943–5; C-in-C Ceylon 1945–6; ret 1946.

434. *Diary*

16 January 1945

... Geoffrey Layton came in at 1500 and told me about Ceylon. He had little good to say about the Navy out there. ...

435. *From Churchill*

18 January 1945

2.   ... Cannot a shell be made which casts out, like a star, obstructions or splinters in all directions? We had a very formidable account from poor Lumsden in his last letter of a bomb falling on an American ship, killing 180, including 40 or 50 high officers and both the Chiefs of Staff of the expedition to Luzon. Please give the utmost stimulus to all inquiries and set your best brains to finding a remedy for this great danger.[1]

436. *To Churchill*

23 January 1945

The suicide bomber poses the same problem as any other form of close-range air attack. In some respects it is simpler, since the shots offered are often easier and weapons, whose performance at longer ranges is poor, can be used to good effect at the short ranges presented.
2.   There is no doubt the first line of defence against suicide bombers or any other airborne attack is, and likely to remain, an adequate number of well-directed fighter aircraft.
3.   An immense variety of miscellaneous AA weapons has been investigated in the last few years, but so far none, except CAP (a long range Guided AA Rocket Projectile controlled throughout its flight), a long term project, shows the least prospect of rivalling the gun.
6.   The HE shell with proximity fuse is the most effective shell against aircraft, as was demonstrated in firing at the flying bomb.
7.   Every assessment of the value of AA weapons brings out the need for accurate control. Substantial progress has been made in producing automatic sights and radar but much still remains to be done.

---

[1]Gen Sir Herbert Lumsden: RA; 2nd Lt 1916; W Front 1916–18; Capt 1925; Maj 1931; staff appt 1930s; Lt Col 1938; Brig 1940; PM's personal reprv on MacArthur's staff.
    Also killed was A/Sub Lt (S) Morton, Fraser's sec.

8. Our most pressing problem is to improve our defence at night or low visibility against all forms of air attack, torpedo, bombing or suicide bombing. This means full radar control but it will be some time before this gear can be supplied and fitted in ships.

9. A message from Admiral Fraser tells us that in the Lingayan Gulf operations the [US] fleet's AA fire was perhaps a little wild but of great volume and many aircraft were crashing into the sea close to the ships.

10. The *Australia* was hit by five suicide bombers on the day of the landings; nevertheless she was able to withdraw at 22 knots at the end of the day, having fulfilled her task and destroyed several aircraft. This compares well with *Dorsetshire's* and *Cornwall's* experience two-and-a-half years' ago when they were sunk by penetrating bombs from about 30 Japanese dive bombers without bringing any down.[1]

437. *To Fraser*

19 January 1945

I was much relieved to hear that in the *New Mexico* crash you had got away safely – very bad luck Lumsden and young Morton being killed. You certainly gained some experience. I found your signal describing the operations off Luzon most interesting. The CO of *Australia* must be a good man. I am not clear why the Americans took three days before they landed; I should have thought they would have gained more by surprise.

7. I am much in agreement with you over forward bases and I feel there is a great danger we may dig ourselves in too deeply in Australia. What I would like – and I think you will agree – is that we should get a base as far forward as possible, if necessary sharing it with the US, and ship all our stores, aircraft, etc., direct there from the UK, using the Torrens Strait or perhaps later going up the west side of New Guinea. This would mean an immense saving in shipping, which is going to be the bottleneck in all operations this next year, especially if the new enemy submarines get really busy. I warned Daniel about this before he left and that he should be prepared to get out of Australia and run his show from a more advanced base, Australia only to be used for such docking and repair as cannot be done forward.

---

[1]*Dorsetshire*: hvy csr, 1930, 9900t, 32.25k, 8×8in, 8×4in, 8×21in tt.
Cornwall: hvy csr, 1928, 10900t, 31.5k, 8×8in, 4×4in, 8×21in tt.
Both sunk by Japanese carrier planes off Ceylon, 5 April 1942.

8.   I hope our people will not get too blinded by American lavishness. We can't compete in either personnel or material, nor do I think we should train our men to expect the same waste as is practised in the American Navy. I am sure that soda fountains, etc., are very good things in the right place but we have done without them for hundreds of years and I daresay can for another year or two. I had hoped that we could get *Richelieu* out to join you, but political reasons may restrict her to the East Indies Station.[1]

438.   *Diary*

22 January 1945

COS meeting at 1100. Discussed how to tackle the US COS over the shipping situation. Leathers in attendance and Metcalfe.[2] The former as slippery as ever but he wisely deprecated dissent on the shipping being used in the Pacific. As usual he attacked the Fleet Train which in view of the later termination of the European war is perhaps a little vulnerable. There is no question the build up of the BPF both physically and logistically must be slowed up. . . .

439.   *To A. J. Power*

23 January 1945

7.   We were much disappointed here at the late date for the operations against Palembang. There was a lot of nonsense talked about the training of the air squadrons. *Indefatigable's* squadrons would not have been in such a bad condition had time on passage been devoted to intensive flying. It is a surprising thing but it was in August that we started to turn over the carriers from Barracudas to Avengers and they were apparently unable to carry out a major operation until the latter part of January. This cannot be considered a satisfactory state of affairs.
10.   The retarded build up in the Pacific will make it necessary to keep the light fleet carriers which are now being commissioned, out of the Pacific until they can be logistically supported there. It is our intention to send them to work up in the Middle East and then they will be

---

[1]CO *Australia*: Capt J. M. Armstrong, RAN: Cdr June 1935; *Penguin* Sept 1939; *Australia* Sept 1940; A/Capt *Manoria* April 1942; Capt *Kattabul*, Garden I, Dec 1942; *Ladava*, Milne Bay; FCapt & CSO, Australian Sqdn, *Australia* Oct 1944.
  Richelieu remained with EF or served off French Indo-China.
[2]Sir Ralph Metcalfe: Dir, W. Cory & Sons; Dir Sea Tpt 1942–5.

passed on to you temporarily until Fraser is able to support them. They might get to you about April – three or four of them with Harcourt as the Flag Officer.[1] Political reasons may also prevent the *Richelieu* going to the Pacific, in which case we shall probably send her back to you.

11. . . . If you do get to Rangoon before the monsoon, if I were you I should press for a rather big leap forward and not play about with small bites.

440. *Diary*

26 January 1945

. . . At 1615 the COS attended the Cabinet. Fleet Train came under heavy attack but the PM listened to my arguments and the points I made were certainly taken by several members of the Cabinet, the Chancellor in particular. Decision to defer any decision for two months. In that time I shall certainly have the figures re-examined.

441. *From A. J. Power*

HMS *Rapid*,
29 January 1945

. . . Up and down the coasts I think you would be satisfied with the RN efforts. The Army has been moved as it wished (sometimes a little quicker) with tanks, lorries and whatnots without a single LST, no HQ ship, and only eight LCTs. Maintenance facilities and spare parts for minor landing craft are practically non-existent. It is in this connection that Martin and his staff have been rather weak – they were soaked in 'Overlord' notions with lavish supplies of everything they needed. They were a little slow in gathering the different conditions out here where dumb lighters are priceless, proper landing craft just do not exist, and we are not 'staffed' as per book. Still they have done well: their difficulties due to weather and enemy opposition were nil, and now I think they realise they must *maintain* their craft or we shall be unable to keep the army moving coastwise. . . .

[1]Light fleet carriers: a notably successful design; 3 classes, 1944–61, 13–18000t, 24–29.5k, 37–42 a/c.

442.   *From A. J. Power*

6 February 1945

7.   She [*Indefatigable*] arrived here with her Avenger aircraft unmodified, and we had to land them and take them all in hand before they were fit to use. This shortcoming was quite unexpected out here, and I imagined she would arrive with Avengers ready to take observers and crews all ready for a battle. Here are the details which may interest the Fifth Sea Lord:
  Fitting oxygen plant (Avengers).
  Fitting Observers' seats and W/T sets (Avengers).
  Training of Seafire pilots, many of whom had never deck landed.
9.   ... I am not expecting any more than Force W before the South West Monsoon breaks. The lack of escort forces has necessitated disabling the Aden Escort Force and running the troopers, etc., free to Bombay and back. There is at present fortunately no risk.
10.   Lack of carriers is a real handicap. These Arakan scrambles have all been done with *Ameer* alone, using just 804 Squadron – and a very good squadron it is.[1]
13.   ... I had hoped conditions would have justified by-passing Burma and getting on to the southward whilst avoiding commitments on the mainland and sticking to the islands. The capture of Manila without a battle seems to indicate that the time has now come to take what may appear to be great risks in this theatre, ...

443.   *To Fraser and Somerville*

12 February 1945

I have discussed employment of the BPF with Admiral King and was disappointed to find that he would not assign BPF to first phase of 'Iceberg'. Reason he gave was the uncertainty of MacArthur's future plans.
2.   King inferred that BPF might be working under MacArthur if it is decided that the latter is to swing left-handed and undertake further operations in the near future. I think this is rather unsatisfactory but there seems to have been some difference of opinion between American Authorities themselves as to what operations, if any, were to be undertaken by MacArthur.

---

[1]*Ameer*: escort carrier, 1943, 11420t, 16k, 2×5in, 20 a/c.

3.   I pointed out to him most strongly undesirability of Fleet remaining idle, with which he agreed. It is probable that BPF will take part in
Phase II of 'Iceberg', but this dependent on decision as to MacArthur's
operations.[1] . . .

444.   *From A. J. Power*

1 March 1945

. . . It is very necessary for everybody on this Station to get out of their
heads all idea of the enemy being strong. He will fight until he is killed
but he has not got the means . . . of seriously interfering with any seaborne expedition. . . .

445.   *To A. J. Power*

13 March 1945

3.   . . . Mountbatten should not let himself be used as a 'cat's paw'.
. . . Try, if you can, to head him off interfering with forces on other
stations about whose operations he can't possibly know anything. . . .
6.   We have now had Mountbatten's future operations. I hope we shall
be able to get sufficient amphibious forces out to you in time but . . .
you will certainly have one complete assault force. I do not see why a
lift of more than one division is required in any of the projected operations. I also thought it was a good thing to assault a place where there
were one or more airfields ready made, and think in the Phuket area
you will have to set to and make some. The second step, the assault on
Port Swettenham, looks to me very difficult. It appears a most uninvit-
ing area to assault from the sea. I should have thought one step to
Penang would have been best. There are already three or four good
aerodromes in that neighbourhood, and it is within flying-in range of
fighters . . .

---

[1] 'Iceberg', phase II: the attack on Okinawa.

446. *Diary*

2 March 1945

COS meeting at 1100. Chief matter for discussion was Mountbatten's future plans. I poured some cold water on the planners' optimistic estimate that his resources could probably be made available. . . .

447. *Diary*

6 March 1945

. . . I got back to the Admiralty to find two infuriating signals, one from Fraser and the other from Mountbatten. The former ignoring the Admiralty and trying to be a law unto himself. The other Mountbatten allowing himself to be made a cat's paw of to help the elements in the [US] Navy Department to prevent the fleet operating in the Pacific.

448. *Diary*

7 March 1945

. . . I got the COS to send off two signals in answer to Mountbatten's. One a pretty sharp rap on the knuckles for addressing the US COS and the other to the JSM saying that we were totally opposed to Mountbatten's suggestions.

449. *Diary*

8 March 1945

. . . Interviewed First Lord at 1230 and discussed Fraser's lapse in making appointments without Admiralty approval. He agreed to sending off a pretty strong signal. Then we discussed the press agitation caused by not so much Fraser's press talk as by what appeared to have been disclosed off the record. The British press or rather the Rothermere lot are demanding statements from those in authority about the alleged opinion of the US authorities that the British fleet is unable to operate with the Americans and so on and so on.[1] . . .

---

[1]Lord Rothermere (1876–1971): 2nd Visct; press baron; RMA 1917; Versailles 1919; Unionist MP, Thanet 1919–29; owner of the *Daily Mail*; Chm, Assoc Newspapers 1932–71.

450. *Diary*

9 March 1945

Very good telegram from James Somerville describing an interview he
had with King. James seems to have spoken with some frankness and
called in question Cooke's activities on his visit to Mountbatten.[1] King
put down the delay in reaching a decision to disagreement in the US
COS committee about forthcoming operations and promised a decision
by 15 March. James says there is some talk of pooling all the Pacific
operations under one commander. Three in the running – King,
MacArthur and Marshall. Nimitz in a press interview in Washington
yesterday also foreshadowed a change in the command and incidentally
backed up Fraser's statement that the BPF is ready for operations.

451. *From Fraser*

14 March 1945

4.   . . . there is no question but that the fortnight in Sydney did them
all a power of good. They boiler-clad, refitted and painted, and coupled
with the overwhelming hospitality of Sydney, went away in good form.
6.   Manus I am afraid is a dismal place when there is operational
inactivity, although the Fleet will be able to do some practices there. Its
facilities are less than Scapa with the addition of no water boats and no
drifters, whilst the airstrip we are to use is on an island outside, some
40 miles away. Then there are all the odd things to compete with in a
strange island, such as labour for unloading the mails from aircraft, and
motor transport to the jetty.
7.   The Americans are most kind and co-operative but look to us to
iron out all these details as soon as possible, and as soon as anything
comes to an official level their hands are rather tied.
8.   All these things will settle themselves, but the fact is that our logistic
support is about two months behind the Fleet. And had we not raided
Force X for ships, personnel and staff, we could not have managed.[2]

---

[1]Adm Charles M. ('Savvy') Cooke (1886–1959) US Navy: grad N Acad 1910; b/ships
1910–14; s/m i/c 1915–20; engr, EO & gun appts 1920s; Bur Nav 1928–31; SubDiv 11
1931–3; N War Coll 1933–4; Cdt, Guantanamo Bay NB 1934–6; staff of C-in-C Fleet
1936–8; War Plans 1938–41; *Pennsylvania* Feb 1941–April 1942; Asst CoS (Plans)
April 1942–Oct 1943; DCoS Oct 1943–Oct 1944; CoS Oct 1944–Aug 1945; DCNO (O)
Oct–Dec 1945; Cdr 7 Fleet Dec 1945–Jan 1947; Cdr N Forces, W Pacific Jan 1947–Feb
1948; ret May 1948.
[2]Force X: unknown.

9.   Again, the Americans have done everything in their power, but while the facilities at Sydney are good for a few ships, the Fleet strained everything to the utmost. . . .

10.   Many of the facilities in Australia come under General MacArthur, with whom I am not able to communicate direct. For example, we asked the RAAF for the use of an airfield at Brisbane for the transport service to Manus. They were quite agreeable but said we must apply to the Americans. So to obtain an airfield at Brisbane, which is agreed to unofficially by the RAAF, I have to ask CINCPAC, who signals General MacArthur, who refers to Brisbane, and then the answer has to come by the same route.

11.   I thought the Palembang operation very well carried out and there is no doubt the aircrews were very pleased with themselves. Rawlings arrived here in excellent form; Vian a little temperamental and with his CSO and Secretary sick, and an urgent requirement to change his SO (O). But I think he left in good form.[1]

12.   I think that the main point is that things which loom large out here apparently seem small at home, and things which seem small out here loom large at home.

13.   I should feel happier could this be reconciled. For example the Admiralty reply concerning the appointment of Carne as Commodore not only greatly perturbed me, but discouraged us all. It seemed such a natural thing to do, to put someone in charge of six to eight escort carriers.[2] . . .

452. *Diary*

14 March 1945

. . . Meeting on shipping for redeployment at 11 Downing Street, Mr Attlee in the chair.

Quickly agreed to let the Americans have a 40,000 lift in our shipping with no strings on it.

---

[1]CSO to RA (Air): Capt J. P. Wright: Cdr June 1936; *Hostile* Aug 1938; Capt June 1940; CSO *St Angelo* (Malta) July 1940; *Mackay* Sept 1941; Dir, Air Co-op Div July 1942; DAWD Sept 1943; FCapt & CSO to RA (Air), BPF, *Indomitable* Dec 1944; FCapt & CSO to VA (Air), BPF, *Formidable* June 1945.

Sec: Cdr (S) W. G. Hewson: Pay Cdr June 1939; *Protector* Sept 1939; *Foliot* Sept 1942; *Drake* (Plymouth) Aug 1943: Sec to RA (Air), BPF Dec 1944.

SO (O): Cdr H. G. Walters: Lt Cdr Feb 1937: *Warspite* June 1937; *Berkeley* Feb 1940; Cdr & *Lightning* Dec 1941; OD Sept 1943; *Striker* May 1945.

[2]Cdre W. P. Carne: Cdr June 1933; FTO, Med F July 1939; Capt June 1941; *Coventry*; BAD 1942–3; *Striker* 1944–5; Cdre 2 Cl 1945.

Then the Secretary of State for War put forward his priority list for our redeployment. His order was Pacific first and then the west and bring home the categories to be re-allocated to civilian work. I disputed this order and said the deployment to SEAC should come before both these. I was supported to some extent by the Minister [of Shipping][,] Law.[1] But obviously political reasons won over military and this order was accepted. A poor show.

453. *Diary*

20 March 1945

... Signal from COMINCH telling me what the BPF are to do in connection with operation 'Iceberg', which is I believe the taking of the Ryuku Islands south of Japan. Their job is to keep the Japanese air in the small islands to the north east of Formosa quiet and perhaps bombard one of the islands. It is pleasant to think they have got going. ...

454. *Diary*

21 March 1945

COS at 1100. ... Discussion on SACSEA's future plans. They are fairly good but rather in the direction of always assuming the best case. One difficulty I foresee is to keep the carrier fighter effort going for nine days while they get the airstrips. I am sure Mountbatten will get frightened and ask for the moon. ...

455. *Diary*

23 March 1945

... The BPF are in action today against the Japanese air on the islands to the north east of Formosa. I am sure they will acquit themselves well.

[1]Richard Law.

456. *Diary*

7 April 1945

Sudden call to COS meeting. The PM neither understood or liked what he called our chilling telegram to Mountbatten about his Rangoon projected operations. Explanations made.

457. *From A. J. Power*

7 April 1945

6. We are keeping up a succession of destroyer sweeps in the Andaman Sea and the Tenasserim Coast which is of excellent training value for all destroyers. They get some night shooting at junks, and occasionally aircraft (frequently friendly) are honoured with a salute from their big ordnances.

7. With the Submarines in the Malacca Straits, these destroyer sweeps in the Andaman Sea and 222 Group (Coastal Command) flying from the Arakan I do not think any appreciable supplies are reaching the Japanese by sea.

8. On Sunday Walker is taking out everything that can steam for a bang at Sabang and then work down the west coast of Sumatra where I hope he will get into some shipping movements which appear to be imminent. . . .

458. *Diary*

12 April 1945

Further telegram from Mountbatten which shows that he proposes to try to take Rangoon from the sea whether or no the army advancing from the north is in a position to support. . . .

459. *Diary*

16 April 1945

COS at 1100. . . . we also discussed the latest plan by the US COS which is to take Brunei in north Borneo as a base for the BPF as a primary object and secondly to get oil. I fear this is just the same story to keep the BPF away to the south. It seems quite ridiculous that in all the Philippines they can't find us a base. They also offered to put the SWPA under us and attach it to SEAC or make it a separate command. If it comes off Fraser might do as Supreme Commander.

460.   *From Rawlings*

18 April 1945

Were you here now you would see a thing you have never seen before – five tankers in line abreast, *King George V* buttoned astern of the right hand one and a Fleet Carrier on each of the others. Alongside two of 'em in addition are two cruisers and the other three have destroyers. It's really rather a notable sight. People are getting very good at it though it will be long before we can get battleships to do it alongside – except in the calmest weather. Too difficult to steer at the low speeds the tankers come down to – indeed fuelling astern at say 5 knots in a swell means bringing a hell of a lot of helm on the whole time.

The hoses and so forth have been an awful headache not helped by the weather the first few times. My principal headache was of course that we couldn't get back to unhitch at the time and date I'd told C-in-C Pacific I would be. We've not had to fall short of our word yet – I trust we won't.

I'm thoroughly enjoying myself: indeed the only fly in the ointment is the fact we must return to harbour after this next strike.

These circular formations are most odd[,] the usual one is like this –
  Ring of destroyers and AA cruisers,
  Four carriers and two 6-inches and two battleboats

  Area is about 60 square miles.

It takes up an enormous mass of ocean and there are all sorts of reasons [?] and distances worked out by clever chaps for flying and close range weapons and this and that. I doubt if without modern helps, the PPI in particular, it would be possible at night in anything like reasonable station; as it is they keep remarkably circular etc. – they're damned good. The PPI amuses me – I lift the lid and look in – throw a bottle by TBS and you see her scurrying back into station. I hope you won't snort at it and say I'm getting instrument minded but I think I can handle this obtuse and odd formation like a flotilla. I've converted to TBS – now we've got 'em drilled. It's quicker than the best drilled aux[iliary?] time I ever had and I used to think the 7th CS was good. But we treat it *exactly* like any other means of signalling – no one talks on it except the proper rating – only signalese is allowed – and everything has to be logged as if it were W/T on V/S. . . .

I really love the PPI – I can get tremendous fun out of it bringing say the whole fleet into position in the dark so one has to make one turn and ships find themselves exactly astern of the oilers at dawn – the two screens amalgamated and all with minimum of talk and pre-warning. As long as one treats it that way – i.e., an aid artistry and not a dictator I think that's right. We couldn't have looked at oiling at sea as we do if we'd had Hun Dönitz on our track! Eight knots, a steady course and a screen frightfully thin – but if you think of today's oiling – five great ships nicely immobilised. . . . because the screen does get deplorably weak I have asked, when you've finished in the west, if I could have two or three frigates or something to do all the DSB stuff.[1] Guns etc. don't matter and speed isn't of huge importance. But they'd save the destroyers a lot of running round and I do want to give them a rest in our oiling times. We shall have been 31 days at sea when we get in – think they earn a rest 'in harbour' – i.e., oiling days.

I'm very proud of the way everyone has come up to scratch. There's been really a lot to learn – it's not too easy to drop things one's been used to all one's life and to hoist in quickly new and sometimes odd terms [as?] V/S and so forth. . . .

The first two or three days were notable for an incredible number of alarms . . . but the FDR and others concerned have tremendously improved. This fighter direction is a very pretty art and there [is] no doubt as to its efficiency particularly at the longer ranges. Last night for example six [-?] manifestly suicides were coming in for a dusk or after dusk attack. The fighters caught two at 55 miles and blasted two and the others lost heart and legged it.[2]

Just had a nice signal from Nimitz – what pleased me about it is that so far there is nothing that they can poke Charlie at the White Ensign over. I do mind very much that we came through high in their opinion – it's so absolutely important for our future – indeed I feel it's the most serious side of my job far and away.

---

[1]DSB: Double Side Band; a form of high frequency communication.
PPI: evidently some form of plot-related communication.
TBS: Talk Between Ships.
[2]FDR: Fighter Direction Radar.

461. *Diary*

19 April 1945

COS meeting at 1030. . . . We approved the Operation 'Dracula' (the taking of Rangoon) though I expressed considerable doubts as to its feasibility. . . .

462. *Diary*

20 April 1945

. . . BPF are having their last strike today and then return to Leyte. They have had very nice signals from Spruance and Nimitz.

463. *Diary*

23 April 1945

. . . Signal from James Somerville describing an interview with King in which they had a royal row. Chiefly about bases in the Pacific and British [Pacific] Fleet.

464. *Diary*

26 April 1945

. . . Some discussion on the Brunei Base. We sent a wire to the US COS saying we did not think it suitable for the BPF. This will cause a storm I think.

465. *Diary*

28 April 1945

Another example of the infuriating delays imposed by the PM insisting on having his hand in everything. The signal re the Borneo operations which the British COS do not favour hung up for 36 hours so missed the COS meeting in Washington yesterday. No wonder the US COS complain of delays in getting things through.

466. *From A. J. Power*

HQ, SACSEA,
Kandy,
4 May 1945

... Rangoon is ours ... but it is quite impossible to pretend that this 'Dracula' operation has been anything more or less than a glorious bounce. ...
5. We also decided our next jump. Agreement was quickly reached as follows:

We must get to Singapore with only one intermediate stage and 'Zipper' was accepted with one qualification ... we must have light fleet carriers. These are required not only to provide fighter protection during the passage of the convoys but also to ferry in RAF aircraft as soon as a 'Zipper' airfield is ready to receive them. ... I know Fraser would like them but should they be taken away before 'Zipper' and 'Mailfist' are finished, I know I should have very great difficulty in getting agreement with the Army and RAF to go as far to the southwards without RAF close support and fighter protection for the Army.[1] ...
6. I tried to get it across to everybody that the Japanese position in this theatre is quite loose; ...
8. ... could we please have 18 LSTs.
9. US representatives are very pleased about Rangoon; ...
10. I am afraid Oliver with his small carriers has never seen a feather. Walker with battleships, cruisers and destroyers had four quite good bombardments on the Andamans and Nicobar. Half of Walker's force will remain in a position to cover Rangoon's approaches for the next few days.[2]

467. *Diary*

11 May 1945

COS at 1030. Directors of Plans present.
Considered operations against Japan. Portal to my surprise came out strongly in favour of directing our main effort of all three services against the main islands of Japan. His argument being that the Dutch

---
[1]'Zipper': planned operations against Ports Swettenham & Dickson, Malaya.
'Mailfist': capture of Singapore.
[2]RAdm G. N. Oliver.

East Indies and Borneo, Celebes, etc., would probably drop into our hands as Denmark, Holland and Norway had. This is the policy I have never wavered from. I cannot see how we are to take a prominent part in the eastern settlement if we have devoted ourselves solely to mopping up operations. . . .

468.   *Diary*

15 May 1945

. . . We [COS] turned down Mountbatten's attempt to steal the light fleet carriers going to the Pacific.

469.   *Diary*

16 May 1945

. . . Good news from East Indies. D26 (Manley Power) with five of his flotilla sank a Japanese 8-inch cruiser last night. She may have had a bomb hit from the *Shah's* aircraft before.[1] . . .

470.   *From Rear Admiral Cecil Harcourt*

HMS *Venerable*,
Melbourne,
16 May 1945

I am glad we are going on as the atmosphere here is just a little too 'peacelike' and it will do my young men a lot of good to be a bit nearer the sound of the guns where there is still a war going on. . . . we have coped successfully with most of our teething troubles. On the flying side our chief difficulty now is supply and fitting of modifications to aircraft so that all aircraft of practically any squadron are the same and as up-to-date as possible. That is making progress. On the ship side, the chief headache is ventilation, which has two aspects:

(a)   The heat under the flying deck is intense and as fitted there was no way for the hot air which collected there to escape. That is now being dealt with as fast as we can.

(b)   Too much ventilation has been badly installed so that intakes are alongside exhausts and for instance hot air exhausted from the

---

[1]*Shah*: escort carrier, 1943, 11420t, 16k, 2×5in, 20 a/c.

galley is sucked in by a supply fan and pumped all over living spaces! We have made some improvement on that.

The flying control and aircraft handling of these ships is good – as is also our endurance – 10,000 miles at 17 knots. We were delighted to see some of our secondary armament arrive, *Anson* and *Duke of York* and we are giving them all the encouragement we can to learn how to shoot down suicide dive-bombers! *Duke of York's* 176 guns are a fine sight even though their fire control system is still based on the illusion that an attacking aircraft flies on a steady course and speed![1]

I can't pretend that we have yet reached a high standard of operational efficiency of our aircraft – but hope to do a great deal on passage – if the monsoon in particular does not stop us. In particular flight deck handling of Corsairs is only in its infancy.[2] Most of them want some more day practices before they embark on the night stuff. All the Barracudas seem pretty happy about it – though I understand that the atmosphere in the tropics will impose a little difference in the handling of the aircraft.

471. *To Somerville*

27 May 1945

. . . I hope we shall not be committed too deeply to an intermediate base which we then find we are unable to develop and support.

2. The main point to my mind is to solve problem of maintaining our effort over next nine months.

3. If during this period our efforts are divided between supporting fleet and supporting construction of a base it will I think further strain our slender resources.

4. Moreover it may result in not having either an intermediate base or necessary facilities in Australia to use during this period.

5. I would recommend in order of priority:

(a) Meeting initial fleet training requirements.

(b) Ensuring facilities in Australia are fully developed and adequate provision is made at Manus. . . .

---

[1] *Duke of York*: b/ship, 1941, 35000t, 28k, 10×14in, 16×5.25in.
[2] Chance Vought Corsair: ftr, 1940, 2450hp, 446mph, 1562m, 6mg, 2000lbs bombs.

472.   *From A. J. Power*

2 June 1945

11.   In addition to the Andaman and Nicobar ideas we are going to carry out a series of operations designed to get such enemy aircraft as exist to attack us and then shoot them down. The Japanese air strength in the SEAC is now very small and if we could get just 30 or 40 down before 'Zipper' it would be a very appreciable reduction on her total air strength. During this operation G. N. Oliver and his carriers will get some excellent working up practices.

13.   I see we are threatened with a very considerable French Squadron on the East Indies Station and very much hope HMG will not think fit to send General de Gaulle with them.

473.   *Diary*

6 June 1945

... Great fight over the fleet train. Leathers as slippery as ever and backed by Cherwell. First Lord put up a good show and I backed him to the best of my ability. Finally PM decided that First Lord and Leathers under the arbitration of Anderson should fight it out.[1]

474.   *To A. J. Power*

15 June 1945

2.   We were delighted about [Captain M. L.] Power's success in sinking the Japanese cruiser. . . . Now we have the other cruiser also, which should relieve you of all worry about naval forces in the Bay of Bengal. *Trenchant's* attack appears to have been a very fine one taking into consideration the shallow water.[2]

3.   . . . It is of the utmost importance that there should be no delay in the capture of Singapore.

4.   I was not overpleased about the attempt to retain the Light Fleet

---

[1]FL: Brendan Bracken.
  CEx: Sir John Anderson.
  [2]*Trenchant*: s/m, 1943, 1090/1575t, 15.25/9k, 1×4in, 11×21in tt; sank *Ashigara*, hvy csr, 8 June 1945. CO: Cdr A. Hezlet: Lt April 1936; *Trident* June 1939; COQC Sept 1940; *St Angelo* (Malta) Sept 1941; *Trident* March 1942; Lt Cdr June 1942; *Thrasher* March 1943; *Trenchant* Oct 1943; Cdr Dec 1944; later VAdm Sir Arthur Hezlet & FO (S).

Carriers as they were passing your front door. You must keep the Supreme Commander in order over these matters; otherwise I shall sail future ships via the Panama Canal. They are wanted for the big operations taking place in the Pacific shortly. I think that you must try to realise that the way to quickly finish the war against Japan is to throw everything that can be used into the main battle. The taking of Singapore appears to me to be the only worthwhile object left in SEAC and nothing must be allowed to interfere with this. The operations after that are really in the nature of mopping up. We are beginning to think here that . . . if the heart of the Japanese empire was to collapse and the Son of Heaven could be induced to give an order the outlying islands, Sumatra, Java, etc., would fall without any loss of life. . . . We are having the greatest difficulty in getting the fleet train for the Pacific and also the cargo ships that are required to support the fleet in the Indian Ocean . . . but we had a good bag in the German ports of some two million tons, which we are getting into action as quickly as possible, so hope for the best.

475. *From A. J. Power*

29 June 1945

5. . . . The light fleet carriers were given to the East Indies Station and, on the understanding that they were to be used in 'Zipper', the Army and Air Force agreed to abandoning any intermediate 'hop'. The next thing that occurred was the light fleet carriers were taken away and I had to get the Army's and Air Force's agreement to do without the intermediate 'hop' in spite of this weakening of our Carrier strength and ability to ferry in RAF aircraft. This they did. Since then I have never advocated holding the light fleets here and the Admiralty have given us two *Smiter* class to do the ferrying. Mountbatten did put in a tardy plea to retain the light fleets and it was a mistake.[1]
6. Your threat to sail future ships by the Panama Canal would be very welcome to us. I have light fleets here now filling up all our aerodromes, using all our training facilities and gobbling up our stores. In justice to Moody may I say that Harcourt and all his party, to use a sailor's expression, 'are very well satisfied'. The whole lot passes on together with *Anson* on 7 July.
7. I can assure you that everyone out here accepts, without question, that the quickest way to finish the war is to put everything into the main battle and that in SEAC Singapore is the only worthwhile target . . .

[1]*Smiter* cl: escort carriers, 1943, 11420t, 16k, 2×5in, 20 a/c.

476. *From Fraser*

15 June 1945

I have briefed VA (Q) I think with all our views, a fairly large bundle for him but which his weight will carry![1]

The Fleet has had a difficult time but are in very good spirits.

There is no doubt however that they are most seriously hoping for conditions to improve which can only be done by meeting our Fleet Train requirements. You will realize that the views I have given VA (Q) on Fleet bases and the signals we have made are founded on what we estimate to be future operations.

So far I have spent most of my time trying to guess what these are going to be and then planning accordingly. This is not easy and we of course may be wrong but there is no question at the moment unless special provision is made we cannot support a Fleet base separate from the Fleet.

If the Fleet is to be used in the east a base to the west is of no value and only an added unit.

BS1 and AC1 have had slight squalls – latter is rather temperamental but everything is OK now.[2]

RAFT and RA (D) in good form.[3]

I must ensure however that all these officers have sufficient staff, the ships are crowded and hot, and there will be more sickness than we [can] cope with if they are continually overworked.

477. *To Fraser*

5 July 1945

We have much benefited from Daniel's visit and he has put your views very clearly.

Where we differ, as far as I can see, is in our conception of what the course of the war in the Pacific will be. You appear to consider a short-

[1]VAdm Daniel.

[2]BS1: VAdm Rawlings.
AC1: RAdm Vian (later VAdm).

[3]RA, Fleet Train: RAdm Douglas Fisher: Capt Dec 1932; *Nelson* April 1938; *Warspite* April 1940; RA & *President* July 1942; RAFT, BPF, *Montclare* Oct 1944.

RA (D): Adm Sir John Edelsten: (1891–1966): Lt 1913; Capt 1933; DPD 1938; SNO, Somaliland 1940; CoS, Med F 1941; RA & ACNS (UT)1942; RA (D), BPF 1945; VA, 1BS 1945; 4CS 1946; VCNS 1947; Adm & C-in-C Med 1950; C-in-C Portsmouth 1952–4; ret 1954.

term policy the most advisable, bringing the greatest force possible to bear during 'Olympic' and 'Coronet' but not really taking much thought for the morrow after these operations. We, on the other hand, while fully agreeing with your views about bringing the greatest force possible to bear in the two operational periods, can find no evidence either in Washington or London which leads us to conclude all will be over as far as the BPF is concerned even if 'Coronet' went according to plan and met with the fullest success. So we are strongly of the opinion that we must continue to press for some sort of forward base. The great difficulty that we are experiencing in getting our demands for the fleet train conceded also makes a forward base with some storage and aircraft facilities essential.[1]

Daniel has also had the opportunity of meeting Somerville who has returned to Washington and will immediately return to the attack.

B.   We are now going ahead with putting before the American COS a plan to use a small amount of our army in 'Olympic'. It won't amount to more than five divisions and the plan is to mount it from SEAC using the assault lift there of about two divisions plus, the idea is that the principal naval support will be given by the East Indies Fleet, though you may be called on to provide some units. Do not regard this as firm – it is only an outline of what is being placed before the American COS and it depends, of course, on our capture of Singapore before the end of this year, which looks to me to be feasible.

I think myself that 'Coronet' and 'Olympic' are going to be rather tougher jobs than we thought some time ago. Your intelligence will doubtless have told you that there are nearly a million first-line troops in Honshu backed up by some seven million Home Guard: it seems to me that, physically, it will take a long time to kill all these.

C.   We have also accepted the US COS suggestions to some extent on taking over the South West Pacific Area. The idea is to divide the area into two, giving SEAC Java, Borneo, the Celebes and the rest of the Netherlands East Indies, and Australia the rest.

We have made some alterations, however, which the US COS may not accept. We have included Indo-China in SEAC's area. . . .

D.   You will probably have seen the most unhelpful signal from the Australian Prime Minister here on the subject of support for the BPF. They seem to wish to take less and less part in the war.

---

[1] 'Coronet': invasion of Honshu.
'Olympic': invasion of Kyushu.

478. *From Fraser*

17 July 1945

2.   I do not think we differ very much on the duration of the war. I have no doubt it will be a tough job.

3.   It is on the facilities and the means of putting schemes into operation that the Admiralty's and our opinion seem to be at variance.

4.   The establishment of a Fleet Base forward, if it is to be of any value, is a vast undertaking. It means wharves, cranes, large stores, supply of water, fresh provisions, airstrips. . . .

5.   To construct this base involves maintaining four to five thousand men in a forward area with all the transport and cargo ships required to supply them whilst the base is building.

6.   I can hardly support the Fleet let alone the people building a base in another area.

7.   Hence my object is to support the Fleet for which the Fleet Train as envisaged is hardly adequate.

8.   If the Admiralty can independent of this supply maintain all the facilities and requirement for building a Fleet Base, I am all for it. It is this part of the project however which remains entirely in the air, and the problems are accentuated by a signal asking for the withdrawal of the *Empire Spearhead*, *Glenearn* and *Lothian*, without which we should have been unable to operate, and unless they are relieved we shall be greatly handicapped.[1]

9.   I realise only too well that it was we who, in the first place, were so keen on this base, but as the war out here has unfolded and the measure of our resources has become clearer, all experience goes to show the tremendous burden we would shoulder in constructing it.

10.   I think we must be very careful about taking over the command of areas out here unless we are fully certain we can meet all the material and manpower commitments. For instance, a great deal of our air transport is dependent on American facilities. At Manus we have been dependent on American victualling and cooking, and for 40% of our harbour transport. If the Americans withdraw entirely, the call on manpower and material will be large.

11.   The Australian Government is being difficult but I haven't yet given up hope of making them see reason. One of the main causes of

---

[1] *Empire Spearhead*: LSI, 1944, 11650t, 14k, 1×4in.

Glenearn: Glen Line, 1938, 8986gt, 18k.

Lothian: (*City of Edinburgh*), City Line, 1938, 8036gt, 16k: (*Lothian*): ldg ship (HQ) large, 4×4in.

the trouble is that the Government has never really had any responsibility for operations. The Americans have run this side of the business and we are now running it for the BPF. In consequence if an operation, or support, fails, they feel they are not to blame.

12.   Today I think is quite historic in a first attack on Tokyo by combined British and American forces. The British force contains Australian, Canadian and New Zealand . . . units.

479.   *From Rear Admiral Edelsten*

HMS *Tyne*,
21 June 1945

. . . The 'suicides' are the devil and leave little time to knock them out of the sky. I claim one for *Quality* and *Queenborough*. The carriers have stuck up to them very well so far and I think the Americans are green with jealousy and sent a detachment to inspect the damage in *Victorious* and *Indomitable*. I think it was *Ulster* had a bit of a bad [time?] with a near miss bomb. The only redeeming feature was the way the ship remained stable with the engine room and one boiler room flooded and a hole 20 by eight feet wide in her side. She had a sticky tow back by *Gambia* and [the ship's company] were on less than a pint of water a day for 10 days which was a bit trying in the heat.[1]

After leaving *Euryalus* I stayed in *Whirlwind* for a week to get a first hand sight of fuelling at sea, transferring cot cases, every [conceivable?] sort of gear to other ships. . . . By and large the destroyers are a damned good lot and we have got a fine *esprit de corps*, and the ships' companies keep in very good heart. All the destroyers are lamentably short of short range weapons but by cannibalising and great efforts by *Tyne* and the people down here, we have increased their fire power by over 50 Bofors and I hope, yet, to get a first class equipment into all of them. The Oerlikon is abso-bloody-lutely hopeless but they are still being sent out. Some astute bloke out here has converted the twin Oerlikon mounting to take a Bofors and it works very well. Busy altering all of them . . . The greatest trouble is water or lack of it. They [the destroyers] have only got one evaporator which never stops intentionally but often by mishap and then it is the devil. The only delicacies

---

[1]*Quality, Queenborough*: destroyers, 1942–3, 1705t, 36.75k, 4×4.7in, 8×21in tt.
Ulster: destroyer, 1943, 1710t, 36.75k, 4×4.7in, 8×21in tt.
Gambia: csr, 1942, 8525t, 33k, 12×6in, 8×4in, 6×21in tt; RNZN 1943.

we have had are dehydrated vegetables! Where are the ice-cream soda fountains!! We have at last got water coolers here but not fitted – I look upon them as an operational requirement.[1]

. . .*Barfleur* has arrived and is a show piece. Eminently suited to this type of warfare we are indulging in but hardly my idea of a destroyer. She can do 32 knots instead of the reported 28. Mike Townsend is her Captain. I know him well from Mediterranean and anti-U-boat war days. I failed to get a cruiser for the next operation and so am hoisting my flag in *Barfleur* instead.[2] . . .

No one likes this war but I am very struck with the excellent way my destroyer ships' companies take it – I try to make them all retain the sense of humour which, without doubt, is one of the greatest of God's gifts, and they do. . . .

480. *Diary*

18 July 1945

[CCS at Potsdam] . . . we took the very thorny subject of control of strategy in the Pacific.

We reached a friendly agreement which assured to us the right of being consulted but the final decision in case of disagreement must rest with US COS. In view of the disparity in the size of the forces to be employed this is I think reasonable. King tried to be rude about it but nobody paid any attention to him[,] Marshall and Arnold going out of their way to be pleasant and friendly.[3] . . .

481. *From Vice Admiral Louis Hamilton*

Navy Office,
Melbourne,
2 August 1945

. . . The staff that Royle turned over to me, both service and civilian, are first class so I don't think there is any trouble about the RAN. . . .

---

[1]*Whirlwind*: destroyer, 1944, 1710t, 36.75k, 4×4.7in, 8×21in tt.
Tyne: destroyer depot ship, 1941, 11000t, 17k, 8×4.5in.
Bofors: 40mm AA gun (Swedish); Oerlikon: 20mm AA gun (Swiss).
[2]*Barfleur*: 'Battle' cl, flotilla leader, 1944, 2325t, 35.75k, 4×4.5in, 1×4in, 8×21in tt.
RAdm M. S. Townsend (1908–84): RA 1956; FO & Pres, Ady Interview Bd 1956–8; CO, Allied N Forces, N Cent Eur 1958–61; ret 1961.
[3]The Potsdam conf was 'Terminal'.

My main job here I look upon as selling a FAA and carriers to this Labour Government . . . I have already experienced how very touchy they are about any advice from UK. . . .

I propose to jockey them into a FAA and at least one carrier, on the principle that they are then committed. I am not optimistic about the result but will do my best. I intend to use the argument that the Fleet of the future must be an Empire Fleet, and that as you are already well advanced in post-war planning it would be of great assistance to know what Australia's contribution is likely to be. . . .

482.   *From Commodore G. H. Faulkner*[1]

Navy Office,
Wellington,
7 August 1945

. . . I expect he [Lake] told you of his troubles with the Navy Board and the Government.

I should like to say at once that the troubles with the Navy Board are over. I have not gone into the reasons for trouble in the past but I am confident that there will be none in the future. I have tackled the other two Naval Members and we all know just how we stand and we all see eye to eye.[2]

As regards my personal relations with the government it is too early yet to speak with certainty but I think they look promising. I think a newcomer who is not a New Zealander is bound to be under suspicion until he is known. . . . Apart from the attitude one would expect Labour men to take towards senior officers (and this is not unduly evident here) my main trouble is the tendency for them to assume that an RN officer is bound to look at problems from an Admiralty point of view . . . I shall hope to live this down without disloyalty to my own service.

---

[1]Cdre G. H. Faulkner (1893–1983): ent RN 1906; destroyers 1914–18; Captain 1935; *Bideford* 1937–8; CoS to C-in-C Nore 1939–41; *Berwick* 1941–3; Cdre 2Cl & CoS to C-in-C S Atl 1943–5; ret 1945; 1st N Mem, NZ 1945–7.

[2]Cdre Sir Atwell Lake, Bt (1891–1972): Eur 1914–18; *Lion* Jutland 1916; Cdre & CoS to C-in-C Portsmouth 1939–42; 1st N Mem, NZ 1942–5.

2 other N Mems: A/Capt M. Taylor: Cdr June 1932; SO (O) *Victory* Oct 1937; A/Capt, ret, 2nd N Mem, RNZN N Bd Sept 1944.

A/Capt (S) W. J. G. Prophit: *Scorpion* Yangtze, Sept 1937; *Aurora* April 1940; *Corinthian* Sept 1943; A/Pay Capt & Sec, RNZN N Bd Sept 1944.

Capt (S) N. H. Beall: PayCdr July 1930; T/Pay Capt, Sec to 2SL Sept 1938; N Sec, RNZN N Bd Sept 1941; Pay Capt (ret) June 1942.

The Government and everyone else are very appreciative of the good work Lake has done, more so I think than they let him know.

There is one major problem here . . . and that is the amount of reduction required in the overall strength in order that we can put a New Zealand land force into the field large enough to keep its identity without undue depletion of civilian manpower particularly in farming and house-building.

This is a major political issue and was debated in the House for a day and half. The net result as far as the Navy is concerned is that we have had to accept a 38% cut bringing our total strength down to 6200. . . .

483. *Diary*

8 August 1945

[Defence Committee] . . . Mountbatten also there. The latter when called upon to speak brought up all the old stories – his great difficulties and how well he has overcome them and then suddenly asked if he could have the light fleet carriers. He is always trying this method of putting pressure on the Admiralty. I said I would look into it. The irritating point of it of course is that he spent 40 minutes with me in the morning and did not mention anything about it. I gave him a pretty good doing but promised to put his name on my recommendations for Rear Admiral next batch.

484. *From A. J. Power*

8 August 1945

2.   I think Walker has got the sea-going fleet in very good heart . . .

10.   'Zipper' orders are now well in hand . . . but . . . I can't bring myself to believe that Singapore will fall quickly. . . . we have not the heavy weapons with which to reduce a fortress of the strength of Singapore should the Japanese decided to stick it out. Maybe they won't and we are working on 'Lightning' [renamed 'Tiderace'] now just in case the atomic bomb . . . upsets the Japanese morale.

11.   We are passing ships through to Fraser almost daily, and we got rid of *Glory*, the last of the light fleets, last week. I had a letter from Fraser today saying that he reckoned that the East Indies Station had done him proud.

12.   . . . We are having considerable success in knocking their aircraft about, destroying locomotives and a few small ships . . .

13.   G. N. Oliver is just off on another run . . . The number of aircraft we destroy is small but when taken as a percentage of the total number of Japanese aircraft in SEAC it is very appreciable. I hope before 'Zipper' starts, the naval aircraft will have written off 30% of the total number of Japanese aircraft.

I feel myself that with the atomic bomb the invasion of Japan will be a very cheap operation as far as expenditure of Allied personnel is concerned. . . .

485. *Diary*

10 August 1945

Rumours of a Japanese surrender. . . . Well it looks like being all over for which we must be profoundly thankful. . . .

486. *To Fraser*

10 August 1945

1.   If surrender of Japan is accepted and this covers all Japanese forces both in and outside the main Japanese islands, it will be important for immediate action with regard to British interests to be taken by the BPF.
2.   Clearly you must be guided by Admiral Nimitz's requirements, but as far as is possible, you should request full British representation in any forces sent to Japan and to

Hong Kong, Shanghai, Tientsin, Dairen, Tsingtao, in that order of priority, Hong Kong being especially important.
3.   At all of these ports there are interned British subjects and considerable British interests.

487. *Diary*

15 August 1945

The announcement of the complete Japanese surrender came through just after midnight. . . .

COS meeting at 1100. We ordered the Hong Kong squadron to proceed. Fraser being at sea and leaving it all to Rivett-Carnac at Sydney is crossing the wires and making things difficult. The latter or it may be Fraser's staff are slow and pedantic and do not realise the need for haste.[1] . . .

488. *To Fraser*

20 August 1945

I was delighted when you were nominated British Government representative with MacArthur – very fitting tribute to the strong finish of the BPF. . . .

With regard to the occupation of Japan, I have told our people here that we shall probably wish to keep a force in Japanese waters and take some part in Japanese naval disarmament. I also told them that we should probably have to have a Japanese port allotted to us where we can have stores, etc. sent and generally for the maintenance of the squadron. . . .

The Hong Kong muddle appears to be clearing up. Our government are quite determined to take possession. I have the feeling that the US wished to have control of it to maintain their Chinese and US forces in the hinterland. I should have thought Canton would have been ample.
. . .

I hope the situation will clear up in a week or so and we may be able to see more clearly what our commitments are going to be.

. . . There is also of course a big outcry here to demobilise everyone and everything and there is no question that our financial situation is so bad that we must reduce to essentials only.

I want to get out of Australia as soon as possible and, if it is practicable, base the BPF on Singapore and Hong Kong.

489. *Diary*

20 August 1945

COS meeting at 1100. The principal paper was the JP's summing up the Hong Kong position.

As I see it although the US COS do not like to say so definitely that they would prefer that we do not go straight in there I believe they hoped to get it under US control and use it for supplying the Chinese

---

[1]RAdm J. W. Rivett-Carnac (1891–1970): Capt June 1934; Cdre 2 Cl, cmdg RNZ Sqdn, *Leander* Nov 1936; DTSD March 1940; *Rodney* July 1941; RA July 1943; FO Br Assault Force, BPF 1944; VA (Q), BPF, *Beaconsfield*, March 1945–7; ret 1947.

and US forces in China. We are being quite firm about it however. . . .
Harcourt is to be in command of the two carriers, two cruisers and
some destroyers and he will be the first military governor.

SEAC has been told to send troops and today I successfully resisted
the War Office idea that Hong Kong should be under SEAC. My view is
that the British COS should be directly responsible. They are directly in
touch with the Colonial Office in London.

Wrote a letter to Fraser . . . pointing out very gently that he should
have Rawlings back to run the fleet. I also gave him an inkling of how
our minds are working, stressing the necessity of sending home all
redundant ships. . . . Further I gave him a bit of a lecture about not
being too parochial about the appointment of admirals.

490. *From Edelsten*

HMS *Tyne*,
29 August 1945

. . . I had a happy time in *Barfleur* for five weeks – grand little ships but
they must have another turret aft. . . .

. . . H. B. [Rawlings] was in great form . . . I liked Halsey very much
and prevailed on him to give our destroyers a chance of running in
shore and doing some bombardment. He readily agreed but the typhoon
stopped all play unfortunately. The destroyers with H. B. [Rawlings]
have now been at sea non-stop for nearly two months and I am now
back in the *Tyne* at Manus (godless spot) trying to collect some reliefs
for them and shuffle the party round the coast to support the China side
commitments. . . .

We had got the fitting of Bofors going hot and strong. *Wakeful* joined
up with seven Bofors instead of her miserable armament of two Bofors
and some obsolescent Oerlikons. I abominate being subservient to the
Yanks – it seems all wrong somehow, but they are *very* nice about it.[1]

491. *From Fraser*

Tokyo,
5 September 1945

It [the formal Japanese surrender aboard USS *Missouri*] was indeed a
great day, MacArthur most dignified and the whole thing well arranged.

---

[1] *Wakeful*: destroyer, 1944, 1710t, 36.75k, 4×4.7in, 8×21in tt.

In the evening I had a musical sunset on board with Halsey and the bands of the Fleet and I think the Americans were very impressed.[1]

The Fleet is grand but undoubtedly tired. The destroyers just coming in have done 60 continuous days at sea. . . .

492.   *From A. J. Power*

HMS *Cleopatra*,[2]
[en route to Colombo],
15 September 1945

. . . Poland at Sabang and Walker at Penang managed their landings and all dealings with the Japanese in a satisfactory manner. These two operations were entirely RN, using the Marines of the fleet as troops.[3]

Holland, with his 'Tiderace' convoy, arrived at Singapore punctually and the personnel was landed very quickly.[4] . . .

. . . I have just got a signal saying *Nelson* is to be relieved by *Howe* and welcome it as the exchange should be the means of getting five to six hundred time-expired men back to the UK. This, together with passage home of the escort carriers and cruiser reliefs, will assist very much. . . .

The activities of the last month have prevented any reaction on the part of our officers and men to the termination of the war. . . . Such luxuries as having decent ventilation at sea and steaming at economical speeds should make conditions for everyone almost those of a yachtsman. Those who have not experienced wartime conditions in our older ships in tropical waters may not appreciate how great is the change from war to peace for all of us out here.

493.   *To A. J. Power*

17 September 1945

. . . It is essential that we reduce our expenditure in the East. The country's financial position is just frightful. So everything that can be

---

[1]*Missouri*: US b/ship, 1944, 48110t, 32.5k, 9×16in, 20×5in.

[2]*Cleopatra*: lt csr, 1941, 5600t, 32.2k, 8×5.25in.

[3]Capt A. L. Poland: Capt *Black Swan* June 1939; *Nile* Feb 1941; *Jervis* Feb 1942; *St George* (I of Man) Feb 1943; Cdre (D), EF *Woolwich* April 1944.

[4]VAdm C. S. Holland: Capt 1932; NA Paris, Brussels, The Hague Jan 1938–May 1940; *Ark Royal* June 1940–April 1941; *Cormorant* (Gibraltar) May 1941; DSD 1942; RA June 1942; RA (Q), EF Nov 1943; VA & ret June 1945.

'Tiderace': the relief of Singapore.

done in the way of reductions in Flag Officers with or without their staffs is welcome.

494. *Diary*

21 September 1945

. . . Rather a disturbing signal from Fraser saying he was off to Chunking to discuss visits of HM ships to the China coast ports.[1] Made a signal to him to do no such thing. Also one from him giving his views on demobilisation. Rather a wild one and threatening us with unrest in the fleet unless the sailors could be assured that all was being done to demobilize them quickly.

Had a talk with First Lord. He made the remark that Fraser's actions were making him doubt if he was fitted for the highest position in the Navy – First Sea Lord.

495. *Diary*

28 September 1945

. . . Fraser being a bit troublesome. He will persist that his ideas are better than those of the Admiralty. A signal from him from Chungking complaining he was not allowed to discuss anything with Chiang [Kai Shek]. He does not see that if he had warned us in time he would have been instructed and so his visit would have been of great use. . . .

496. *From Lieutenant J. Wells*[2]

HMS *Swiftsure*,[3]
[Hong Kong],
n.d., September 1945

. . . On the forenoon of 30 August Admiral Harcourt decided to go in. He came aboard *Swiftsure* at 1100 and with everyone at Action Stations we went through the Lie Mun Pass at 1145. Batteries on the heights of the many small islands could be discerned quite easily. Apart from a few meaningless flags at local signal stations, our entry was uneventful.

---

[1]Chunking was the Chinese Nationalist capital at the time.
[2]Lt J. Wells: Mid (Air) Sept 1939; Lt Sept 1945.
[3]*Swiftsure*: csr, 1944, 8800t, 31.5k, 9×6in, 10×4in, 6×21in tt.

We were astern of D27 in *Kempenfelt* and had scores of fighters over-head that seemed cross at finding no opposition.[1] *Euryalus* followed us in and we both anchored off a badly battered dockyard at 1230, to disgorge about 500 Seamen and Marines. They went ashore with our Commander in charge. Leading a troop of bloodthirsty Royal Marines armed to the proverbial teeth, he was greeted on the jetty by the re-sourceful Commander Craven (PoW) and a benign Japanese officer, hissing gently, and the last British Governor's ADC (PoW) called MacGregor.[2] By sunset the yard was completely occupied and aboard we felt reasonably secure. . . .

. . . I spent the next two hours talking to a bunch of ex-PoWs who had just come out of a camp on the mainland called Shan Shio Po. Pretty groggy on their feet, rather haggard to look at, they were eager for news out of England more than anything else. They had never heard of Radar, V2s, Buzzbombs or jet propulsion and I had to explain them all very slowly indeed. . . .

. . . One morning a small patrol became involved in a shindy near the Queen's Pier where the Chinese had caught the Japanese High Execu-tioner in disguise, trying to escape to Kowloon. They couldn't prevent his quick and unpleasant death but they managed to get his body carted away in record time by two rick-shaw boys. It was a horrid sight, but could not have been worse than Cenotaph steps where the Japanese carried out daily executions.

497. *Diary*

3 October 1945

COS at 1100. We sent off a message to Fraser telling him to get the British force under Servaes out from Kinkaid's command.[3] The latter is not playing the game – anyway from our angle and with I suspect Wedemeyer is trying to keep the British out of China.

---

[1]*Kempenfelt*: flotilla leader, 1943, 1730t, 36.75k, 4×4.7in, 8×21in tt.
[2]Cdr D. H. S. Craven: Cdr Dec 1937; SO, 1BS, *Barham* July 1938; Sqdn Navig O, *Manchester* Nov 1939; CoS *Tamar* (Hong Kong) Oct 1940.
McGregor: not identified.
[3]RAdm R. M. Servaes: Capt 1935; DDLD 1938; DLD Oct 1939; *London* Oct 1940; RA & ACNS (F) 1943–5; RA 2CS, BPF June 1945.

498.   *To Fraser*

9 October 1945

A.   The PoW situation appears to be clearing up and I cordially agree with the use of carriers to carry them about.

We are going to turn *Victorious* round quickly and use her and two new light fleets for trooping; also we hope to have six CVEs and two more 8-inch cruisers in the trooping fleet in a few weeks. . . .

C.   Nothing has yet been settled about our share in the control and disarmament of Japan. . . .

I have asked Somerville to find out what fleet the Americans are keeping in Japanese waters, and we will base our numbers on theirs. If they keep, say, three or four battleships we must have one, and so on. I hope you will not have any difficulty with the Americans about sending one back there and I should say it would be advisable to do so as soon as you have one rested and ready. . . .

499.   *From Lieutenant J. Wells*

HMS *Swiftsure*,
[Japan],
n.d., October 1945

. . . I was appointed British Naval Representative, Yokohama, and Officer of the Guard at the Consulate. . . .

. . . The Japanese seem particularly unresentful at the Allied occupation. They go about looking rather dejected but their labour gangs work well and they always appear keen to help one out. . . . Tokyo has several large buildings still standing but the effect of incendiary bombs has been devastating. . . .

Arriving at Nagasaki at 0900 on 18 [October] . . . Imagine an area as big as Portsmouth and Southsea looking like a big mass of dirty rubble. Not a building stood upright within an area of a mile radius of the bomb burst at a height of 1400 feet. That one missile, the size of a melon, could do incalculable harm, was a staggering thought. Charred heaps of bones marked the areas of massed housing; here and there the blackened and blasted stumps of trees remained as if to signify the terrific heat that was generated. I picked up two bottles that had been melted together and one of the sailors found a stone impaled in a piece of metal. After half an hour I was glad to leave such a sickening yet terribly impressive spectacle.[1] . . .

[1]Site of second atomic bomb, 9 Aug 1945.

500. *From Fraser*

23 January 1946

. . . May I say how grateful the Navy will be for all the great work you have done and also I would like to wish your successor the very best of good fortune in the difficult tasks which lie ahead.

One has differences with the Admiralty from time to time (far fewer I think than when you were afloat!!) but they are bound to arise from the difference of outlook of those far away giving an order and those on the spot having to execute the order. The sailors are behaving remarkably well principally because (a) we have been able to keep them busy on worthwhile jobs; (b) the success of the A and SG scheme; and (c) the occasional relaxation in the bright lights of Sydney and the better climate.[1] . . . For myself I reckon my job here is done and I told the First Lord that I would much like to leave about April and if as a last privilege I could come home in the *Duke of York* it would be giving me great pleasure.

501. *To Fraser*

c.7 March 1946

3. *Commitments*

. . . I consider it important, anyway for the immediate future, to maintain as strong Naval forces as practicable in the Western Pacific and to make an adequate show of force in Japanese and Korean waters. The Foreign Secretary has supported me strongly in this view.[2] We must do all we can to counter the impression held in some quarters that we tacitly admit the right of America to claim over-riding interest in, and probably responsibility for, affairs, commercial and political, in the Western Pacific. This is necessary in order not only to foster our considerable commercial interests in China, which are so dependent on our prestige with the Chinese who set much store by a display of strength, but also to maintain our prestige with the Australians who count themselves a Pacific power. Moreover, the Australian sense of Commonwealth unity would best be encouraged by the realisation that we are not abandoning to the Americans overall responsibility in the Western Pacific.

[1]A & SG Scheme: unknown.
[2]Ernest Bevin.

Bases

... With regard to Singapore, there is a great deal to be said on strategic grounds for restricting its use to the support of cruisers and below and for using Australia and New Zealand as the 'solid background' for Fleet operations and resources. ...

SECTION H

THE POST-WAR NAVY

MAY 1943–MAY 1946

Being First Sea Lord was uncongenial to Cunningham, for he was primarily a seaman, an admiral who led from the front in classic line-of-battle actions. It is true that he had adapted well to shore-based command during the Mediterranean expeditions of 1942–43 (in which much of his travelling was done by air), but he had a rooted distaste for the desk-bound job at the top of the Admiralty. Even less acceptable was the task of whittling down the post-war fleet from the huge establishment of war time, but the issue was inescapable and urgent. Cunningham, forever a man of duty, would not retire from the First Sea Lord's post until he had reshaped the post-war fleet.

For the most part he had conventional ideas. The advances in nuclear weapons and rocket science did not affect his thinking – unsurprisingly because, although both rockets and atomic bombs had given dire warning of their destructive effect, their eventual implications were still unclear and demanded further experiments, like the one at Bikini atoll in 1946, and rocketry depended on capturing a raft of German scientists and persuading them to work on the West's behalf [508]. The Russians were equally keen to get their hands on them and, as has been seen, there was a 'great game' to acquire U-boat scientists and materials.[1]

Cunningham, along with most naval officers, thought in terms of a large Imperial fleet, directed from the Admiralty, consisting of a variety of types yet with few concessions to modern advances. Cunningham's concern for the types of destroyer he had commanded since 1911 and the actions he recalled from the early days of the war in the Mediterranean led him to an early expression of disgust at the proposed design for the 'Battle' class destroyers. They were state-of-the-art ships, intended for Pacific service and packed with instruments and short-range AA weapons. Though they had a conventional outfit of torpedo tubes, they had only four 4.5in guns, on a displacement about twice that of pre-war destroyers. In Cunningham's view, they were less handy and suitable for the sort of encounters common in the Mediterranean in 1940–42. Moreover, the Admiralty seemed to have neglected another

[1]See Nos. 328, 330, 332–5.

form of destroyer, which Cunningham had championed in 1938 and which he had used widely as C-in-C, Mediterranean – the 'Hunt' class of escort destroyers [502, 529].[1]

He was equally attached to battleships and had subordinates refute Cherwell's claims that the bomber had put paid to dreadnoughts – though he had felt at first that *Vanguard* was a waste of resources [506, 517–18, 521, 523, 526].[2] Proposals for the post-war fleet initially were expansive, with large and small cruisers prominent, with conventional broadside armaments but enhanced AA weaponry [502, 504–7, 512, 514–16, 519, 521, 523, 525–6, 529]. Capital ships dating from pre-war days were scheduled for modernisation [503, 510, 512]. Reality soon curbed these dreams, however, and it was decided to complete only ships that could fight in the war or be completed in 1946 [515, 519]. By the end of the war in August 1945, the pressures of inadequate man-power and shortage of money forced the post-war fleet to be scaled down successively, and the Army and RAF claimed greater shares of the pared-down defence budget and scarce manpower than before the war [514, 524–5, 527]. After initial scepticism, Cunningham came to see that the Royal Navy would have to make its case for a reasonable share of both money and men and women [513–14, 520].

The international position in 1945 was as threatening as it had been in 1939, the Soviet Union, a war-time ally, rapidly replacing Nazi Germany as the main potential enemy, a development which the COS saw much more quickly than many politicians. At the same time, Brit-ain's capacity to defend itself and its Empire was greatly reduced. Cunningham was much exercised in re-orienting the Royal Navy to face the Soviet threat, though much of the defence in the new Cold War had to be on the ground in Germany or by airborne nuclear weapons. He became aware of the financial, resource and manpower constraints on Imperial security and his answer, like most senior Royal Navy officers, was to ask Commonwealth countries to shoulder more of the burden, at least locally, while remaining under the Admiralty umbrella. This was a pious hope, for those countries were now much more identi-fied with the United States, had developed their own independent sentiments, sought to rein in their outlay on finance and manpower and remained immune to Admiralty requests [509, 511, 525, 528, 530].

In two respects, the Royal Marines and the Fleet Air Arm, Cunningham was very forward-looking. As a result of his experience with the United

---

[1]There were several sub-types but they all displaced 1000–1175t, made 26–28k, carried 4–6×4in, and some had 2–3×21in tt. There were 86 in all, completed 1939–43.
[2]*Vanguard*: b/ship, 1946, 44900t, 30k, 8×15in, 16×5.25in.

States Corps of Marines, he was adamant that the Royal Marines should have a sharper focus in post-war years. They should reposition themselves as the cutting edge of Britain's amphibious forces. This had two parents – the wish to see an end to 'private navies' (Combined Operations, unloved by most of the Royal Navy's hierarchy), and the desire to find a role for the Royal Marines, which had become somewhat vague in the two World Wars [531–4].

The question of air power in the post-war fleet was one on which Cunningham had definite views. In 1943 he had been characterised by Churchill as a dinosaur, unappreciative of air power at sea. That might have been true before his introduction to carrier aviation in 1935, but in the fleet exercises of that year he had become aware of its power and potential. In the Mediterranean in 1940–43, he had made optimum use of the naval aviation at his disposal. He became convinced that the Fleet Air Arm would become the spearhead of the post-war fleet, though it needed to be reminded of its naval basis and shorn of its lengthy training, operational shortcomings and long supporting tail [507, 522, 535–47]. He was pragmatic about Coastal Command, for he was opposed to a long wrangle with the RAF over its actual ownership and was committed to Naval operational control over it, which would include shore-based air power on overseas stations [523, 526].

At the war's end, Cunningham resolved to oversee the trimming down of the great war-time fleet but once that was well underway by the spring of 1946, and assisted by a heart attack, he decided that the time had come to step down.

502.   *To the Admiralty*

Algiers,
31 May 1943

I am astonished that the name of 'Battle' Class should have been chosen for such under-gunned and defensively minded destroyers.

2.   I am unable to understand how it is that US designers are able to mount 8×5-inch HA/LA guns and eight torpedo tubes on a displacement of 1850 tons while we can only produce 4×4.5-inch, eight Bofors and eight tubes on a displacement which I understand will be 2300 tons. I can only assume that our British margins of safety in structural design are excessive.[1]

3.   It seems necessary to clear our minds as to the functions of Fleet Destroyers. In my opinion they are (A) to seek out and destroy enemy vessels of all types by gun, torpedo or A/S armament as the occasion requires. (B) To provide a screen for fleet units. (C) To have sufficient AA armament, speed and endurance to fulfil function (A) and (B) satisfactorily.

4.   A minimum suitable armament for such vessels should be (A) at least six dual purpose main armament guns of a calibre which approaches five inches as closely as is compatible with standard production and avoidance of yet another type of ammunition.

    (B)   at least six, preferably eight, torpedoes.

    (C)   as much simple close range armament as can be maintained consistent with (A) and (B).[2]

5.   Main gun armament considering the weight of 4.5-inch shell is superior to the old 4.7-inch and equivalent to American 5-inch [thus] our adoption of the 4.5-inch mounting is not the retrograde step it may appear. If considerations of production and the maximum fixed ammunition size which can conveniently be handled require this course, I consider this calibre acceptable and provided

    (A)   at least six guns are fitted.

    (B)   ammunition outfit is sufficient for prolonged operations.

---

[1]US destroyers of the 1930s and 1940s varied considerably in displacement and armament. The only ones which came near Cunningham's claim were the *Porter* class of 1936–7, which carried 8×5in on 1834t. The *Somers* class of 1937–8 had 8×5in on 2047t. Both classes lost two guns during the war, the *Somers* class proving top heavy. Other American destroyers of the period 1935–45 carried 4–6×5in on 1358–2616t.

[2]This sounds like the 'cover' for the 'J', 'K' & 'N' classes, with which Cunningham was familiar in the Mediterranean: 1760–1773t, 6×4.7in, 10×21in tt, completed 1939–42. The 'L' & 'M' classes were 1920–1935t, had 6×4.7in & 8×21in tt, but their guns were an improved mark.

6.   Torpedo armament. I fully appreciate the value of the torpedo in Pacific operations, but in spite of the possibilities of RDF control at night I am strongly opposed to long range bombardments by torpedo and I am not impressed by arguments about zone densities. The correct range to use the torpedo remains the closest range at which it will not miss. There may be a requirement for a proportion of the torpedo armament to be made to fire ahead, and the mounting of two tubes[,] possibly light close fitting mark 2 capable of this plus a quadruple mounting amidships[,] is worth investigating.

7.   Close range AA armament. All arguments of stopping and hitting power and range favour a weapon of the Bofors type but after bitter experience of power mountings of coastal craft in operation 'Retribu-tion' I am profoundly mistrustful of the complications in the Twin Bofors stabilized mountings. The only Mediterranean experience of this type was for a few weeks with *Isaac Sweers* when it appeared that the repair of any fault in this complicated mounting would be far beyond the capabilities of ship and flotilla staffs operating in the Pacific far from any dockyard. If the merits of the gun justify its acceptance the design must be kept simple and adequate spares to enable a complete bodily change of the whole power units will be necessary.

8.   In general I consider that in all these proposed designs defensive mindedness and extra gunnery complication have produced an escort vessel rather than a fleet destroyer.

9.   While on the subject of destroyer design I understand that any further building of 'Hunt' class destroyers has been abandoned even for replacements of ships sunk. I should have thought that this class had proved their worth beyond any argument more especially in confined waters such as the Mediterranean even though endurance and speed fall far short of what was promised and expected at their inception. I would suggest that it would be profitable to investigate as to whether with a small increase in tonnage the above mentioned shortcomings could not be overcome, a good design perpetuated and perhaps produce a more suitable vessel than what I understand to be the present design of medium destroyers.

503.   *To A. V. Alexander*

9 November 1943

4.   It is necessary to modernise all the four *King George V* Class battleships in addition to the *Rodney* and *Nelson*. Controller's proposals

for carrying out the modernisation of the *King George V* Class are on the attached diagram [not reproduced].[1]

5.   When the programme for the *King George V* Class has been settled, we shall be in a position to ask the US authorities whether they can help us with the *Nelson* and *Rodney*, but it is very improbable that they will be willing to undertake either ship.

6.   If *Rodney* is to continue in service a short refit is essential soon, but she cannot be taken in hand before the *King George V* Class are completed.

7. (a)   Every step has been taken to ensure that the calls of 'Overlord' are met. In making the calculations to ensure this, allowance has been made for the modernisation of the *King George V* Class.

(b)   The attached new plan for modernisation will involve only two of the *King George V* Class being taken in hand at a time. I shall be surprised if the *Tirpitz* is repaired in under six months.

(c)   The difficulty which the Director of Dockyards has to contend with is too many ships and too few men, so he has made suggestions to the Controller giving his views as to where the additional ships can be taken in hand. The Controller, having additional information available so that he can judge future problems, makes the decision whether the Director of Dockyards' suggestions must be adopted.

To stop new construction would not provide the type of labour required for modernisation work.

(d)   Our refitting resources are so stretched that the only possibility of refits at present is for ships which are damaged. If they are in hand for that reason long enough, modernisation may be put in hand.

504.   *Diary*

10 April 1944

. . . Drove to Chequers with the Controller for a meeting about the 1944 programme and the Fleet Train.

Agreement reached on the whole. Every item of the 1944 building programme came under heavy fire but was finally accepted. . . .

---

[1]Adm Wake-Walker.

505. *Diary*

21 April 1944

... A very interesting Sea Lords' meeting on subjects dealt with during the last month. After the Controller produced plans of the projected heavy cruiser we all plumped for the big one about 14,000 tons, 12×6-inch main armament, 12×4.5-inch HAA, 10 twin Bofors and innumerable Oerlikons as LAA. A formidable ship but undoubtedly the criticism will be made that a ship of that tonnage should have larger guns but I think the 6-inch gun is right for the cruiser.[1] ...

506. *Diary*

18 May 1944

... Attended Cabinet meeting at 1640 subject this year's building programme. Some opposition to battleships (by S[ecretary] of S[tate] for Air and Lord Cherwell – only to be expected).[2] The PM carried the whole thing through on his own. He is very sound on the battleship question and had evidently been reading the Staff memorandum on the post-war fleet. Anyway the programme went through.

507. *Diary*

19 May 1944

... Meeting with the Sea Lords, Secretary and DCSR. ... discussed the Air Branch demand that the new carriers should be redesigned to allow of the whole number of aircraft to be flown off in one flight. Result will be at least six months delay in laying down. There is no doubt the air staff made a mess of it in not pressing for this nine months ago. The difference is in having an open hangar or closed ditto. The former means that the strength deck is the floor of the hangar and the hangar just a box built on top of it. The latter has no armoured deck as the top or flight deck. We decided to accept the delay and have the more up-to-date article.[3]

---

[1]This cruiser never got beyond this stage. See E. J. Grove, *From Vanguard to Trident: British Naval Policy since World War II* (London, 1987).

[2]Sir Archibald Sinclair.

[3]Ironically, the British adopted the American fashion for unarmoured flight decks in the interest of stowing more a/c, while the US Navy embraced the armoured flight deck in consequence of the better experience of British carriers in dealing with *kamikazes*.

508. *Diary*

10 July 1944

... Dr Goodeve the research and development expert came and told me about future developments. There is some chance of a rocket-type projectile which will home on to a plane. Also several new types of propulsion for warships are under investigation.[1] ...

509. *Diary*

26 July 1944

COS meeting at 1100. Long and interesting discussion on security of the British Isles in the post-war world. It became clear that if sufficient defence in depth was to be obtained the whole or part of Germany would have to be in any organisation or union of the Western powers. The treatment of Germany in the immediate post-war years would thus have to be related to the ultimate aim of including her in the Western powers' organisation. This should be taken into consideration in the policy of partition or non-partition. It was generally agreed that Russia would be the only danger in the foreseeable future.

510. *Diary*

11 August 1944

... Much discussion on the future of *Nelson*. *Valiant* looks to be permanently out of it and would take two years to repair. King has also let us down over the modernisation of *Nelson*. We decided to bring her home after repair and she can go as full back to the Home Fleet while the German war goes on.[2]

---

[1]Dr (Sir) Charles Goodeve (1904–80): b Canada; chemistry, metals; Cdr, RNVR, ret; DD Dept of Misc Weapon Dev 1940–2; D Cntrlr (R & D) 1942–5.
[2]*Nelson* & *Valiant* served with EIF 1944; *Valiant* was irreparably damaged by the collapse of a dry dock; *Nelson* suffered from mine damage.

511. *Diary*

4 October 1944

... Portal, Ismay and I met the Foreign Secretary at 1600. Orme Seargeant there. We had taken exception to the Foreign Secretary saying, in his paper on the dismemberment of Germany, that the COS must not consider Russia as a possible enemy. Such an ostrich-like attitude. One can't close one's eyes and by not thinking of it remove the potential danger of a hostile Russia. The upshot was that he withdrew his paper, we rewrite ours and then he puts out another paper after seeing ours.[1] ...

512. *Diary*

6 October 1944

... Sea Lords' meeting ... We then had a useful discussion on small cruisers and how to get greater efficiency on a smaller tonnage. Discussion also on refitting and modernising ships. The general idea had been that the technicians were having too much of their own way in laying up ships for long periods to fit the latest gadgets. Had a talk with Markham about the shortcomings of our construction branch.[2]

513. *Diary*

27 October 1944

... Had a meeting with the Parliamentary Secretary Bruntisfield, Markham and Willis on the subject of publicity. We came to little decision but thought it would be wise to consult a prominent press man about naval publicity and also to get an organisation going now for the publicity of the eastern war. Bruntisfield said it would take about 80 officers. Well they must be found.[3] ...

---

[1]FS: Eden.
   Sir Orme Sargent (1884–1962): FO 1906; Paris, Bern, FO, Versailles 1914–19; C Dept, FO 1926; Asst US Aug 1933; DUS Sept 1939; Permnt US Feb 1946; ret Feb 1949.
   [2]H. V. Markham (1897–1946): RGA, W Front; Ady 1921; PPS to FL 1936–8; PS 1940–6.
   [3]Lord Bruntisfield was Parl Secy, Ady.

514. *Diary*

10 November 1944

. . .Sea Lords' meeting at 1600. Long discussion about building a monster carrier. Decided to seek more information before deciding. Publicity also discussed. Manpower, etc., etc.

515. *Diary*

22 November 1944

. . . Discussion on proposal by Controller and CSMR to slow down and even cancel warship building. I pointed out certain disadvantages to the post-war fleet and perhaps to the conduct of the Japanese war.[1] . . .

516. *Diary*

24 November 1944

. . . Sea Lords' meeting. Discussed design of new big cruiser. All Sea Lords except Patterson agreed to the design.[2] . . . Also provision of small harbour craft for the Pacific and manpower. . . .

517. *Diary*

27 November 1944

Cabinet at 1830. Before going in Cherwell told me that he had just written a letter or paper on the subject of the impossibility of the survival of the battleship against bombing. I pointed out that he had written much the same before this war!! . . .

518. *Diary*

30 November 1944

[To Glasgow for the launching of the *Vanguard*].
. . . At noon left for John Brown's shipyard. . . . The *Vanguard* looked mighty impressive with her raked up bow. . . . After a short service the

---

[1]CSMR: Controller of Shipbuilding Maintenance & Repair: Sir James Lithgow (1883–1952): s/bldr; RGA 1914–19; Dir S/bldg Prodn 1917; CSMR 1940–6.
[2]VAdm Wilfrid Patterson: ACNS (Weapons) March 1943–Feb 1945.

launch was performed. Everything went very smoothly and after the tremor the great ship slid quietly into the river being brought up gently by the chains and wire pendants. Though a foul overcast day as she took the water and made her curtsey the sun broke through and lit her up. A good omen and an impressive sight. . . .

519. *Diary*

23 February 1945

. . . Board meeting at 1530. Discussion on future constructional programme. General aim to press on with all ships that can be in commission by end of 1946 and space out the construction of others already approved so as to allow of increased building of merchant vessels and also in the lean years following the war to keep the industry going.

520. *COS Minutes*

25 February 1945

COS 31: Service Newspapers

[Admiral Cunningham thought the] quality and type of contributions . . . left a great deal to be desired . . . [and] suggested that the regulations governing such contributions should be so framed to prevent irresponsible or undesirable articles.

521. *Diary*

28 February 1945

. . . Sea Lords' meeting at 1700. . . . Discussed size of carriers. Final decision to build X1 about same as *Hood* on waterlines. 41,000 tons.[1] Then discussed the reply to Cherwell's blast against battleships. . . . decided that Captains Parham and Dick would set about it and write the reply from the three drafts already in hand.[2]
    Second Sea Lord again stressed the manpower situation.[3]

[1]*Hood*: b/csr, 1920, 46680t, 31k, 8×15in, 12×5.5in, 8×4in. The carriers were either *Eagle* & *Ark Royal* (1951, 1955, 36800t, 32k, 16×4.5in, 78 a/c), or the *Malta* class (4 ships, never laid down; 46900t, 32.5k, 16×4.5in, 81 a/c).
[2]Capt F. R. Parham: Cdr June 1934; *Gurkha* Dec 1938; DD, NOD March 1940; *Belfast* Sept 1942; DOD (F) Aug 1944.
[3]Adm Willis.

522.   *Churchill to A. V. Alexander*

10 March 1945

You must realise that after the war the Air will take over a large part of the duties hitherto discharged by the RN.

523.   *Diary*

13 March 1945

. . . Meeting with the Sea Lords and others at 1715 to examine Captains Parham and Dick's memorandum on battleships in reply to the Paymaster General.[1] Approved with some minor amendments. Further considered a paper put forward by Plans Division on the Post-War Fleet and Organisation. Distributed the work.

It was gratifying to find general agreement about the attitude to be taken up by the Admiralty about the Coastal Command. Briefly the Admiralty should make no claim to have the Coastal Command turned over to the Navy. They should request that the same system should be extended to foreign stations, that they should have a voice in the training and that there should be some permanency in the Coastal Command personnel.

524.   *Minute by Cunningham*

27 March 1945

Growth of War Complements of Ships – Overcrowding

I fully concur with the Second Sea Lord. We have gone equipment mad. Some of the fault may be laid to the account of inflated staffs. . . .

His para. 8. Gideon chose his men more for their drinking habits than for what he knew about their morale!

I suggest this would not be a good way of choosing a ship's company.

[1]Lord Cherwell.

525. *To Louis Hamilton*[1]

29 April 1945

... as a result of the war this country is no longer in a position either from the manpower or the financial point of view to undertake the major share in Empire defence, which we previously did. The lines on which our minds have been running are that the world must be divided into a number of strategic zones, comprising Home, Middle East, India, South East Asia, Australia and New Zealand, South Africa and Canada. The UK will presumably still have to undertake the defence of the first four, but it is our idea that each Dominion should undertake virtually the whole of the defence commitment for the area surrounding it and we feel it might not be too much to ask that they might bear some share in the zones contiguous to their own.

The commitment for the defence of a zone includes, in our opinion, the maintenance of facilities for the repair and logistic support of a major portion of the Commonwealth Navies, should it prove necessary for them to operate in that area. ... As regards the Fleet of each individual Dominion, ... in view of the importance of our sea communications it should clearly be of the greatest size possible and capable of rapid expansion in war. Further, to ensure that tactical doctrines are common, it is most necessary that the make-up of the Dominion Fleets should approximate in organisation to that of our own.

It appears desirable that Australia and New Zealand should work together in a common strategic zone ...

... the preliminary target should be in the order of two light fleet carriers, together with the necessary aircraft and reserve squadrons, three cruisers and 18 destroyers. ... I think that the squadron outlined above would be a very adequate operational unit, particularly if complemented and supported by a squadron from New Zealand of one light carrier, one cruiser and four destroyers ...

There are three *Majestic* Class which have been launched but which it is not intended to complete in the near future. It would probably be possible to transfer two of them to the Australians on loan, on the basis that they would pay for the remaining cost of completion.

As regards Cruisers, no post-war design has yet been finally evolved, the general trend of design being toward a ship of some 10,000 tons with a dual purpose armament of some 8–10 6-inch guns. The first of these is unlikely to take the sea before 1952 at the earliest. In the

[1]VAdm Louis Hamilton, 1st N Mem, Australian Commonwealth N Bd.

meantime it would appear desirable to go with what you already have, modernised as much as is required for training purposes.[1]

Destroyer design is at present equally uncertain. We want to recoil from the overgrown and under-armed 'Battle' to some more satisfactory type, but at present it appears well nigh impossible to fit in all the requirements of the various Staff Divisions into a hull of reasonable size. It would, however, be perfectly possible to transfer a flotilla of comfortably up to date destroyers to Australia without prejudice to the requirements of the RN.

526. *Diary*

1 June 1945

. . . Sea Lords' meeting at 1500.

Discussed design of smaller battleships. The fact is that our ports, docks, etc., will not allow our building of a ship bigger than about 45,000 tons.

Some debate about whether the constructors are putting enough into this suggested ship which will only mount six guns in two turrets. In fact we are down again to the doubt of [whether] our constructors are skilled enough. On the face of it the French and US ships are better than ours.

Discussion on the Coastal Command.

Two alternatives: (1) to go all out for the control of all maritime air craft and not only control but possession; (2) to accept present system of Admiralty operational control, administration by RAF. But under conditions. We must have a say in the training and the operational control must extend to foreign stations. All the Sea Lords are agreed on the second alternative. . . .

527. *COS: Provisional Personnel Requirements for Post-War Forces*

25 July 1945

Naval Establishment

7.   From preliminary appreciation of the numbers and types of ships and naval aircraft which will be required to fulfil the Royal Navy's

---

[1]The RNZN was loaned the cruisers *Bellona* (replaced by *Royalist*) & *Black Prince*. The RAN acquired the light fleet carriers *Melbourne* (ex-*Majestic*) & *Sydney* (ex-*Terrible*).

world-wide commitments in peace, it is estimated that a minimum of 170,000 long-service officers and ratings will be required, excluding any assistance by the Dominions and Colonies.

This estimate is an increase of 37,000 over the 1939 figure of 133,000. The principal reasons for this are:

(a)   The technical and scientific developments and the increased weight of air attack have brought about a considerable increase in the complements of ships, notably to man the radar warning equipment and the large number of AA weapons which are now so essential.

(b)   It will be necessary to maintain nucleus organisations for forces such as minesweeping and coastal forces which are now an integral part of the Fleet, and also a nucleus organisation to maintain the mobility of the Fleet, i.e., the Fleet Train.

(c)   Inter-Service co-operation must continue so the post-war Navy must include a nucleus of amphibious forces both for training and for development.

(d)   Carrier-borne air forces are fundamental to sea warfare and an integral part of the Royal Navy. A large proportion of the Navy's manpower must be devoted to this end. Besides the requirements of ship-borne aircraft, naval airfields must be maintained for flying training, and for the accommodation of disembarked aircraft.

The necessity for all these increases has been proved during the war, and it will be necessary to maintain organisations in peace to train personnel and to provide scope for technical progress.

If conscription continues into the peace years a further number of long-service officers and ratings will be required to train and administer the conscripts.

528.   *From Admiral Burrough*

British Naval Representative,
Germany,
25 February 1946

First of all I want you to know how happy I am at the prospect of going to The Nore.[1] I confess I shall not be sorry to leave this country with all its Quadripartite complications. The Field Marshal returned from Switzerland yesterday and I went over to see him this morning. As you

[1] Adm Burrough became C-in-C, The Nore, in 1946.

know I was Acting Commander-in-Chief for the three weeks of his absence, thanks to the firm stand I took over the Naval C-in-C's position over here. I considered it my duty to take the Field Marshal's position at the Control Council in Berlin, rather than leave it to Robertson.[1] The experience was very worthwhile and I think succeeded in maintaining the prestige of the Royal Navy *vis-à-vis* Zhukov, Koenig and Macnarney.[2] The Control Council meeting on 11 February was a tricky one and I had a fairly fierce duel with Zhukov, while that on 20 February was mainly concerned with signing laws. Robertson throughout has been most helpful and the soul of loyalty. We have had some repercussions over here of the Bevin-Vishinski duels at UNO and our Russian allies have been very sticky on the Naval side.[3] I was getting on very well (perhaps too well in their eyes) with Admiral Levchenko so they withdrew him on a plea of illness (or that is what I think) and sent Admiral Sibelnikov with orders to make demands and with no powers to negotiate.[4] I need not bother you with details but most of it concerns inaccuracies in the Red Book, which up to date they have refused to have corrected. Things reached such an impasse that I asked for an interview with Zhukov and last Thursday we did some straight talking for an hour and a half – after which he gave me a two-hour Russian lunch. It's difficult to gauge the reactions of a Crocodile whether you chuck it under the chin or stick pins into it, but I came away with the feeling that I had made a hole in some very thick ice! This morning I hear that Levchenko is returning, which I think is a good sign and they may at last drop their unco-operative attitude. . . .

[1]FM: Montgomery.
Gen Sir William Robertson (1896–1974): s of FM Sir W. Robertson, CIGS in WWI; RE 1914; France 1914–19; India; Staff Coll 1926–7; industry 1935–40; Abyssinia 1940; Brig (Admin), 8 Army; Lt Gen, Chief Admin O, Italy 1944; D Mil Govr, Germany 1945–7; C-in-C, Germany 1947–9; H Cmnr, Germany 1949–50; C-in-C ME Land Forces 1950; ret 1953.
[2]Mshl G. Zhukov, Soviet A: victor over Japanese, Outer Mongolia 1939; Moscow, Stalingrad; D Sup Cdr Aug 1942; victor of Kursk 1943; occupied Berlin 1945; head of Soviet forces in occupied Germany.
Gen Koenig, Fr A: Cmdg Fr occupation forces.
Gen Joseph Macnarney, US Army: Air Corps; DCoS 1942–5; Cmdr US occupation forces.
[3]M. Vishinsky: Soviet Ambassador to UN.
[4]Adm Levchenko (1897–1981) Soviet N: ent N 1918; CO. destroyers, *Aurora* 1929–31; cdr Baltic F 1938–9; cded Leningrad, Kronstadt; cdr S Baltic F 1946–7; DC-in-C 1947–50, 1956–8; VAdm Sibelnikov (1902–52), Soviet N: ent N 1921; s/m 1925–37; chf N Div, Sov Mil Admin, Germany, 1946–7.

529. *Diary*

18 March 1946

... These 'Battles' fulfil my worst anticipations. An erection like the Castle Rock, Edinburgh, on the bridge they call a director all to control four guns firing a total weight of about 200 lbs.

We must get back to a reasonably sized destroyer well-gunned.

530. *From Admiral Willis*

Office of the C-in-C, Mediterranean,
Malta,
8 May 1946

I have just returned from the Eastern Mediterranean and you may be glad to have my impression of the goings on in Cairo. I found when I got there that the Cabinet had accepted the 'clear out as a gesture policy' and I must confess after talking to everyone I came to the conclusion that this is the only thing to do. Not only because of the loss of goodwill and the flare up if we don't, but because in the estimation of the Army there aren't enough British troops to deal with the resulting situation. . . .

3.   However, I'm not so pessimistic about the eventual outcome because I'm quite sure the reasonable Egyptians don't want us to withdraw altogether and if only the Army can clear Cairo and Alexandria of troops and Union Jacks or most of them, I believe the atmosphere will improve greatly. Then it's quite on the cards that they might let us keep a footing in the Canal Area. Anyway I think we should keep a small Naval organisation going in Navy House at Port Said for as long as we possibly can and this I understand conforms with Admiralty Policy.

4.   I paid short visits to Alexandria and Port Said. We shall be practically clear of the former next month and I have had the process speeded up a bit. . . .

The Royal Marines

531. *Diary*

21 July 1944

. . . CCO Laycock came in to see me about the Admiralty comments on the report of the future of the amphibious warfare organisation.[1] The Admiralty do not wish to perpetuate the present system and contrary to the committee's opinion want the whole question re-examined after the war. I am not sure that this is not a wise suggestion.

532. *COS 132: Memorandum by First Sea Lord*

22 July 1944

In the Admiralty view the present system of responsibility for the command of amphibious warfare has the inherent defect that advice to the COS is divorced from the provision of personnel and material, and indeed from the planning and execution of operations, all of which must lie with the Service Ministries. A comparison can be made with the Joint Planning organisation, which in effect performs similar functions to the Combined Operations HQ, but in which the members of the JPS remain a part of their own Ministries and have the weight of Ministries' operational and technical staffs behind them. Combined Operations are not a black art, in fact they are normal operations of war, and it is felt that their conduct should be governed by similar principles. The Admiralty considers, therefore, that the present system is not the best that it is possible to evolve, and do not agree that it should be perpetuated in its present form. No major change in the organisation is, however, advocated at the present time, when changes not vital to the prosecution of the war are to be deprecated, and since under existing war conditions, the CCO and the Service Ministries are making it work in a satisfactory manner.

2. . . . the Admiralty considers the responsibility vested in CCO should be that of advice to the COS on policy, etc., and that the organisation should be as closely as possible related to the three Service Ministries. . . .

3. In particular, the new directive appears to endow DCOs abroad with an undesirable degree of independence.[2] Their main duty must be to advise their C-in-C, and to act only with his approval.

[1] Gen Sir Robert Laycock.
[2] DCOs were Dirs of Combined Ops.

4.   The Committee's broad recommendations as to the part to be played by the Royal Marines in the inter-Service organisation are considered satisfactory. . . .

533.   *COS 133: Inter-Service Responsibility for Amphibious Warfare*

24 July 1944

2.   This memorandum [no. 132, above] recommends that after the war an Inter-Service Committee should be charged with the responsibility for seeing that our amphibious technique and requirements remain up-to-date and sufficient. . . . Past experience suggests that where normal Service requirements conflict with amphibious requirements, there is a tendency for the latter to be curtailed in favour of the former. In the post-war period, when there are bound to be severe limitations in manpower and finance, there is likely to be an increased tendency for each Service to concentrate on its own immediate and evident requirements;
. . .

3.   . . . I am doubtful whether in peace an Inter-Service Committee, representing as it would the views of the three Service Ministries, would be able to watch the interests of amphibious preparations as impartially as an independent organisation.

4.   Nor do I think that it will be easy for a small Committee to formulate policy for and in some cases administer, the Combined Operations Establishments or Units. . . .

6.   The Admiralty does not consider that it is either necessary or desirable to come to a decision now as regards the future organisation responsible for amphibious warfare. I would suggest that there are considerable advantages in reaching a broad decision at a time when the importance of amphibious operations is evident and the matter can be viewed impartially, rather than at a later date when the need for amphibious preparedness is less evident, and when, owing to post-war economies, normal Service requirements are likely to take precedence.

7.   . . . it would be demanding a Utopian degree of impartiality if we adopted a system which, if it is to work, relies on the voluntary acceptance of considerable sacrifices and inconveniences by an individual Service for the good of a combined technique.

534.   *To Major General Laycock*

6 March 1945

... the Royal Marines should provide the basic elements of the three Beach Brigades required for the war against Japan, and should man those amphibians which are employed in support, assault and build-up roles, including amphibians employed in connection with Beach Brigades. ...

The Fleet Air Arm

535.   *From Vice Admiral Boyd*[1]

6 November 1943

... It is true to say that there are very few Members of the Board who can talk aviation to any Air Marshal, and they are therefore under the impression ... that we are not 'air minded'. My answer is that few Air Marshals have been so intimately connected with air warfare as those Admirals who have served at sea during this war with inadequate air cover and that if we are not air minded, then nobody is. ...

I have very few first-class brains on whom I can call to do anything. The FAA consists entirely of junior Lieutenants, a smattering of very good Commanders, one or two very good Captains and the rest are rather deadbeats. All the real cream were expended in the first two years of the war.[2]

536.   *Diary*

12 July 1944

... Lyster came to see me and we talked of carriers and fishing.[3] As I thought our FAA pilots are getting contaminated by the RAF and want leave after so many operational hours. And I suppose a carrier with a crew of 1500 lies idle while these temperamental young men go on leave. ...

---

[1]5SL: VAdm Boyd.
[2]Notably Capt Caspar John, later a FSL.
[3]Adm Sir Lumley Lyster.

537. *Diary*

25 July 1944

. . . Boyd came to see me and we had a most useful talk. He brought models of the next Firebrand, the improved *ditto* and the Seafire XV. The improved Firebrand [is] a single seater, torpedo plane, looks a beautiful machine but we shall not get it for two years and in one year we shall get the 1st Firebrand, good but awkward looking.[1]

Discussed fitting fleet carriers with Avengers in lieu of Barracudas, paying off of escort carriers to provide men for light fleets, personnel and their vagaries. It appears that the preliminary training given to our lads by the RAF though good in itself does not instil discipline or naval ideas. . . .

538. *Diary*

18 October 1944

Drove to Heath Row aerodrome and embarked in an FAA Hudson. Landed at Inskip at 1100. This station is devoted to A/S and torpedo training and we saw Avengers landing and taking off every minute. I liked the look of the Avengers. Saw also a Seafire take off rocket assisted.

Had lunch and afterwards looked at Wrens' and sailors' quarters. Then talked to young pilots in the cinema. Took as my text that the Navy looked on them as an important part of the Service and they must also remember that they belong. Heath the CO appears a good man.[2]

Next flew to Hinstock. The CO an RNVR Commander called Pugh, formerly running an airline in the Singapore district. An enthusiast on blind, instrument flying to the instruction of which this station is devoted.[3] Saw countless planes – Oxfords – landing and taking off blind.[4] Pugh told me his crash rate was the lowest of any naval air station. There is no doubt he is doing good work. His aim is to enable pilots to fly on and off a carrier however thick the weather.

---

[1]Blackburn Firebrand: strike ftr, 1942; not in service till Sept 1945.

[2]Inskip: *Nightjar* (Preston, Lancs).

Cdr J. B. Heath: ret Dec 1936; A/CO, *Blackcap* (Stretton, Warrington, Lancs) Aug 1943; *Nightjar* May 1944.

[3]Hinstock: *Godwit* NAS, Mkt Drayton, Shropshire.

T/A/Capt (A) J. B. W. Pugh, RNVR: Lt (A) July 1940; 782 Sqdn *Merlin* Oct 1940; *Blackcap* Aug 1942; T/A/Cdr (A), CO *Godwit* June 1943; T/A/Capt (A), Jan 1945.

[4]Airspeed Oxford: trnr, 1937, 2×355hp, 182mph, 550m, 3 crew.

539. *Diary*

19 October 1944

. . . Had a long talk with MDG on the subject of FAA flying personnel. I put forward my view that the MO's duty was to keep them flying and not make reports that whole squadrons were suffering from operational fatigue and required leave. As a corollary the MDG's department and Naval Air Staff should lay down the number of hours flying to be undertaken by a squadron before being stood off. Of course nothing to prevent the medico from standing off pilots who are obviously unfit. I found the MDG much of my way of thinking and rather frightened of some of his young doctors.[1]

540. *Diary*

1 November 1944

. . . Boyd came in in the afternoon. He is alarmed about the way his supply of aircraft from USA has been cut down and about the suggestion that after the war each service must be responsible for its own supply. He thinks as regards aircraft this would be tantamount to handing us over to the Air Ministry.

541. *Diary*

6 December 1944

COS meeting at 1100. . . . Portal asked for five minutes' conversation at the end. His reason was to ask the Admiralty to withdraw their opposition to the Air Ministry taking over the design and production of all aircraft instead of MAP functioning.[2] He promised full guarantees that Navy interests would be looked after and proposed a meeting between Sinclair, First Lord, CAS and myself.

I had a talk on the subject with the First Lord after lunch. Hitherto he has taken up the attitude that the weapons users must control the production in the case of the Army and Navy but has reserved his

---

[1]MDG: Surgeon Adm Sir Sheldon Dudley (1884–1956): SCapt 1930; DMDG 1935–8; MO Chatham 1938–40; MDG 1941–5. The issue is discussed by A. H. Goddard, 'Operational Fatigue: The Air Branch of the Royal Navy's Experience during the Second World War', *The Mariner's Mirror* (Feb 2005), pp. 52–66.

[2]M Aircraft Prodn.

position in regard to the RAF. Boyd and Slattery came and saw me and most strongly urged that we should oppose aircraft production being taken from MAP.[1] Their arguments were impressive. Of course past experience must lead us to view with distaste the Navy again being dependent on the RAF for the design and production of their aircraft.

The question is: Is this a question for us to take sides or shall we gain by remaining neutral? I can't think that we could ever be brought to support the RAF contention but we could leave MAP and the Air Ministry to fight it out alone. Is this wise? Should we throw our weight on the side of the MAP from whom we get a square deal? Should we antagonise the RAF bitterly if we do with consequent evil influence on future difficulties? The truth is the Navy mistrusts deeply the RAF, with reason! But are we without sin? . . .

542. *Diary*

7 December 1944

. . . Had a further talk with Portal on the subject of post-war arrangements for the production of aircraft. I told him that though I could not commit the First Lord it was probable that the First Lord would not oppose the Air Ministry's claim to [become?] the authority for production. Although at first he was not too happy when I pointed out that he could not expect the First Lord to go completely contrary to his naval air advisors and directly support the Air Ministry he appeared to be content and said he thought the Air Secretary would be proposing a meeting. I think we are doing the right thing taking a long view. We do not want eternal friction between the services.

543. *To Fifth Sea Lord*

12 December 1944

I do not understand C-in-C, East Indies' 111343Z [not reproduced].[2] *Indefatigable* has been in commission some six months, has carried out operations on the Norwegian coast. Her Avengers have been on board some months.

---

[1]RAdm Sir Matthew Slattery (1902–90): ent RN 1916; Capt Dec 1938; Dir Air Matl Oct 1940; *Cleopatra* June 1941; Dir Gen, N A/c Eqpt Dev & Prodn, M Prodn, & Chief N Reprv 1943; V Cntrlr (Air) & Chief N Air Eqpt 1945–8; aviation business 1948.
[2]VAdm Sir Arthur Power.

Why are a proportion of her Seafire pilots untrained?

Why are the Avenger squadrons not ready for operations?

Indefatigable was 10 weeks in dockyard hands, were the squadrons not given training during that period?

It appears that the NAA are now so occupied with training that they are seldom ready to operate.[1]

The position is most unsatisfactory.

544. *Diary*

6 March 1945

. . . Had a talk with Fifth Sea Lord and VCNS about alterations in the Admiralty organisation to meet the recommendations of the Evershed report. Both VCNS and I though we agree with some of them [the recommendations] were not inclined to swallow the whole report. The impression left on my mind was that he had taken too little evidence from non-air sources and that though his object was to integrate the air with the Navy very thoroughly his method tended to keep them apart. We called in Markham to help us and had a most useful discussion.[2] . . .

545. *Diary*

22 March 1945

. . . Meeting with the First Lord and others interested in the Evershed report as a preliminary to the Board meeting tomorrow. General agreement on several important matters of principle. Fifth Sea Lord will be mostly on the staff side. FONAS will be relieved by a FO (Air). The basic training of the young pilots must be taken from the RAF and done by the Navy. Some re-organisation on the material side which [will] make the Controller responsible for Air Material and make CNR a Deputy Controller under him.[3]

[1]NAA: Naval Air Arm was another title for FAA.
[2]VCNS: VAdm Syfret.
5SL: VAdm Boyd.
Lord Justice Evershed (1899–1966): RE 1918–19; bar 1928; Judge in Chancery 1944; Lord of Appeal 1947; Mr of Rolls 1949–62; Lord of Appeal in Ordinary 1962–5; he had reported on the future of the FAA in 1944 but Cunningham made little use of his recommendations.
[3]CNR: Chief N Reprv, M of A/c Prodn.

546. *Diary*

17 April 1945

. . . Settled the new appointments for the Naval Aviation with the First Lord. Boyd will become FO (Air), Troubridge Fifth Sea Lord and Mackintosh FO (Air Training).[1] We have to find a new ACNS (Air). Denny, Lambe or G. N. Oliver spring to the mind.[2] We must get some acute brains on to the Air side to withstand the attack of the Air Ministry that will surely come, and lead the counter-attack.

547. *Diary*

30 April 1945

. . . Boyd came in to say goodbye on relinquishing duties of Fifth Sea Lord. He has done a good job and now will have as FO (Air) better opportunities. I wonder whether Troubridge will make the grade. . . .

[1] RAdm L. D. Mackintosh: Capt June 1938; *President* (for 'Torch') Aug 1942; *Implacable* Oct 1943; ACNS (Air) Nov 1944; FO Air Trng.

[2] Adm Sir Michael Denny (1896–1972): ent RN 1909; m/s 1914; Capt 1936; DDN Ordc 1937–40; *Kenya* 1940–2; CoS Home F 1942–3; *Victory* 1944–5; RA 1945; DPS 1946–7; VA 1948; 3SL 1949–53; Adm 1952; C-in-C Home F 1954–5.

SECTION I

SUNSET RETREAT:

RETIREMENT AND SUCCESSION
MAY 1945–JUNE 1946

With the end of the Far Eastern war in August 1945, like other service chiefs in Britain and America, Cunningham felt his job was done. After putting the Royal Navy in reasonably good shape for the post-war years, he looked forward to retirement. He was acutely conscious of not blocking the promotion of other men, having had nearly half a century of very satisfying service life. He experienced a psychological exhaustion once the guns fell silent, he and his wife were troubled by depression, and wartime strain in high positions told in a severe heart attack early in 1946 and he was hospitalised in Haslar for several weeks [548, 552].[1] Rather against his wishes, he was created a Viscount in the New Year's Honours List of 1946 (he was concerned at the financial implications of the arms and the robes, and his natural modesty made him shy away from it). On 7 January 1946 he celebrated his 63rd birthday with the observation that the sea still called him [554–5].

Who should follow him? The possibilities included Bruce Fraser, who had been offered the post ahead of Cunningham in October 1943, Jack Tovey, who had been considered briefly at the same time, James Somerville, Cunningham's old term mate, and John Cunningham, for whose many talents Andrew Cunningham had a high regard. Andrew Cunningham canvassed several highly-placed military officers and the First Lord, Albert Alexander, re-installed in that office after Labour's massive win in the General Election of 1945. All of those mentioned in his diary – his colleagues on the COS [Brooke and Portal], Jack Tovey at The Nore, Geoffrey Blake, liaison officer with the US Naval forces in London, and Alexander – plumped for John Cunningham and the Prime Minister, Clement Attlee, readily agreed [548, 550–1, 553–4, 556]. Bruce Fraser, so widely touted in 1943, had exasperated Cunningham by his constant complaints and wilfulness, both as C-in-C, Home Fleet, and as C-in-C, British Pacific Fleet. Both Cunningham and Alexander thought his judgment suspect and that he needed further experience as C-in-C of a home port before acceding to the highest post [550].[2]

[1]Haslar RN Hospital, Portsmouth.
[2]Fraser served as FSL 1948–51. Blake might well have been First Sea Lord in place of Cunningham if his poor health had not forced his retirement in 1938.

At the end of May 1946 Cunningham drew the curtains on a naval career embracing nearly half a century of vivid memories, exciting actions, much humdrum steaming, grand strategy and finally the leadership of the Royal Navy. He was celebrated, justly, as Britain's outstanding sailor of the Second World War and one of the greatest the country has ever produced. Most of his glory resulted from the brief period June 1940 to March 1942, when he led the Mediterranean Fleet, but, as this collection of his papers has tried to show, he deserves much praise and admiration for his leadership in the period June 1942 to May 1946. In those years he impressed the Americans (even Ernie King!), worked selflessly under a junior and very green Supreme Commander, Eisenhower, in 'his' sea, the Mediterranean, and toiled conscientiously as First Sea Lord for nearly three years, steering the Royal Navy and its allies in other services and countries to eventual victory.

His memorandum on 'The Organisation of Command' appears to have been written in the spring of 1946, a sort of parting broadside on a matter on which, clearly, he had strong feelings. He opted for a triumvirate of the three services, reflecting his own happy experience with Wavell and Longmore in the Middle East in 1940–41.[1] With a single nation involved, he thought a supreme commander superfluous but conceded, somewhat reluctantly, that with allies, one was probably necessary. He was going against the trend, but he made a last-ditch stand on behalf of the committee system, applying the pragmatic test of efficiency, underpinned by his characteristic consideration for others [558].

It was a weary and ailing Cunningham who retreated to his 'little house in the country', the Palace House at Bishop's Waltham, which he and Lady Cunningham had acquired before the war. Even after they moved in as permanent residents in late 1943, the war prevented them from really enjoying the experience. It was, therefore, with much anticipation that he and Nona went to their home, near Portsmouth, in June 1946. They had a very busy retirement. Nona was active in the local church, while the new Viscount attended the House of Lords from time to time, lent his name occasionally to press statements about the Royal Navy (drafted for him by Stephen Roskill, author of the official histories), busied himself with duties as various (and as enjoyable) as Lord High Commissioner to the Church of Scotland's annual assembly

[1]ACM Sir Arthur Longmore (1895–1970): b Australia; ent RN 1900; pilot 1910; CO, 1 Sqdn, RNAS Dunkirk 1914; Lt Cdr, *Tiger*, Jutland 1916; i/c air ops, Med F 1918; RAF 1918; Grp Capt, Iraq 1923; Cdt Cranwell; AM & Cdt, IDC 1933; C-in-C, Trng Cmd 1939; AOC-in-C ME 1939–41; Inspr Gen 1941–2; ret 1942. See his *From Sea to Sky* (London, 1946).

in 1950 and 1952, the naval pipers, the Royal College of Naval Constructors, chairing the Trustees of the Imperial War Museum, and carrying
the crown at the Queen's Coronation in 1953.[1] He was especially active
in seeking justice for his old acquaintance from Mediterranean days,
Admiral Sir Dudley North, controversially dismissed from his command at Gibraltar in late 1940. In this he was joined by most of the
surviving Admirals of the Fleet, headed by Lord Chatfield. They secured a partial vindication for North in 1957.[2] Cunningham, never one
to seek publicity, was prevailed on to write his memoirs, *A Sailor's
Odyssey*, standing writing diligently at an old-fashioned desk for two
hours every morning for two years. They were polished by his old
friend from destroyer days, Captain Taprell Dorling – 'Taffrail'.[3]

Cunningham and his wife enjoyed their extensive garden, entertained
family and friends (including his wife's three nephews, the Byatt broth-
ers, and his own great-nephew by marriage, Jock Slater, a junior officer
at the time but later also a First Sea Lord), along with naval colleagues.[4] It was reputed that the Admiral played a mean game of
croquet and manoeuvred the resident flock of geese like a destroyer
flotilla. After a very full life, of which the Service and the nation can
feel proud and for which they can be grateful, he fell asleep on 12 June
1963, aged 80.[5]

---

[1]Capt S. W. Roskill (1903–82): tec expert; served in Ady, BAD & CO *Leander*
(RNZN); author, *The War at Sea*, 3 vols (London, 1954–61); founder, Churchill Archives Centre & Fellow of Churchill College, Cambridge.

[2]Adm Sir Dudley North (1881–1961): ent RN 1896; Lt 1903; Heligoland 1914; Cdr
1915; Dogger Bank 1915; Jutland 1916; Capt 1919; 'C' cl csrs 1922–4; R tours; FCapt,
Atl & Rsv F's; DOD 1930; RA & CoS to Adm Sir J. Kelly, Home F 1932; Cmd R Yachts
1936; VA 1936; FOC, N Atl, Gibraltar Nov 1939–Nov 1940; Ret; Home Guard; RA (ret)
& FO Yarmouth 1943; Adm Cmdg R Yachts 1946–7.

AoF Lord (Sir Ernle) Chatfield (1873–1967): ent RN 1886; FCapt, *Lion*, Jutland 1916;
RA & 4SL 1919; C-in-C Atl & Med F's 1929–32; FSL 1933–8; M for Co-ordn Dfc 1939–
40. See E. J. Grove, 'Admiral Sir Ernle Chatfield', in M. H. Murfett (ed.), *The First Sea
Lords: From Fisher to Mountbatten* (London & Westport, CT, 1995), pp. 157–71.

The other AoF's were the two Cunninghams, Lord Cork & Sir A. Willis. Fraser, who
had been a member of the Board of Admiralty in 1940 as 3SL, declined to serve. AoF
Lord Mountbatten was still serving as Chief of the Defence Staff. Somerville, who
would have been outspoken and vigorous about the whole sorry affair, had died in 1949.
See M. A. Simpson (ed.), *The Somerville Papers*, pp. 47–51, 142–66.

[3]Capt Taprell Dorling ('Taffrail') (1883–1968): ent RN 1897; S Af, China; destroyer
cmds 1914–18; ret 1929; M of Info 1939–42, on ships; staff of C-in-C Med Dec 1942–5;
b/caster, N correspdt.

[4]Now Sir Hugh (a former Lt RNVR), Mr Robin and Mr David Byatt. Admiral Sir Jock
Slater was from the Edinburgh 'heartland' of the Cunningham clan.

[5]There is a bust of Cunningham in Trafalgar Square, by Franta Belsky, unveiled by AoF
HRH Prince Philip, Duke of Edinburgh, in the presence of Lady Cunningham and many of
Cunningham's old associates, on 2 April 1967. There is also a tablet in St Paul's Cathedral
and one in *Britannia* RNC; *Warspite's* Battle Ensign hangs in St Giles, Edinburgh.

548. *Diary*

5 July 1945

... curious that he [Geoffrey Blake] agrees with me that John Cunningham would make a better First Sea Lord than Bruce Fraser.

549. *Diary*

10 August 1945

... I have now my own position to consider. I do not wish to hang on here keeping other people back so as soon as the fleet gets a bit sorted out I will go. My relief requires thought.

550. *Diary*

14 August 1945

... Discussed future appointments with the First Lord. He seemed to agree that someone to come here as my relief before Fraser was desirable. I suggested James Somerville or John Cunningham and to my surprise found he was favourable to the latter.

551. *Diary*

23 August 1945

... I had told the First Lord that I wish to go between January and June [1946]. Admiralty candidates are James Somerville, Jack Tovey, John Cunningham and Bruce Fraser and that I favoured John Cunningham. Both Portal and Brooke also seemed to welcome the idea of John [Cunningham].

552. *Diary*

3 November 1945

... I find myself that I have to fight depression all the time. ...

553. *Diary*

6 December 1945

. . . [When] I asked him [Tovey] who should succeed me without hesitation he said John Cunningham.

554. *Diary*

1 January 1946

Well we start the new year as a Viscount.
   I recommended John Cunningham . . . he [A. V. Alexander] consented. . . .
   First Lord came in in the evening and told me that the PM had consented to John Cunningham. . . . Fraser and Jack Tovey barons. . . .

555. *Diary*

7 January 1946

. . . 63 today!! Well I don't feel like it though I am a bit tired of this desk work. I always feel I could go to sea again. . . .

556. *From John Cunningham*

18 January 1946

. . . Thank you for your advance information about my future – it is very flattering and I know very well who I have to thank for it – and do. . . .

557. *To Aunt Connie May*

The Palace House,
Bishop's Waltham,
17 June 1946

. . . I turned over the Admiralty to John Cunningham next morning and we came down here . . . and glad to come.[1]

---

[1]Aunt Doodles had died.

558. *The Organisation of Command*

Spring 1946

In this war we have used two main systems of command.

(i)   The Triumvirate, that is with the C's-in-C of the three Services working together;

(ii)   A Supreme Commander appointed over the C's-in-C of the three Services.

The Triumvirate

This worked well in the Middle East up to a point, though at the beginning of the war in the Mediterranean there was no sign that any of the three C's-in-C fully understood each other's problems. I think that the Navy had a fairly good idea of what the Army was trying to do; I looked at the Desert Campaign as essential to knock out the Italian bomber bases and push these further away from Alexandria and so assist in the supply of Malta; but I do not think the Army had any idea, at the start, of the Navy's problems and did not even know how their bread and butter arrived.

When Wavell undertook his first advance he had no idea of how the Navy could help him, and I had to force Naval assistance, such as battleship bombardments of Bardia, on him. So it cannot be said that we understood each other's problems.

At Benghazi the Army did not understand the importance of defending this town which was the supply port for the front line, they could not spare any AA guns or fighters for its defence and the only AA defences in this place for 14 days were provided by the *Terror* and the *Coventry*.[1] The three C's-in-C should have flogged out together whether we should have defended it to the full as our front supply port, or whether we should have used one further back.

The Air always understood naval problems better than the Army.

There was not sufficient touch and co-operation between the three C's-in-C.

The Army began to understand Naval problems about the time we were going to Greece, though they never understood the necessity for Malta. By March, the time of Matapan, the three C's-in-C were starting to get together well and by the time of the evacuation of Greece and Crete were working together as one man, and Wavell was beginning to

---

[1]*Terror*: monitor, 1916, 8450t, 12k, 2×15in; sunk off N. Africa, 24 Feb 1941.

Coventry: lt csr, 1918, 5240t, 29k; conv to AA csr 1935–6, 10×4in; bombed off N Africa 14 Sept 1942.

understand the sea problem. During the evacuation of Greece, first Baillie-Grohman and then Pridham-Wippell, sat alongside Maitland Wilson and then co-operation worked well.[1]

Then Wavell went and Auchinleck came. He was all for the three C's-in-C working together but his idea of this co-operation was to dictate to the other services what was to be done. The supply of Malta meant just nothing to him, he did not realise how important Malta was in the interception of the enemy's supplies and at one time asked why we did not let Malta go. Though we were working together closely, Auchinleck was jealous of any Naval movement which would deprive him of fighters. The co-operation was still not perfect and again at Benghazi we ran in 3,000 tons of petrol two days before the Army left which the enemy then used against us.[2]

I think, however, that there is very little that cannot be settled by the three C's-in-C around a table. It must be remembered, however, that I was in Alexandria while the other two were in Cairo. At the time of the Abyssinian crisis it was decided that the three C's-in-C should be at Alexandria and that this arrangement would be used in any future war.[3]

I think that the Triumvirate system is in accordance with the British spirit of compromise. In this method, there will develop a spirit of comradeship and a conviction that each will not let the other down, and that the three C's-in-C will spend their time thinking what they can do to help the others.

A fine example of this comradeship and co-operation lies in the work of the COS committee. If a Supreme Commander is necessary, surely one would expect one to be needed here.[4]

The Supreme Commander

The object of a Supreme Commander is presumably to co-ordinate the three services and to make decisions when there are differences

---

[1]VAdm Tom Baillie-Grohman (1888–1978): ent RN 1903; Lt 1909; Med & China; N Sea & Channel 1914–18; Persian Gulf & Red Sea 1922–3; Capt 1930; SO, RN Mission to China 1931–3; Capt (D) 1DF, Med F 1934; *Ramillies* 1939; RA Jan 1941; FOAM March 1941; Comb Ops Sept 1943; VA & FO Harwich Nov 1943; ret 1946.

[2]FM Sir Claud Auchinleck (1884–1981): most of career in India; Maj Gen 1939; IV Corps; Norway Spring 1940; V Corps; S Cmd; Lt Gen July 1940; Gen & C-in-C India Nov 1940; C-in-C ME July 1941–Aug 1942; C-in-C India 1943–7; FM 1946.

ACM Tedder replaced Longmore just before Auchinleck replaced Wavell.

See M. A. Simpson (ed.), *The Cunningham Papers*, vol. I.

[3]Alexandria would have been a better joint HQ, as it was much nearer the front line & adjoined the Med F's domain.

[4]As has been the case since 1957. See W. Jackson & Lord Bramall, *The Chiefs: The Story of the UK Chiefs of Staff* (London, 1992).

between them. But how are we to select a Supreme Commander? What are the requirements of such a man?

He must have great energy and ability, a knowledge of all three services and be a man of great experience in war. He must be a man acceptable to all three services and able to hold his own with the politicians, and finally, he must be possessed of a supremely balanced judgement, which is probably the greatest need of all.

These are the requirements for a man who is to be Supreme Commander over the Forces of his own country, where allies are concerned there are other questions to be considered.

Now let us consider our experiences of Supreme Commanders during the war.

Wavell (ABDA)

He had all the qualifications we have listed, he had *learnt* about the three Services in the hard school of war, he could deal with the politicians, had energy, drive and was honest. He was a great and experienced soldier, had very good judgement and could discount the smaller things. An excellent choice with a hopeless job.

Eisenhower ('Torch')

He had no military knowledge and knew nothing about the Navy, he was a pilot and knew something about the air; he was an untried man except that he was known to have great staff ability.

What effect did he have on 'Torch'? Some on his American soldiery perhaps, otherwise none. I was never given any instructions or advice by him, nor was I consulted, nor did I consult him. He had no political experience and his negotiations with Giraud at Gibraltar were pitiable. Some Americans knew he was a good man who would possibly develop. But what did Churchill and Roosevelt know of him when he was selected? It was purely a political appointment.

The real inter-service work for 'Torch' was done on the level of Commanders in charge of the landings; Troubridge and Burrough did excellent work with their respective American Generals; it was on this level that all questions as to the work of the Command ashore, and how the troops were to be put ashore, were settled.

At Algiers, Eisenhower came on a lot and though much blamed for his negotiations with Darlan, I think he did these well. I made a point of seeing him for half an hour every day but I still had little connection with him, though I talked with him a good deal about the necessity for Sea/Air, as the airman on our staff was not very strong. Then Alexander and Tedder were appointed. The American papers said it looked as if Eisenhower was to be the stooge and that the Tunisian campaign was to be run by Alexander, Tedder and Cunningham – which was what happened.

Tunis finished, and then there was Sicily. Eisenhower was getting better, he was integrating his staff, and was showing signs of the very great man that he became. By then he had command of himself; in the tunnel at Gibraltar he had not, and he afterwards referred to this as his worst hour. It must be remembered that he had been appointed to take charge of a very critical amphibious operation and had not developed the necessary qualities; it took eighteen months to make him.

The planning for Sicily was again done by Alexander, Tedder and Cunningham, and again I was not conscious of Eisenhower having ever stated any requirements to me or of having asked my opinion. The Navy was still apparently a closed book to him, though it may be that in our daily half hour talks he was beginning to pick up all he wanted to know. The Naval problem in the Sicilian landing was a very difficult one as convoys starting from Sfax, Gibraltar, Port Said and other places all had to meet at the right time.

Eisenhower was rather ignored in Naval matters by Admiral King in Washington.

Maitland Wilson

He was a makeweight though he had some of the qualifications of a Supreme Commander which few of the others possessed. He had great experience, knowledge of all three Services in war and good judgement. He held Alexander's hand in the Italian Campaign.

Alexander

He was not fit to be a Supreme Commander. He had no opinions of his own that he was not prepared to change and he took what the last man said. He had no knowledge of the sea and little of the air.

Mountbatten

He had energy and drive and a reasonable naval reputation as a young captain. He had shown great drive and ability and frightful extravagance in building up Combined Operations. He did not know much of the higher side of naval warfare and nothing of soldiery or of the air, *and he had no judgement.*

In SEAC, he fought with Somerville, Giffard and Peirse, but he was quick to learn. By the time Fraser arrived he was learning, and by the time Power arrived he had learnt.[1]

---

[1]Gen Sir George Giffard (1886–1964): Queen's R Regt 1906; King's African Rifles, E Africa, 1913–18; A/Col 1917; Staff Coll 1919; SO 1920; IDC 1931–2; Lt Col, 2 Bn,

But what effect had he on the Campaign? If it had been left to Power, Park and Slim would not the results have been just the same?[1]

When you have a Supreme Commander you lose something. You wait for the Supreme Commander to tell you to do something and you are not always thinking how you can help your brother C's-in-C. How are you to choose these Supreme Commanders? The time may come when we can *train* them, but they do not exist, and I think that our experience of choosing them in this war would rather put us off.

Must you have this huge organisation? Can't you get an integrated staff with a Triumvirate?

The Supreme Commander was invented by the Americans because the Army and Navy could not agree, and when they reached the point in the Pacific, they still could not agree, and did not have a Supreme Commander.[2]

Surely the lesson of this dissertation is that our Supreme Commanders were not picked men. Only one passes the test. None of the others were experienced, and some were by no means acceptable to all three Services. The answer is that they were picked as a political job! Where is the real argument for having one? With Allies a Supreme Commander is probably necessary, but otherwise I am against it.

•

Queen's R Regt 1932; SO; Maj Gen, African Col Forces 1936; Mil Sec to S St War 1939–40; GOC Palestine 1940; C-in-C W Africa; Gen 1941; E Army 1943; C-in-C, 11 Army Group; fell out with Mountbatten 1944; ret 1946.

A/ACM Sir Richard Peirse (1892–1970): pilot 1913; Sub Lt, RNR; Flt Cdr, Belgian coast 1915; Sqdn Cdr 1916; Wing Cdr Dover; Sqdn Ldr 1919; W Cdr, Staff Coll 1922–3; Air Min 1926–7; ME & Palestine; DDO 1, 1931; AOC Palestine 1933–6; AVM 1936; D Ops & Igc & DCAS 1937; A/AM 1939; VCAS April 1940; C-in-C Bbr Cmd Oct 1940–Jan 1942; A/ACM & AOC-in-C India 1942–4.

[1]ACM Sir Keith Park (1892–1975): b NZ; SASO, Ftr Cmd, July 1938–April 1940; AVM & 11 Ftr Group July 1940; 23 Group, Flying Trng Cmd Dec 1940; AOC Egypt Jan 1942; AOC Malta July 1942; C-in-C MEAF Jan 1944; A/ACM & C-in-C SEA Air Force Feb 1944.

FM Visct (Sir William) Slim (1891–1970): RE 1914–18; Indian A 1919; Bdr Sept 1939; 10 Indian Div, Syria 1941; Lt Gen Burcorps March 1942; XV Indian Corps, Arakan 1943; C-in-C, 14 A Oct 1943; Gen & C-in-C SEA Allied Land Forces 1945; FM & CIGS 1948–51; Gov Gen, Australia 1953–60; Visct 1960.

[2]Responsibility for the Pacific in 1945 was divided, judiciously, between MacArthur in the S & Nimitz in the C & N.

DOCUMENTS AND SOURCES

The British Library

The Papers of Admiral of the Fleet Viscount Cunningham of Hyndhope (BL Add Mss 52559–52581B). [Listed here as BLAM.]

Churchill Archives Centre, Churchill College, Cambridge

The Papers of Admiral of the Fleet Viscount Cunningham of Hyndhope [CUNN]
The Papers of Admiral of the Fleet Sir Dudley Pound [DUPO]
The Papers of Admiral of the Fleet Sir James Somerville [SMVL]
The Papers of Admiral of the Fleet Sir Algernon Willis [WLLS]
The Papers of Admiral Sir John Edelsten [EDSN]
The Papers of Admiral Sir George Oliver [OLVR]
The Papers of Admiral Sir Bertram Ramsay [RMSY]
The Papers of the Rt Hon Earl Alexander of Hillsborough [AVAR]

The National Archives (formerly The Public Record Office), Kew, Richmond, Surrey

Admiralty Papers [ADM]
Cabinet Papers [CAB]
Premier's Papers [PREM]

The National Maritime Museum, Greenwich, London

The Papers of Admiral of the Fleet Baron Fraser of North Cape [FRASER]
The Papers of Admiral Sir Howard Kelly [KEL]

NOTE: Other collections were consulted at the above archives and also at *The Imperial War Museum, London.* In the United States, the archives at *The Franklin D. Roosevelt Presidential Library*, Hyde Park, NY; *The Library of Congress (Manuscripts Division)*, Washington, DC;

The National Archives, College Park, MD; *The Naval Historical Center*, Washington Navy Yard; and *The Library and Archives*, Naval War College, Newport, RI, were consulted.

Numbered Document Sources

Part I: British Admiralty Delegation, 1942

1.	To Admiral Sir H. Kelly	29 March 1942	KEL 43
2.	A. V. Alexander to Churchill	3 June 1942	PREM 3/478/4
3.	Churchill to A. V. Alexander	4 June 1942	PREM 3/478/4
4.	Admiral Sir D. Pound to Alexander	8 June 1942	ADM 205/14
5.	Alexander to Churchill	9 June 1942	PREM 3/478/4
6.	Alexander to Sir K. Wood	10 April 1943	PREM 3/478/4
7.	To Aunt Doodles	11 June 1942	BLAM 52559
8.	To Aunt Doodles	16 June 1942	BLAM 52559
9.	From Pound	1 June 1942	ADM 205/1
10.	To Aunt Doodles	29 June 1942	BLAM 52559
11.	To Aunt Doodles	6 July 1942	BLAM 52559
12.	To Aunt Doodles	13 July 1942	BLAM 52559
13.	To Aunt Doodles	25 July 1942	BLAM 52559
14.	To Pound	31 July 1942	BLAM 52561
15.	To Pound	12 August 1942	BLAM 52561
16.	From Pound	24 August 1942	BLAM 52561
17.	To Kelly	17 August 1942	KEL 43
18.	To Aunt Doodles	23 August 1942	BLAM 52559
19.	To Aunt Doodles	30 August 1942	BLAM 52559
20.	To Aunt Doodles	6 September 1942	BLAM 52559

Part II: A. Return to North Africa, 1942–43

21.	To Pound	21 July 1942	CAB 121/490
22.	To Pound	31 July 1942	BLAM 52561
23.	To Pound	12 August 1942	BLAM 52561
24.	From Pound	24 August 1942	BLAM 52561
25.	CCS 38th Meeting	28 August 1942	CAB 121/490
26.	To Pound	12 September 1942	CAB 121/491
27.	Admiral Sir B. Ramsay to Lady Ramsay	22 September 1942	RMSY 8/19
28.	From Ramsay	2 November 1942	BLAM 52570
29.	To Ramsay	3 November 1942	RMSY 5/21
30.	From General Eisenhower	10 May 1945	BLAM 52572
31.	To Lady Cunningham	10 November 1942	BLAM 52581B
32.	From Ramsay	11 November 1942	BLAM 52571
33.	To Ramsay	12 November 1942	RMSY 5/21
34.	Ramsay to Lady Ramsay	14 November 1942	RMSY 8/19
35.	To Aunt Doodles	19 November 1942	BLAM 52559

36.	To Ramsay	21 November 1942	RMSY 5/21
37.	From Pound	27 November 1942	BLAM 52561
38.	To British warships	7 November 1942	ADM 223/568
39.	To Vice Admiral Sir H. Burrough	11 November 1942	ADM 223/568
40.	To Pound	11 November 1942	ADM 223/568
41.	To Ramsay	12 November 1942	RMSY 5/21
42.	From Admiral Sir H. Harwood	14 November 1942	ADM 223/568
43.	To Lady Cunningham	15 November 1942	BLAM 52581B
44.	From Admiral Sir W. Whitworth	16 November 1942	BLAM 52570
45.	To Pound	18 November 1942	ADM 223/568
46.	To Pound and Harwood	18 November 1942	ADM 223/568
47.	To Lady Cunningham	29 November 1942	BLAM 52581
48.	To Ramsay	21 November 1942	RMSY 5/21
49.	From Pound	27 November 1942	BLAM 52561
50.	To Lady Cunningham	28 November 1942	BLAM 52581B
51.	To Lady Cunningham	1 December 1942	BLAM 52581B
52.	From Field Marshal Sir J. Dill	1 December 1942	BLAM 52570
53.	From Harwood	3 December 1942	BLAM 52570
54.	To Ramsay	4 December 1942	RMSY 5/21
55.	To Pound	5 December 1942	BLAM 52561
56.	From Harwood	9 December 1942	BLAM 52570
57.	From Whitworth	15 December 1942	BLAM 52570
58.	To Lady Cunningham	26 December 1942	BLAM 52581B
59.	From Pound	28 December 1942	BLAM 52561
60.	COS (42) 357	28 December 1942	CAB 79/24
61.	From Vice Amiral Godfroy	24 May 1943	BLAM 52570
62.	To Aunt Doodles	6 June 1943	BLAM 52559
63.	To Aunt Doodles	13 June 1943	BLAM 52559
64.	To Aunt Doodles	29 June 1943	BLAM 52559
65.	To Aunt Doodles	5 September 1943	BLAM 52559
66.	Diary	14 March 1945	BLAM 52578
67.	To Admiral J. Godfrey	26 April [1954?]	DUPO 6/1
68.	To Pound	20 November 1942	PREM 3/274/2
69.	Ramsay to Lady Ramsay	21 November 1942	RMSY 8/19
70.	To Ramsay	4 December 1942	RMSY 5/21
71.	To Pound	5 December 1942	BLAM 52561
72.	Churchill to Pound	6 December 1942	ADM 178/323
73.	From Pound	6 December 1942	PREM 3/274/2
74.	To Pound	8 December 1942	PREM 3/274/2
75.	To Lady Cunningham	13 December 1942	BLAM 52581B
76.	To Lady Cunningham	25 December 1942	BLAM 52581B
77.	From Pound	28 December 1942	BLAM 52561
78.	To Aunt Doodles	10 January 1943	BLAM 52559
79.	Pound to Churchill	12 January 1943	ADM 205/27
80.	To Lady Cunningham	21 January 1943	BLAM 52581B
81.	To Pound	31 January 1943	BLAM 52561

82.	To Lady Cunningham	1 February 1943	BLAM 52581B
83.	From Rear Admiral Pegram	1 February 1943	BLAM 52570
84.	From Commodore Norman	1 February 1943	BLAM 52570
85.	COS (43) 35	2 February 1943	CAB 80/39
86.	To Lady Cunningham	14 February 1943	BLAM 52581B
87.	Ramsay to Lady Ramsay	15 February 1943	RMSY 8/23
88.	To the Admiralty	17 February 1943	ADM 199/953
89.	From Pound	27 February 1943	BLAM 52561
90.	To Aunt Doodles	3 March 1943	BLAM 52559
91.	To Pound	15 March 1943	BLAM 52561
92.	Ramsay to Lady Ramsay	15 March 1943	RMSY 8/23
93.	To Lady Cunningham	25 March 1943	BLAM 52581B
94.	To Lady Cunningham	20 April 1943	BLAM 52581B
95.	From Pound	23 April 1943	BLAM 52561
96.	To Pound	28 April 1943	BLAM 52561
97.	To Pound	8 May 1943	BLAM 52561
98.	To Captain Edelsten	15 June 1943	EDSN 1/2
99.	To Aunt Doodles	16 May 1943	BLAM 52559
100.	To Aunt Doodles	6 June 1943	BLAM 52559
101.	From Dill	11 June 1943	BLAM 52570
102.	To Aunt Doodles	13 June 1943	BLAM 52559
103.	To Aunt Doodles	24 June 1943	BLAM 52559
104.	From Rear Admiral Hall, US Navy	3 December 1943	BLAM 52571
105.	Report on 'Torch'	30 March 1943	ADM 199/902
106.	Report on 'Retribution'	13 November 1943	CAB 106/673
107.	Diary	9 July 1945	BLAM 52578

Part II: B The Landings in Sicily, 1943–44

108.	To Pound	15 March 1943	BLAM 52561
109.	Ramsay to Lady Ramsay	19 March 1943	RMSY 8/23
110.	Ramsay to Lady Ramsay	7 April 1943	RMSY 8/23
111.	Ramsay to Lady Ramsay	14 April 1943	RMSY 8/23
112.	Ramsay to Lady Ramsay	28 April 1943	RMSY 8/23
113.	To Pound	28 April 1943	BLAM 52561
114.	Ramsay to Lady Ramsay	6 May 1943	RMSY 8/23
115.	To Pound	8 May 1943	BLAM 52561
116.	Ramsay to Lady Ramsay	10 May 1943	RMSY 8/23
117.	Ramsay to Lady Ramsay	11 May 1943	RMSY 8/23
118.	Ramsay to Lady Ramsay	28 May 1943	RMSY 8/23
119.	From Pound	30 May 1943	BLAM 52561
120.	To Pound	25 June 1943	BLAM 52561
121.	From Pound	3 July 1943	BLAM 52561
122.	To Aunt Doodles	14 August 1943	BLAM 52559
123.	To Ramsay	20 September 1943	RMSY 9/4
124.	Combined Ops. HQ	October 1943	ADM 199/858
125.	To the Admiralty	14 November 1943	ADM 199/497
126.	Report on 'Husky'	1 January 1944	ADM 199/2497
127.	Diary	17 April 1944	BLAM 52577

Part II: C. The Landings in Italy 1943–45

128.	To General Alexander	26 August 1943	BLAM 52571
129.	General Montgomery to Ramsay	26 August 1943	RMSY 9/4
130.	To the Admiralty	1 September 1943	BLAM 52566
131.	To Aunt Doodles	12 September 1943	BLAM 52559
132.	To Vice Admiral Willis	14 September 1943	WLLS 6/1
133.	To Aunt Doodles	19 September 1943	BLAM 52559
134.	To Ramsay	20 September 1943	RMSY 9/4
135.	Cunningham-de Courten Agreement	23 September 1943	ADM 199/641
136.	Cunningham to Cdre Oliver	n.d., [September 1943]	OLVR 7/3
137.	From A. V. Alexander and Cunningham to Admiral Sir P. Noble	7 October 1943	ADM 205/27
138.	To C-in-C, Mediterranean, etc.	3 March 1944	ADM 199/954
139.	From Admiral Stark, US Navy	5 April 1944	BLAM 52571
140.	Admiral Hewitt, US Navy: Report on 'Avalanche'	11 January 1945	ADM 199/947

Part III: A. First Sea Lord: Appointment

141.	Rear Admiral Dalrymple-Hamilton to A. V. Alexander	14 September 1943	AVAR 5/8/33a
142.	Minute by Churchill	25 September 1943	AVAR 5/8/36
143.	A. V. Alexander to Churchill	25 September 1943	AVAR 5/8/37
144.	A. V. Alexander and Churchill: Minutes of Conversation	26 September 1943	AVAR 5/8/38
145.	Churchill: Draft Signal	27 September 1943	AVAR 5/8/39b
146.	Churchill to the King	4 October 1943	AVAR 5/8/42f
147.	From Noble	1 October 1943	BLAM 52571
148.	From Admiral Sir J. Tovey	5 October 1943	BLAM 52571
149.	From Dill	18 October 1943	BLAM 52571
150.	To Aunt Doodles	23 October 1943	BLAM 52559
151.	To Aunt Doodles	1 November 1943	BLAM 52559
152.	To Admiral Sir J. Somerville	19 December 1943	SMVL 8/2
153.	From Noble	23 December 1943	BLAM 52571
154.	To Aunt Doodles	15 March 1944	BLAM 52559

Part III: B. Churchill, etc., 1943–46

155.	To Somerville	19 December 1943	SMVL 8/2
156.	To Noble	3 Jan 1944	BLAM 52571

157.	To Vice Admiral Sir G. Blake	18 January 1944	CUNN 5/1
158.	Diary	29 May 1944	BLAM 52577
159.	Diary	9 June 1944	BLAM 52577
160.	Diary	6 July 1944	BLAM 52577
161.	Diary	11 August 1944	BLAM 52577
162.	Diary	29 August 1944	BLAM 52577
163.	Diary	5 September 1944	BLAM 52577
164.	Diary	8 September 1944	BLAM 52577
165.	Diary	12 September 1944	BLAM 52577
166.	Diary	13 September 1944	BLAM 52577
167.	Diary	14 September 1944	BLAM 52577
168.	Diary	15 September 1944	BLAM 52577
169.	Meeting between Admiral King, US Navy, and Cunningham	15 September 1944	ADM 205/37
170.	Diary	16 September 1944	BLAM 52577
171.	Diary	3 October 1944	BLAM 52577
172.	Diary	3 November 1944	BLAM 52577
173.	Diary	4 November 1944	BLAM 52577
174.	Diary	7 November 1944	BLAM 52577
175.	Diary	4 December 1944	BLAM 52577
176.	Diary	10 December 1944	BLAM 52577
177.	Diary	11 December 1944	BLAM 52577
178.	Diary	13 December 1944	BLAM 52577
179.	Diary	16 January 1945	BLAM 52578
180.	Diary	30 January 1945	BLAM 52578
181.	Diary	4 February 1945	BLAM 52578
182.	Diary	5 February 1945	BLAM 52578
183.	Diary	6 February 1945	BLAM 52578
184.	Diary	8 February 1945	BLAM 52578
185.	Diary	9 February 1945	BLAM 52578
186.	Meeting between King and Cunningham	9 February 1945	ADM 205/46
187.	Diary	12 April 1945	BLAM 52578
188.	Diary	13 April 1945	BLAM 52578
189.	From Field Marshal Alanbrooke	7 June 1946	BLAM 52573

Part III: C. Command and Manpower

190.	From Admiral Sir C. Kennedy-Purvis	15 October 1943	ADM 205/32
191.	From Captain E. Brind	24 October 1943	ADM 205/28
192.	Manpower Situation	16 November 1943	ADM 205/36
193.	To Somerville	19 December 1943	SMVL 8/2
194.	Diary	13 April 1944	BLAM 52577
195.	Diary	17 April 1944	BLAM 52577
196.	To A. V. Alexander	18 April 1944	ADM 205/39
197.	Memo. by Cunningham	26 May 1944	ADM 205/52

198.	Diary	31 May 1944	BLAM 52577
199.	Diary	30 June 1944	BLAM 52577
200.	Diary	18 July 1944	BLAM 52577
201.	Diary	26 July 1944	BLAM 52577
202.	Diary	31 July 1944	BLAM 52577
203.	Diary	4 August 1944	BLAM 52577
204.	Diary	10 August 1944	BLAM 52577
205.	Diary	11 August 1944	BLAM 52577
206.	Diary	30 August 1944	BLAM 52577
207.	Diary	31 August 1944	BLAM 52577
208.	Diary	4 September 1944	BLAM 52577
209.	Diary	21 September 1944	BLAM 52577
210.	Diary	24 November 1944	BLAM 52577
211.	Diary	5 December 1944	BLAM 52577
212.	Diary	10 January 1945	BLAM 52578
213.	Diary	11 January 1945	BLAM 52578
214.	Diary	12 January 1945	BLAM 52578
215.	To Admiral Sir B. Fraser	19 January 1945	BLAM 52572
216.	Diary	8 March 1945	BLAM 52578
217.	Diary	13 March 1945	BLAM 52578
218.	Diary	29 May 1945	BLAM 52578
219.	Diary	26 June 1945	BLAM 52578
220.	Diary	24 September 1945	BLAM 52578
221.	Diary	5 October 1945	BLAM 52578
222.	Manpower Meeting	28 January 1946	ADM 205/65

Part III: D. 'Neptune' and After

223.	To Somerville	19 December 1943	SMVL 8/2
224.	Diary	1 April 1944	BLAM 52577
225.	Diary	7 April 1944	BLAM 52577
226.	Diary	10 April 1944	BLAM 52577
227.	Diary	14 April 1944	BLAM 52577
228.	Diary	24 April 1944	BLAM 52577
229.	Diary	25 April 1944	BLAM 52577
230.	Diary	29 April 1944	BLAM 52577
231.	Diary	4 May 1944	BLAM 52577
232.	Diary	2 June 1944	BLAM 52577
233.	Diary	4 June 1944	BLAM 52577
234.	Diary	5 June 1944	BLAM 52577
235.	Diary	6 June 1944	BLAM 52577
236.	From Montgomery	6 June 1944	BLAM 52571
237.	Diary	7 June 1944	BLAM 52577
238.	Diary	8 June 1944	BLAM 52577
239.	Diary	9 June 1944	BLAM 52577
240.	Diary	10 June 1944	BLAM 52577
241.	Diary	11 June 1944	BLAM 52577
242.	Diary	12 June 1944	BLAM 52577
243.	Diary	13 June 1944	BLAM 52577
244.	Diary	16 June 1944	BLAM 52577

245.	Diary	21 June 1944	BLAM 52577
246.	Diary	22 June 1944	BLAM 52577
247.	Churchill to A. V. Alexander	22 June 1944	ADM 205/35
248.	To Churchill	22 June 1944	ADM 205/35
249.	Diary	23 June 1944	BLAM 52577
250.	Diary	26 June 1944	BLAM 52577
251.	Diary	28 June 1944	BLAM 52577
252.	Diary	30 June 1944	BLAM 52577
253.	From Churchill	10 July 1944	ADM 205/35
254.	To Churchill	11 July 1944	ADM 205/35
255.	From Churchill	13 July 1944	ADM 205/35
256.	Diary	12 July 1944	BLAM 52577
257.	Diary	15 July 1944	BLAM 52577
258.	From Churchill	4 August 1944	ADM 205/35
259.	To Churchill	7 August 1944	ADM 205/35
260.	Diary	4 August 1944	BLAM 52577
261.	Diary	5 August 1944	BLAM 52577
262.	Diary	7 August 1944	BLAM 52577
263.	To Blake	17 August 1944	BLAM 52571
264.	Diary	2 September 1944	BLAM 52577
265.	Diary	5 September 1944	BLAM 52577
266.	Diary	7 September 1944	BLAM 52577
267.	Diary	20 September 1944	BLAM 52577
268.	Diary	4 October 1944	BLAM 52577
269.	Diary	6 October 1944	BLAM 52577
270.	To Churchill	16 October 1944	ADM 205/35
271.	To Churchill	15 November 1944	ADM 205/35
272.	Diary	21 December 1944	BLAM 52577
273.	From Ramsay	1 January 1945	BLAM 52572
274.	Diary	2 January 1945	BLAM 52578
275.	Diary	6 January 1945	BLAM 52578
276.	Diary	7 January 1945	BLAM 52578
277.	Diary	9 March 1945	BLAM 52577
278.	Diary	21 March 1945	BLAM 52577
279.	Diary	23 April 1945	BLAM 52577
280.	Diary	4 May 1945	BLAM 52577

Part III: E. The German Navy, 1944–45

281.	To Aunt Doodles	1 January 1944	BLAM 52559
282.	Anti-U-Boat Warfare Committee	12 January 1944	CAB 86/6
283.	From Burrough	31 January 1944	BLAM 52571
284.	Anti-U-Boat Warfare Committee	15 March 1944	CAB 86/6
285.	To Tovey and Ramsay	17 March 1944	ADM 205/40
286.	Diary	3 April 1944	BLAM 52577
287.	Diary	13 April 1944	BLAM 52577
288.	Diary	14 April 1944	BLAM 52577
289.	Diary	25 April 1944	BLAM 52577

290.	Diary	17 May 1944	BLAM 52577
291.	Diary	22 May 1944	BLAM 52577
292.	Diary	14 July 1944	BLAM 52577
293.	Diary	17 July 1944	BLAM 52577
294.	Diary	20 July 1944	BLAM 52577
295.	Diary	24 July 1944	BLAM 52577
296.	Meeting held by Cunningham	24 July 1944	ADM 205/40
297.	Diary	1 August 1944	BLAM 52577
298.	Diary	4 August 1944	BLAM 52577
299.	Diary	11 August 1944	BLAM 52577
300.	Diary	3 October 1944	BLAM 52577
301.	From Churchill	26 October 1944	ADM 205/35
302.	To Churchill	27 October 1944	ADM 205/35
303.	Anti-U-Boat Warfare Committee	31 October 1944	CAB 86/6
304.	Diary	12 November 1944	BLAM 52577
305.	Diary	13 November 1944	BLAM 52577
306.	Diary	27 November 1944	BLAM 52577
307.	Diary	19 December 1944	BLAM 52577
308.	Anti-U-Boat Warfare Committee	19 December 1944	CAB 119/133
309.	Diary	11 January 1945	BLAM 52578
310.	Diary	15 January 1945	BLAM 52578
311.	Cunningham: Minutes on Anti-U-Boat Warfare	15 January 1945	ADM 205/44
312.	Diary	18 January 1945	BLAM 52578
313.	To Fraser	19 January 1945	BLAM 52572
314.	Diary	22 January 1945	BLAM 52578
315.	To Admiral G. Jones, RCN	25 January 1945	ADM 205/44
316.	Anti-U-Boat Warfare Committee	26 January 1945	CAB 119/133
317.	Diary	26 January 1945	BLAM 52578
318.	CCS Directive	2 February 1945	CAB 119/133
319.	Cunningham on DAUD Memo.	22 February 1945	ADM 205/44
320.	Diary	26 February 1945	BLAM 52578
321.	Diary	1 March 1945	BLAM 52578
322.	Diary	2 March 1945	BLAM 52578
323.	From Captain Dundas	9 March 1945	ADM 205/44
324.	Diary	13 March 1945	BLAM 52578
325.	Diary	28 March 1945	BLAM 52578
326.	Diary	4 April 1945	BLAM 52578
327.	Diary	9 May 1945	BLAM 52578
328.	To Stark	17 May 1945	ADM 205/48
329.	Minute on 'Halfback'	25 June 1945	ADM 205/49
330.	COS (45) 172	9 July 1945	CAB 79/32
331.	Diary	10 July 1945	BLAM 52578
332.	Diary	22 July 1945	BLAM 52578
333.	To Vice Admiral Miles	13 August 1945	ADM 205/54

334.	From Vice Admiral Miles	n.d. [1945]	BLAM 52572
335.	Diary	21 August 1945	BLAM 52578
336.	Minute on 'Foxchase'	24 August 1945	ADM 205/49

Part III: F. The Mediterranean, 1943–46

337.	From John Cunningham	23 March 1943	BLAM 52562
338.	From John Cunningham	19 September 1943	BLAM 52562
339.	To Vice Admiral Syfret	9 October 1943	CAB 120/500
340.	From Willis	19 October 1943	BLAM 52571
341.	From Willis	27 October 1943	BLAM 52571
342.	From Kelly	4 December 1943	BLAM 52571
343.	To Kelly	17 December 1943	BLAM 52571
344.	From John Cunningham	27 January 1944	BLAM 52562
345.	To John Cunningham	6 February 1944	BLAM 52562
346.	From John Cunningham	11 February 1944	BLAM 52562
347.	From John Cunningham	17 February 1944	BLAM 52562
348.	From John Cunningham	4 March 1944	BLAM 52562
349.	To John Cunningham	21 March 1944	BLAM 52562
350.	From Kelly	3 April 1944	BLAM 52571
351.	Diary	5 April 1944	BLAM 52577
352.	Diary	10 April 1944	BLAM 52577
353.	Diary	22 April 1944	BLAM 52577
354.	Diary	23 April 1944	BLAM 52577
355.	To John Cunningham	6 May 1944	BLAM 52562
356.	From John Cunningham	23 May 1944	BLAM 52562
357.	From John Cunningham	26 May 1944	BLAM 52562
358.	Diary	2 June 1944	BLAM 52577
359.	Diary	9 June 1944	BLAM 52577
360.	To John Cunningham	1 September 1944	BLAM 52562
361.	From John Cunningham	25 September 1944	BLAM 52562
362.	Diary	1 September 1944	BLAM 52577
363.	From Vice Admiral Rawlings	27 September 1944	BLAM 52571
364.	Diary	10 October 1944	BLAM 52577
365.	Diary	20 November 1944	BLAM 52577
366.	Diary	1 December 1944	BLAM 52577
367.	Diary	18 December 1944	BLAM 52577
368.	Diary	28 May 1945	BLAM 52578
369.	From John Cunningham	7 June 1945	BLAM 52562
370.	Diary	15 September 1945	BLAM 52577
371.	From John Cunningham	25 October 1945	BLAM 52579
372.	Diary	16 February 1946	BLAM 52579

Part III: G. Pacific and East Indies

373.	From Admiral Sir G. Layton	10 November 1943	BLAM 52571
374.	To Churchill	24 November 1943	ADM 205/27
375.	To Layton	1 January 1944	BLAM 52571

376.	From Noble	29 February 1944	ADM 205/37
377.	To Churchill	18 March 1944	CAB 119/153
378.	From Admiral Sir G. Royle	25 March 1944	ADM 205/37
379.	From Noble	2 April 1944	BLAM 52571
380.	Diary	3 April 1944	BLAM 52577
381.	To Noble	8 April 1944	BLAM 52571
382.	Diary	10 April 1944	BLAM 52577
383.	Diary	19 April 1944	BLAM 52577
384.	Diary	20 April 1944	BLAM 52577
385.	Diary	5 May 1944	BLAM 52577
386.	Diary	8 May 1944	BLAM 52577
387.	Diary	16 May 1944	BLAM 52577
388.	Diary	17 May 1944	BLAM 52577
389.	Diary	18 May 1944	BLAM 52577
390.	From Layton	20 May 1944	BLAM 52571
391.	Diary	26 May 1944	BLAM 52577
392.	Diary	2 June 1944	BLAM 52577
393.	Diary	7 June 1944	BLAM 52577
394.	Diary	14 June 1944	BLAM 52577
395.	Diary	21 June 1944	BLAM 52577
396.	Diary	7 July 1944	BLAM 52577
397.	Diary	14 July 1944	BLAM 52577
398.	Diary	7 August 1944	BLAM 52577
399.	Diary	8 August 1944	BLAM 52577
400.	Diary	9 August 1944	BLAM 52577
401.	Diary	10 August 1944	BLAM 52577
402.	Diary	11 August 1944	BLAM 52577
403.	Diary	14 August 1944	BLAM 52577
404.	Diary	18 August 1944	BLAM 52577
405.	Diary	29 August 1944	BLAM 52577
406.	Diary	31 August 1944	BLAM 52577
407.	Diary	2 September 1944	BLAM 52577
408.	To Marshal of the RAF Sir C. Portal	4 September 1944	ADM 205/42
409.	Diary	20 September 1944	BLAM 52577
410.	To Churchill	26 September 1944	ADM 205/35
411.	Diary	2 October 1944	BLAM 52577
412.	Cunningham: Minutes	5 October 1944	ADM 205/39
413.	Diary	5 October 1944	BLAM 52577
414.	Diary	23 October 1944	BLAM 52577
415.	Cunningham: Minutes	24 October 1944	ADM 205/40
416.	Diary	24 October 1944	BLAM 52577
417.	A. V. Alexander to Churchill	25 October 1944	ADM 205/35
418.	Diary	26 October 1944	BLAM 52577
419.	Churchill to A. V. Alexander	29 October 1944	ADM 205/35
420.	To A. V. Alexander	30 October 1944	ADM 205/35
421.	Diary	30 October 1944	BLAM 52577
422.	Diary	13 November 1944	BLAM 52577
423.	Diary	18 November 1944	BLAM 52577

424.	From Fraser	14 November 1944	BLAM 52571
425.	Diary	20 November 1944	BLAM 52577
426.	To Vice Admiral Sir A. J. Power	19 November 1944	BLAM 52562
427.	Diary	29 November 1944	BLAM 52577
428.	To Churchill	1 December 1944	ADM 205/35
429.	From A. J. Power	1 December 1944	BLAM 52562
430.	Diary	13 December 1944	BLAM 52577
431.	Diary	22 December 1944	BLAM 52577
432.	From A. J. Power	3 January 1945	BLAM 52562
433.	From A. J. Power	11 January 1945	BLAM 52562
434.	Diary	16 January 1945	BLAM 52578
435.	From Churchill	18 January 1945	ADM 205/43
436.	To Churchill	23 January 1945	ADM 205/43
437.	To Fraser	19 January 1945	BLAM 52572
438.	Diary	22 January 1945	BLAM 52578
439.	To A. J. Power	23 January 1945	BLAM 52562
440.	Diary	26 January 1945	BLAM 52578
441.	From A. J. Power	29 January 1945	BLAM 52562
442.	From A. J. Power	6 February 1945	BLAM 52562
443.	To Fraser and Somerville	12 February 1945	ADM 205/50
444.	From A. J. Power	1 March 1945	BLAM 52562
445.	To A. J. Power	13 March 1945	BLAM 52562
446.	Diary	2 March 1945	BLAM 52578
447.	Diary	6 March 1945	BLAM 52578
448.	Diary	7 March 1945	BLAM 52578
449.	Diary	8 March 1945	BLAM 52578
450.	Diary	9 March 1945	BLAM 52578
451.	From Fraser	14 March 1945	BLAM 52572
452.	Diary	14 March 1945	BLAM 52578
453.	Diary	20 March 1945	BLAM 52578
454.	Diary	21 March 1945	BLAM 52578
455.	Diary	23 March 1945	BLAM 52578
456.	Diary	7 April 1945	BLAM 52578
457.	From A. J. Power	7 April 1945	BLAM 52562
458.	Diary	12 April 1945	BLAM 52578
459.	Diary	16 April 1945	BLAM 52578
460.	From Rawlings	18 April 1945	BLAM 52572
461.	Diary	19 April 1945	BLAM 52578
462.	Diary	20 April 1945	BLAM 52578
463.	Diary	23 April 1945	BLAM 52578
464.	Diary	26 April 1945	BLAM 52578
465.	Diary	28 April 1945	BLAM 52578
466.	From A. J. Power	4 May 1945	BLAM 52562
467.	Diary	11 May 1945	BLAM 52578
468.	Diary	15 May 1945	BLAM 52578
469.	Diary	16 May 1945	BLAM 52578
470.	From Rear Admiral Harcourt	18 May 1945	BLAM 52572
471.	To Somerville	27 May 1945	ADM 205/50

472.	From A. J. Power	2 June 1945	BLAM 52572
473.	Diary	6 June 1945	BLAM 52578
474.	To A. J. Power	15 June 1945	BLAM 52562
475.	From A. J. Power	29 June 1945	BLAM 52562
476.	From Fraser	15 June 1945	BLAM 52572
477.	To Fraser	5 July 1945	BLAM 52572
478.	From Fraser	17 July 1945	BLAM 52572
479.	From Rear Admiral Edelsten	21 June 1945	BLAM 52572
480.	Diary	18 July 1945	BLAM 52578
481.	From Vice Admiral L. Hamilton	2 August 1945	BLAM 52572
482.	From Commodore Faulkner	7 August 1945	BLAM 52572
483.	Diary	8 August 1945	BLAM 52578
484.	From A. J. Power	8 August 1945	BLAM 52562
485.	Diary	10 August 1945	BLAM 52578
486.	To Fraser	10 August 1945	ADM 205/51
487.	Diary	15 August 1945	BLAM 52578
488.	To Fraser	20 August 1945	BLAM 52572
489.	Diary	20 August 1945	BLAM 52578
490.	From Edelsten	29 August 1945	BLAM 52572
491.	From Fraser	5 September 1945	BLAM 52572
492.	From A. J. Power	15 September 1945	BLAM 52562
493.	To A. J. Power	17 September 1945	BLAM 52562
494.	Diary	21 September 1945	BLAM 52578
495.	Diary	28 September 1945	BLAM 52578
496.	From Lt J. Wells	September 1945	BLAM 52572
497.	Diary	3 October 1945	BLAM 52578
498.	To Fraser	9 October 1945	BLAM 52572
499.	From Lt J. Wells	October 1945	BLAM 52572
500.	From Fraser	23 January 1946	BLAM 52573
501.	To Fraser	c.7 March 1946	ADM 1/18691

Part III: H. The Post War Navy, 1943–45

502.	To the Admiralty	31 May 1943	ADM 205/29
503.	To A. V. Alexander	9 November 1943	ADM 205/39
504.	Diary	10 April 1944	BLAM 52577
505.	Diary	21 April 1944	BLAM 52577
506.	Diary	18 May 1944	BLAM 52577
507.	Diary	19 May 1944	BLAM 52577
508.	Diary	10 July 1944	BLAM 52577
509.	Diary	26 July 1944	BLAM 52577
510.	Diary	11 August 1944	BLAM 52577
511.	Diary	4 October 1944	BLAM 52577
512.	Diary	6 October 1944	BLAM 52577
513.	Diary	27 October 1944	BLAM 52577
514.	Diary	10 November 1944	BLAM 52577
515.	Diary	22 November 1944	BLAM 52577
516.	Diary	24 November 1944	BLAM 52577

517.	Diary	27 November 1944	BLAM 52577
518.	Diary	30 November 1944	BLAM 52577
519.	Diary	23 February 1945	BLAM 52578
520.	COS (45) 31	25 February 1945	CAB 79/45
521.	Diary	28 February 1945	BLAM 52578
522.	Churchill to A. V. Alexander	10 March 1945	ADM 1/19056
523.	Diary	13 March 1945	BLAM 52578
524.	Cunningham: Minute	27 March 1945	ADM 205/51
525.	To L. Hamilton	29 April 1945	ADM 205/66
526.	Diary	1 June 1945	BLAM 52578
527.	COS (45) 154	25 July 1945	CAB 80/54
528.	From Burrough	25 February 1946	BLAM 52573
529.	Diary	18 March 1946	BLAM 52579
530.	From Willis	8 May 1946	BLAM 52573
531.	Diary	21 July 1944	BLAM 52577
532.	COS (44) 132	22 July 1944	CAB 80/44
533.	COS (44) 133	24 July 1944	CAB 80/44
534.	To Major-General Laycock	6 March 1945	ADM 205/58
535.	From Vice Admiral D. Boyd	6 November 1943	ADM 205/31
536.	Diary	12 July 1944	BLAM 52577
537.	Diary	25 July 1944	BLAM 52577
538.	Diary	18 October 1944	BLAM 52577
539.	Diary	19 October 1944	BLAM 52577
540.	Diary	1 November 1944	BLAM 52577
541.	Diary	6 December 1944	BLAM 52577
542.	Diary	7 December 1944	BLAM 52577
543.	To Boyd	12 December 1944	ADM 205/44
544.	Diary	6 March 1945	BLAM 52578
545.	Diary	22 March 1945	BLAM 52578
546.	Diary	17 April 1945	BLAM 52578
547.	Diary	30 April 1945	BLAM 52578

Part III: I. Retirement and Succession, 1945–46

548.	Diary	5 July 1945	BLAM 52578
549.	Diary	10 August 1945	BLAM 52578
550.	Diary	14 August 1945	BLAM 52578
551.	Diary	23 August 1945	BLAM 52578
552.	Diary	3 November 1945	BLAM 52578
553.	Diary	6 December 1945	BLAM 52578
554.	Diary	1 January 1946	BLAM 52579
555.	Diary	7 January 1946	BLAM 52579
556.	From John Cunningham	18 January 1946	BLAM 52562
557.	To Aunt Connie May	17 June 1946	BLAM 52559
558.	The Organisation of Command	Spring 1946	BLAM 52573

INDEX

NAVY RECORDS SOCIETY
(FOUNDED 1893)

The Navy Records Society was established for the purpose of printing unpublished manuscripts and rare works of naval interest. Membership of the Society is open to all who are interested in naval history, and any person wishing to become a member should apply to the Hon. Secretary, Robin Brodhurst, Pangbourne College, Pangbourne, Berks, RG8 8LA, United Kingdom. The annual subscription is £30, which entitles the member to receive one free copy of each work issued by the Society in that year, and to buy earlier issues at reduced prices.

A list of works, available to members only, is shown below; very few copies are left of those marked with an asterisk. Volumes out of print are indicated by **OP**. Prices for works in print are available on application to Mrs Annette Gould, 1 Avon Close, Petersfield, Hampshire, GU31 4LG, United Kingdom, to whom all enquiries concerning works in print should be sent. Those marked 'TS', 'SP' and 'A' are published for the Society by Temple Smith, Scolar Press and Ashgate, and are available to non-members from the Ashgate Publishing Group, Gower House, Croft Road, Aldershot, Hampshire GU11 3HR. Those marked 'A & U' are published by George Allen & Unwin, and are available to non-members only through bookshops.

Vol. 1. *State papers relating to the Defeat of the Spanish Armada, Anno 1588*, Vol. I, ed. Professor J. K. Laughton. **TS**.

Vol. 2. *State papers relating to the Defeat of the Spanish Armada, Anno 1588*, Vol. II, ed. Professor J. K. Laughton. **TS**.

Vol. 3. *Letters of Lord Hood, 1781–1783*, ed. D. Hannay. **OP**.

Vol. 4. *Index to James's Naval History*, by C. G. Toogood, ed. by the Hon. T. A. Brassey. **OP**.

Vol. 5. *Life of Captain Stephen Martin, 1666–1740*, ed. Sir Clements R. Markham. **OP**.

Vol. 6. *Journal of Rear Admiral Bartholomew James, 1752–1828*, ed. Professor J. K. Laughton & Cdr. J. Y. F. Sullivan. **OP**.

Vol. 7. *Hollond's Discourses of the Navy, 1638 and 1659*, ed. J. R. Tanner. **OP**.

Vol. 8. *Naval Accounts and Inventories in the Reign of Henry VII*, ed. M. Oppenheim. **OP**.

Vol. 9. *Journal of Sir George Rooke*, ed. O. Browning. **OP**.

Vol. 10. *Letters and Papers relating to the War with France 1512–1513*, ed. M. Alfred Spont. **OP**.

Vol. 11. *Papers relating to the Spanish War 1585–1587*, ed. Julian S. Corbett. **TS**.

Vol. 12. *Journals and Letters of Admiral of the Fleet Sir Thomas Byam Martin, 1773–1854*, Vol. II (see No. 24), ed. Admiral Sir R. Vesey Hamilton. **OP**.

Vol. 13. *Papers relating to the First Dutch War, 1652–1654*, Vol. I, ed. Dr S. R. Gardiner. **OP**.

Vol. 14. *Papers relating to the Blockade of Brest, 1803–1805*, Vol. I, ed. J. Leyland. **OP**.

Vol. 15. *History of the Russian Fleet during the Reign of Peter the Great, by a Contemporary Englishman*, ed. Admiral Sir Cyprian Bridge. **OP**.

Vol. 16. *Logs of the Great Sea Fights, 1794–1805*, Vol. I, ed. Vice Admiral Sir T. Sturges Jackson. **OP**.

Vol. 17. *Papers relating to the First Dutch War, 1652–1654*, ed. Dr S. R. Gardiner. **OP**.

Vol. 18. *Logs of the Great Sea Fights*, Vol. II, ed. Vice Admiral Sir T. Sturges Jackson.

Vol. 19. *Journals and Letters of Admiral of the Fleet Sir Thomas Byam Martin*, Vol. II (see No. 24), ed. Admiral Sir R. Vesey Hamilton. **OP**.

Vol. 20. *The Naval Miscellany*, Vol. I, ed. Professor J. K. Laughton.

Vol. 21. *Papers relating to the Blockade of Brest, 1803–1805*, Vol. II, ed. J. Leyland. **OP**.

Vol. 22. *The Naval Tracts of Sir William Monson*, Vol. I, ed. M. Oppenheim. **OP**.

Vol. 23. *The Naval Tracts of Sir William Monson*, Vol. II, ed. M. Oppenheim. **OP**.

Vol. 24. *The Journals and Letters of Admiral of the Fleet Sir Thomas Byam Martin*, Vol. I, ed. Admiral Sir R. Vesey Hamilton.

Vol. 25. *Nelson and the Neapolitan Jacobins*, ed. H. C. Gutteridge. **OP**.

Vol. 26. *A Descriptive Catalogue of the Naval MSS in the Pepysian Library*, Vol. I, ed. J. R. Tanner. **OP**.

Vol. 27. *A Descriptive Catalogue of the Naval MSS in the Pepysian Library*, Vol. II, ed. J. R. Tanner. **OP**.

Vol. 28. *The Correspondence of Admiral John Markham, 1801–1807*, ed. Sir Clements R. Markham. **OP**.

Vol. 29. *Fighting Instructions, 1530–1816*, ed. Julian S. Corbett. **OP**.

Vol. 30. *Papers relating to the First Dutch War, 1652–1654*, Vol. III, ed. Dr S. R. Gardiner & C. T. Atkinson. **OP**.

Vol. 31. *The Recollections of Commander James Anthony Gardner, 1775–1814*, ed. Admiral Sir R. Vesey Hamilton & Professor J. K. Laughton.

Vol. 32. *Letters and Papers of Charles, Lord Barham, 1758–1813*, ed. Professor Sir John Laughton.

Vol. 33. *Naval Songs and Ballads*, ed. Professor C. H. Firth. **OP**.

Vol. 34. *Views of the Battles of the Third Dutch War*, ed. by Julian S. Corbett. **OP**.

Vol. 35. *Signals and Instructions, 1776–1794*, ed. Julian S. Corbett. **OP**.

Vol. 36. *A Descriptive Catalogue of the Naval MSS in the Pepysian Library*, Vol III, ed. J. R. Tanner. **OP**.

Vol. 37. *Papers relating to the First Dutch War, 1652–1654*, Vol. IV, ed. C. T. Atkinson. **OP**.

Vol. 38. *Letters and Papers of Charles, Lord Barham, 1758–1813*, Vol. II, ed. Professor Sir John Laughton. **OP**.

Vol. 39. *Letters and Papers of Charles, Lord Barham, 1758–1813*, Vol. III, ed. Professor Sir John Laughton. **OP**.

Vol. 40. *The Naval Miscellany*, Vol. II, ed. Professor Sir John Laughton.

*Vol. 41. *Papers relating to the First Dutch War, 1652–1654*, Vol. V, ed. C. T. Atkinson.

Vol. 42. *Papers relating to the Loss of Minorca in 1756*, ed. Captain H. W. Richmond, R.N. **OP**.

*Vol. 43. *The Naval Tracts of Sir William Monson*, Vol. III, ed. M. Oppenheim.

Vol. 44. *The Old Scots Navy 1689–1710*, ed. James Grant. **OP**.

Vol. 45. *The Naval Tracts of Sir William Monson*, Vol. IV, ed. M. Oppenheim.

Vol. 46. *The Private Papers of George, 2nd Earl Spencer*, Vol. I, ed. Julian S. Corbett. **OP**.

Vol. 47. *The Naval Tracts of Sir William Monson*, Vol. V, ed. M. Oppenheim.

Vol. 48. *The Private Papers of George, 2nd Earl Spencer*, Vol. II, ed. Julian S. Corbett. **OP**.

Vol. 49. *Documents relating to Law and Custom of the Sea*, Vol. I, ed. R. G. Marsden. **OP**.

*Vol. 50. *Documents relating to Law and Custom of the Sea*, Vol. II, ed. R. G. Marsden.

Vol. 51. *Autobiography of Phineas Pett*, ed. W. G. Perrin. **OP**.

Vol. 52. *The Life of Admiral Sir John Leake*, Vol. I, ed. Geoffrey Callender.

Vol. 53. *The Life of Admiral Sir John Leake*, Vol. II, ed. Geoffrey Callender.

Vol. 54. *The Life and Works of Sir Henry Mainwaring*, Vol. I, ed. G. E. Manwaring.

Vol. 55. *The Letters of Lord St Vincent, 1801–1804*, Vol. I, ed. D. B. Smith. **OP**.

Vol. 56. *The Life and Works of Sir Henry Mainwaring*, Vol. II, ed. G. E. Manwaring & W. G. Perrin. **OP**.

Vol. 57. *A Descriptive Catalogue of the Naval MSS in the Pepysian Library*, Vol. IV, ed. Dr J. R. Tanner. **OP**.

Vol. 58. *The Private Papers of George, 2nd Earl Spencer*, Vol. III, ed. Rear Admiral H. W. Richmond. **OP**.

Vol. 59. *The Private Papers of George, 2nd Earl Spencer*, Vol. IV, ed. Rear Admiral H. W. Richmond. **OP**.

Vol. 60. *Samuel Pepys's Naval Minutes*, ed. Dr J. R. Tanner.

Vol. 61. *The Letters of Lord St Vincent, 1801–1804*, Vol. II, ed. D. B. Smith. **OP**.

Vol. 62. *Letters and Papers of Admiral Viscount Keith*, Vol. I, ed. W. G. Perrin. **OP**.

Vol. 63. *The Naval Miscellany*, Vol. III, ed. W. G. Perrin. **OP**.

Vol. 64. *The Journal of the 1st Earl of Sandwich*, ed. R. C. Anderson. **OP**.

*Vol. 65. *Boteler's Dialogues*, ed. W. G. Perrin.

Vol. 66. *Papers relating to the First Dutch War, 1652–1654*, Vol. VI (with index), ed. C. T. Atkinson.

*Vol. 67. *The Byng Papers*, Vol. I, ed. W. C. B. Tunstall.

*Vol. 68. *The Byng Papers*, Vol. II, ed. W. C. B. Tunstall.

Vol. 69. *The Private Papers of John, Earl of Sandwich*, Vol. I, ed. G. R. Barnes & Lt. Cdr. J. H. Owen, R.N. Corrigenda to *Papers relating to the First Dutch War, 1652–1654, Vols I–VI*, ed. Captain A. C. Dewar, R.N. **OP**.

Vol. 70. *The Byng Papers*, Vol. III, ed. W. C. B. Tunstall.

Vol. 71. *The Private Papers of John, Earl of Sandwich*, Vol. II, ed. G. R. Barnes & Lt. Cdr. J. H. Owen, R.N. **OP**.

Vol. 72. *Piracy in the Levant, 1827–1828*, ed. Lt. Cdr. C. G. Pitcairn Jones, R.N. **OP**.

Vol. 73. *The Tangier Papers of Samuel Pepys*, ed. Edwin Chappell.

Vol. 74. *The Tomlinson Papers*, ed. J. G. Bullocke.

Vol. 75. *The Private Papers of John, Earl of Sandwich*, Vol. III, ed. G. R. Barnes & Cdr. J. H. Owen, R.N. **OP**.

Vol. 76. *The Letters of Robert Blake*, ed. the Rev. J. R. Powell. **OP**.

*Vol. 77. *Letters and Papers of Admiral the Hon. Samuel Barrington*, Vol. I, ed. D. Bonner-Smith.

Vol. 78. *The Private Papers of John, Earl of Sandwich*, Vol. IV, ed. G. R. Barnes & Cdr. J. H. Owen, R.N. **OP**.

*Vol. 79. *The Journals of Sir Thomas Allin, 1660–1678*, Vol. I *1660–1666*, ed. R. C. Anderson.

Vol. 80. *The Journals of Sir Thomas Allin, 1660–1678*, Vol. II *1667–1678*, ed. R. C. Anderson.

Vol. 81. *Letters and Papers of Admiral the Hon. Samuel Barrington*, Vol. II, ed. D. Bonner-Smith. **OP**.

Vol. 82. *Captain Boteler's Recollections, 1808–1830*, ed. D. Bonner-Smith. **OP**.

Vol. 83. *Russian War, 1854. Baltic and Black Sea: Official Correspondence*, ed. D. Bonner-Smith & Captain A. C. Dewar, R.N. **OP**.

Vol. 84. *Russian War, 1855. Baltic: Official Correspondence*, ed. D. Bonner-Smith. **OP**.

Vol. 85. *Russian War, 1855. Black Sea: Official Correspondence*, ed. Captain A.C. Dewar, R.N. **OP**.

Vol. 86. *Journals and Narratives of the Third Dutch War*, ed. R. C. Anderson. **OP**.

Vol. 87. *The Naval Brigades in the Indian Mutiny, 1857–1858*, ed. Cdr. W. B. Rowbotham, R.N. **OP**.

Vol. 88. *Patee Byng's Journal*, ed. J. L. Cranmer-Byng. **OP**.

*Vol. 89. *The Sergison Papers, 1688–1702*, ed. Cdr. R. D. Merriman, R.I.N.

Vol. 90. *The Keith Papers*, Vol. II, ed. Christopher Lloyd. **OP**.

Vol. 91. *Five Naval Journals, 1789–1817*, ed. Rear Admiral H. G. Thursfield. **OP**.

Vol. 92. *The Naval Miscellany*, Vol. IV, ed. Christopher Lloyd. **OP**.

Vol. 93. *Sir William Dillon's Narrative of Professional Adventures, 1790–1839*, Vol. I *1790–1802*, ed. Professor Michael Lewis. **OP**.

Vol. 94. *The Walker Expedition to Quebec, 1711*, ed. Professor Gerald S. Graham. **OP**.

Vol. 95. *The Second China War, 1856–1860*, ed. D. Bonner-Smith & E. W. R. Lumby. **OP**.

Vol. 96. *The Keith Papers, 1803–1815*, Vol. III, ed. Professor Christopher Lloyd.

Vol. 97. *Sir William Dillon's Narrative of Professional Adventures, 1790–1839*, Vol. II *1802–1839*, ed. Professor Michael Lewis. **OP**.

Vol. 98. *The Private Correspondence of Admiral Lord Collingwood*, ed. Professor Edward Hughes. **OP**.

Vol. 99. *The Vernon Papers, 1739–1745*, ed. B. McL. Ranft. **OP**.

Vol. 100. *Nelson's Letters to his Wife and Other Documents*, ed. Lt. Cdr. G. P. B. Naish, R.N.V.R.

Vol. 101. *A Memoir of James Trevenen, 1760–1790*, ed. Professor Christopher Lloyd & R. C. Anderson. **OP**.

Vol. 102. *The Papers of Admiral Sir John Fisher*, Vol. I, ed. Lt. Cdr. P. K. Kemp, R.N. **OP**.

Vol. 103. *Queen Anne's Navy*, ed. Cdr. R. D. Merriman, R.I.N. **OP**.

Vol. 104. *The Navy and South America, 1807–1823*, ed. Professor Gerald S. Graham & Professor R. A. Humphreys.

Vol. 105. *Documents relating to the Civil War, 1642–1648*, ed. The Rev. J. R. Powell & E. K. Timings. **OP**.

Vol. 106. *The Papers of Admiral Sir John Fisher*, Vol. II, ed. Lt. Cdr. P. K. Kemp, R.N. **OP**.

Vol. 107. *The Health of Seamen*, ed. Professor Christopher Lloyd.

Vol. 108. *The Jellicoe Papers*, Vol. I *1893–1916*, ed. A. Temple Patterson.

Vol. 109. *Documents relating to Anson's Voyage round the World, 1740–1744*, ed. Dr Glyndwr Williams. **OP**.

Vol. 110. *The Saumarez Papers: The Baltic, 1808–1812*, ed. A. N. Ryan. **OP**.

Vol. 111. *The Jellicoe Papers*, Vol. II *1916–1925*, ed. Professor A. Temple Patterson.

Vol. 112. *The Rupert and Monck Letterbook, 1666*, ed. The Rev. J. R. Powell & E. K. Timings.

Vol. 113. *Documents relating to the Royal Naval Air Service*, Vol. I (1908–1918), ed. Captain S. W. Roskill, R.N.

*Vol. 114. *The Siege and Capture of Havana, 1762*, ed. Professor David Syrett.

Vol. 115. *Policy and Operations in the Mediterranean, 1912–1914*, ed. E. W. R. Lumby. **OP**.

Vol. 116. *The Jacobean Commissions of Enquiry, 1608 and 1618*, ed. Dr A. P. McGowan.

Vol. 117. *The Keyes Papers*, Vol. I *1914–1918*, ed. Professor Paul Halpern.

Vol. 118. *The Royal Navy and North America: The Warren Papers, 1736–1752*, ed. Dr Julian Gwyn. **OP**.

Vol. 119. *The Manning of the Royal Navy: Selected Public Pamphlets, 1693–1873*, ed. Professor John Bromley.

Vol. 120. *Naval Administration, 1715–1750*, ed. Professor D. A. Baugh.

Vol. 121. *The Keyes Papers*, Vol. II *1919–1938*, ed. Professor Paul Halpern.

Vol. 141. *The Channel Fleet and the Blockade of Brest, 1793–1801*, ed. Roger Morriss. A.

Vol. 142. *The Submarine Service, 1900–1918*, ed. Nicholas Lambert. A.

Vol. 143. *Letters and Papers of Professor Sir John Knox Laughton (1830–1915)*, ed. Andrew Lambert. A.

Vol. 144. *The Battle of the Atlantic and Signals Intelligence: U-Boat Tracking Papers 1941–1947*, ed. Professor David Syrett. A.

Vol. 145. *The Maritime Blockade of Germany in the Great War: The Northern Patrol, 1914–1918*, ed. John D. Grainger. A.

Vol. 146. *The Naval Miscellany: Volume VI*, ed. Michael Duffy. A.

Vol. 147. *The Milne Papers*, Vol. I *1820–1859*, ed. Professor John Beeler. A.

Vol. 148. *The Rodney Papers*, Vol. I *1742–1763*, ed. Professor David Syrett. A.

Vol. 149. *Sea Power and the Control of Trade. Belligerent Rights from the Russian War to the Beira Patrol, 1854–1970*, ed. Nicholas Tracy. A.

Occasional Publications:

Vol. 1. *The Commissioned Sea Officers of the Royal Navy, 1660–1815*, ed. Professor David Syrett & Professor R. L. DiNardo. SP.

Vol. 2. *The Anthony Roll of Henry VIII's Navy*, ed. C. S. Knighton and D. M. Loades. A.